THE PERFECT MILE

ALSO BY NEAL BASCOMB

*Higher: A Historic Race to the Sky and
the Making of a City*

THE PERFECT
MILE

THREE ATHLETES, ONE GOAL, AND
LESS THAN FOUR MINUTES TO ACHIEVE IT

NEAL BASCOMB

HOUGHTON MIFFLIN COMPANY

BOSTON · NEW YORK · 2004

For information about permission to reproduce selections
from this book, write to Permissions, Houghton Mifflin Company,
215 Park Avenue South, New York, New York 10003.

Visit our Web site: www.houghtonmifflinbooks.com.

ISBN-13: 978-0-618-39112-7
ISBN-10: 0-618-39112-6

Library of Congress Cataloging-in-Publication Data
Bascomb, Neal.
The perfect mile : three athletes, one goal, and less than four
minutes to achieve it / Neal Bascomb.
p.   cm.
ISBN 0-618-39112-6
1. Bannister, Roger. 2. Landy, John, 1930– 3. Santee, Wes.
4. Runners — Biography. I. Title.
GV1061.14.B38 2004
796.42'092'2 — dc22   [B]
2004040535

Book design by Melissa Lotfy

Printed in the United States of America

QUM 10 9 8 7 6 5 4 3 2 1

Lines from "If" by Rudyard Kipling are reprinted by
permission of A. P. Watt Ltd. on behalf of the National Trust
for Places of Historic Interest or Natural Beauty.

To Diane

CONTENTS

PROLOGUE

OW DID HE KNOW he would not die?" a Frenchman asked of the first runner to break the four-minute mile. Half a century ago the ambition to achieve that goal equaled scaling Everest or sailing alone around the world. Most people considered running four laps of the track in four minutes to be beyond the limits of human speed. It was foolhardy and possibly dangerous to attempt. Some thought that rather than a lifetime of glory, honor, and fortune, a hearse would be waiting for the first person to accomplish the feat.

The four-minute mile: this was the barrier, both physical and psychological, that begged to be broken. The number had a certain mathematical elegance. As one writer explained, the figure "seemed so perfectly round—four laps, four quarter miles, four-point-oh-oh minutes—that it seemed God himself had established it as man's limit." Under four minutes—the place had the mysterious and heroic resonance of reaching sport's Valhalla. For decades the best middle-distance runners had tried and failed. They had come to within two seconds, but that was as close as they were able to get. Attempt after spirited attempt had proved futile. Each effort was like a stone added to a wall that looked increasingly impossible to breach.

But the four-minute mile had a fascination beyond its mathematical roundness and assumed impossibility. Running the mile was an art form in itself. The distance—unlike the 100-yard sprint or the marathon—required a balance of speed and stamina. The person to break that barrier would have to be fast, diligently trained, and supremely aware of his body so that he would cross the finish line just at the point of complete exhaustion. Further, the four-minute mile had to be won alone. There could be no teammates to blame, no coach during halftime to inspire a comeback. One might hide behind the excuses of cold weather, an unkind wind, a slow track, or jostling competition, but ultimately these obstacles had to be defied. Winning a footrace, particularly one waged against the clock, was ultimately a battle with oneself, over oneself.

In August 1952 the battle commenced. Three young men in their early twenties set out to be the first to break the barrier. Born to run fast, Wes Santee, the "Dizzy Dean of the Cinders," was a natural athlete and the son of a Kansas ranch hand. He amazed crowds with his running feats, basked in the publicity, and was the first to announce his intention of running the mile in four minutes. "He just flat believed he was better than anybody else," said one sportswriter. Few knew that running was his escape from a brutal childhood.

Then there was John Landy, the Australian who trained harder than anyone else and had the weight of a nation's expectations on his shoulders. The mile for Landy was more aesthetic achievement than footrace. He said, "I'd rather lose a 3:58 mile than win one in 4:10." Landy ran night and day, across fields, through woods, up sand dunes, along the beach in knee-deep surf. Running revealed to him a discipline he never knew he had.

And finally there was Roger Bannister, the English medical student who epitomized the ideal of the amateur athlete in a world being overrun by professionals and the commercialization of sport. For Bannister the four-minute mile was "a challenge of the human spirit," but one to be realized with a calculated plan. It required scientific experiments, the wisdom of a man who knew great suffering, and a magnificent finishing kick.

All three runners endured thousands of hours of training to shape their bodies and minds. They ran more miles in a year than many of us walk in a lifetime. They spent a large part of their youth struggling for breath. They trained week after week to the point of collapse, all to shave off a second, maybe two, during a mile race—the time it takes to snap one's fingers and register the sound. There were sleepless nights and training sessions in rain, sleet, snow, and scorching heat. There were times when they wanted to go out for a beer or a date yet knew they couldn't. They understood that life was somehow different for them, that idle happiness eluded them. If they weren't training or racing or gathering the will required for these efforts, they were trying not to think about training and racing at all.

In 1953 and 1954, as Santee, Landy, and Bannister attacked the four-minute barrier, getting closer with every passing month, their stories were splashed across the front pages of newspapers around the world, alongside headlines about the Korean War, Queen Elizabeth's coronation, and Edmund Hillary's climb toward the world's rooftop. Their performances outdrew baseball pennant races, cricket test matches, horse derbies, rugby matches, football games, and golf majors. Ben Hogan, Rocky Marciano, Willie Mays, Bill Tilden, and Native Dancer were often in the shadows of the three runners, whose achievements attracted media attention to track and field that has never been equaled since. For weeks in advance of every race the headlines heralded an impending break in the barrier: "Landy Likely to Achieve Impossible!"; "Bannister Gets Chance of 4-Minute Mile!"; "Santee Admits Getting Closer to Phantom Mile." Articles dissected track conditions and the latest weather forecasts. Millions around the world followed every attempt. When each runner failed—and there were many failures—he was criticized for coming up short, for not having what it took. Each such episode only motivated the others to try harder.

They fought on, reluctant heroes whose ambition was fueled by a desire to achieve the goal and to be the best. They had fame, undeniably, but of the three men only Santee enjoyed the publicity, and that proved to be more of a burden than an advantage. As for riches, financial reward was hardly a factor—they were all amateurs. They had to scrape around for pocket change, relying on their hosts at races for decent room and board. The prize for winning a meet was usually a watch or a small trophy. At that time, the dawn of television, amateur sport was beginning to lose its innocence to the new spirit of "win at any cost," but these three strove only for the sake of the attempt. The reward was in the effort.

After four soul-crushing laps around the track, one of the three finally breasted the tape in 3:59.4, but the race did not end there. The barrier was broken, and a media maelstrom descended on the victor, yet the ultimate question remained: who would be the best when they toed the starting line together?

The answer came in the perfect mile, a race fought not against the clock but against one another. It was won with a terrific burst around the final bend in front of an audience spanning the globe.

If sport, as a chronicler of this battle once said, is a "tapestry of alternating triumph and tragedy," then the first thread of this story begins with tragedy. It occurred in a race 120 yards short of a mile at the 1,500-meter Olympic final in Helsinki, Finland, almost two years to the day before the greatest of triumphs.

PART I
A REASON TO RUN

1

I have now learned better than to have my races dictated
by the public and the press, so I did not throw away a
certain championship merely to amuse the crowd and be
spectacular. —JACK LOVELOCK,
1936 Olympic Gold Medalist

On July 16, 1952, at Motspur Park in South London, two men
were running around a black cinder track in singlets and
shorts. The stands were empty, and only a scattering of people
watched former Cambridge miler Ronnie Williams as he tried to stay
even with Roger Bannister, who was tearing down the straight. It was
inadequate to describe Bannister, who was eating up yards at a rate of
seven per second, as simply "running." His pacesetter for the first half of
the time trial, Chris Chataway, had been exhausted, and the only reason
Williams hadn't folded was that all he needed to do was maintain the
pace for a lap and a half. What most distinguished Bannister was his
stride. Terry O'Connor, a *Daily Mail* journalist, tried to describe it:
"Bannister had terrific grace, a terrific long stride, he seemed to ooze
power. It was as if the Greeks had come back and brought to show you
what the true Olympic runner was like."

Bannister was tall—six foot one—and slender of limb. He had a
chest like an engine block and long arms that moved like pistons. He
flowed over the track, the very picture of economy of motion. Some
said he could have walked a tightrope as easily as a track, so balanced

and even was his foot placement. There was no jarring shift of gears when he accelerated—as he did at the end of the three-quarter-mile time trial—only a quiet, even increase in tempo. Bannister loved that moment of acceleration at the end of a race when he drew upon the strength of leg, lung, and will to surge ahead. Yes, Bannister ran, but it was so much more than that.

As he sped to the finish with Williams at his heels, Bannister's friend Norris McWhirter prepared to take the time on the sidelines. He held his thumb pressed firmly on the stopwatch button, knowing that because of the thumb's fleshiness, having it poised lightly above added a tenth of a second at least. Bannister shot across the finish—McWhirter punched the button. When he read the time, he gasped.

Norris and his twin brother, Ross, had been close to Bannister since their days at Oxford University. They were three years older than the miler, having served in the British navy during World War II, but they had been teammates together in the university's athletic club. Norris had always known there was something special about Roger. Once, on an Italian tour with the Achilles Club (the combined Oxford and Cambridge athletic club), which Bannister had dominated, McWhirter had looked over with amazement at his friend sleeping on the floor of a train heading to Florence and thought, "There lies the body that perhaps one day will prove itself to possess a known physical ability beyond that of any of the one billion other men on earth." But as McWhirter stared down at his stopwatch that July afternoon he could hardly believe the time: Bannister had run three-quarters of a mile in 2:52.9, four seconds faster than the world record held by the great Swedish miler Arne Andersson.

After gathering his breath, Bannister walked over to see what the stopwatch read. Cinders clung to his running spikes. At the time, athletic shoes were simply a couple of pieces of thin leather that molded so snugly to the feet that when the strings were drawn tight one could see the ridges of the toes. The soles were embedded with six or more half-inch-long steel spikes for traction. Running surfaces had advanced very little over the years. They were mostly oval dirt strips layered on top with ash cinders that were taken from boilers at coal-fired electricity plants. Track quality depended on how well the cinders were maintained, since in heat the cinders became loose and tended to blow away and in rain the track turned to muck. Motspur Park's track benefited from having the country's best groundskeeper, and it was one of the fastest, which was why Bannister had chosen it for this time trial.

He always ran a three-quarter-mile trial before a race to secure in his mind his fitness level and pace judgment. This trial was particularly important because in ten days, provided he qualified in the heats, he would run the race he had dedicated the past two years to winning: the 1,500-meter Olympic final. A good time this afternoon was crucial for his confidence.

"Two-fifty-two-nine," McWhirter said.

Bannister was taken aback. Williams and Chataway were just as incredulous. The time had to be wrong. "At least, Norris, you could have brought a watch we could rely on," Bannister said.

McWhirter was cross at such a suggestion. But he knew one way to make sure his stopwatch was accurate. He dashed to the telephone booth near the concrete stadium stands, put in a penny coin, and dialed the letters T-I-M. The phone rang dully before a disembodied voice came onto the line, tonelessly reading, "And on the third stroke the time will be two-thirty-two and ten seconds— bip— bip— bip— and on the third stroke the time will be two-thirty-two and twenty seconds— bip — bip— bip. . . ." Norris checked his stopwatch: it was accurate.

After McWhirter returned and told the others the result, they agreed that Bannister was certain of a very good show in Helsinki. They dared not predict a gold medal, but they knew that Bannister considered a three-minute three-quarter-mile the measure of top racing shape. He was now seven seconds under this benchmark. All of his training for the last two years had been focused on reaching his peak at exactly this moment—and what a peak it was. He was in a class by himself. The critics—coaches and newspaper columnists—who had condemned him for following his own training schedule and not running in enough pre-Olympic races would soon be silenced.

There was a complication, however, that McWhirter had yet to tell Bannister. As a journalist for the *Star,* he kept his ear to the ground for any breaking news, and he had recently heard something very troubling from British Olympic official Harold Abrahams. Because of the increased number of entrants, a semifinal had been added to the 1,500-meter contest. In Helsinki Bannister would have to run not only a first-round heat but also a semifinal before reaching the final.

The four men bundled into McWhirter's black Humber and headed back to the city for the afternoon. When the twenty-three-year-old Bannister was not racing around the track, where he looked invincible, he appeared slighter. In pants and a shirt, his long corded muscles were no longer visible, and it was his face that one noticed. His long cheekbones, fair complexion, and haphazard flop of straw-colored hair across the forehead gave him an earnest expression that turned boyish when he smiled. However, there was quiet aggression in his eyes. They looked at you as if they were sizing you up.

As Norris McWhirter turned out of the park, he finally said, "Roger . . . they put in a semifinal."

They all knew what he meant—three races in three days. Bannister had trained for two races, not three. Three required a significantly higher level of stamina. But Bannister had concentrated on speed work. With two prior races, the nervous energy he relied on would be exhausted by the final—if he made the final. It was as if he were a marksman who had precisely calibrated the distance to his target, then found that his target had been moved out of range. Now it was too late to readjust the sights.

Bannister looked out the window, saying nothing. Away from Motspur Park, with its trees and long stretches of open green fields, the roads were choked with exhaust and bordered by drab houses and abandoned lots overgrown with weeds. The closer they got to London, the more they could see of the war's destruction, the bombed-out walls and craters that had yet to be bulldozed and rebuilt. A fine layer of soot clouded the windows and grayed the rooftops.

The young miler didn't complain to his friends, although they knew he was burdened by the fact that he was Britain's great hope for the 1952 Olympics. He was to be the hero of a country in desperate need of a hero.

To pin the hopes of a nation on the singlet of an athlete seemed to invite disaster, but Britain at that time was desperate to win at something. So much had gone wrong for so long that many questioned their country's standing in the world. Their very way of life had come to seem precarious. "It is gone," wrote James Morris of his country in the 1950s: "Empire, forelock, channel and all . . . the world has overtaken [us]. We are getting out of date, like incipient dodos. We have reached, none too soon, one of those immense shifts in the rhythm of a nation's history which occur when the momentum of old success is running out at last." The First World War had seen the end of Britain's economic and military might. The depression of the 1930s had slowly drained the country's economic reserves, and its grasp on India had started slipping away. The country moved reluctantly into the Second World War, knowing it couldn't stand alone against Hitler's armies. Once the British joined the fight, they had to throw everything into the effort to keep the Nazis from overrunning them. When the war was over, they discovered, like the blitz survivors who emerged onto the street after the sirens had died away, that they were alive but had grim days to face ahead.

And grim days they were. Britain owed £3 billion, principally to the United States, and the sum was growing. Exports had dried up—in large part because half of the country's merchant fleet had been sunk. Returning soldiers found rubble where their homes had once stood. Finding work was hard, finding a place to live even harder. Shop windows remained boarded up. Smog from coal fires deadened the air. Trash littered the alleys. There were queues for even the most basic staples, and when one got to the front of the line, a ration card was required for bread (three and a half pounds per person per week), eggs (one per week), and everything else (which wasn't much). The children needed ration books to buy their sweets. Trains were overcrowded and hours off schedule, and good luck finding a taxi. If this was victory, asked a journalist, why was it "we still bathed in water that wouldn't come over your knees unless you flattened them?"

And the blows kept falling. The winter of 1946–47, the century's worst, brought the country to a standstill. Blizzards and power outages ushered in what the chancellor of the Exchequer called the "Annus Horrendus." It was so cold that the hands of Big Ben iced up, as if time itself had stopped. The spring brought severe flooding, and the summer's temperatures were scorching. Adding to the misery was a polio scare. Throughout the next five years "austerity" remained the reality, despite numerous attempts to put the country back in order. Key industries were nationalized, and thousands of dreary prefabricated houses were built for the homeless. In 1951 the Festival of Britain was staged to brighten what critic Cyril Connolly deemed "the largest, saddest and dirtiest of the great cities, with its miles of unpainted half-inhabited houses, its chopless chop-houses, its beerless beer pubs . . . its crowds mooning around the stained green wicker of the cafeterias in their shabby raincoats, under a sky permanently dull and lowering like a metal dish-cover." The festival, though a nice party, was an obvious attempt to gloss over people's exhaustion from years of hardship. Those who were particularly bitter said that the festival's soaring Skylon was "just like Britain," standing there without support. To cap it all, on February 6, 1952, London newspapers rolled off the presses with black-bordered pages: the king was dead. Crowds wearing black armbands waited in lines miles long to see King George VI lying in state at Westminster Abbey. As they entered the hall only the sound of footsteps and weeping was heard. A great age had passed.

The ideals of that bygone age—esprit de corps, self-control, dignity, tireless effort, fair play, and discipline—were often credited to the country's long sporting tradition. It was said that throughout the empire's history "England has owed her sovereignty to her sports." Yet even in sport she had recently faltered. The 1948 Olympic Games in London began badly when the Olympic flame was accidentally snuffed out on reaching England from Greece. America (the "United, Euphoric, You-name-it-they-had-it States," as writer Peter Lewis put it) dominated the games, winning thirty-eight gold medals to Britain's three. After that the country had to learn the sour lesson of being a "good loser" in everything from cricket to rugby, boxing, tennis, golf, soccer, track and field, and even swimming the Channel. It looked as though the quintessential English amateur—one who played his sport solely for the enjoyment of the effort and never at the cost of a complete life—simply couldn't handle the competition. He now looked outdated, inadequate, and tired. For a country that considered its sporting prowess symbolic of its place in the world, this was a distressing situation.

Roger Bannister, born into the last generation of the age that ended with George VI's death, typified the gentleman amateur. He didn't come from a family with a long athletic tradition, nor one in which it was assumed that he would go to Oxford, as he did, to study medicine and spend late afternoons at Vincent's, the club whose one hundred members represented the university's elite.

His father, Ralph, was the youngest of eleven children raised in Lancashire, the heart of the English cotton industry and an area often hit by depression. Ralph left home at fifteen; after taking the British civil service exams and qualifying as a low-level clerk, he moved to London. Over a decade later, after working earnestly within the government bureaucracy, he felt settled enough to marry. He met his wife, Alice, on a visit back to Lancashire, and on March 23, 1929, she gave birth to their first son and second child, Roger Gilbert. The family lived in a modest home in Harrow, a suburb of London. Forced to abandon their education before reaching university (his mother had worked in a cotton mill), Roger's parents valued books and learning above everything else. All Roger knew of his father's athletic interests was that he had once won his school mile and then fainted. Only later in life did he learn that his father carried the gold medal from that race on his watch chain.

Bannister discovered the joy of running on his own while playing on the beach. "I was startled and frightened," he later wrote of his sudden movement forward on the sand in bare feet. "I glanced round uneasily to see if anyone was watching. A few more steps—self-consciously . . . the earth seemed almost to move with me. I was running now, and a fresh rhythm entered my body." Apart from an early passion for moving quickly, nothing remarkable marked his early childhood. He spent the years largely alone in typical boyhood pursuits—building models, imagining heroic adventures, and dodging neighborhood bullies. When he was ten, this world was broken: an air-raid siren sent him scrambling back to his house with a model boat secured under his arm. The Luftwaffe didn't come that time, but soon they would. His family evacuated to Bath, but no place was safe. One night when the sirens sounded and the family took refuge underneath the basement stairs of their new house, a thundering explosion shook the walls. The roof caved in around them, and the Bannister family had to escape to the woods for shelter.

Although the war continued to intrude on their daily lives, mostly in the form of ration books and blacked-out windows, Roger had other problems. As an awkward, serious-minded twelve-year-old who was prone to nervous headaches, he had trouble fitting in among the many strangers at his new school in Bath. He won acceptance by winning the annual cross-country race. The year before, after he had finished eighteenth, his house captain advised him to train, which Bannister did by running the two-and-a-half-mile course at top speed a couple of times a week. The night before the race the following year, he was restless, thinking about how he would chase the "third-form giant" who was the favorite. The next day Bannister eyed the favorite, noting his cockiness and general state of unfitness. When the race started, he ran head down and came in first. His friends' surprise would have been trophy enough, but somehow this race seemed to right the imbalance in his life as well. Soon he was able to pursue his studies, as well as interests in acting, music, and archaeology, without feeling at risk of being an outcast—as

long as he kept winning races. Possessed of a passion for running, a surfeit of energy, and a preternatural ability to push himself, he won virtu-
ally all of them, though he was usually wheezing for breath by the end.

Before he left Bath to attend the University College School in London, the headmaster warned: "You'll be dead before you're twenty-one
if you go on at this rate." His new school had little regard for running,
and Bannister struggled to find his place once again. He was miserable.
He tried rugby but wasn't stocky or quick enough. He tried rowing but
was placed on the third "eight" team. He had never had a problem
knowing what he wanted, and after a year he knew he wanted out. So at
sixteen he sat for the Cambridge exam. At seventeen he chose to take a
scholarship to Exeter College, Oxford, since Cambridge had put him off
for a year.

Bannister intended to study to become a doctor, but he knew he
needed a way not only to fit in but to excel among his fellow students,
most of whom, in 1946, were as much as eight years older than him,
having deferred placement because of the war. A schoolboy among ex-
majors and brigadiers, he realized that running was his best chance to
distinguish himself.

The year before his father had taken him to see the gutsy, diminutive
English miler Sydney Wooderson take on the six-foot giant Arne Andersson at the first international track and field competition since the
war's end. White City Stadium was bedlam as Andersson narrowly beat
Wooderson. "If there was a moment when things began, that was it for
me," Bannister later said. In a footrace, unlike other sports, greatness
could be won with sheer heart. He sensed he had plenty of that.

Before he had even unpacked his bags at Oxford, Bannister sought
out athletes at the track. Finding no one there, he uncovered a notice on
a college bulletin board for the university athletic club. He promptly
mailed a guinea to join but received no response. He decided to go running on the track anyway, although one of the groundskeepers advised, "I'm afraid that you'll never be any good. You just haven't got the
strength or the build for it." Apparently the groundskeeper thought
everyone needed to look like Jack Lovelock, the famous Oxford miler:
short, compact, with thick powerful legs. The long-limbed, almost un-
gainly Bannister persisted nonetheless. Three weeks later, having finally
received his membership card, he entered the Freshman's Sport Mile
wearing an oil-spotted jersey from his rowing days. He thought it best
to lead from the start—a strategy he would later discard—and fin-

ished the race in second place with a time of 4:52. After the race the secretary of the British Olympic Association advised him, "Stop bouncing, and you'll knock twenty seconds off." Bannister had never before worn running spikes, and their grip on the track made him, as he later described it, "over-stride in a series of kangaroo-like bounds."

The cruel winter of 1946–47, with its ten-foot snowdrifts, meant that someone had to shovel a path on the track so the athletes could train; Bannister took to the yeoman's task and, for his effort, won a third-string spot in the Oxford versus Cambridge mile race on March 22, 1947. On that dreary spring day, on the very track at White City where he had watched Wooderson compete, Bannister discovered his true gift for running. He stepped to the mark feeling the pressure to run well against his university's archrival. From the start Bannister held back, letting the others set the pace. The track was wet, and the front of his singlet was spotted black with the cinder ash kicked up by the runners ahead of him. After the bell in the final lap Bannister was exhausted but still close enough to the leaders to finish respectably. All of a sudden, though, he was overwhelmed by a feeling that he just had to win. It was instinct, a "crazy desire to overtake the whole field," as he later explained. Through a cold, high wind on the back straight, he increased the tempo of his stride, and to the shock of everyone, teammates and competitors alike, he surged past on the outside. In the effort inspired by the confluence of body and will, he felt more alive than ever before. He pushed through the tape twenty yards ahead of the others in 4:30.8. It wasn't the time that mattered, but rather the rush of passing the field with his long, devouring stride. This was ecstasy, and it was the first time that Bannister knew for sure that there was something remarkable in the way he ran — and something remarkable in the feeling that went with it.

After the race he met Jack Lovelock, the 1936 gold medalist in the 1,500-meter race and the former world-record holder in the mile. "You mean *the* Jack Lovelock," Bannister said on being introduced. Lovelock was a national hero, an Exeter graduate, and a doctor, and he was blessed with tremendous speed. It didn't take much insight on his part to see in Bannister the potential resurrection of British athletics.

Bannister didn't disappoint. Six weeks later, on June 5, 1947, he clocked a 4:24.6 mile, beating the time set by his hero Wooderson when he was the same age, eighteen. That summer Bannister traveled with the English team on its first postwar international tour, putting in several good runs. In November he was selected as a "possible" for the 1948 Olympics, then turned down the invitation. He wasn't ready, he decided—to some criticism.

It was in his nature to listen to his own counsel, however, not that of others. He had taken a coach, Bill Thomas—who once trained Lovelock—but Bannister soon became disgruntled with him. Thomas attended to Bannister on the track while wearing a bowler hat, suit, and waistcoat. He barked instructions at the miler on how to hold his arms or how many laps to run during training. When the young miler asked for the reasoning behind the lessons, Thomas simply replied, "Well, you do this because I'm the coach and I tell you." When Bannister ran a trial and inquired about his time, Thomas said, "Oh, don't worry about that." Soon Bannister dropped him, preferring to discover for himself how to improve his performances.

The next year he became Oxford University Athletic Club secretary, then quickly the club's president. He won the Oxford versus Cambridge meet for the second year and competed in the Amateur Athletic Association (AAA) championships in the summer, learning the ropes of first-class competition. Increasingly the newspapers headlined his name. He even saved the day at the Olympic opening ceremony when it was discovered that the British team hadn't been given a flag to march with into the stadium. Bannister found the backup flag, smashing the window of the commandant's car with a brick to retrieve it.

Four years later he intended to save the British team's honor again.

Preparations for the Helsinki Olympics began in the autumn of 1950. Bannister had spent the two previous years studying medicine, soaking up university life, hitchhiking from Paris to Italy, and going on running tours to America, Greece, and Finland. His body filled out. He won some races and lost others, but most important, he turned the corner from being an inexperienced, weedy kid to being a young man who clearly understood that Oxford and running had opened up worlds to him that otherwise would have remained closed. He was ready to make his Olympic bid and afterward put away his racing spikes for a life devoted to medicine.

Bannister's plan was to spend one year competing against the best international middle-distance runners in the world, learning their strengths and weaknesses and acclimatizing to different environments. Then, in the year before the Helsinki games, he would focus exclusively on training to his peak, running in only a few races so as not to dull his edge. The plan was entirely his own. After speaking to Lovelock about his preparations for the 1936 Olympics, Bannister felt he needed no other guidance. First he flew to New Zealand over Christmas for the Centennial Games, where he beat the European 1,500-meter champion Willi Slijkhuis and the Australian mile champion Don Macmillan, both of whom he was likely to face in Helsinki. His mile time was down to 4:09.9, a reduction of more than forty seconds from his first Oxford race three years before. While in New Zealand, he visited the small village school that Lovelock had attended; there he noticed that the sapling given to the Olympic gold medal winner had now grown into an oak tree. The symbolism wasn't lost on him. Back in England Bannister continued his fellowship in medicine through the spring of 1951 at Oxford, where he investigated the limits of human endurance and chatted with such distinguished lecturers as J.R.R. Tolkien and C. S. Lewis.

He then flew to Philadelphia to compete in the Benjamin Franklin Mile, the premier American event in middle-distance running. The press fawned over this foil to the American athlete, commenting on his traveling alone to the event: "No manager, no trainer, no masseur, no friends! He's nuts — or he's good." In front of forty thousand American fans, Bannister crushed the country's two best milers in a time of 4:08.3. The *New York Herald Tribune* described him as the "worthy successor to Jack Lovelock." The *New York Times* quoted one track official as saying, "He's young, strong and fast. There's no telling what he can do."

The race brought Bannister acclaim back home. To beat the Americans on their own turf earned one the status of a national hero. When he followed with summer victories at the British games and the AAA Championships, it seemed that track officials and the press were ready to award him the Olympic gold medal right then and there. They praised his training as "exceptional," an "object lesson." The British press gushed that his long fluid stride was "immaculate" and "amazing." He left rivals standing; he was a "will-o'-the-wisp" on the track. After a race where the crowd laughed at how effortlessly Bannister won, a British official predicted: "Anyone who beats him in the Olympics at Helsinki will have to fly."

Then the positive press quickly turned negative. Following his own plan, Bannister stopped running mile races at summer's end. Tired from competition, he felt he had learned all he needed during the year and should now dedicate himself to training. When he chose to run the half-mile in an international meet, the papers attacked: "Go Back to Your Own Distance, Roger." This was only the beginning of the criticism, but Bannister remained focused on his goal.

To escape the attention he journeyed to Scotland to hike and sleep under the stars for two weeks. One late afternoon, after swimming in a lake, he began to jog around to ease his chill. Soon enough he found himself running for the sheer exhilaration of it, across the moor and toward the coast. The sky was filled with crimson clouds, and as he ran a light rain started to fall. With the sun still warming his back, a rainbow appeared in front of him, and he seemed to run toward it. Along the coast the rhythm of the water breaking against the rocks eased him, and he circled back to where he had begun. Cool, wet air filled his lungs. Running into the sun now, he had trouble seeing the ground underneath his feet, but still he rushed forward, alive with the movement. Finally spent as the sun disappeared from the horizon, he tumbled down a slight hill and rested on his back, his feet bleeding, but feeling rejuvenated. He had needed to reconnect to the joy of running, to get away from the tyranny of the track.

Throughout the winter of 1951–52, Bannister immersed himself in his first year of medical school at St. Mary's Hospital in London, learning the basics of taking a patient history and working the wards. He was also training for the Olympics. By springtime he had developed his stamina and begun speed work on the track. When he announced that he wouldn't defend his British mile championship, the athletic community objected: It was unthinkable. He had obligations to amateur sport. He had to prove he deserved his Olympic spot. He must take a coach now. He couldn't duck his British rivals. Bannister made no big press announcements defending his reasons. He simply stuck to his plan, trusting it. As isolating as this plan was, it had taken him exactly where he wanted—so far. Meanwhile, most other athletes trained under the guidance and direction of the British amateur athletic officials.

On May 28, 1952, Bannister clocked a 1:53 half-mile at Motspur Park with his "space-eating stride." Ten days later he entered the mile at the Inter-Hospitals Meet and won by 150 yards. Maybe he knew what he was doing. The press turned to writing that he would silence his critics at Helsinki and that his training was "well advanced." Compared to the rest of the top international 1,500-meter men, his times were sufficient. His "pulverizing last lap" would probably win the day. Even L. A. Montague, the *Manchester Guardian*'s esteemed athletics correspondent, trotted out to explain that Bannister was the "more sensitive, often more intelligent, runner who burns himself up in giving of his best in a great race." Bannister was Britain's best chance at the gold medal; did critics, Montague wondered, "really think that they suddenly know more about him than he knows himself?"

Although he lost an 800-meter race at White City Stadium in early July, the headlines exclaimed: "Don't Worry About Bannister's Defeat —He Knows What He Is Doing!" Ably assisted by the press, Bannister had painted himself into a corner. He was favored to bring back gold by everyone from the head of the AAA to revered newspaper columnists —and, by association, by his countrymen as well. Of course, there weren't going to be any scapegoats if he failed. "No alibis," as Bannister said himself. "Victory at Helsinki was the only way out." A part of him suspected that he had maneuvered himself into this tight position on purpose. Come the Olympic final, he would have an expectant crowd, the rush of competition, two years of dedicated training, the expectation that it was his last race before retirement, and nobody to blame but himself if he lost. *This* was motivation.

On July 17, even though most of the British Olympic team had already left for Finland, Bannister was still in London. He would have to join the team soon. The team manager, Jack Crump, declared upon arriving in Helsinki: "We will not let Britain down."

But like a few other athletes, Bannister wanted to avoid the media frenzy in the prelude to the games. There was also the inevitable waiting around, worrying about upcoming events. His friend Chris Chataway, the 5,000-meter hopeful, had also delayed his departure. The two scoured London for dark goggles to curtain the twenty-one hours of Scandinavian daylight. Given that one rarely saw the sun in London, it proved a difficult search. In the meantime Bannister sought out a morning newspaper.

It didn't take Bannister long to find a story headline that would change everything—"Semi-Finals for the Olympic 1,500 Metres." This confirmed what Norris McWhirter had told him the day before about the added heat. "I could hardly believe it," Bannister later explained. "In just the length of time it took to read those few words the bottom had fallen out of my hopes." Worse, he had drawn a tough eliminating heat in the first round.

As he went about his day in the smog-choked London streets, the crisp air and fast tracks he expected to enjoy in Helsinki seemed threateningly close at hand. One could hardly have blamed him if he didn't want to go at all.

2

The essential thing in life is not so much conquering as fighting well.
— BARON DE COUBERTIN,
founder of the modern Olympic Games

I N THE NARROW concrete tunnel, Wes Santee stuck to his position in the seven-man line, waiting to move forward as the first athletes on the American team marched into Helsinki's Olympic Stadium through the Marathon Gate. The applause from the stands reverberated in the tunnel, sounding as if the whole of mankind had come to watch the opening ceremony parade. Santee, his feet more accustomed to cowboy boots or track spikes, stepped ahead in white patent leather shoes. His outfit was a departure from his typical attire of western-style shirts and jeans. Like the rest of his teammates, he wore a dark flannel jacket with silver buttons, gray flannel slacks, and a poplin hat, whose brim he had folded to make it look more like a cowboy hat.

The twenty-year-old University of Kansas sophomore towered over most of those around him. At six foot one, and with much of that height in his legs, he looked the part of the clean-cut American athlete, buzz cut included. His shoulders were wide, and he bristled with energy. His face easily lit with a smile, and he almost always said what he thought, with a midwestern twang. One had the sense that he wore his emotions out in the open, but that this vulnerability had a limit buttressed with steel.

That afternoon of July 19, he was nothing but a bundle of nervous anticipation as he moved toward the tunnel's mouth. Rain streaked across the opening. He peered past it into the stadium, where hundreds of athletes circled the track. They were dressed in a kaleidoscope of colors and styles: pink turbans, flower-patterned shirts, green and gold blazers, black raincoats, orange hats. It was impossible to tell where each team was from because all the flags were in Finnish. Santee could not even pronounce the translation for the United States: *Yhdysvaltain.* The Soviets were already settled in the infield, wearing their cream suits and maroon ties and lined up as neatly as an army regiment. It was their first Olympics since 1912, and they had made no secret of the fact that they were out to beat the Americans.

Finally Santee cleared the tunnel and moved in file toward the track, his head swiveling about to take in the three-tiered stadium and its seventy thousand spectators. It was an awesome sight, like nothing he had ever witnessed. So many people from so many places, charged with excitement and speaking so many different languages. And they had all come this afternoon simply to watch the athletes march around the track, not even to see them compete. On an electric signboard, the likes of which Santee had seen only a few times, were the words *Citius, Altius, Fortius*—Faster, Higher, Stronger. He had made it. He was an Olympic athlete representing his country.

After marching around the mud-soaked track, he followed the row of athletes to his spot on the infield for the ceremony's beginning. He felt as if his eyes weren't wide enough to take in everything happening around him. This was a long way from Ashland, the farming town deep in the southwestern part of Kansas where he was raised. The size of the Helsinki stadium alone was enough to marvel at. He remembered arriving at the University of Kansas for the first time and going to the big auditorium for freshman orientation. He was with his teammate Lloyd Koby, who also came from the kind of small town where electricity was just on its way in and a rooster's crow was the only wake-up call one knew. Koby looked across the numerous tiers of seats and gauged the height of the rafters; he turned to Santee and said, "Boy, this building would hold a lot of hay." It was less a joke than a reference to the only context they knew. But that auditorium was nothing compared to this place, its steep concrete stands seeming to reach the sky.

At a rostrum on the track in front of Santee, the chairman of the organizing committee began to speak, first in Finnish, then in Swedish, French, and English, about the Herculean efforts that had gone into these games. His countrymen had cleared forests, put up hundreds of new buildings of stucco, granite, and steel, enlisted thousands of volunteers, and opened their homes to strangers from around the globe. The stadium in which the opening ceremony was taking place had been the chief target of Russian bombers at the start of the Second World War because of its symbolic value. Now it was once again alive with people, who were anxious for the competition to commence.

The chairman finished his speech by introducing Finland's president, who stood at the microphone and announced: "I declare the Fifteenth Olympic Games open!" To the sound of trumpets, the Olympic flag with its five interlocking circles was raised on the stadium flagpole. Then a twenty-one-gun salute boomed. As its echo dissipated, 2,500 quaking pigeons were released from their boxes to swoop and pivot in the air. Santee looked skyward as the pigeons escaped one by one, carrying the message that the Olympics had begun. Before the last pigeon soared away, the scoreboard went blank and then appeared the words: "The Olympic Torch is being brought into the Stadium by . . . P-A-A-V-O N-U-R-M-I."

Pandemonium ensued. Santee had passed the bronze statue of Nurmi at the stadium entrance and had seen his classic figure on posters wallpapered throughout Helsinki, but few had expected to see *the man* himself. Peerless Paavo, the Phantom Finn, the Ace of Abo. Nurmi was a national hero in Finland and the godfather of modern track and field. At one time he owned every record from 10,000 meters down to 1,500. At the 1924 Paris Olympics he claimed three gold medals in less than two days. Put simply, he was the greatest. Bald-headed, slight of stature, and fifty-five years old, Nurmi ran into the stadium in a blue singlet with the torch in his right hand, his stride as graceful and effortless as ever. Photographers maneuvered into position. The athletes, Santee included, broke ranks, storming to the track side to catch a glimpse of the unconquerable Nurmi.

The fire leaping from the birch torch Nurmi held had been lit in Olympia, Greece, on June 25, and had since weathered a five-thousand-mile journey across land and water. When Nurmi finished his run around the track, as athletes and spectators alike jostled one another to get a better look, he passed the flame to a quartet of athletes at the base of the 220-foot-tall white tower at the stadium's south end. While they ascended the tower, at the top of which another Finnish champion, Hannes Kolehmainen, waited, a white-robed choir stood to sing. The stadium was reverently silent. Kolehmainen took the torch and tilted it to light the Olympic flame, which would burn until the games ended.

Santee and the other athletes returned to their places in the field. From a distance each team looked uniform, its athletes dressed in matching outfits and standing side by side. On closer inspection, they were an odd assembly of men and women: stocky wrestlers, tall sprinters, wide-shouldered shot putters, cauliflower-eared boxers, miniature gymnasts, crooked-legged horsemen, and weather-beaten yachtsmen — all with their own ambitions for victory in the days ahead.

As Santee stood in the middle of this medley of people, looking at the Olympic flame and hearing the jumble of voices all around him, the strangeness of the scene overwhelmed him. He had been overseas only one other time. Except for traveling to athletic meets, he had never left the state of Kansas. Now he was in this enormous amphitheater in a country where night lasted only a few hours. He didn't have his coach with him and had few friends among the athletes. Not only had he rarely faced international competition, but he was scheduled to run in the 5,000-meter race, even though the 1,500 was his best distance. Filled with these thoughts, Santee gulped. The tightness in his throat felt like a stone. Indeed, he was a long way from Kansas now.

If his father had had his way, Wes would still be pitching hay, fixing fence posts, and plowing fields back in Ashland. Most fathers want their sons to have a better life, but Wes Santee didn't have such a dad.

David Santee was born in Ohio in the late 1800s. He lived a helter-skelter childhood, never advancing past the second grade. He was a keen braggart and adept at the harmonica, but his only employable skill was hard labor. Over six feet tall and weighing 220 pounds, he had the size for it. After his cousin married a ranch owner named Molyneux in western Kansas, David Santee went out to work the eight thousand acres as a hired hand. He met Ethel Benton, a tall, gentle woman who had studied to be a teacher, on a blind date. They were soon married and shortly after that were expecting the first of three children. On March 25, 1932, the town doctor was called to the ranch to deliver Wes Santee. He came into the world kicking.

Santee was raised on the Molyneux cattle and wheat ranch five miles outside of Ashland. It was practically a pioneer's existence, with an out-house, no running water, no electricity. If you wanted to listen to the radio, you had to hook it up to the car battery. Farm life was vulnerable to the often cruel hand of nature. The Santees lived through the drought of the Dust Bowl years, when sand squeezed through every crack in the house and made the sky so dark that the chickens went to roost in midafternoon. They survived tornadoes and storms of grasshoppers that ate everything they could chew, including the handle of a pitchfork left out against a fence post. In good times and bad, Mr. Molyneux ruled the ranch. He liked the Santee boy's spirit and was more of a father to Wes than David Santee ever was. Molyneux was a successful rancher and businessman; he owned Ashland's dry goods store and enjoyed taking the boy into town to buy him a double-dip ice cream cone at the drugstore. Molyneux died when Wes was in the fourth grade, and his happy childhood ended abruptly. From that point forward he was his father's property, suffering his bad temper while working a man's day on the ranch. His only freedom was running.

For Santee, running was play. He ran everywhere. "I just don't like to fiddle around," he said. "If I was told to get the hoe, I'd run to get it. If I had to go to the barn, I'd run." The only bus in town was a flatbed truck, so instead of riding, Santee ran the five miles to school. When he returned in the early afternoon, he ran from his house into the fields to help with the plowing or to corral one of the four hundred head of cattle. At dusk, when his father called it a day, an exhausted Santee didn't walk home for supper. He ran—fast—wearing his cowboy boots. As the distance from his father lengthened, a weight lifted from his shoulders, and by the time he washed up and changed clothes he was as fresh as if he hadn't worked at all. Later, when a remark, a look, or seemingly nothing at all set off his father's rage, this freshness was torn from Wes. He took the brunt of his father's anger, saving his younger brother Henry, who suffered from rickets as a child, and his younger sister Ina May from the worst of it. David Santee dispensed his cruelty with forearm, fist, rawhide buggy whip, or whatever else was at hand—once it was a hammer. Wes considered himself lucky that his old man didn't drink or the situation could have been really bad. Some sons of abusive fathers want to become big enough to fight back; Santee wanted to become fast enough to get away.

Very early he recognized that he had a gift for running. He was never very good in the sprint, but if the game was to run around the block twice, he always won. In eighth grade the high school coach came down to evaluate which kids were good at which sports. That was how a small town developed its athletes. The coach threw out a football to see who threw or kicked it the farthest, threw out a basketball to see who made a couple of jump shots. Then he told Santee and the other twenty kids in his class to run to the grain elevator. Within a few hundred yards, Santee was all alone and knew he had the others whipped. This was "duck soup," he said to himself as he ran to the grain elevator and back and took a shower before the others returned. Most walked half the distance.

When a new kid named Jack Brown, who was rumored to be quite a runner, arrived in town, the townspeople urged Santee to race him. The first day of his freshman year Santee joined Brown at the starting line of the half-mile track used for horse races and had almost lapped him by the finish. It felt good to be better than everybody else at something. What had started as fun—running to chase mice or the tractor—and then became a way to escape from his father's clutches, was now a way to excel. Each race he won bolstered his pride.

J. Allen Murray was there to help him on this path. Murray was Ashland's high school athletics coach (as well as history teacher and basketball/football coach). He believed Santee could be the next Glenn Cunningham, the most famous U.S. middle-distance runner and a Kansas native. The problem was that Santee barely had enough time for classes, let alone running, because his father wanted him home to work. Murray told Wes that if he didn't have time to train, he should just continue to run everywhere he went. That was fine with Santee.

Finally the time came for his first track meet. Scheduled for a Saturday, the meet was delayed until Monday because of a thunderstorm. Unfortunately, Santee worked on Mondays, and he knew his father would object to losing an afternoon of his free labor. Murray told him he would take care of it.

The next evening Coach Murray walked up the steps to the Santees' house. He had invited himself to dinner. His father normally greeted visitors with a .22-caliber pistol and an offer of five minutes to get off his property. This time David Santee at least pushed the door open, but his hospitality ended there. Through dinner and dessert, Coach Murray explained to Wes's parents why they should allow their son to attend the track meet—how it was good for the boy to be challenged in competition. David Santee didn't utter a word the entire evening: not a yes, not a no. Murray left without an answer, and Wes disappeared into the fields afterward. Alone in the dark, he clawed at the dirt and grass, wondering how he would get out of this place. If he hadn't learned to hate his father before this night, he did so now.

The next day Coach Murray told him to get up early on Monday to do his chores; he would pick him up at seven o'clock. Santee rose at four, hauled feed, milked the cows, and did everything required of him before his coach arrived. Santee's father was working in the fields and thought his son simply left for school. It was the first time Wes had left the county, and although he was the youngest in the mile race, unaware of tactics of competition, and scared of having disobeyed his father, he placed third. Awarded a red ribbon, Santee could barely stand still from the excitement. But then he had to go home. When he entered the house, his father was sitting at the table. From the grim look on his face, it was obvious that he knew that Wes had gone to the meet.

"I won third place," he said with sheepish excitement.

"If you have time to miss school and do all this," his father bit off each word, "then you have time to get all the rest of the plowing done."

For the next twenty hours Wes Santee sat on the tractor, plowing miles of fields without a break for lunch, and certainly not for school. His throat burned from thirst, his spine ached from the jarring movements of the tractor on uneven terrain, and his hands were rubbed raw from gripping the wheel. Working from dawn until ten o'clock at night, Wes finished two days of plowing in one. For a boy who spent most of his youth laboring on the farm, he would remember that day as the hardest he had ever endured. When he finally returned to school, Murray asked if he was all right. Santee nodded. Murray then asked him if he wanted to go to the next meet in Mead, Kansas. Santee said yes.

After Wes left, Murray called the ranch to say one thing to Santee's father: "I want you to bring your truck in and haul some kids to Mead." David Santee didn't reply, but the tone in Coach Murray's voice made him understand that he didn't have a choice in the matter. Like most bullies, David Santee folded when someone finally stood up to him. The next week he showed up on time with his truck, and though it angered him that his son was wasting time that would be better spent on the ranch, he never got in the way of Wes's running again. Over the next four years Wes Santee scorched up tracks throughout Kansas. He won two state mile championships, broke Glenn Cunningham's state high school record, became the favorite son of Ashland, and was targeted by college track recruiters from coast to coast. He had found his way out, and there was nothing that could stand in his way. He trained as much as possible, studied hard to keep his grades up, and decided not to let things get too far with his high school girlfriend because recruiters were not interested in athletes with wives or children. Shutting himself down with her was not easy, but he had to get out of Ashland.

When Bill Easton, the University of Kansas track and field coach, offered him a scholarship in 1949, Santee accepted. Over the previous two years Easton had won Santee's confidence, probably because he was everything Santee's father was not: he wore a coat and tie, spoke intelligently, won friends easily, and backed up his words with action. Under Easton's guidance and encouragement, the KU track team had become one of the country's best.

The summer before he left for college Wes had his last confrontation with his father. While he dug yet another six-foot-deep hole in the hard ground for the soon-to-arrive electricity poles, his father started pounding on his back with his fists because he was digging too slowly. That was it. The seventeen-year-old, his shirt soaked with sweat and his hands blistered from the work, stormed back to the house, informed his mother he was leaving, and said good-bye to Henry and Ina May. In the stable he saddled Bess, the horse his father had given him, and put a halter on a second mare, which Wes had yet to name. A local farmer had given her to Wes in exchange for breaking some horses. He led his two horses toward the front gate. A cloud of dust from their hooves trailed behind them.

Suddenly his father appeared from behind the barn and blocked his way. "You're not taking that horse anywhere," he said, gesturing toward Bess.

Seeing the coiled violence in the way his father stood rigid in front of him, Wes grimly said, "Okay," and then unstrapped his saddle from Bess. He then threw it over the other horse, which had never been ridden before, and led her through the gate, leaving his father without a good-bye. When he was two hundred yards away, Santee carefully hoisted himself up on the horse and rode into town. He stayed with a friend who owned the local ice plant and had once told him that he could stay with him if things ever got too bad at the ranch. Santee lived there until college began.

In Lawrence Santee fell under the protection of Bill Easton. The coach invited the youth, who had almost nothing with him but the clothes on his back, to stay at his house until his dormitory was ready. Santee may have been bold-talking and powerful, but he needed someone to care for him. The first morning, over a breakfast of bacon and eggs, Easton told Santee that he needed to set a good example and help lead the team. Easton spoke to him like an equal, and Santee listened.

Coach Murray had given him the opportunity to run; Coach Easton showed Santee how to turn his raw talent as a runner into greatness. It had little to do with changing his short, clipped stride, which had become ingrained in his youth while running along plow furrows and in pastures where a long stride would have been dangerous on the uneven terrain. Santee did not bring his arms back in a normal long arc, nor did he drive to the extreme with his kicking foot, as most distance runners did. Instead, he had the quick arm swing and knee action of a sprinter. But with his native speed, coordination, long legs, strong shoulders, and ability to relax, he was able to sustain this sprinter style over long distances. Easton was convinced that reshaping his stride into a more classical motion would do more harm than good. Rather, Easton taught Santee to harness his power through training, pace judgment, and focus. Soon enough, seniors on his team struggled to keep up with him in practice and competition.

Led by Santee, the freshman squad won the Big Seven cross-country and indoor championships. He set the national collegiate two-mile record in 9:21.6 and began to win headlines as the "long-legged loper" who would "play havoc" with most, if not all, of Glenn Cunningham's records by the time he was finished. In the spring of 1951, at the Amateur Athletic Union (AAU) Championships, he took seventeen seconds off the 5,000-meter record in the junior division, and the next day he placed second in the senior division. By the end of his freshman year his mile time hovered in the four-minute-teens (4:15, 4:16, 4:17). He earned a spot on an AAU-sponsored tour to Japan in the summer and found himself running in Osaka, Sapporo, and Tokyo. There he met the American half-miler Mal Whitfield, who had won two gold medals at the 1948 Olympic Games. While some athletes were hesitant to share a hotel room with the black track star, Santee gladly jumped at the opportunity. Whitfield taught the young miler to make sure to keep his toes pointed straight ahead when striding so as not to lose even a quarter-inch of distance with each stride. He also taught Wes that in the mile race there was time for only one offensive and one defensive move, so it was of utmost importance to run strategically. When Santee returned to Kansas in August, he felt certain that he was ready for more international competition. He announced to local reporters, "I want to make the Olympic team and go to Helsinki, Finland."

In his sophomore year this "sinewy-legged human jet," as one reporter described Santee, proved that he was on his way. Some began to compare him to Emil Zatopek, the Czech star who ran everything from the mile to the marathon at world-class levels. This was the level of enthusiasm that Santee generated on and off the track. He loved racing in front of large crowds and never tired. His talent just barely outmeasured his confidence.

On a flight to a meet a Jayhawk teammate held out a newspaper article to show Wes. "Look what it says here . . . Billy [Herd] hasn't been beaten in any kind of a race for almost two years. That includes relay carries. . . . He's gobbled up some pretty good boys too, Wes."

Santee stretched his boots out into the aisle. "Yeah, he's a good boy. But he hasn't tried to digest me yet."

In two-mile races during his sophomore year Santee lapped his competitors. In cross-country meets he was slipping into his sweats before other runners had finished. During the indoor season he set record after record in the mile, leading his team to a host of dual meet victories. It was almost too easy. On campus he ran from class to class, and professors set their watches by the precise time he started his training sessions.

In April 1952 at the Drake University Relays in Des Moines, Iowa, one of the year's most important outdoor track meets, Santee anchored the four-mile relay for his team. When the baton was passed to him, Georgetown's Joe LaPierre was sixty yards ahead. Santee blazed three sixty-two-second quarter-miles, yet had trouble gaining ground because LaPierre was running brilliantly. As Santee sped into the first turn of the last lap Easton yelled out, "He's wilting in the sun." Santee was finally gaining. Stride after stride he closed the gap. When he burst through the tape yards ahead of LaPierre, setting a national collegiate mile record in 4:06.8, he had officially arrived. "Santee's not human," said the Georgetown coach. The *Des Moines Register* quipped, "Santee stuck out above every other athlete like the Aleutian Islands into the Bering Sea." And the national papers picked up the best quote from the Drake coach: "Santee is the greatest prospect for the four-minute mile America has yet produced. He not only has the physical qualifications, but the mental and spiritual as well."

But Santee first turned his sights to the Olympics. As the holder of national titles in the 1,500 and 5,000 meters, Santee by right qualified for the American trial in each. In mid-June he went to California with Easton to spend a week training. They decided together that he would participate in both trials. "I just want to make the Olympic team," he told his coach. "Time or race isn't important." On June 27, at the Los Angeles Memorial Coliseum, Santee placed second in the 5,000-meter trial, guaranteeing a trip to Helsinki. That night he dined on his customary steak and potato dinner and enjoyed quiet conversation with Easton back at the hotel. The next day, braving one of the coldest June days in Los Angeles history, he readied himself for the 1,500-meter trial in front of forty-two thousand spectators. Santee looked around for Easton but couldn't find him. A whistle was blown, the race was called, and Santee approached the starting line alongside milers Bob McMillen and Warren Druetzler, both of whom he was sure he could beat. In the program listing the qualifiers for the 3:40 P.M. race, Santee was predicted to "win as he pleases—he has all year." He was revved to go.

Suddenly two AAU officials grabbed his arm, shuffling him off the track before he could protest. "Wes, they're not going to let you run," one official said.

"What do you mean? What's going on?" Santee shrugged off their hold on him. Out of the corner of his eye he saw Easton running across the field. Though wearing a jacket, tie, and dress shoes, he was moving fast.

The race starter called, "Runners to your mark!" and then the gun fired. Santee watched helplessly as the trial started without him.

Easton finally made it to his side. "Wes, I'm sorry. We've been in a meeting for over an hour, and they're saying you're not good enough to run both races, and they won't let you drop out of the 5,000 meter to run the 1,500 meter."

This wasn't right. Only the previous week he had run the third-fastest 1,500-meter time in AAU history, 3:49.3. It was the fastest time by an American in years. Santee welled with anger, and with balled fists he looked ready to act out his frustration.

Easton pulled him to the side. The coach had the stocky build of a wrestler, and even then, in his late forties with a fleshy, oval face, he looked capable of stopping this tall athlete if necessary. His voice was calm. "They told me you were only twenty—not good enough to run the 5,000 against Zatopek followed up with the 1,500. I told them we don't particularly want to run the 5,000; we want to run the 1,500. Their only response was 'You qualified for that, and you have to stay with it.'"

There was nothing to be done. Easton knew that no Olympic rule forbade an athlete to participate in two events. If Santee qualified, he qualified. Those were the rules, but the AAU ran the show, and if a rule interfered with what the AAU wanted, its leaders either ignored the rule or changed it. This was the first time the AAU would stand in Santee's way, and unfortunately not the last. Yes, he was off to Helsinki to race in the 5,000 meter, but his best chance of coming home with a medal was in the 1,500 meter.

The three weeks between the trial and the opening ceremony in Helsinki were a whirlwind. Santee nearly died on a flight from Los Angeles to St. Louis when the plane carrying America's Olympic athletes went into a tailspin and passengers were thrown from their seats. When the plane finally righted itself, the preacher and pole vaulter Bob Richards walked down the aisle asking for confessions. After a long layover in St. Louis, they arrived in New York. Santee participated in the national TV show *Blind Date*, hosted by Arlene Francis, as well as the first Olympic telethon with Bob Hope and Bing Crosby. He ran in an exhibition three-quarter-mile race on Randalls Island and set a new American record of 2:58.3, not to mention leaving the Olympic 1,500-meter qualifiers far behind. The effort was born of frustration: he wanted to show the AAU officials his speed and prove their decision wrong. After a flurry of press interviews, he flew from New York to Newfoundland, to London, and finally to Helsinki. By the time Santee arrived in Finland he was a jumble of excitement, jet lag, hope, aggravation, patriotism, fear, and confusion—a very different cocktail of emotions from what he needed to perform at his best.

But there he was at the opening ceremony, right in the middle of it all and wanting to prove that he deserved to stand side by side with the best runners in the world. When the ceremony ended, the 5,870 athletes from sixty-seven nations filed out of the stadium, soaked and cold. Santee had only a few more days to pull himself together for his qualifying round. His legs had never failed him before, and no matter the obstacle or his state of mind, he expected them to see him through once again.

3

To be great, one does not have to be mad, but definitely
it helps.
—PERCY CERUTTY

A LL WAS QUIET in Kapyla, the Olympic Village in a forest of
pine trees twenty miles outside of Helsinki. John Landy and
three of his four roommates, Les Perry, Don Macmillan, and
Bob Prentice, lay in their iron-framed beds. The Arctic twilight crept in
around the edges of the window, the sheets were as coarse as burlap,
and the piles of track clothes and shoes reeked, but the Australians were
resting easily, exhausted from being thousands of miles from home and
trying to prepare for the most important athletic competition of their
lives. In the days before an Olympian's event, he felt as if he were looking over the edge of a cliff: the nerves, upset stomach, and general un-
ease took a lot out of an athlete. The anticipation was almost as trying
as the event itself. Sleep was the only relief offered, if one could finally
fall asleep.

"Wake up! Wake up! You don't need all this sleep!" Percy Cerutty
yelled as he burst into the room, swinging the door wide and switching
on the lights.

"Bloody hell, Percy!" groaned one of his athletes. "Thanks for waking us."

"You blokes don't need all this sleep," their coach shouted back. At
fifty-seven Cerutty was a whirling dervish, a short, fit man with a flowing white mane of hair, goatee, toffee-colored face, blue eyes, and the

kind of voice that could wake up the dead when raised. It was often raised.

"All *what* sleep?" his athletes retorted.

"Ah, you're hiding in here. You're avoiding reality!" He bounced around the floor, kicking up little wakes of cement dust. "The world is gathered here just outside that doorway, and all you fellas can think of is sleep. Sleep won't get you anywhere." He was really getting going now. When Cerutty started a rant, he went on for a while. They had to stop him.

It may have been a single voice, but it was their collective annoyance that finally said, "Look, shut the hell up, Percy. It's all right for you to wander around grandstanding, but we're the ones who have to run. You've been carrying on nonstop since we got here, when all we're trying to do is prepare to race. You're supposed to be here to help us."

Les Perry had to face the mighty Emil Zatopek; Bob Prentice would run a marathon; and Macmillan and Landy would toe the line with the greatest field of middle-distance runners in Olympic history. Cerutty had chosen to crash with his protégés, whether they liked it or not. They had been patient with him, and he would have to excuse them for finally taking a stand against his antics.

After the athletes joined him for a series of pre-Olympic races in London on June 20 (as an unofficial, nonsponsored coach, Cerutty had to pay his own way and could afford the journey from Australia only by slow boat), Cerutty had provoked incident after incident. They knew he needed to attract attention to promote his coaching techniques — but at what cost? Prancing around Motspur Park wearing only a pair of white shorts, he heckled other runners. At White City he walked up to Roger Bannister, close enough to feel his breath, and said, "So you're Bannister. . . . We've come to *do* you." He showboated to the journalists: "Others can run faster," he boasted, "but none can run harder than I." He was dragged off screaming from a meet because he wouldn't leave the track. On arriving in Helsinki, Cerutty had made a beeline to visit Paavo Nurmi without an invitation, and he had stayed so late with Zatopek that the Czech runner was forced to offer his bed to the Australian coach and sleep in the woods himself. Cerutty's athletes were used to him, but couldn't he have left his eccentricities in Australia? This was the Olympics. Enough was enough.

While Cerutty scrambled about the room, Landy and the others shielded their eyes from the light. Earlier that evening Landy had scaled the fence surrounding the Olympic training arena to get in some extra training, so he was particularly tired. Compared to Don Macmillan, the miler in the bed next to him, who had long legs and a powerful chest, Landy was small. His 150 pounds were stretched over a narrow, five-foot-eleven frame, and with his quiet voice, soft brown eyes, and shag of curly hair, he hardly stood out in a room. Yet he had a strong presence. In part it was because of his intelligence, which was lively, well-rounded, and quick. He also possessed a deep and infectious laugh. But mostly it was an intangible quality that people noticed, a feeling that Landy possessed a reservoir of calm, uncompromising will. In conversation with him one immediately had the sense that he would be a rock in the storm, and that a friendship with him would endure.

Although Landy had been last on the list to make the Australian team, an honor that earned him a chance to compete but not the funds to make the trip, he had done very well in the six weeks since leaving Melbourne. In London he had placed second in the British AAA Championship mile race—a surprise to himself and everybody else in White City Stadium. He followed that race with meets in Belfast, Glasgow, Middlesborough, and another in London. Back home in Australia the press began to pay attention, commenting on his "paralyzing burst" and noting that many experts "had not seen a runner over the last fifteen years with such relaxation, smoothness, and style." He had even set a new two-mile record with a time of 8:54, a feat that resulted in his inclusion in the 5,000-meter heats on top of the 1,500 meter. It also improved the odds posted on him to bring back a medal. Now he just needed some sleep.

Landy and his three friends knew they owed their presence in Helsinki mainly to Cerutty, this madcap little man with his strange ideas about pushing oneself to the limit. After all, they were Cerutty's gang. Unfortunately, enlightenment came at a cost.

To develop four Australian distance runners to Olympic standards had taken more than a sleep deprivation regime. Unlike Finland, Australia wasn't a country known for investing either attention or dollars in track and field. The six state amateur athletic associations ran perpetually in the red. Training methods were years behind European and American advances. Some Australians even thought too much exercise was bad for one's health. As an athlete from the 1950s explained: "Runners were oddities; long-distance runners were very peculiar people; and those who ran the marathon were crazy." The country had a long track and field tradition, but it was marked by neglect, a focus on gambling in professional footraces, lackadaisical training, a dearth of talent, and very little international success. Spectators and athletes alike had to pay at the gate, yet the expense of running meets consistently fell short of revenues. In promoters' jargon, the sport "didn't sell."

Facilities for training and events were lacking as well. Australia, nearly the size of the continental United States, had only two standard athletic fields. One of those was in Melbourne, Landy's hometown, but as Joseph Galli, a cigar-chomping, omnipresent athletics reporter of the time, wrote: "Olympic Park [was] a depressing shambles—lank grass covers the earth banking, dressing rooms are dirty and primitive, and the burnt-out stand remains as mute testimony of the unwillingness of Government and civic leaders to give amateur athletes the small, permanent stadium they need for the future." The track itself was a disaster; runners would have posted better times circling a potholed city block through rush-hour traffic.

This is not to say that Australia cared little for sport in general: among sport-crazed nations, it reached the height of bedlam. Early in their history Australians had imported the English love of sport and over the years had taken it to an entirely different level. It has been noted that for every thirty words in the Australian language, one has to do with sport. In the early 1950s a *Saturday Evening Post* correspondent explained that the country's sports heroes were accorded a respect greater than that given to "ministers of State or Gospel" and their fans were among the world's most avid. Total attendance in the minor rounds of Australian football matches typically reached over two million spectators. And when one of their great athletes died, he or she was accorded all the trappings of a state funeral. On the international stage Australians couldn't claim military might, economic superiority, cultural influence, political power, or historical greatness, but they could make their country known in the sporting arena. Success there fostered pride that was wanting in a nation built by convicts and gold prospectors. In cricket and football, tennis and swimming, Australians were respected, but in track and field much less so. And in distance running not at all.

Young men like John Landy needed to be convinced to take up running seriously; for most it was just something one played at. Born on April

12, 1930, Landy showed early promise by winning the sprint race at Malvern Grammar School's annual sports meeting. When his proud father, Gordon, who had been a fine footballer in his day, turned to his wife, Elva, and said that one day John would be a "world champion," she laughed. He was six.

Landy enjoyed a comfortable childhood. His family lived in a gracious, five-bedroom house in East Malvern, an upscale suburb a few miles southeast of Melbourne, a city of one and a half million born of the Gold Rush. The Landy family dated back to the mid-nineteenth-century influx of immigrants from England and Ireland. Along with his two brothers and two sisters, John Landy was loved and supported by his parents, who were neither too strict nor too lenient. His father, a disciplined man, well respected in the community, was a successful accountant and served on the Melbourne Cricket Club board. His mother had a great interest in history and literature. The children attended private schools and were urged to pursue their own interests. They vacationed in Dromana, a seaside town outside Melbourne. If one asked about the Landy family, the response was that they were "good people."

Young John Landy was more interested in butterfly collecting than in running. When he was ten years old, he met a beetle specialist in the neighborhood who introduced him to entomology. With three other local kids, Landy often rode his bike twenty miles into the bush to chase after butterflies with a net and a pair of fast legs. At home he would carefully secure his latest find on a mounting board and add the butterfly's taxonomic classification for identification.

Only when Landy was fourteen and had entered Geelong Grammar, an elite boarding school outside the city where the "prefects whack[ed] the boys," did he begin to distinguish himself in sport. It was the height of the war in the Pacific, and his father was away from Melbourne handling logistics for the air force. John was part of a group called the Philistines, boys who, as he described it, weren't regarded as "intellectual powerhouses" but who knew their way around the playing fields. Like the others, Landy preferred Australian rules football, and he excelled by being quick on his feet and a fierce competitor. In the off-season Landy proved to be pretty good at track and field events. In his final year at Geelong he won the school cross-country, 440-yard, 880-yard, and one-mile track titles—a clean sweep. He then claimed the All Public Schools Mile Championship in a time of 4:43.8. That was impressive, but two years earlier at the same championship Don Macmillan had posted a better time by seventeen seconds, so not much attention was paid to Landy's future as a miler outside the small circle of devoted Australian running fans. Still, a handful of people were watching Landy's efforts on the track.

When he enrolled at Melbourne University to take his degree in agricultural science, Landy continued to dabble in running, but he considered his prospects limited. He had a good head for numbers and was aware of the times of Australian and international stars; given his progress to date, he thought his best time in the mile would be 4:20. In whatever sport he pursued, he wanted to be the best, and running laps around the track didn't appear to repay the effort involved, particularly as he began to lose more races than he won. During his second year in college—one spent 120 miles northeast of the city to learn the more practical side of agricultural science (mending fences, driving tractors, tending to sheep and cattle)—Landy won the Hanlon "Best and Fairest" footballer trophy, a distinguished prize. While there, he didn't win any footraces. More than ever, playing center half back looked to be the right choice for his undergraduate sporting activities. He liked being part of a team as well. Like many Australian athletes before him who had great potential, he was losing interest in running from a lack of encouragement and insightful training.

But in late 1950 everything changed. Like many Geelong students, Landy had joined the school's athletic club after graduation in order to participate in meets. The club captain, marathoner Gordon Hall, had advised him to alternate days of cross-country and sprint running. Landy took that advice. After a race at Olympic Park, however, Hall approached him and said, "You're not fit." Hall suggested that Landy speak to his own coach, Percy Cerutty, who was a fixture at Olympic Park; to find him all one had to do was listen for his piercing voice. The two went over to Cerutty, and Hall introduced Landy, who, though not exceptionally tall, towered over the bantam 116-pound coach.

Cerutty stroked his chin and finally said, "Never heard of you."

The coach liked to press an athlete's buttons in order to gauge his reaction and strength of will. Usually he invaded the young man's space in the process, setting him further on edge. Landy fell for the bait, commenting that he was truly a footballer and only played at running. That attitude was anathema to Cerutty, who demanded 100 percent commitment from his athletes. Before the conversation had barely begun, Cerutty was walking away. Nonetheless, he told Landy that if he was interested in learning how to run — seriously interested — then he should come by the house in South Yarra for another talk. They didn't set a date.

Cerutty knew what he was doing; an athlete needed to choose to be taught. Only when Landy went to him could Cerutty show what Landy would gain by listening to him. He had already recruited two of Australia's brightest young stars and helped them to achieve astounding results.

The first was Les Perry, the "Mighty Atom," as some called him, because of his short stature and indefatigable energy. Perry had first caught the Cerutty show at the annual professional footrace known as the Stawell Gift. On the infield Cerutty waved his arms about while explaining to a crowd how he had just run seventeen miles to the nearest mountain range and back. "Endurance? You've only got to get out there and do it. Face up to it: man was meant to run."

A year later, upset at his progress in running, Les Perry answered an advertisement that Cerutty had posted in the local Melbourne paper. He went to the house in South Yarra, and over the course of the afternoon Cerutty lifted weights and ran around the house ranting about prehistoric man and the survival of the fittest. But his ideas on fitness made sense. Perry enlisted his help and then urged his friend Don Macmillan to see him as well.

When Macmillan, one of the most naturally gifted milers to appear on the Australian scene for years, showed up at Cerutty's door on a Sunday morning, he was in a terrible state. He was failing his exams, having trouble finding time to train, and worried about his direction in life. Cerutty sat him down to talk about books, discuss the Bible, and argue philosophy. Then he gave Macmillan an ultimatum: "If you want to come work with me, be part of my gang, I'll tell you straight out, I'm not interested in failures. You have to pass all your exams. That bit's up to you, but if you want, I'll tell you how to do it." He gave Macmillan an hour-by-hour schedule, directing him when to get up, drink his tea, run, study, take a shower, eat, run again, read the paper, and go to bed. Within a few months Macmillan had passed his exams and won the Australian mile title in record time. At that same championship Les Perry came in first in the three-mile race.

When John Landy decided to make his way to South Yarra, Cerutty's reputation was well established. As he led Landy up the stairs to his study overlooking Melbourne's botanical gardens, the coach paused and, with a befuddled look, asked, "What did you say your name was? Landy? Gordon Hall told me you won the Combined Public Schools mile last year, and I always study the results. . . . What was the time you ran?"

"About four-forty-four."

"I have never heard the name," Cerutty said, looking him straight in the eye. He sensed that Landy would resist taking direction. "It seems to me, young man, it is time you put the name of Landy on the world map."

In a study that measured seven feet by seven feet and was crowded with books, cherry red velvet couches, dumbbells, a decanter of port, a typewriter, and a hodgepodge of papers and magazines, Landy sat in silence as Cerutty dispelled the notion that Landy would burn out, or worse, harm himself if he trained too much. The "human organism" is built to handle stress, he said; the body actually welcomes it. Through continuous effort, superior fitness is guaranteed. Look at the rigorous training of Emil Zatopek or the Finnish runners Arne Andersson and Gundar Haegg, he told Landy. Look at Percy Cerutty.

Landy was fired by Cerutty's ideas. Nobody had ever spoken to him in this way. He told Cerutty that he would train with him. When Landy left, Cerutty simply noted on a card the young man's date of birth and the mile time of 4:43.8 that he had run in the 1948 Victorian Public Schools Championship. He filed it in his athletic card catalog, unaware that it was John Landy who would launch him into the international arena as a coach.

It took three weeks of hard training and a few lessons on running style for Landy to realize results. On January 20, 1951, he dropped his mile time by six seconds. Cerutty then gave Landy a training outline and set him out on his own, never inquiring as to whether the young runner was following his guidance. And Landy did not feel the need to offer the information himself. The proof was in his performances. Two months later, after upper body strengthening with dumbbells and hundreds of miles of conditioning work, his time was down another ten seconds. On May 22, 1951, he ran a 4:16 mile, an extraordinary improvement. It was the first time Landy thought he might have a shot at the Olympics, though the qualifying time was 4:10. This "Conditioner of Men," as the brass plate outside Cerutty's house read, had discovered his greatest athlete yet. Landy had natural coordination and very strong leg muscles, and most important, he could sustain punishing levels of training. In this last respect, coach and athlete were much alike.

Almost from the day he was born in 1895, Percy Cerutty was a sickly child. His father was an alcoholic, and his mother barely kept her son from malnourishment. Cerutty was plagued by pneumonia; his lungs barely functioned. Much of his youth was spent reading. He was continually nursed back to health by his mother and sisters. At fifteen, when he took a job as a telegraph messenger boy, he had to ride his bicycle many miles into the suburbs — and he found that he enjoyed this. At eighteen he won his first footrace. At twenty-one he was experiencing brutal headaches that blurred his vision and made him vomit, yet he still raced, posting his best mile time in 4:34, just behind the fastest middle-distance runner in Australia at the time.

After he married and took up a career as a telephone technician, he hung up his racing shoes for the serious business of adult life. But soon the dreariness of that life began to sap his strength; he took to smoking and inactivity. The migraines worsened, his health deteriorated, and depression overpowered him. One day at the age of thirty-nine he stumbled into an empty church with tears pouring from his eyes. He had reached bottom: thin, weak, and with no hope but for an early death.

His doctor recommended a six-month leave from the telephone company and gave Cerutty one prescription: "I can't heal you with medicines, Percy. . . . You have to save yourself. If you want to do anything about yourself, you'll get off that bed under your own will and spirit." Cerutty took that advice seriously. He restricted his diet to raw foods and quit smoking. Perhaps most important, he started reading. He read everything from poetry to religious texts, weightlifting advice, Eastern philosophy, scientific treatises, and long-distance training guides. He developed a new approach to life, one that was unencumbered by fear and defined by exerting himself fully — physically, intellectually, and spiritually.

Mostly, though, he exercised. He lifted weights. He joined a walking club and began taking longer and longer hikes through the bush. Within a year he had completed a seventy-mile hike, to his wife's shock. The outdoors exhilarated him. It was not long after that hike when he started to run. Soon he ran constantly and his body was transformed into that of a much younger man. In 1942, at forty-seven, he showed up at the Malvern Harriers locker room and announced, "I've come down to have a run with you. I used to be a member here."

Gone were the migraines, rheumatism, and spells of depression. The road hadn't been easy, though. When Cerutty first began exercising, he would return home on the brink of total collapse, his heart racing. He could hardly push open the front door. He would lie down on the floor, eyes glued to the ceiling as his breath and heart rate gradually returned to normal. He learned to appreciate the torture that his body endured because he always recovered and returned stronger the next day. "Thrust against pain. Pain is the purifier," he said.

Within a year of joining the Harriers he was regularly clocking mid-four-minute miles. Then came the marathons—hundred-mile races in twenty-four hours and two hundred miles in forty-eight hours. Such feats by a man of his age brought attention, and Cerutty adored it. He also welcomed the chance to expound his theories. As he codified his philosophy of training and life in the late 1940s, athletes were beginning to pay heed. In 1946 Cerutty purchased three acres in Portsea, a town south of Melbourne on the easternmost point of Port Philip Bay. There he began building a ten-by-fourteen-foot hut and a larger shack out of lumber dismantled from shipping boxes. He would be a teacher.

By Christmas 1951, when John Landy walked up to the gate for his first and only visit at the Portsea property, Cerutty's buildings and philosophy were complete. He didn't train athletes; he guided "Stotans."

The gate to the property was shut. Unlike the rest of the athletes at the camp, Landy had come down to Portsea on his own for the ten-day training session. His parents were circumspect about Cerutty, particularly because of his outlandish antics, but their son's improvement as an athlete was undeniable, so they didn't object to his visit. Seeing no lights on, Landy realized that it was too late to catch anybody awake. He had brought a sleeping bag, and not wanting to disturb anyone, he found a hollow to sleep in. Because of the chill in the air, he donned every item of spare clothing he had brought, including his football socks, before slipping into his bag. He was all right until rain began to pelt his bag. Then it turned into a downpour. Shaking, wet to the bone, he stuck it out. By first light the hollow had turned into a streambed, and Landy stumbled into the camp, half in shock from the cold. The Portsea training had begun.

In the year since Landy had first called on Cerutty he had paid close attention to the coach's direction. He had paid ten shillings for lessons on how to move his arms and how to run like a rooster, clawing at the air. He had strengthened his upper body by lifting dumbbells. He had participated in running sessions on a two-and-a-half-mile horse path named the Tan (after the four-inch layer of tree bark discarded from tanneries, which cushioned the dirt), and he had bounded up and down Anderson Street Hill with the others under Cerutty's watchful eye. Their runs provoked gasps from the Melbourne residents nearby. They couldn't understand what these young men, hounded by a shirtless older man, were doing. Running for exercise was odd in and of itself, but a group doing so through the botanical gardens carrying bamboo poles in each arm and shrieking like banshees as Cerutty called to them to run like "primitive man" was pure scandal.

What Cerutty had in mind for the ten-day training camp in Portsea would definitely have been beyond the observers' comprehension. Landy was skeptical as well, yet there he was. By following Cerutty's grueling regimen, Landy hoped to win a spot on the Olympic team.

Before breakfast the men ran the Hall Circuit, a course that threaded through tea trees, up hills, down steep slopes, and across sand dunes for one mile and 283 yards; the runners were timed and pitted against one another with handicaps and a threepence-bet apiece. The winner won the pot, and Cerutty didn't hesitate to direct runners around the wrong bend so he could claim the prize himself. Sometimes he clocked their runs and badgered them to go faster, questioning their manhood or dedication, often both. He ridiculed and taunted them mercilessly, particularly Landy, who he thought needed toughening up. Often he shouted encouragements to his runners such as "Move your bloody arms. . . . Too slow! Too slow! . . . Come on, you lazy bastards! You're hopeless bloody dogs! Children could run faster than that!"

Other training sessions were held on nearby golf courses, where Cerutty had his charges accelerate up hills to achieve the kind of energy explosion they needed in a race. They ran up sand dunes for the same effect, an exercise that Landy particularly disliked. He preferred the rhythmic flow of running on flat ground. For resistance training they sprinted along the beach in knee-deep surf. When not running, they swam, surfed, or hiked along the coast. They were always in a state of movement until Cerutty stopped to give a lecture on the grass beside the 300-meter Portsea Oval. There he taught his Stotan (part Stoic,

part Spartan) philosophy. Cerutty had coined the term and its requirements:

1. Realization that, as Wordsworth the poet says, "Life is real, life
   is earnest," which denotes there is no time for wasteful ideas
   and pursuits.
2. In place of wasteful hobbies there commences a period of supervised and systematic physical training, together with in-
   struction in the art of living fully. This replaces previously
   undirected life.
3. Swimming will be done all the year round. . . . This especially
   strengthens the will and builds resistance to quitting the task
   ahead.
4. The cessation of late hours. Amusements both social and entertaining should be reduced to a minimum and then only in
   the nature of relaxation from strenuous work.

Cerutty delivered this philosophy along with quotes from Plato,
Buddha, Jesus, Freud, Einstein, and St. Francis of Assisi, among others.
He stressed the importance of yoga, nonconformity, a diet of oats, the
study of nature and animals, and running barefoot to connect with the
Earth. There were also the impromptu lessons after their meals, like the
time when Cerutty lectured them on warming up. A cat was sitting on a
ledge outside one of the huts when their coach snuck over and emptied
a bucket of water over it. The cat leapt away and disappeared in a flash.
Cerutty then expounded: "There. Did the cat do stretches? Did the cat
jog around? Did the cat do knee bends? Did the cat have a track suit on
before racing? No, the cat just got up and went. No more warming up.
Forget it."

For Landy, the son of an accountant and the product of private
schools, this was wild stuff. He laughed off most of it, but there was
wisdom in what Cerutty said about training hard. The body had amazing limits that most people never tested; Cerutty drove Landy to try.
He had helped bring out a discipline and focus that the young runner
never suspected he had. This ability had been dormant, but now it revealed itself. The other athletes at Portsea were impressed by Landy's
discipline. During the hard runs that seemed to last forever they also
realized they could never match it.

There was no sense of jealousy, however. In fact, Landy took away
from this time with Cerutty more than important lessons. He became

one of a tightly knit group of friends at Portsea—among them Perry and Macmillan as well as three-milers Geoff Warren and Trevor Robbins. The hard training and rustic setting combined to create a sort of boot camp, one that forged friendship and brought the athletes together. Landy, Robbins, Warren, and two others bunked in the "ski hut," which was a modified wooden container that was originally used to import Volkswagen cars. The first night Landy stayed there he had a bad dream about trying to get out of a hole. The nightmare was so vivid that he literally clawed his way out of his top bunk and crashed to the floor. The next night Landy agreed to be roped into his bed. Meanwhile, Perry and Macmillan, the two more established Stotans, were staying with Cerutty in an old cabin nicknamed after the luxury hotel "Menzies" because of its superior accommodations. One morning after a particularly cold night Landy came up to Macmillan and explained, "It's pretty tough out here. Nobody will get up and get the breakfast. If you do and get everything out and ready, the second you turn your back, suddenly all these vultures"—and Landy then jokingly mimicked a vulture poised to strike with its claws—"and little monkeys come down and eat it all up and go back up to their bunks, and yours is gone." By the end of the story he had Macmillan in hysterics. With each such episode at Portsea the others liked Landy more and more.

By the tenth day of camp the gang of runners had bonded. They were both exhausted and inspired. As for Cerutty, he came away with a better understanding of what made his runners tick. Of Landy he wrote: "He undervalues himself, his achievements, and his possibilities, merely because he measures himself not against mediocrity but against the highest levels. . . . Courage and desire to excel without undue display of effort, much less suffering, causes him to run well within himself. . . . What his highest potential level is I can only guess at." Though Cerutty thought it unlikely that Landy would ever become a true Stotan, they both knew who had set him on the path to athletic greatness.

On January 12, 1952, in Melbourne, Landy set out to break 4:10 in the mile, the time established by the Australian Olympic organizers to qualify for Helsinki. Without "Big Mac" Macmillan to push him, Landy led from the start, pushing harder than ever before, but he crossed the finish line a second short. "It is bad luck," he said after the race. "I don't suppose there will be enough finance to send us both [Macmillan and Landy] to the Olympics." He swallowed his disappointment and only a few hours later ran a 3,000-meter race in 8:53, breaking the Australian open record. The training at Portsea had increased his endurance but not his speed at shorter distances. Two weeks later in Sydney he beat Macmillan by inches, but again the time was too slow to qualify.

By the cutoff date for selection, Macmillan and Landy had both run the qualifying time in the 1,500 meter, but only Macmillan had run the requisite speed for the mile. When the list of sponsored Olympic team members was published in March, Landy's name was missing. There was a loophole, however. If Landy and a few others could come up with $750 each, they could join the team. It was a lot of money—a year's wages for some—but the Geelong Guild Athletic Club rallied to raise it for Landy. The club held Saturday night dances and "chook" raffles, which awarded the winner a dressed hen. With a lot of work and good intentions, the club members raised most of the money, but they were still $250 shy. Landy's father made up the difference. His son was going to the Olympics. John heard the news while driving a tractor on his family farm on the South Gippsland coast, 130 miles southeast of Melbourne. He had only eight weeks to train.

Before Landy left for Europe, Joseph Galli published an article whose title mirrored what many were thinking: "Victorian John Landy May Soon Become Our Greatest Middle-Distance Runner." It was the reason so much effort had been made to send him. Landy was quoted thanking Cerutty for his guidance, and then the miler made a prediction, not of future success but rather of his untapped potential. "I don't know just what my body can stand up to," he said—not yet.

At Kapyla Village in Helsinki, Cerutty finally quieted down. Landy lay in bed, uncertain how he would stack up against the world's best. He had made great strides in his development and had run well in England, but still he was unsure. And he was very sensitive to the fact that he owed his Olympic ticket to the generosity of family and friends. He felt pressure to live up to the efforts they had made to get him there in the first place. Yet each day he spent on the track, observing the speed and fluid style of other athletes, his confidence in his ability to compete against them weakened. His coach may have believed that he had the greatest insight into running and training, but Landy knew these Europeans and Americans had pretty good ideas of their own about what it took to be world-class. He knew he would soon find out how good.

4

If you can meet with Triumph and Disaster
And treat those two imposters just the same . . .
If you can fill the unforgiving minute
With sixty seconds' worth of distance run —
Yours is the Earth and everything that's in it,
And — which is more — you'll be a Man, my son!

— RUDYARD KIPLING, "If"

THE RAIN OF the opening ceremonies left the red-brick-dust track a soupy mess. During the night Finnish groundskeepers spread petrol over it and lit hundreds of small fires to burn off the water. Smoke billowed into the sky over the stadium, and its acrid scent permeated the surrounding streets. By dawn on Sunday, July 20, the track had dried, and it was rolled and leveled before the first athletes arrived.

Wes Santee awakened in his room unsure of what to do. Throughout the morning tens of thousands of people descended on the stadium. Scores of athletes, many of whom represented countries that had been at war a few years before, milled about the Olympic Village, passing the time between training sessions, meals, and their competitions. Santee dared not step outside Kaplya, certain he would get lost or run into trouble. He was one of the youngest members of the track and field team. It was his first Olympics, and for the life of him, he could not find out what he needed to know. When was he competing? Against whom?

And when could he train? Remarkably, this fundamental information proved elusive. Everyone had their own races to worry about, and even though this Olympics was being built up as a contest for national pride, particularly between the Americans and the Soviets, Santee was beginning to realize that this did not necessarily mean team leadership and cooperation were priorities.

He was left to fend for himself, a situation that was utterly foreign to him. At the University of Kansas he was used to being surrounded by teammates who looked after each other. He was also used to his coach telling him when to arrive for practice, whom he was competing against the next weekend, how to run the race, what to eat beforehand, when to arrive at the stadium, and where he was allowed to warm up. This management of the details allowed him to concentrate on the one thing he had supreme confidence in: his running. As a member of the U.S. Olympic team, however, directions to the dining hall and bedroom were about the most useful bits of information he had been given. He felt alone and, as the games commenced, increasingly panicked. The pit in his stomach was less from thoughts of his upcoming race than from worry over how he was going to find out when it was set to take place.

After a day spent scrambling about trying to track down team officials, he cornered a few older American athletes who had a schedule of events and listings about who was competing in which heats. Santee was scheduled to run in the 5,000-meter qualifying round on July 22 at five o'clock, and yes, there would be an announcer calling out the lap times so that he would know the pace he was running. But they had no idea what kind of competitors he would be facing or whether it would be a slow or fast race. It was quite certain, however, that as part of the American team, which had won half of all the gold medals presented in track and field in 1948, Santee was expected to win. Late that afternoon, when he went to work out on the training track, he was the only American to neglect wearing his "U.S.A.—Helsinki—1952" jersey, having chosen instead to appear in his orange-red pants and blue University of Kansas jersey. He wanted to win for his country as much as anyone, but at the moment he felt a lot more comfortable in his KU colors.

On the first day of the Olympics, Czech star Emil Zatopek stormed to victory in the 10,000-meter championship, beating British hopeful Gordon Pirie to win the first of what many assumed would be two gold medals. The United States captured its first gold in track and field thanks to high-jumper Walter Davis, the six-foot-eight-inch Texan who set a new Olympic record in the process. The Soviets countered by sweeping the women's discus. The second day of events saw an American stranglehold in track and field. The Soviets ruled gymnastics. By the third day newspapers around the world were headlining the points table: the United States was in first position, the Soviet Union was second, and Czechoslovakia was third. Great Britain ranked fourth and had yet to capture a gold. As promised, the fifteenth Olympiad was shaping into a battle between the Americans and the Soviets.

National pride had always played a role in the Olympics, but never as much as it did in the 1952 games. In the four years leading up to Helsinki, the Soviets had "mobilized to win the Olympic War," as *Life* magazine put it. They combed the countryside for athletes, hired hundreds of coaches, built stadiums, and poured billions of rubles into training programs. No effort was spared. In Helsinki, Russia (along with the Eastern Bloc countries Poland, Bulgaria, Hungary, Romania, and Czechoslovakia) demanded separate "Reds Only" housing and training quarters, and they afforded their athletes every luxury, including platters of caviar and smoked salmon. In their camp in Otaniemi they hung a huge portrait of Stalin over the entrance and erected a wooden scoreboard to post their point totals. The cold war, which was developing on the Korean peninsula and through the atomic arms race, had entered the sporting arena with a decided chill.

The United States was equally focused on winning, and when it came to preparations, they were hardly lacking. After all, the team was primarily composed of scholarship-funded college athletes who had devoted endless hours to training under the guidance of full-time coaches. One needed simply to look for the jugs of vitamins available for "Americans Only" in the Kapyla dining halls to appreciate the special treatment they enjoyed. Many complained that countries like Britain, which invented the idea of the amateur athlete, didn't stand a chance in the face of what amounted to a "professional" approach to sport. Right or wrong, sport was changing, and Helsinki marked a symbolic shifting point. The only remaining questions were who would win this particular matchup and by what margin.

Santee had a front seat to this battle, particularly since one of the greatest rivalries between the two countries was in basketball. Half of the American team comprised University of Kansas players, and he was privy to the stories of seven-foot Russian stars and how long they had trained together. But Santee had his own concerns about winning for his country, particularly since the track and field team was considered one of the big point scorers for the American team.

By Tuesday, July 22, the day of his qualifying round, Santee had learned little about his race, and he desperately wished Easton could have been there. Santee discovered that he could not warm up on the track before the race, which was part of his normal routine, so he jogged around outside the stadium before returning to the locker room to be called out for his heat. All around him athletes were speaking in unrecognizable languages, and he had no idea who among them he was competing against or what times they usually ran. His biggest fear was falling too far behind the leaders. There was no coach to speak to about strategy. He could not help thinking that he should not have even been in this race. The 1,500 meter was his best distance, and one he certainly had much more experience running. Seldom did a runner, even one as naturally talented as Santee, have the speed and stamina to compete at a world-class level in both the 1,500 and 5,000 meters. With each passing minute his apprehension grew.

When he saw Fred Wilt, the Indiana University alumnus who had competed extensively overseas, Santee hurried across the locker room to speak to him. Wilt would know what Santee should do.

"I really don't know much," Wilt said after Santee told him who was in the heat against him. "Except that Schade guy. He'll probably run a steady even race. Follow him."

And with this information, Santee was called to the track for his heat by an Olympic official. He jogged into the stadium, feeling only slightly comforted by this one piece of advice. With Easton he would have gone over the race on the blackboard in Easton's office at KU, his coach indicating lap times to shoot for, how the other runners traditionally ran, and when to move with the pack or ahead of it. His race was literally drawn out for him in chalk. Only when Santee approached the starting line did he notice the German ace Herbert Schade. Except for the Canadian runner Richard Ferguson, the rest of the field was a mystery. What if the German started out too fast or too slow? What was the best time Schade was capable of running? There were many questions he needed answered, and it was only seconds before the race started. By the time the athletes were called to their marks, Santee was overwhelmed. This was the Olympics. He was representing his country, and perhaps more important, Kansas. He had to do well, and yet he felt displaced, like he had been blindfolded, led out into a dark field, and left alone to find his way out.

Soon enough the starting gun fired, and Santee was running. Going into the first turn, he was in good position behind Schade, right where he wanted to be. The first lap went well: Schade led, and Santee kept back by several runners but stayed close enough. By the third lap Santee and the German were alone. The others had fallen back on the pace. Halfway through the race Santee sensed his legs tiring, but he held on to second position. At 3,000 meters he heard Schade's time called — 8:23 — and then his own, two seconds slower. It was too fast. The best he had run this distance was 8:44, and he was 150 yards ahead of that pace. Santee began to lose confidence. The pace was too fast. He couldn't maintain this kind of speed. What he should have known before this point in the race was that the German was using this heat to show his speed to Czechoslovakia's Zatopek and France's Alain Mimoun, both of whom were in separate heats and would likely prove Schade's stiffest competition in the final. An Olympic record would be broken if Schade continued at this pace, and he meant to continue.

Half a lap later Santee lost momentum. His arms and legs leadened; his chest couldn't bring in enough breath. His pace slackened. By 4,000 meters he hardly felt like he was moving — the sensation was more like running through water than over a track. Everything seemed to be in slow motion. He couldn't drive his legs. Runner after runner passed him, and there was nothing — even if he had been suddenly infused with all the willpower in the world — that he could do. His body had given out. He finished at a dismally slow pace, thirteenth overall, in a time of 15:10.4 — the worst showing at this distance of his career.

As he put on his sweatsuit he was exhausted physically, but the fear and dread before the race had taken an even greater toll. Emotionally he was a wasteland. He didn't want to speak to anybody. He was embarrassed when he left the stadium, wanting to hole up in his room until they flew out of Helsinki. As he later said, "Not only did I lose, I wasn't even in the race." For an athlete who had seldom known defeat, particularly at this level, this was agony. It was like the loss of a first love: his heart literally ached.

Sitting in the stands at the Olympic stadium on July 24, Landy did not like his chances in the 1,500-meter race set to take place in less than an hour. He was in the fourth, and probably most difficult, heat in the qualifying round. Only the top four finishers in his race would move forward to the semifinal, and his eight-man heat included French and Yugoslav champions, Patrick El Mabrouk and Andrija Otenhajmer, respectively, as well as America's Bob McMillen and England's Roger Bannister, the latter of whom Landy had met briefly while competing in London. Landy knew that his best time in the distance (3:52.8) was several seconds slower than his competitors', plus he was much more accustomed to running a mile than 1,500 meters.

Although only 120 yards shorter than the mile, the 1,500 meter was an awkward race. Standard European tracks, Helsinki included, were 400 meters in length, meaning that runners competed over three and three-quarters laps. Landy disliked the race, as he later explained, because "there's nothing graceful about it. You don't start where you finish, it's ugly." The split times were difficult to understand, and given the incomplete first lap, he found it hard to get into his rhythm.

At the moment, however, Landy was more interested in watching the 5,000-meter final about to start. He had failed to qualify for the longer event, finishing over thirty seconds behind the winner of his heat, Alain Mimoun, in tenth position overall. It was a poor showing, but his personal best, achieved in early February, had been only two seconds faster. He had to settle for watching his friend and countryman Les Perry try to take home a medal in an event featuring the "Human Locomotive" Emil Zatopek, former gold medal winner Gaston Reiff, new Olympic record holder Herbert Schade, and English up-and-comer Chris Chataway, as well as the fearsome French-Algerian Mimoun. It promised to be a must-see battle.

When the gun went off, the redheaded Chataway moved into an early lead, at the head of the pack for the first lap, with Schade behind him and Perry in the middle of the pack. The Australian team cheered on the "Mighty Atom," but by the end of the third lap, with the first four runners averaging sixty-seven seconds per lap, Perry looked like a minor player on a great stage. Soon enough Zatopek was setting the pace.

The very sight of the thirty-year-old Czech army major was frightening. His bony five-feet-eight-inch frame sped down the track in an unrhythmic mess of arms and legs. His head rolled back and forth as he ran; his tongue protruded from his mouth; his face contorted as if, one sportswriter noted, he was experiencing an "apoplectic fit." Yet the runners knew that he was more fit than they were, and Zatopek did not hesitate to inform them of the matter, midrace. While his competitors gasped for air, the Czech considered it a good time for a conversation. During his 10,000-meter final in which he broke his own world record, Zatopek ran alongside the Russian Alexander Anoufriev, who had set a rapid early pace, and admonished him on the dangers of going out too fast. As Zatopek blazed into the lead in the 5,000-meter final, he yelled back at Schade in German: "Herbert, do two laps with me!"

Two thousand meters from the finish, the tactical race began. Schade, answering Zatopek's taunt, burst into the lead, with Chataway and Reiff staying close behind. Zatopek faded back. Then Pirie picked up his tempo, shifting easily past the Czech and the rest of the field. Schade quickly regained his first position, pushing Pirie aside, and then Mimoun started to make his move. Five hundred meters to go, and it was Schade, Chataway, Mimoun, Zatopek, and Pirie. At the bell Zatopek kicked. From the stands the spectators could almost feel the excruciating effort required of him to make the move. But it was to no advantage. Chataway cruised past him one hundred meters down the track, with Schade and Mimoun breathing down his neck. Zatopek trailed in fourth position, looking altogether finished. Schade then regained the lead, only to have Chataway steal it right back at the final turn.

"ZAT-O-PEK, ZAT-O-PEK, ZAT-O-PEK!" The cry erupted from the stands. The crowd was on its feet. Face twisted, mouth open, arms flailing, eyes split wide, Zatopek found another spurt. Suddenly Chataway caught the track's edge with his foot, and he went crashing onto the red-brick surface, churning up a cloud of dust behind him. Mimoun and Schade attempted to hold off Zatopek as he drove around the turn, but there was nothing they could do to keep him from victory. The crowd boomed again when the Czech sprinted down the straight, every step looking like his last, yet somehow he found a way to continue forward. He snapped the tape with a new Olympic record time, Mimoun was second, Schade third, Reiff fourth, Chataway fifth (after picking himself up off the track), and Perry finished in an exhausted sixth place.

Announcers, journalists, spectators, and athletes alike understood that they had just witnessed greatness in the form of Emil Zatopek. He had now claimed his second gold medal, and with his participation in the marathon a few days later, a race he had never run, Zatopek was proving he deserved the acclaim of being the finest distance runner since Nurmi. Although Perry had not medaled, he had run his best time, and Landy had to believe that his friend was proud simply to have competed in the same race as his hero Zatopek. Landy himself was impressed by the Czech's tactical skill, but more than that, he had never seen someone of such overpowering physical fitness.

Everyone in the stadium was still reveling in the Zatopek victory when the 1,500-meter qualifying round began. While Landy warmed up with a light jog on the infield, his countryman Don Macmillan placed fourth in his heat, qualifying for the semifinal the next day. Of the runners in the three heats before Landy's who advanced to the next round, all had run better than his fastest 1,500-meter time. He had his work cut out for him.

Landy stepped to the line. Three minutes and fifty-seven seconds later his Olympic hopes were dashed. El Mabrouk came from behind to finish first with a time of 3:55.8, an unexceptional pace. Macmillan, Bannister, and the Hungarian V. Tolgyesi followed, in that order, with Landy one second behind in fifth position. As Landy later described it, the last one hundred meters of the race was a "mad scramble," but he was too tired in the final straight to overtake Tolgyesi.

The Australian miler was disappointed in himself, regardless of his doubts before the race. He had traveled all this way and failed to make even the semifinals. He knew the reason too: since his good runs in England, he had come off his peak, a consequence of incomplete training. Cerutty took his athlete's loss as a personal affront, and after the race he was not exactly comforting to Landy. The exact form of his vitriol is probably best left forgotten, but his coach's general attitude toward Landy—right or wrong—was that he lacked a "killer instinct." And worse, throughout the Australian team, which was not performing well except for sprinters Shirley Strickland and Marjorie Jackson, there were grumblings that many athletes had not deserved to make the Olympics in the first place. In fact, the team manager issued a report after returning to Australia that bluntly stated, "No man or woman should be selected for future Australian teams who is not prepared to undergo the Spartan-like period of self-denial and rigorous training as practiced in other countries."

Unfair as this attitude was, it stung Landy, who was one of the last athletes to make the team. However, he refused to wallow in his failure to qualify for the 1,500- or 5,000-meter finals. He thought there was a lot he could learn while in Helsinki, especially from the athletes who dominated the games. Observing Zatopek, for instance, tempered the disappointment that Landy felt.

Long before his 5,000-meter win and subsequent marathon victory, Zatopek was of interest to Landy. Cerutty often talked about him, and Les Perry idolized him because of his infamously hard training schedule and unrivaled record in distance running. When Perry first arrived in Helsinki, he had put on his track suit and run the three miles across to Otaniemi, where the iron curtain countries were housed. Once past the guards at the gate, he found Zatopek down on the track and ran alongside him until he mustered the nerve to say, "I'm Les Perry from Australia." Zatopek put his arm around the bespectacled fan and said in English, "You come from the other village to see me? You honor me! Join me. We will run together." After working out, they had a shower, dinner, and tea. Then Zatopek invited Perry to watch the Bolshoi Ballet performing in the camp. When Perry finally returned to Kapyla, he regaled his roommates with the experience.

After his 1,500-meter loss, Landy made it his job to study other athletes at the old track near the stadium where they trained. He spent hours there, mentally noting how they ran and learning about their training methods. Zatopek, whom Landy later referred to as the "Piped Piper of Hamelin," fascinated him the most. With a pack of other devotees at the track, Landy followed the Czech as he jogged forward and backward, speaking about running. There was a lot to jot down afterward because Zatopek talked almost as fast as he ran, so there was much to take in. Zatopek shared his love for the sport and told how he had achieved so much since taking up running at the age of nineteen. "When I was in the 1950 European Championships . . ."—he began one story, talking about the race and the athletes he competed against. "Last year I was doing twenty four-hundreds in training . . . ," he would say, or, "I was running in the snow in my army boots. . . ." Zatopek's training methods were based on making running a way of life. He believed in training one's willpower in small steps, every day. Discipline was the key. As for style, which he was accused of lacking, he was plainspoken: "I shall learn to have a better style once they start judging races according to their beauty. So long as it's a question of speed then my attention will be directed to seeing how fast I can cover the ground." His three gold medals proved to Landy that Zatopek was on the right track.

Zatopek wasn't about antics, Eastern philosophy, recriminations, or wild theories—unlike Cerutty, who had Don Macmillan preparing for the 1,500-meter final by jogging around the track wearing two track suits and a towel wrapped around his head. Zatopek had devised schedules and methods of maintaining the balance between speed and endurance throughout the year. Landy liked his analytical approach. Cerutty disliked schedules: he felt they confined the soul. The two men were opposites, and Landy had the intelligence and independence to understand that he owed his coach his achievements to date, but not his future. While in Helsinki, Landy plotted this future.

Roger Bannister was too exhausted to sleep. No amount of tossing, turning, shuffling, or kicking his feet against the sheets would allow him to drop off. Every second and minute brought the 1,500-meter final closer; every hour a new wave of anxiety swept over him. At 4:30 P.M. the next day he would line up against eleven of the best middle-distance men in the world. His confidence was torn by having already run two races instead of the one he had expected to run to qualify for the final. He feared that he was already beaten.

The past week had brought only restless days and nights. He and his roommates—sprinter Nicholas Stacey, quarter-miler Alan Dick, and three-miler Chris Chataway—had tried to relieve the constant churning of their thoughts about victory or defeat and about what would make the difference between the two. Resting on their unkempt beds, they spoke of politics and history, read books, or joked around with each other. One evening Stacey mounted a wooden box, as though it were an Olympic podium, to accept his imaginary gold medal and offer a congratulatory speech. Other times they discussed their competitors, particularly Zatopek, who they thought inhuman in ability. "While he goes for a twenty-mile training run on his only free day," Chataway said, "we lie here panting with exhaustion, moaning that the gods are unkind to us, and that we're too intelligent to train hard. It's all nonsense." Inevitably, the four thought again and again about that second when the starting gun would fire and whether they would prove good enough. Regardless of what happened, they promised each other that once the Olympics had ended they would never put themselves through this torture again.

By the morning of Saturday, July 26, Bannister was the only one of the roommates who was still tense, though he tried as much as possible not to show it, keeping his doubts about being able to win the race to himself. The others had finished their events, nobody in triumph, and Chataway most disastrously by falling in the final lap of the 5,000-meter final. Bannister had watched the race, and its conclusion impressed on him how important his finishing kick would be.

Absence of victory was the story for the entire British team. Two days remained in the track and field competitions, and they had won only a handful of medals, not one of them gold. Nor had any British athlete won gold in any of the other events. The British reporter who had said before the games that he would "eat a pair of spiked shoes if our team doesn't win twelve gold medals" was dangerously close to having a mouthful of leather. Headlines cried out, "Don't Worry, We Are Still in the Fight," yet column after column reported failures and missed chances.

There was one hope left, though: Bannister. Now more than ever his countrymen rallied around him. A few days before the *Daily Mirror* columnist, Tom Phillips, had compared Bannister to a great racehorse trainer who "rarely bothered about picking minor honors here and there. If he wished to win a classic race, he got his horse perfectly fit for that day and nearly every time his horse was first past the post." Phillips concluded: "I believe Bannister will win and teach some of our other athletes, and the officials and coaches, a lesson in strategy and tactics."

If confidence could be drawn from the amount of column space guaranteeing his victory, Bannister was a sure thing. Most sportswriters considered him their favorite. But his legs hurt. He hadn't slept soundly in days. He was plagued by worries, both real and otherwise. His qualifying round and semifinal in the previous two days had been brutal. To avoid the jostling and elbowing of a crowded field, he ran both races in the second and third lanes, adding at least twenty yards to each and exhausting himself even more. The semifinal was especially taxing because there was a fight to the finish that placed him only a narrow four-tenths of a second ahead of Stanislav Jungwirth from Czechoslovakia, who failed to qualify. Usually Bannister required three or four days of recovery after such a race because of his limited training regime, but now he had been given only twenty-four hours.

As he waited in the room and the minutes ticked past, Bannister knew that the 1,500-meter final would draw the world's attention. He knew that the stands would be jammed to capacity. He knew that his competitors had also trained thousands of hours for this day and that they would strive with every muscle and ounce of will to claim victory.

It was impossible not to rehearse the coming race over and over again in his head: How quickly should he start? Should he stay on the inside lane or move to the outside? Where must he be by the third lap? How close to the finish could he start his burst?

When Bannister made his way down the tunnel underneath the stadium that afternoon, he was no less tortured. His face was blanched, his step uncertain. Australian miler Don Macmillan walked alongside him. Macmillan was in bad shape as well, dehydrated and soaked with perspiration after the voodoo warm-up imposed by his coach, yet he noticed that Bannister, whom he had run against in New Zealand in 1950, was pale and nervous.

"Good luck, Don," Bannister said, heading up into the stadium.

"Thanks, Roger," Macmillan choked out.

The time had come. When the Duke of Edinburgh arrived in the stands for the 1,500-meter event, the crowd cheered. The sun even broke through the clouds to honor this signature Olympic race. While the other athletes stretched and jogged around the infield to warm up, Bannister rested on the bench. Chris Brasher, the British steeplechaser and former president of the Cambridge University Athletic Club, watched from the stands and later described his friend's appearance: "There was a peculiar loneliness about Roger. He stood apart from the others, looking drawn and white, as if he were about to go into a torture chamber." Chris Chataway was also in the stands. He had written his mother the day before to tell her how concerned he was about Bannister's state in the days before his race. As Chataway waited for the race to begin he worried that his roommate had already defeated himself in his mind.

Though tense and sapped of energy from two heats, Bannister still felt that he had a chance. Every race was imperfect, and he had always come through in the past. After Finnish middle-distance runner Denis Johansson took a presumptuous pre-race victory lap, the starter called the race. With the eleven others, Bannister came to the line. The crowd hushed for the gun. He had prepared his whole athletic career for this moment. Suddenly they were off.

The German Rolf Lamers carried the field through the first 400-meter lap in 57.8 seconds, looking like he might be pacing for his countryman and the favorite to win, Werner Lueg. Throughout this first lap Bannister stayed to the inside. He did not have the energy to battle in the middle of the pack. Lamers soon faded, and Lueg took the lead, finishing the second lap at a slower pace in 2:01.4. Bannister had managed to come up through the field and was running in fifth place. By the bell Lueg was still leading. He finished 1,200 meters in 3:03, a slow pace given the field's talent. Only three-quarters of a lap to go.

In the radio broadcast booth BBC announcer Harold Abrahams was worried for Bannister, despite the fact that he was in the right position —third—for making his break: "He is not running as well as one would hope. He is looking rather tired."

In the back straight of the last lap the race heated up. Two hundred meters from the finish, the whole field was nearly sprinting. Down the straight Olle Aberg of Sweden and then El Mabrouk of France tried to surge to the head of the pack. Bannister was next, deciding to strike at the same time Lovelock had in the 1936 Olympics to win the gold.

"Bannister is in third position with 180 meters to go," said Abrahams. "Bannister fighting magnificently. Bannister now trying to get into the lead."

This is it, Bannister thought. Although he had suffered nothing but dread since learning of the added semifinal, he was in the ideal spot to win the gold. He had managed the jostling field, kept with the pace, and avoiding tripping. As he moved into the final turn, now in second place, he called on the full speed of his finishing kick, his most potent weapon. He gave the order to his legs to go. But for the first time in his life his kick wasn't there. When he should have leapt ahead, he stalled. His legs just didn't have the energy. It was a shock. Little Josey Barthel from Luxembourg swept by him, unbelievably, impossibly. Then the American, Bob McMillen, passed him as well. Bannister felt drained and helpless, knowing he had lost.

"Bannister is fading!" Abrahams called into the microphone.

Lueg held strong, stretching his lead by three yards at the end of the turn. Barthel then struck, delivering the finish Bannister wanted for his own. The Luxembourg miler cruised past Lueg in the final fifty meters with McMillen also coming up fast.

"And it's Barthel wins. Second the American. Third Lueg. Fourth Bannister. Time 3:45.2."

It was a new Olympic record and the surprise upset of the games. Bannister was so exhausted by the end of the race that he had to hold on to the back of Lueg's singlet to keep from pitching to the track. He hadn't even claimed a bronze. The British team was distraught. Columnists began to sharpen their pencils. This was a betrayal of trust.

Barthel was handed roses, and then he rested on a bench to take off his shoes. *The New Yorker's* A. J. Liebling described the scene: "He had had no trainer and no compatriot with him when he came into the stadium, and he was still alone. It must have been a great solace to him on the night before the race, knowing he had nobody to disappoint." How different it was for Bannister who, full of emotion, watched Barthel later mount the victory dais and weep tears of joy while Luxembourg's anthem played throughout the stadium.

The Helsinki final was a disaster. Bannister told his friend Brasher years later: "A disaster is something which is shared between you and the public which expects something of you and which you cannot or have not fulfilled."

As he headed back to the Olympic Village later that afternoon, fending off the press, who were preparing to excoriate him for his insufficient preparations, Bannister needed to find a way to overcome what had happened. He couldn't go out a loser. His answer would be to attempt a challenge that had been in the making for a very long time: the four-minute mile. He would not be alone in the effort either.

5

The man who has made the mile record is W. G. George
. . . His time was 4 minutes 12.75 seconds and the proba-
bility is that this record will never be beaten.

— HARRY ANDREWS, 1903

To the farthest limit he searches out . . .

— JOB 28:3

BEFORE STOPWATCHES, cinder tracks, and perfect records, man
ran for the purest of reasons: to survive. The saying goes that
"every morning in Africa, an antelope wakes up. It knows it must
outrun the fastest lion, or it will be killed. Every morning in Africa, a
lion wakes up. It knows it must run faster than the fastest antelope, or it
will starve. It doesn't matter whether you're a lion or an antelope —
when the sun comes up, you'd better be running." There are few in-
stincts more natural than the body in full motion as it races across a
field or through the trees. From the beginning, we were all made to run.
In days past, when "survival of the fittest" meant exactly this, the only
measure of the race was whether the hunted reached safety before
being overtaken. Seconds and tenths of seconds had no meaning.

Sport evolved from this competition to survive. In ancient Egypt
newly chosen kings went on a ceremonial run, as historian Edward
Sears wrote, that "symbolized laying claim to his domain and proved
that he was fit enough for the demands of his position." Thirty years

after the king's coronation, and every three years thereafter, he was challenged to run the same long distance he had run as a young man. If he failed, he lost his power to rule. Other early societies proved status by skills such as hitting targets with a bow and arrow, lifting heavy rocks, or jumping across streams, but the ability to run faster and farther than others remained a dominant standard.

It is fitting that the first event in civilization's earliest and greatest celebration of sport, the Olympic Games in 776 B.C., was a footrace. A Greek citizen named Coroebus sprinted two hundred yards across a meadow alongside the river Alpheus and was crowned winner with a garland made from the leaves and twigs of an olive tree. Sporting ability was integral to Greek life, and the Greeks were the first to promote what would later be phrased *mens sana in corpore sano*—a sound mind in a sound body.

Ancient Olympic champions were treated like gods—worthy of worship and great odes. The athletes ran their races naked and barefoot, and as the years passed they instituted ten-month training regimes and specialized in certain distances. Longer races involved running from one end of the stadium to the other and back, the distances varying from stadium to stadium. Success was recorded by how many victories an athlete had claimed over his fellows, not by their times (crudely measured in those days by sundial or water clock). The Romans favored gladiator contests over athletics, but they made two important contributions to the story of the four-minute mile: first, they were devoted to statistics and detailed the results of their sporting heroes (namely chariot racers); second, they were the first to come up with the distance of the mile. Roman soldiers calculated their long marches in *mille passus* (*mille:* one thousand; *passus:* a two-step stride). Given that each stride was roughly two feet, five inches—shorter than average because the soldiers carried over fifty pounds of provisions and weapons—the earliest mile translated into roughly 1,611 yards.

In sixteenth-century England, footmen, who traveled long distances by the sides of heavy coaches, steering their masters away from dangerous spots in the road, were the first to race—often at the bidding of their masters. They used the mileposts, first installed by the ruling Romans, as starting and finishing lines. This tradition developed throughout the seventeenth and eighteenth centuries into "freak runs," part of village festivals, where the competitors ran on stilts or carrying a load of fish. Endurance contests, whether walking or running, were also popular.

By the nineteenth century "pedestrians," as the English runners were known, were running on the roads for cash. Events were often organized by local pubs in order to draw a crowd. Since the mile race was a favorite, it paid to specialize in that distance. The idea of competing for a mile record instead of simply against one's opponent in a particular race evolved gradually from the standardization of the mile at 1,760 yards, advances in timekeeping, and an early industrial society's passion for quantifying everything in sight. It so happened that a quarter-mile grass track fit nicely around a cricket ground or football field, and it was much safer racing there than on increasingly busy roads. Technology, progress, and coincidence had all played a part. Now all the mile race needed was a few fast souls.

Running a mile in less than five minutes was considered the breaking point until Scottish landowner Captain Robert Barclay came along. Famous for his cheerful disposition, predilection for lifting heavy objects, and walking a thousand miles in a thousand hours, Barclay won five hundred guineas by posting a 4:50 mile in 1804. Then, in 1825, James Metcalf, "a tailor by trade, but a pedestrian by profession," who trained by chasing hounds, beat Barclay's time by a margin of twenty seconds. Over the next sixty years various milers chipped away at the record, second by painful second, the best runners earning championship belts for their efforts. Over time the stakes wagered rose into the thousands of pounds.

For most of the nineteenth century the "gentleman amateur" was absent from this scene. This British public school ideal, favored by the universities of Oxford and Cambridge, was indeed a noble thought, but the runners who subscribed to its strict rules were no match for the best of the professionals. That was, until chemistry apprentice Walter George began training seriously and reduced his mile time to 4:18.8 in 1884. Since this was two seconds shy of the record held for the previous eight years by the professional William Cummings, a showdown between the two was inevitable.

To test himself against Cummings, George was forced to forfeit his amateur status, despite having offered his earnings from the races to a hospital charity. After a series of preliminary races in which they both had a share of the victories, Cummings and George faced off for the

"Mile of the Century" on August 23, 1886. Twenty-five thousand spectators crowded around a bicycle track to watch George run so fast that he left Cummings unconscious behind him on the last lap. His record of 4:12.8 lasted three decades and set the stage for Paavo Nurmi to introduce the four-minute mile to the world, establishing an irresistible challenge to athletes that would guarantee their place in history.

It was impossible to know who first uttered the challenge of running the mile in less than four minutes. Reports date back to 1770 of an English runner who made the distance from Charter House Wall to Shoreditch Church in the City of London in this time, but even nineteenth-century historians cast a skeptical eye on the account. In 1915, when American Norman Taber broke George's record by less than two-tenths of a second, the track and field world was not set on fire. It was too slim a difference to warrant much more than a passing remark in the record books. Then, on August 23, 1923, Paavo Nurmi, a twenty-six-year-old farm engineer from Turku, Finland, was drawn into a faster first lap than he would have liked by Swedish miler Edvin Wide. Nurmi, who always ran with a large stopwatch in his hand and preferred an even-paced race, kept up with Wide's fast start. By the third lap Wide faded and Nurmi continued the pace. He broke Taber's record by two seconds with a 4:10.4. It was a giant step forward given how long it had taken Taber to reduce Walter George's mark by just a fraction of a second. Suddenly the mile record was in play again, and when Nurmi won gold medals at the 1924 Paris Olympics in the 1,500 and 5,000 meters in the space of forty-two minutes, he looked capable of anything. Joseph Binks, a noted journalist and former British miler, suggested to Nurmi that the mile barrier was within grasp. Nurmi replied, "No, four minutes four seconds, maybe!" Self-deprecation or not, the Finnish miler had put the possibility of a four-minute mile on the table.

Inspired by Nurmi, a new wave of talented milers appeared in the 1930s, and their races packed stadiums around the world. Races at Madison Square Garden rivaled modern-day prizefights. The air was dense with smoke, the crowds rowdy and devoted to their favorite runners, and the stands so close to the track that fans felt the rush of air when the field surged past. The first miler to run four minutes and single digits was Frenchman Jules Ladoumegue. An orphan who first competed in village-to-village races, Ladoumegue competed on pure emotion. Before races he was so agitated that he had to be pulled to the starting line.

If a door closed suddenly behind him, he nearly jumped out of his skin. Once he was running, though, he loved the heat of battle and became a national treasure for his efforts. On October 4, 1931, he took advantage of a windless, sunny Parisian afternoon and the pacemaking of half-miler Rene Morel to reduce the mile record to 4:09.2.

Jack Lovelock, the New Zealand–born and British-adopted miler with a compact frame and a keen idea of his abilities and limitations, was next to lower the record. In his youth Lovelock had developed his smooth running style by striding alongside a stone wall while a friend on the opposite side chastised him when he saw Lovelock's head moving up or down. On July 15, 1933, in Princeton, New Jersey, he ran a 4:07.6 while representing Oxford University against the Americans. After the race the New York Herald Tribune praised his effort: "It was all so easily accomplished, with so little outward evidence of stress and strain, as to make a four-minute mile seem just around the corner." Lovelock never reduced this time, but his Olympic gold medal in the 1,500 meter, his epic races against Glenn Cunningham and Sydney Wooderson, and his insight about training and tactics added to his legacy.

With a time of 4:06.8, Lovelock's rival, the American Glenn Cunningham, seized the mile record only eleven months after the New Zealander had claimed it. The "Kansas Powerhouse" was a legend long before he ran the fastest mile in the world. At seven years of age he and his brother tried to stoke the fire in their small schoolhouse's stove by dousing the coals with kerosene. His brother died as a result of the accident, and Glenn's legs were burned almost beyond repair. During recovery he found walking more painful than running, and an athlete was born. Cunningham learned to work around his disability, and at his first intervarsity mile at the University of Kansas he exploded on the last lap to win the field. His running inspired a generation of Kansas farm boys and gave Americans the hope that the four-minute mile could be theirs.

Sydney Wooderson brought the mile record back to England in 1937. Walter George, now seventy-nine years old, was there to see it. Wooderson, at five feet six inches and 126 pounds, was an atypical miler. When he stepped onto the track in his thick glasses and with the meek demeanor of a solicitor's clerk, he looked the underdog. Once he set off running, however, he was a force of indomitable energy. He dealt with his loss to Lovelock at the 1936 Olympics by staging an attempt to beat Cunningham's mile time. On August 28, 1937, at Motspur Park, he arranged for pacemakers from his athletic club to lead him around the first three laps. Using his famed kick, he handled the last lap alone and registered a time of 4:06.4.

Slowly, by investing more and more time and energy in training, milers approached the goal of four laps of the track in four minutes. Six and a half seconds was a long time off, and the small reductions in the record made by the best runners were just that—small reductions. The possibility of seeing "the other side" of four minutes was looking increasingly uncertain.

When Swedish runners Gundar Haegg and Arne Andersson finished their epic battles at the end of World War II, the four-minute mile appeared unattainable. Of the two, Haegg had a more natural, flowing stride, but Andersson trained harder. A year apart in age, they reached their peak at the same time. Separately, they were the finest milers, in fitness and form, possibly to have ever graced the track; racing against each other, they looked to be the best who ever would. Over the course of three and a half years Haegg and Andersson passed the mile record back and forth to each other.

DATE	RUNNER	PLACE	TIME
January 1, 1942	Haegg	Gothenburg, Sweden	4:06.2
October 7, 1942	Andersson	Stockholm, Sweden	4:06.2
April 9, 1942	Haegg	Stockholm, Sweden	4:04.6
January 1, 1943	Andersson	Gothenburg, Sweden	4:02.6
July 18, 1944	Andersson	Malmo, Sweden	4:01.6
July 17, 1945	Haegg	Malmo, Sweden	4:01.4

Their duels inspired great performances, yet the barrier still stood untouched. Journalists and statisticians tried to convince the athletics world that the barrier would inevitably be scaled. They calculated that the average world-class miler could sustain a speed of 7.33 yards per second (or 15 miles per hour). This meant that the difference between Haegg's best time and the four-minute mile was a short twelve yards— less than 1 percent of the race's total distance. That was nothing, they maintained. But others disagreed, and quite publicly. Coach Brutus Hamilton, one of the most revered figures in track and field, published "The Ultimate of Human Effort," listing the perfect records beyond which man could never go for the javelin, the shot put, the 100 meter, the 400 meter, the mile, the 5,000 meter, and the 10,000 meter. Hamilton backed up his analysis with detailed statistics, but many would have considered his word final even if he had jotted these "perfect records" down on a cocktail napkin. To the question, can the mile be run in four minutes flat? Hamilton replied, not quite. The fastest time that would ever be possible, he stated, was 4:01.6. Although Hamilton, who wrote the article in 1935, had been disproved by two-tenths of a second, he still found the idea of anyone running faster difficult to imagine.

Many wanted the bogey to go away, including the 1912 Olympic 1,500-meter champion, Colonel Strode Jackson, who wrote at the height of the Haegg-Andersson struggle: "When we stop this nonsense of running like a metronome and with the watch always in mind, we will get back to real racing, the triumph of one runner over another. That is what racing was meant to be and what it will be when we get the four-minute myth out of the way."

Myth or not, twelve yards or many more, the barrier remained, and with each passing year, as runners attempted to break through its walls and failed, the mile barrier grew in fame. By 1952, as Frank Deford, one of the finest writers to report on the challenge, described, "The Poles had been reached, the mouth of the Nile found, the deepest oceans marked, and the wildest jungles trekked but the distance of the ground that measured a mile continued to resist all efforts to traverse it, on foot, in less than four minutes."

The 1952 Olympic flame had barely been snuffed out in the Helsinki stadium when the editorials and reviews of the games began spinning off the presses. Two points were indisputable: the Finns had proved to be fine hosts of the competition, and more records were broken in these games than in any other Olympics in history. Less than forty-eight hours after the closing ceremonies in Helsinki, another competition was held, this time in London's White City Stadium, pitting a British Empire team against the United States. The stadium had staged an Olympic Games itself in 1908 and was infamous for setting the official marathon distance at 26 miles, 385 yards—instead of simply 26 miles —so that the race would finish in front of Queen Alexandra's royal box. The stadium was now used for greyhound racing and an assortment of other events, including track and field. The Americans beat the British Empire team, as they had beaten the world a few short days before.

In the 4 x 1 mile relays, where four runners from each team ran a mile, Roger Bannister earned the Empire team an early lead. But the second member of his team lost this advantage. Running third leg for the Americans, Wes Santee looked like he would stretch a lead for his team too great to overcome, but John Landy, running in the same leg for the Empire team, managed to close on Santee in the final 440. The anchors for each team traded leads, but in the end the Americans won. It was the first time Bannister, Santee, and Landy had competed in the same race. None of the three would remember much of the other two from that race, retaining neither a memory of a conversation nor an impression of one another's abilities. Yet as these three milers went their separate ways — Bannister back to life at St. Mary's Hospital a short distance by Underground, and Landy and Santee on long flights to their respective countries — they each charted a course in the days ahead that would bring them back together again. It would be a struggle that they and tens of millions would never forget.

Santee flew back with an American team ripe from victory. Although the Soviets had fought well in their events, and for a few days had looked like they might actually win the most medals, they couldn't match the strength of the U.S. track and field team, which won fourteen gold medals and thirteen silver and bronze. Of his teammates, Santee was in the minority of those who did not medal. Watching the 1,500-meter final, knowing he had beaten the second-place finisher Bob McMillen "every time we had stepped on a track," left him feeling empty and helpless as a puppet. He was certain he could have won the race if he had been given the chance the amateur officials had stolen from him in Los Angeles.

Before heading back to the University of Kansas, Santee went to visit his parents in Ashland for the first time since he had ridden away on that unnamed horse. If he was waiting for his father to say how proud he was of his son, Wes left empty-handed. Either his father simply didn't understand what his son had accomplished through his running, or the man just couldn't express any feeling other than bitterness. Either way, his silence stung. Over the past two years Wes had tried to convince his mother to leave his father, but she told Wes that since he had left, his father had mended his "negative ways and stopped being so mean." Regardless, Wes wanted nothing to do with the man.

Back in Lawrence, Santee sat down with Coach Easton, who expressed his pride where Wes's father had not. Easton suggested that Santee could learn a great deal from his Olympic experience, but Santee was less philosophical. It was not in his nature to suffer defeat. In his high school senior year he had lost the mile race in the state finals to Bill Tidwell. Although expected to win, particularly since he had won his sophomore and junior years, Santee refused to be crestfallen. His close friend Don Humphreys was surprised at his indifference. "I couldn't understand how you could be up after losing the mile by a stride or two. I know Tidwell was a good distance runner, but it never occurred to me that he could beat you." Santee explained in a matter-of-fact tone, "Oh, Tidwell, he's not a miler." It took a while for Humphreys to understand this response. Then he thought of a football player who gets knocked down in a game and gets right back up and sets out to return the favor. Santee had that killer instinct. As Humphreys later said, "Guys like that never get whipped in their minds. Even when they get beat, they're not beat."

In Helsinki, Santee felt, he had learned how to fend for himself and compete against the best. He wanted to prove what a big mistake it had been to prevent him from running in the 1,500 meter, and more important, he wanted to show how good he really was. He set his sights on a goal that had always been on the horizon for him: the four-minute mile. In the list of high school prophecies published when he graduated was the following: "Wesley Santee has recently broke the world mile record in a time of 3 min., 58.3 sec. And it should stand for many years to come." Since his win at the Drake University Relays the previous spring, the prediction by sportswriters that he was a sure bet for the world mile record had brought the goal closer in sight. His blistering three-quarter-mile run in New York before leaving for the Olympics made him realize just how close he was. Only days after returning to campus, Santee marched into the office of the University of Kansas newspaper. He had an announcement to make: Wes Santee was going to be the first to run the four-minute mile. For years he had known he was capable. Now his intention was a matter of public record.

John Landy had a different announcement to make when he landed in Melbourne, but one equally telling. Directly after the British Empire versus the United States match, he boarded a flight to Australia. He had declined to join Macmillan and Perry, who, accompanied by Cerutty, were running in a series of competitions in Scandinavia. Landy needed to get back to his agricultural science studies, which had fallen by the wayside as he strove to make the Olympic team. He also wanted to start training again.

Landy wanted to show that his trip to Helsinki had been worth the time and money it had taken to get him there. This desire to redress his failure to qualify in either of his events, a failure that had been met with what he believed was unwarranted criticism, was also woven into his excitement about the prospect of becoming a faster and stronger runner. He felt he had been given the lessons—namely, in improving his stride and his training methods—to reach this new level. Zatopek and other European middle-distance runners had shown him how.

For his stride, he would be helped by a pair of European track shoes he had bought. Landy wanted nothing more to do with the kangaroo-hide track shoes made in Melbourne. They were designed primarily for sprinting on grass tracks. Therefore, the spikes were built up in the front, so much so that it was awkward to lower the heel of the foot to the ground. They required him to run on his toes. In Helsinki Landy noticed that the European middle-distancers, running in spikes with flat soles and a heel, had a smoother, more relaxed stride. Shoes alone, however, would not change his running style: he would have to practice the arm and leg action of the Europeans until it became habit.

But as Zatopek had shown, style was not what separated the Czech from every other distance runner in the world. It was his demanding training, and Landy felt that if achieving fast mile times was mostly a question of working hard, he was willing to make the sacrifice. On the flight back to Australia Landy spent many hours rehashing in his notebook the type of training sessions that Zatopek had discussed with him and other runners. Landy concocted a plan to achieve for himself the kind of fitness that Zatopek revealed in Helsinki. By doing so, he hoped to beat Don Macmillan's national record in the mile—4:08.9—and win the Australian Championships in early 1953.

When Landy arrived at Melbourne's airport, journalists herded around the athletes, asking for their comments on the Olympics and on the future. Some complained of having traveled too far with too little rest. Others denied they were ready to retire. Many defended their achievements or lack thereof. Landy spoke of Emil Zatopek. He explained how the Czech had proven his superiority, earning three gold medals. "He thoroughly deserved his success because he is the hardest trained athlete in the world," Landy said. It was obvious to those who knew the young Australian miler that he meant to claim this distinction for himself. Though his goals had nothing yet to do with a four-minute barrier, unwittingly they had set him on its path, and he would soon show that nothing was safe from his determination.

Of the three runners, Bannister suffered the worst for not having lived up to expectations. Save for a horse named Foxhunter, whose winning jump came eight minutes before the closing ceremonies began, the British would have managed to go the whole games without a single gold medal. For track and field enthusiasts, this single medal provided little solace. They wanted revenge. The press provided an outlet for their anger. "Hang out the crepe and lower the flag to half mast," the *Sunday Express* bellowed. "Right now I feel like suing British athletes for breach of promise," the *People* commented. Editorials questioned whether amateurism was dead. Some thought the sooner the British realized this was true, the sooner they would have a fighting chance against the Americans and Soviets. Others defended the ideal but belittled the athletes for a lack of commitment to excellence. Journalist Hyton Cleaver wrote, "Britain was failing to win, not because she was paying the price of amateurism but because she had lost the art of being spectacular."

Bannister was a lightning rod for most of this criticism, and the same journalists who first condemned, then praised, his independent training methods had shifted back again. Their vitriol tormented him. Headlines read, "Bannister Fails!" The *Daily Mirror* hurt the worst:

> Roger Bannister could have won the 1,500 meters if the AAA had persuaded him to compete regularly in Britain. Instead, they ignored the advice of their chief coach, Mr. Geoffrey Dyson, and allowed Bannister to have only one actual race in a year before going to Helsinki.
>
> He ran like a "green" three-year-old thoroughbred having its first race in a classic—running all over the track, on the inside, then the outside, accelerating and slowing up before making his final effort, to finish fourth. We heard wonderful stories in Helsinki that Bannister would win because he had done a world-shattering time in a secret trial before leaving. MAYBE HE DID. ANYONE CAN RUN QUICKLY PAST TREES!

Not only did Bannister have to read about how he let down his country, but he also had to suffer those who stopped him on the street, demanding to know what went wrong. This scrutiny was a difficult thing to bear at twenty-three years of age.

Throughout his life Bannister sensed that he had a "greater degree of self-determination" than others, but the Olympics seemed to rudely disprove this notion. He was human like everybody else. Ridiculed and defeated, he decided that only an ambition greater than an Olympic gold could absolve him of what had happened in Helsinki. He couldn't just walk away from running after such a defeat.

Days after returning from Helsinki, Bannister sent letters to miler Brian Hewson and to Chris Chataway, asking if they would push him in a four-minute mile attempt—not next year, as they might have expected, but now. He still planned on retiring before the start of his second year of medical school. The Motspur Park time trial showed he had the legs for a record attempt, and Bannister wanted to silence his critics with an achievement most thought insurmountable. Then they would know what kind of athlete he was. Even more than answering for his failure, Bannister wanted to capture the four-minute mile to show how one could achieve athletic greatness without the sacrifice of everything else in life. This was the ideal that the Greeks first promoted, that the British later advanced, and that the world was ready to discount. The four-minute mile wasn't an end in itself. Rather, it was a challenge Bannister wanted to embrace as a proof of his theorem of sport and life.

By the end of August 1952, with Bannister exhausted from competitive strain and Chataway and Hewson unable to help him because of other commitments, this challenge had to wait. Though Bannister knew the demands on him at St. Mary's would only increase, retirement from running was out. He had not yet lined up everything he needed for the effort, but he was confident that the moment would come. The four-minute mile had a long history and could wait a few more months to be broken.

PART II
THE BARRIER

6

A man who sets out to become an artist at the mile is something like a man who sets out to discover the most graceful method of being hanged. No matter how logical his plans, he can not carry them out without physical suffering. —PAUL O'NEIL, "A Man Conquers Himself," *Sports Illustrated*, May 31, 1956

I N MELBOURNE'S Central Park, opposite his East Malvern house, John Landy watched his shadow. As he ran around a bluestone gravel path in flat-soled sand shoes, he studied the rhythm of his legs and the movement of his arms. He might never catch his shadow, but he could learn from it. Over the course of his run he balanced the action of his arms and legs. The higher he carried his arms, the more distance he won from his stride. However, the technique he was developing was more complicated than simply swinging his arms out and up as far as possible. If he overextended, he lost equilibrium in his stride and wasted energy. Rather, he was looking for symmetry of form—the place where his arm action was completely in sync with his knee lift and consequently the drive from his hips. His head needed to remain level, his center of gravity still, his shoulder muscles relaxed, and his feet landing from heel to toe, nearly flat-footed. And all of this needed to occur effortlessly. Slowly he was shaping his running style into one worthy of an "Inca courier," as a sportswriter later commented, one in which he would seem to almost float over the track.

By mid-September 1952, one month after returning from Helsinki, Landy was fast moving beyond Cerutty's teachings. Cerutty had promoted a low arm carriage, believing that man should run like a rooster, clawing at the air, or like African warriors, who carried spears by their sides over great distances. Landy preferred to mimic the European runners, who had proven themselves superior in style and performance at Helsinki. "They don't run on their toes like sprinters and paw the track with their spikes as I used to," Landy said. "With a higher arm carriage your knees automatically lift and you get a slightly longer stride. But, most important, there is no tension in the leg muscles. When it comes to the final spurt you have so much extra strength to get on your toes and sprint home. Try standing on your toes and feel the tension in your calf and thigh muscles, and see what I mean." With each passing day, his body grew more accustomed to this new style, and he was getting more return for his effort.

And there was a great deal of effort involved, particularly in the intensity of his training. Landy never wanted to step to the starting line again unless he was the fittest person on the track. His training sessions required intense dedication, and they were run smarter and harder than any guided by Cerutty. Before Helsinki his improvements resulted from a grab-bag collection of endurance work. Because Cerutty despised schedules, he had his gang run until they hurt and then he pushed them further. This was the crux of his training method. However, running a fast mile required more than simply putting up with pain. This conditioning worked only to a certain point. Middle-distance running was about more than stamina. According to Zatopek, one had to train for speed. Improvement there was won by subjecting the body to periods of high stress at a fast pace while reducing the recovery time between these periods. Zatopek sold this theory of repetition running by dint of his Helsinki success. His theory was now Landy's practice.

The training ideas that Landy had scribbled into his notebook had translated into hard regimen. Through the early Australian spring (while it was fall in the Northern Hemisphere), with Cerutty and his running mates still away on tour, Landy ran alone. His agricultural science studies demanded that he train at night, after he had finished with his papers and reading. At eleven o'clock or past midnight he slipped quietly out of his house, making sure not to wake his parents or four siblings, who had little idea of the extreme effort he was making. Many nights it was difficult to force himself to put on his shoes and get out there. As he put it, "The mind is always selling the body." He often rationalized that he was too tired and might better put off the run until the next day, or that he deserved a day off. But then he would convince himself to run at least a few laps. "It's like a car starting. There's an immense amount of energy you need to start the car, but once you're rolling, it's easy." Since he had returned from the Olympics, Landy hadn't missed a single training session: this was a pure exercise of will.

On a typical night Landy walked across the street to Central Park and began a series of alternating fast and slow laps around the 600-yard oval path made of gravel. A few streetlights illuminated the make-do track, but even blindfolded, he would have known every inch of the way. Alone, the only sound his footsteps hitting gravel, he concentrated solely on how much faster he could push himself. He didn't carry a watch; his effort was measured by the interplay of exhaustion and recovery. For most of the lap he would maintain a fast even pace, but not all-out effort. Then he would burst ahead at the end and sprint until his legs felt uneasy below him. Next he reduced his pace to a jog, feeling his breath return and the pain ebb, but he slowed his pace only enough so that on the next lap he could repeat the fast even pace and surge. By stressing his legs and lungs to such an extreme point, he was immunizing himself to the pain.

An hour and a half into the session Landy had usually run eight to twelve 600-yard laps at a pace of roughly ninety seconds each (or a sixty-five-second 440-yard lap). Between each, he jogged a lap of the oval path in four minutes. He repeated these sessions—pushing himself to the limit of his physical abilities—five nights a week. On the remaining two nights in the week he ran seven miles, sometimes more, at a five-and-a-half- to six-minute pace, along the roads leading out of Melbourne. This was to build endurance. Regardless of weather, sore tendons, blistered feet, or fatigued muscles, Landy trained like this religiously.

It was the stringing together of session after session, without compromise of effort, that most tested his discipline. On a typical day he left his house by 8:00 A.M., walking a mile to the Caulfield railway station, where he took a train into the city. Occasionally some people remarked on how slowly he walked, but they had no idea of the limits to which he had pushed his body the previous night. At the University of Melbourne he attended classes on subjects like soil science, bacteriology, and farm economics, broke for lunch with his classmates, and then attended more lectures until he returned to East Malvern to have dinner with his family. Except for drinking a great deal of milk, his diet was utterly normal. He might relax briefly after dinner, but soon withdrew to his room to study for several hours before he sneaked out of the house to train again. Returning to the house long after midnight, he took a shower and then collapsed into bed.

In this schedule there were no spare moments for girlfriends or a social life, much to the dismay of his sisters. There was little time for a generous night of sleep either—he got six or seven hours at the most. Still Landy persisted, convinced that he was on the right path. Of the rigors of training he told *Track and Field News:* "The harder, the better." Of his motivation he told the *Sydney Morning Herald,* "I just go out there and work. I've got to punish myself to get anywhere." Of pain and injury he told *Sports Illustrated,* "There is no gray—just black and white. . . . If you're hurt enough to limp, you can't run at all. If you aren't, it makes no difference."

Landy's resolve was extraordinary. It was sustained by a still-developing attraction to running. Unlike the experience of playing football with a team, he was the sole master of how well he ran the mile. And the harder he trained, the more control he had over his body to dictate this performance. He may not have noticed the dramatic change in his fitness, because he had experienced it slowly, but others certainly did. One weekend afternoon he invited eighteen-year-old up-and-comer Robbie Morgan-Morris out to train with him. The young runner, who had recently won a cross-country championship, was agog at the opportunity to run with an Olympian. He had seen Landy race against Macmillan before Helsinki but was astonished at what he saw in Central Park. Morgan-Morris followed behind Landy for a few laps but was soon run off his feet. Landy kept going and going, faster and faster. Nobody in all of Australia ran this way. Morgan-Morris thought to himself, How fast is this bloke doing this?

In October Les Perry returned from his Scandinavian tour. Perry had probably seen Landy run more than any other person. He knew how much his friend had improved under Cerutty, but when he visited Landy at Central Park, he was shocked to see Landy run so well. His legs and arms were more defined. His running style had been transformed. And the speed . . . Perry tried to keep up with Landy on several laps, but couldn't.

"This is terrific sort of training," Perry said. He knew Landy had been disappointed about Helsinki, that it was in his nature to try to right the wrong of not performing at the level some might have expected, but this kind of speed and repetition work was beyond his imagination. "Is this the sort of thing you've been doing?"

"I've had a bit of a routine."

Later Landy told Perry that he had been following Zatopek's advice. Perry suspected that the Australian track and field community, Cerutty included, was in for a surprise when Landy next took to the track. When their coach tried to lasso Landy back into his fold, the runner was polite but clear: "I'm taking no more advice from anyone. I simply want to put together the best of what I've seen."

In the history of athletic training, selecting the best course for how to train, for how long, and at what intensity, has been a matter of intuition. Ancient Greek athletes trained by running in every direction save skyward. They skipped, jogged, hopped, and, on occasion, sprinted while rolling a large hoop in front of them. Their coaches carried forked sticks for motivating them. The Greeks understood the importance of increasing exertion over time, but their use of this theory lacked sophistication. Milo of Croton walked every day with a calf in his arms in order to gain strength in his arms and legs slowly as the cow matured. Hellenic runners trained on indefinite four-day schedules called *tetras:* the first day consisted of light exercise; the second, intense effort; the third, rest; and the fourth, moderate exercise. Before competitions they seasoned their meals with special herbs and mushrooms. Aristotle recommended training one's breath by holding it for increasing lengths of time; this improved strength and allowed the body to retain its spirits and humors.

The ancient Romans had their own ideas about how to prepare their athletes, whether gladiator or runner. In early training their diet was limited to dried figs, boiled grain, and fresh cheese. Later they added meat to their diet, generally pork, because, as one Roman advised, "If they lived but one day on any other food, [they] found their vigor manifestly impaired the next." They were allowed only small portions of water and were forbidden to engage in sexual intercourse. To familiarize themselves with pain, slaves flogged their backs with rhododendron branches until they bled. They exercised in the open air no matter the weather. They followed these sessions with tepid baths and copious amounts of sleep. The latter was supposed to enliven the athlete and promote muscular strength.

By the seventeenth century athletes were having their spleens removed to increase their speed, an operation with a one-in-five chance of death. Training techniques looked like they would never move beyond the arcane and bizarre until Captain Barclay of mile fame set down his ideas in writing in 1813. Generations of "pedestrians" followed his advice. Some of his suggestions, like purging the body by the use of Glauber salts, eating a breakfast of "beef-steak or muttonchops under-done, with stale bread and old beer," and lying in bed naked for a half-hour after exercise, were nonsensical. However, he also advised a rigorous regime of exercise that started at five o'clock in the morning and lasted throughout the day:

1. Sprint half-mile up a hill.
2. Walk six miles at a moderate pace.
3. Eat breakfast at seven o'clock.
4. Walk six miles at a moderate pace.
5. Lie in bed without clothes for a half-hour at twelve o'clock.
6. Walk four miles.
7. Eat dinner at four o'clock (same meal as breakfast).
8. Sprint half-mile immediately after dinner.
9. Walk six miles at moderate pace.
10. Retire to bed at eight o'clock.

Barclay had little understanding of why his regime produced results, but it had worked for him, so others suspected they would benefit from it as well. In subsequent years athletes replaced walking with more running, and both their fitness and speed continued to improve. Barclay's theories had provided a solid foundation.

Nonetheless, in the nineteenth century the general public still believed that too much exercise guaranteed an untimely death. In 1864 *London Society,* a widely read journal of the time, commented in regard to amateur athletics: "Not all training is good or desirable; very much is unquestionably injurious. The honour of a place in the representative eight of the Universities has been purchased in many instances at the cost of years of life." Some physicians thought that the heart had a limited number of beats over a lifetime and that speeding up the heart rate during exercise was a foolish waste of a very precious resource.

That athletes persisted in their efforts to see what was physically possible was testament to mankind's innate tenacity and desire to succeed. Walter George further stretched boundaries, explaining, "First, I figured out the time I thought the mile should be run in. Second, I started testing my theories and particularly my own constitution and capabilities; the result of this study soon convinced me that the then existing records at the distance were by no means good." His methods included speed drills, running on his toes in place, and extensive walks. Both speed and stamina were gradually built up as knowledge about the human body's limits and possibilities accumulated. In Britain and the United States, track and field manuals espousing the latest techniques began to appear on a regular basis. One published by an "athletic instructor" at Harvard in 1904 provided a typical schedule. Runners a century later would deem this laughable:

Monday a mile with a fairly good three-quarters and the last quarter easy. Tuesday a half mile in about two minutes ten seconds, a rest, and then another easier half mile, sprinting the last hundred yards. Wednesday jogging up and down the straightaway, rather quicker than if running a mile, followed by an easy one and one-half miles. Thursday a fast half, followed by a rest and an easy three-quarters. Friday an easy two miles, sprinting the last hundred yards. Saturday a mile trial on time. Sunday some walking.

The trials and the errors continued. In 1910 runner Alf Shrubb suggested walking sixteen miles three or four times a week to get in optimum shape. Paavo Nurmi proved that much longer training runs over the course of years would bring further improvements in time. Plus, he was an advocate of even-paced runs—keeping lap times consistent throughout to level out expenditure of effort. In the late 1920s marathoner Arthur Newton propagated continuous year-round exercise, including sessions of twenty miles a day. Jack Lovelock believed that hard work was necessary, but that an athlete risked staleness if he ran too many races. To combat this, he espoused "peak training"—building oneself up with stamina, then speed work, and then saving the best for race day. In the 1930s German physiologist Dr. Woldemar Gerschler promoted "interval training": he advised athletes to run a fast lap followed by a slow lap on the track. These were timed to ensure strict routine. Zatopek came up with the same idea by himself but refused to time his runs. Meanwhile, the Swedes, led by Haegg, believed that the key to training lay in "speed-play," known as *Fartlek*. This also included fast and slow combinations of running, but always away from the track. With Fartlek, to stay fresh, athletes needed the joy and freedom of running through forests, up and down hills, judging for themselves when to accelerate and when to hold back. The track was to be visited only for races.

Throughout the development of new techniques, doctors and laypeople alike continued to advise against the perils of so much running. In 1927 British physiologist and Nobel laureate Archibald Hill wrote that "it's not unusual for an athlete to tear a tendon, or to strain a muscle, and not unknown even for him to pull off a piece of a bone by an exceedingly violent effort. We are obviously not far from our limit of safety. If we doubled our speed of movement . . . athletics would become a highly dangerous pastime." Despite studies proving otherwise, the general belief was that overtraining could permanently damage the heart and other essential organs. Madness was assigned to those who pushed the boundaries of what was possible. Yet athletes continued to push to improve.

Timers, no timers, on the track, in the woods, schedules, no schedules, staleness, peaks, plateaus, stamina versus speed, the Stotan life, long walks, runs of ten miles a week, twenty, thirty, fifty—training had advanced a long way from carrying calves and flogging backs, but not to the point of certainty. By the 1950s coaches and former athletes had started a cottage industry out of giving (often conflicting) advice. Fads were common, and the latest champions were proclaimed to have the perfect method—until they were beaten by others. The only sure thing was that questions about how to train had many answers, and every athlete had to find his own way.

Landy had found his own way since returning from Helsinki, and he followed it mercilessly. His new running style and Zatopek-inspired training routine promised great returns, yet he had no idea how great. By Saturday, October 25, 1952, ten weeks had passed without a race or even a timed trial. In his training he had run over five hundred miles, many at near race pace, and he was slowly reducing the recovery time between fast laps to increase the pressure on his body. He knew how well he compared against his friends on Central Park's gravel path, but not against the clock.

In the first race of the outdoor season between Victoria's amateur athletic clubs, Landy crossed the finish line for Geelong Guild in 4:17. He looked back to see his nearest competitor over a hundred yards behind. The *Melbourne Argus* reporter Ken Moses believed that Landy had held back and could have run at least five seconds faster. Moses predicted that Landy would break Don Macmillan's Australian mile record of 4:09 by season's end. The next week Landy ran a three-mile race, beating the Australian cross-country champion Neil Robbins by three hundred yards and trimming Les Perry's record by sixteen seconds. On November 8 he drew away from his competitors, including Perry, in the second lap of a 2,000-meter race, winning easily and setting another record. During the week Landy continued to train, harnessing more strength with each session. It was clear that he was on the verge of something extraordinary.

On November 15, in the mile at Olympic Park, Landy "spread-eagled the field," as Moses described the race in which Landy led from the middle of the first lap and finished half a lap ahead of his competitors in 4:14.8. After the race he entertained questions from the small herd of Melbourne athletics reporters. He said that he ran in his oldest pair of shoes because he wanted to save himself for a really good time in early December. "Two- and three-mile events are my objective at the moment," he said. "I am out to build up stamina and only racing in those events will help me. It was stamina that beat me when I was away at the Games, and I do not want it to happen again." Three days later he entered one of those two-mile races and broke another record. Keenly aware of Landy's early season success, the Melbourne press sensed more records would soon fall. Athletics reporters made the rounds of his friends to see what they expected to happen. Perry commented that there was "nothing surer" than Landy breaking Macmillan's record and that Landy might even get his mile time down to 4:06. Steve Hayward of the *Melbourne Herald* suspected that in a couple of years Landy could equal Gaston Reiff, who had recently run a 4:02.8 mile, the first sub-4:03 mile since Haegg and Andersson had competed over seven years before. Hayward would not have to wait that long.

On December 12, Landy attended a reunion of Australian Olympians held at Bob Prentice's house. It was a Friday night, a chance to let off some steam, take a break from training, and relax with friends. They drank Foster's lager, ate sausage rolls, and reminisced about Zatopek and other stars they had met. They also joked about Cerutty's behavior in London and Helsinki. They avoided talk of their defeats by much more capable European and American runners, though these memories would always color their time together. At one point in the evening the conversation shifted to Landy and his season to date. Many knew of his increased training, but they were unaware of the specifics and certainly had no idea of the full scale of the effort involved. They were simply excited about how much he had improved, and they guessed that once he had someone to give him chase in a race, a good mile time was inevitable. Landy shrugged off the suggestion, preferring not to be the focus of attention. "I can only do what I can do," he said.

The next day brought a welcome break from a weeklong summer storm that had flooded highways throughout Victoria. Tales of families marooned by the floods led the news. John Landy put in his half-day filing land titles and finished at noon, feeling a bit queasy from the long night and a lack of food. After grabbing his bag with his track clothes, he decided to get some fresh air and walk to Olympic Park. He had a race at half past two.

On his way to the stadium he stopped for a chocolate ice cream sundae. When that failed to satisfy his appetite, he ate a pair of meat pies to hold him over until after the race. It wasn't the diet that Cerutty or the Greeks would have suggested, but for Landy this day was no more special than the next. He then strolled down the banks of the Yarra River for a few kilometers until he reached the track.

Though Melbourne had come a long way from its foundation in 1835 as a British outpost, the city remained mostly a collection of villages connected by tram lines. Car traffic was seldom a problem, and church steeples still ranked as the tallest buildings on the skyline. Bars closed at 6:00 P.M., television had not yet invaded living rooms, and along with barbeques, town hall dances, and private parties, local sport was one of the main entertainment outlets.

The athletes who belonged to Landy's Geelong Guild and its competing clubs ranged from students to opticians, accountants, hairdressers, and milkmen. Few Melbourne athletes, let alone Melbourne itself, ever made international news, and among the stories in the morning papers — about potato prices dropping, city budget improvements, a thwarted gold heist, and a mile race at Olympic Park — nobody could have expected the last item to launch Melbourne onto front pages around the world, least of all Landy himself. It was too absurd to imagine.

Olympic Park was the center of the city's amateur athletics and the site of one of the two international-standard tracks in Australia. The flat stretch of land next to the river on which it stood had been used over the years for everything from farming to army training and motorcycle races. In the 1920s a local businessman upgraded the grounds, installing a track that he laid with crushed scoria (a porous rock cinder produced from volcanic eruptions). The track was set within a natural bowl surrounded by grass-covered hills on three sides and concrete tiers of seats on the fourth. At best, the place was unremarkable, and despite its name, it had never hosted an Olympic Games.

By two o'clock Landy had switched into his Geelong Guild singlet and the white European track shoes that he had brought back with him from Helsinki. They had served Landy well on his previous runs this season. He warmed up at the grass oval track adjacent to the main track, a routine involving a few stretches, some jogging, and a couple of sprints. Since the previous week's three-mile race had been rained out, he felt as though he had some nervous energy to burn off. In the back of his mind he thought he might have a fast run in him today. Nevertheless, he planned to wait until halfway through the race to decide whether he should make an all-out effort. It depended on his rhythm and how he was feeling. There was no sense going into the race weighed down by the expectation of a good time.

"I think they called your race," another athlete said.

Lost in thought, Landy had missed the track official's announcement for the mile event. If he was late to the line, he would be disqualified. He raced over the hill toward the track and hustled into the pack of milers getting into their places for the start, making it just in time. There were enough milers in the race to warrant a line two men deep. Landy was placed in the second row. The starter gave his usual instructions: "Nobody will cross over in front of another, unless you're two clear yards in front. . . . We have a mile race, four laps. You'll get the bell with one lap to go." The runners jockeyed into position.

Each club team stood together alongside the track. The stands were lightly scattered with family and friends, including Landy's parents. Only a few reporters were on hand. There were no programs, concession stands, or banners. Many spectators chose to sit on the hill along the finishing straight. They had spread wool rugs across the grass and sipped from flasks of cordial or tea. Rarely through the afternoon had they broken out in more than subdued applause. The meet, like many others, felt like a "country picnic," as Cerutty gang member Trevor Robbins described it.

"On your marks . . . set . . ." The starter's gun fired.

Les Perry went out fast, faster than normal. Without Landy's knowledge, Perry had decided to pull his friend around the track for as long as he could. A sixty-second lap was flat out sprinting for him, and three-quarters of the way through the first lap he was still in the lead, but fading. There was no way he could keep it up much longer. As Landy passed him on the straight before the end of the first lap, Perry whispered to himself, "Do it, John," hoping that his friend would break Macmillan's record.

Landy was on his own. He ran on the outside of the first lane because the track to the inside edge had been chewed up from prior events and a week's worth of heavy rain. He finished a very good first lap in 59.2 seconds. He was running easily. In the lead, with the rest of the field behind him, he relaxed into the rhythm of the run. For him relaxation came from the fingers; he liked to keep his hands soft, almost open as he strode around the track. Once in the rhythm, he could then increase his tempo if needed. As he finished the second lap, he heard a time called out: two minutes. Trevor Robbins and Malvern Harrier half-miler Len McRae, who studied agricultural science with Landy, had positioned themselves on the straight to call out times so their friend would know how fast he was going. Fast. Landy thought the time was either wrong—or that he was about to run an incredible mile. The time was wrong, but only by one second. Landy finished the half-mile in 2:01.

For the past ten weeks he had run countless laps at a hard pace and was nearly immune to the pain caused from exertion. He continued to run relaxed, despite the blistering pace. As the bell for the final lap rang Robbins shouted out, "Three minutes and three seconds." No way would he run a sixty-five-second last lap, Landy thought—no way. His mile would be good, at least good enough to break Macmillan's record. He was hardly exhausted and felt he had a fair bit of acceleration still in his legs.

"Then I went," Landy later said of the start of his fourth lap. He put every gain from his months of training into that last lap. The crowd of two hundred people rose and cheered as he entered the back straight. He increased his tempo but maintained rhythm. He pressed harder and harder, his stride lengthening in the final turn. McRae and Robbins rushed down to the head of the straight to get a closer look. They knew Landy was about to run an incredible time. When he passed the 1,500-meter mark in a little over 3:45, they shouted themselves hoarse for Landy to go faster as he tore down the straight. Robbins sensed that history was about to be written in Olympic Park. Trailing far behind, Perry urged Landy on in his mind. In full stride, Landy broke the tape and slowed to a jog. His breath was heavy, but he was nowhere near the point of collapse. Turning, he saw the timekeepers huddled together. Landy thought there was something wrong.

Half-miler Len McRae ran toward him. "You ran 4:03," he said.

"What?" Landy exclaimed.

"We've been timing it."

Within moments, before he had regained his breath, reporters crowded around Landy, asking questions. The loudspeakers announced the time: 4:02.1. Everyone in Olympic Park gave Landy a standing ovation. It was the third-fastest mile in history.

Reporters' pencils flew across notebooks while he came to terms with what he had accomplished: he had brought his best mile time down by eight seconds and approached Haegg's long-standing world record by seven-tenths of a second. Landy told reporters about his new running style and said that for the first time in his athletic career he had the confidence in his conditioning to lead from the front.

"Most of the credit must go to Perce," Landy said, generous despite his split with his former coach. "Had it not been for him I would not have got anywhere near my time today. Only hard work gets results. Perce has been telling us that all the time, and our trip to the Games confirmed what he said."

While Landy explained the genesis of his run and the timekeepers and track officials nervously followed protocol to secure the record time, Percy Cerutty entered the stadium with his wife for the first time since arriving back in Australia. He couldn't understand why crowds of people were bustling about the track and infield. Events should be taking place. Something had happened. He spotted Les Perry by the stands.

"What . . . what's going on? What's all the excitement?" Cerutty asked.

"Landy just ran a four-two mile," Perry said.

Cerutty registered the time like a blow. His face fell. Then he exploded. "Here's a bloke who's come home like a whipped dog from the Olympics—couldn't qualify for a final in 4:14. And then he comes back and does this! After all the effort to get the money together to get him over there, he's bloody well wasted the fare!" Sitting in the stands, Landy's parents heard what Cerutty said and stepped away so they wouldn't have to listen to any more of his remarks. Only later would they tell their son. He deserved to enjoy his moment.

After Landy signed the necessary forms to ratify the record (which included verification that the track distance and official watches were accurate), the festivities continued in the bar underneath the stands. Landy and his friends had some beers and talked more about the race. This was the best race of his life—the most unexpected and therefore the most rewarding as well. Landy was overjoyed.

When he went home to have dinner with his parents, it was clear that his 4:02.1 run had changed everything for Landy. Winning the Australian Championships and owning the Australian mile record were minor in comparison to what was possible now—and to what would be expected from him. From the most unlikely of places, by the most unlikely of athletes, the world was put on notice that the mile barrier was in play.

7

An average man's body weighing ten stone is constructed of enough water to fill a ten-gallon barrel; enough fat for seven bars of soap; of carbon sufficient for 9,000 lead pencils, and of phosphorus to make 2,200 match heads; enough magnesium to provide one dose of salts; iron to make one medium-sized nail; lime to whitewash a chicken coop; potassium to explode a toy cannon; sugar to fill a shake; and sulphur to rid a dog of fleas. The whole could be purchased for the few shillings that accord with contemporary prices.

—SIR ADOLPHE ABRAHAMS,
The Human Machine (1956)

ON DECEMBER 14, 1952, Norris and Ross McWhirter passed through Victoria Station in London and stopped by the newsstand to pick up a copy of *L'Equipe*, the Parisian-based sporting paper that collected wire services from around the world and had correspondents of its own in many countries. Newspaper sportswriters themselves, the twins were also beginning to make a small publishing industry out of their fascination with facts and figures, not only in athletics but in fields that stretched from archaeology to zoology. To them *L'Equipe* was a necessity. After they opened its pages and saw the news from Australia, they called Bannister's flat.

"The Australian, John Landy, just ran 4:02.1," Norris McWhirter said.

Bannister was stunned. He had met John Landy through his countryman Don Macmillan in England and then run against him in the first round of the 1,500 meter in Helsinki, and certainly he was no 4:02.1 miler back then. Not at all. This kind of progress was difficult to imagine. Bannister wasn't alone in his surprise. In the days that followed British and American newspapers doubted reports that a miler who failed to qualify for the 1,500-meter Olympics final had dropped eight seconds from his best mile in the span of a few months. Arthur Daley of the *New York Times* wrote, "Never in the history of footracing have strangers come up from nowhere to shatter or approach marks. They always bore credentials first, a background of other high-class performances. . . . [Landy is] either one of the seven wonders of the age or something's wrong somewhere. It would indeed be nice to hear that Landy's 4:02.1 is a completely legitimate performance. For the present, please pass the salt." Three weeks later, when Landy clocked a 4:02.8 in a stiff wind, mea culpas were offered by his doubters, Daley included.

Bannister continued to follow the Australian as he entered race after race through the early part of 1953. It would have been hard to ignore Landy, given how much media attention was focused on the acclaimed "Meteor Miler." Melbourne papers started the fervor with headlines proclaiming there was "no hope of catching him, even in taxis." The *Sydney Morning Herald* followed by profiling the miler and publishing his photograph across several columns. The wires picked up this story from Australia's flagship newspaper, and suddenly Landy was a lead item in sports pages around the world.

Bannister didn't have to read the papers to stay up to date on Landy's progress. The McWhirter twins provided everything he wanted to know and more. They wanted an Englishman to be the first to break the four-minute mile, and Bannister was their best hope, not to mention a close friend. Having recently launched the track and field publication *Athletics World,* the twins made it their business to get as much on Landy as they could. These future founders of the *Guinness Book of World Records* were adept at culling information, a skill that dated back to age seven when they began systematically clipping newspapers to gather facts. In December 1952 they detailed Landy's "brutal assault" on the record and then announced: "Ever since Irving and Mallory in 1924 got ninety-six percent the way up Mount Everest, and the year before Paavo Nurmi went within 10.4 seconds of the Four Minute Mile, these two goals have fired men's minds. The year 1953 is going to see the greatest assault ever made on either." They published fractional times of Landy's mile runs and wrote to him, asking about his training methods. The Australian dutifully sent them the details, and the Mc-Whirters published his letter for Bannister and all to see. Every week one of the twins stopped by to see Bannister, apprising him of the latest Landy news and insisting that it would be "no good being second to run the four-minute mile."

How the Australian miler had run the weekend before and his chances for the weekend to come were far from being Bannister's only concerns. He had a ward of patients to examine, lectures to attend, cases to study, and books to read. His days as a second-year intern at St. Mary's Hospital started at 8:30 A.M. and sometimes lasted through the night. He shoehorned some time in between to prepare for the season's first race in May. Studying medicine took a gargantuan effort. Doing so while trying to accomplish the impossible in athletics was asking too much—for most people.

Bannister's days started in a small basement apartment in the London neighborhood of Earl's Court. He lived a self-described "chaotic" existence, cooking for himself (usually a quick meat stew as well as pickled herring for protein) and trying to find spare moments for laundry and the like before heading to St. Mary's Hospital near Paddington Station. Originally founded in 1845 to serve the impoverished "Stinking Paddington" area, St. Mary's had evolved into one of England's finest medical schools and research facilities, noted most famously for Alexander Fleming's discovery of penicillin. To study at the small teaching hospital, Bannister had won the scholarship established by Lord Moran, a decorated medical officer in World War I who later served as Winston Churchill's doctor.

While dean of the school, Moran was known for recruiting amateur athletes because he believed that sport teaches character and makes for good doctors. In the middle of interviews with prospective medical students Moran would bend down below his desk and retrieve a rugby ball, which he then threw at his interviewee. If the interviewee caught the ball, he was admitted. If he threw it back, he earned a scholarship. Those days were long past, but St. Mary's remained committed to recruiting well-rounded students, and Bannister had the undergraduate marks, seriousness of purpose, and athletic pedigree to warrant admittance on scholarship. Shirking his studies for the sake of athletics was out of the question.

When Bannister arrived at the hospital each morning by subway, he was besieged by responsibilities. He oversaw a ward of forty beds; under the guidance of consultants, he interviewed patients and prescribed treatments. This clinical training was supported by lectures and post-mortem examinations. Bannister rarely had the chance to sit down. Every few months he went on a different rotation offering new challenges to manage on little sleep: junior medicine, junior surgery, gynecology, obstetrics, and emergency medicine, among other specialties. During lunch—his only break in a day of making rounds, studying, and writing papers—he hurried from the hospital with his running gear and took the Underground train two stops to Warwick Road Station. There it was a quick walk to the Paddington Recreation Ground, where he trained throughout the week amid a group of overweight middle-aged men who panted around the track to trim off a few pounds during lunchtime. He paid his sixpence, changed, and within a few minutes was into his routine of fast laps on the poorly kept black cinder track. There was no time to waste with stretches and a jog. He had thirty-five minutes to train before showering, grabbing a bite to eat, and returning to the hospital.

From the day Landy burst onto the scene with his 4:02.1 mile, Bannister had stepped up his training. Clearly the ambition he had held since Helsinki—to break the four-minute mile—was in jeopardy. With a year and a half left of medical studies, his running days were numbered, and an Olympic gold was simply never going to be his. His failure in Helsinki had left him with a need to redeem himself—to deal with "unfinished business," as he said.

The more he thought about the mile barrier, the more he recognized its significance. Since Landy had revived interest in it, Bannister had been bombarded with questions from the press and public about whether breaking the four-minute mile was possible. Bannister was certain it would be done, since it was not physiologically impossible. Yet as he later wrote: "To say, however, 'Four minutes is only a time' was presumptuous, unless I had an answer for the inevitable follow-up question—'Well, if it's possible, why don't you do it?'"

The "Dream Mile," as the Scandinavians deemed the achievement, had a mythical enchantment. Until broken, it would stand as a limit to human endeavor. The idealist in Bannister wanted to break the barrier to show that no such limit existed. More important, he wanted to demonstrate that an amateur athlete was capable of the effort. And the defeated Olympian in him wanted to be the one to do it first.

Since mid-December, before Bannister hit the track in late February, he had been developing his stamina in earnest, mostly on the cricket field at Harrow School near his parents' house. After jumping a fence to get into the school grounds, he set off on his run. There was no strict method to his routine. The fifteen acres of fields and hills gave him the freedom to run at will. He liked to train at night, when the trees and other static objects were out of sight. Then he had the feeling that there was no ceiling to his speed. His running had no measure other than the energy exerted. But the darkness was not without perils. The year before he had run into some concrete blocks left in the grass and gashed his leg down to the bone. Only after climbing back over the fence and flagging down a car was he able to get to a hospital.

Nonetheless, the sessions on the cricket field were exhilarating. They were best described as Fartlek: he ran fast at times, slow at others, up hills and down slopes, judging for himself when to force his legs or when to hold back, not using a stopwatch. But it was more involved than that. In certain moments he projected a finishing line fifty or a hundred yards down the field and sprinted to break through the imaginary tape. At another moment there seemed no end point to his running, just a feeling of pushing himself to exhaustion. After twenty minutes he had usually worked himself up to a peak where he ran eight hundred yards at near-maximum speed. When he ascended hills, he focused on gaining strength in his legs. On descent he focused on his balance. Some nights the sessions were so hard that it took several days to recover. Other nights he held back.

Two months later he was ready for more severe training on the track. By early March he was only beginning to see the results. He didn't enjoy track work: the grind took much of the thrill out of running. Ever since he had begun training at Oxford University in 1946 he had been indoctrinated with the idea of "effortless superiority." This was the modus operandi of the gentleman amateur: one never gave the impression that one had worked for one's success. Oxford sprinter Bevil Rudd illustrated this when he arrived at a quarter-mile race with a lit cigar in his mouth, put it down on the track's edge, won the event in record time, and picked up the still-smoking cigar when finished. For six years Bannister had steadily reduced his mile time without abandoning the principle that running should be one part of a much larger life. But to continue to improve his fitness while balancing his studies he needed to get more from each training session without lengthening its duration. This meant grinding out harder and harder sessions on the track.

Bannister trained alone and without coaching, convinced that he alone could get the best out of himself. His track time was limited exclusively to interval training. It was a method he had used previously to develop his speed, but he had never applied it with such pressure. His theory of training was simple: he needed to run the same distances faster each week. He had speed, but not the kind of enduring speed that he would need to break four minutes. Helsinki had shown him this. In one session he ran as many as ten laps at sixty-three seconds each with only two to three minutes' rest in between. Occasionally one of the McWhirter twins would show up to time his laps; mostly, though, Bannister carried a stopwatch himself.

Each day was a test against the one before. Although the track work stole the joy from running, he was fascinated by the daily adjustments in speed and effort that he made to get the most from his body. He liked the intellectual challenge of determining for himself what was needed in each session. His approach to training was decidedly scientific:

> Does it work? Does it not? You learn by your mistakes. It's so subtle. If you run so hard that you can't recover, you haven't done any good. It's stressing the machinery to the point where if you had a graph and plotted performance against stress, the line at first will proceed smoothly upwards, but there comes a point when more stress becomes counterproductive and the line falls.

Few had examined the human body's capacity to withstand punishment as Roger Bannister had. In addition to the grueling life of a medical student and the rigors of hard-core athletic training, Bannister had a third job: finishing his research scholarship at Merton College, Oxford, where he was investigating the physiological effects of running. Bannister said that running the mile was an "art of taking more out of yourself than you've got." He first based this art on science.

Arterial pCO_2, blood lactate, pulmonary ventilation, carotid chemoreceptors, oxygen mixes, hyperpnea, and gas tensions — this was how Bannister described the effects of training on his body. In March 1953 it was the language he used while preparing two papers: "The Carbon

Dioxide Stimulus to Breathing in Severe Exercise" and "The Effects on the Respiration and Performance During Exercise of Adding Oxygen to the Inspired Air." Atypical expertise for your average miler. Bannister was aswim in a sea of lactate counts, carbon dioxide readings, and oxygen consumption levels from his experiments. His task was to make sense of the numbers.

Over two and a half years had passed since he began the postgraduate research project supervised by two Oxford professors, and Bannister had learned as much about the impact of exercise on the body as it seemed possible to know. "The efficient integration of the human body, in order to achieve something like the four-minute mile," he said, "is way ahead of our capacity to measure how much is breathing, how much is heart or how much is circulation."

This understanding of what was known and what was unknown came at the expense of a lot of sweat, and blood, from Bannister himself and his test subjects — or guinea pigs, as Norris McWhirter referred to them.

"Do you think you could come along and help me with an experiment?" Bannister had asked. Without much reflection or investigation, McWhirter had replied, "Oh, yes."

McWhirter found himself in a small room crowded with a motorized treadmill and a frightening array of attachments: gas bags, meters, valves, pipes, tubes, and pumps. It looked thrown together on a tight budget and a prayer. The door closed swiftly behind him. Stripped down to a pair of shorts and running shoes, McWhirter winced as the assistant took his hand and shot a spring gun attached to a scalpel blade into his finger to draw blood. His singlet was already stained with blood before the experiment began. He stepped onto the treadmill and secured his mouth around a rubberized tube that jutted out over the front of the adjustable platform. From what he understood, the experiment measured the effects that different oxygen mixes (from a normal level of 21 percent to as much as 75 percent) have on the body when running to exhaustion. By using the mouthpiece, he inhaled enriched air. His exhalation was then measured for a variety of factors too complicated to explain to every guinea pig.

Wearing a white lab coat, Bannister fired up the "diabolical machine," as McWhirter referred to the treadmill, and the sprinter began to run. The whole contraption made a terrible clatter, but the noise was the least of his worries. From what Bannister had told him, the treadmill had a gradient steep enough to ascend the thirty thousand feet of Everest within six hours. Bannister had even tested the team members of the latest Everest expedition and discovered their fitness wanting. After a couple of minutes McWhirter was not only exhausted but hurting as well. Granted, he wasn't a distance runner, but the treadmill's speed and gradient were ridiculously harsh. His difficulties were worsened by the fact that he was running with a rubber mouthpiece attached to his face and the lab assistant was repeatedly taking his hand midstride and shooting the blade into another finger to draw more blood. Oxygen-enriched air or not, he was struggling, badly. Wooden bars to his left and right kept him from pitching over the side, and a strategically placed electric fan prevented overheating.

Five minutes into the experiment, McWhirter was weakening. He was out of breath, his legs felt like they were buckling, and he experienced what one runner called the "black waves of nausea" from too much effort. At six minutes he was finished. His spine went to rubber, his chin fell to his chest, and his knees went up to his face. Suddenly he was shot from the treadmill into a pile of blankets and duvets positioned behind him. He was in a total state of collapse, barely able to lift his head. The assistant then set upon him once again with the spring gun. Breathless and splattered with blood, McWhirter finally pulled himself back together after ten minutes. His *friend* needed him for three more "damn near terminal" sessions. That was all.

In the course of his research Bannister put himself through this same experiment on fifteen separate occasions. He managed to stay on the machine for at least three times as long as his other subjects, driving himself into collapse again and again. His results were to be included in the papers as well. Afterward, in the laboratory, he analyzed the exhaled gas to see what elements influenced breathing during exertion. This analysis required painstaking exactness, the kind that made everything else in the world drift into insignificance while he worked. Under his professors' guidance, he began to make sense of the results. When he noticed that he and his subjects sustained themselves longer on the machine by breathing 66 percent oxygen rather than 100 percent, he tried to deduce why. He read scores of physiology papers and research reports, some on such esoteric topics as carbon monoxide and oxygen uptake by sheep's corpuscles.

Oxygen was the key. A distance runner was limited by his ability to uptake and then use it. This limit could be extended through training.

Bannister knew from studies done on him that he had natural gifts. Based on body types first categorized by Hippocrates, measures could be taken of three components of the human body: ectomorphy (thinness), mesomorphy (muscularity), and endomorphy (fatness). Like many middle-distance runners, Bannister enjoyed high degrees of ectomorphy and mesomorphy with no endomorphy. One scientist who used these components—and several others, including height, weight, and heart size—gave Bannister 18,869 points in terms of potential athletic prowess, a number that was relevant only when it compared favorably with the numbers of others. But natural gifts could carry him only so far. In the mile's history, success had come for athletes of all shapes and sizes. Good distance runners had to be made. In contrast, sprinters were born with their talent; training helped only to economize their movements. If Bannister wanted to run the four-minute mile, he had to harness his potential by tuning his body to best handle strenuous effort. After all, running in a bubble of enriched air wasn't an option.

His experiments and secondary research showed that once the body suffers from a lack of oxygen, the muscles stop using oxygen for energy and switch to a mechanism that can be sustained only for a narrow window and that causes the release of lactic acid into the blood. When too much lactic acid is present, it results in withering pain and ultimately causes muscle contractions (a self-defense mechanism). Since oxygen was the problem, Bannister set himself two goals: reducing the amount of oxygen consumed by eliminating unnecessary movements and running at an even pace, and increasing the efficiency of his uptake, delivery, and use of oxygen.

Bannister had long since perfected his stride so that his movements were neither wasted nor restricted by tension. A few awkward and clumsy strides could steal momentum, and to regain it a runner needed to use oxygen for more energy. To keep his head poised and level Bannister had accustomed himself to looking at a point fifteen yards ahead on the track. To maintain evenness of stride he had practiced accelerating while staying relaxed. Natural body lean and arm lift were individual to the runner, and he had found his groove over many years of training. Voluntary action was now reflex. As to even pace, Bannister knew this was critical for his mile attempt. He lost more energy by accelerating at one point in a race than he saved by running slower at another point. In the mile more energy was used running laps of fifty-eight, sixty-two, sixty-four, and sixty-six seconds than four successive sixty-second laps. The difference was slight, but critical to breaking a record separated by a few strides.

For the second goal, improving the uptake of oxygen, Bannister knew that his body was already functioning at a level equaled by few— from first inhalation to the lungs' diffusion of oxygen into his blood, to his heart pumping this blood down into the capillaries of his legs, to the cells in his muscles converting digested food and oxygen into energy, to the firing of his muscle contractions, and finally to the elimination of the by-products of these reactions. In 1953 Bannister had a pulse rate of fifty beats per minute—twenty-two beats lower than the average man. His lungs absorbed 5.25 quarts of oxygen a minute— twice the standard. In other words, when he ran, his body was operating nearly 50 percent more efficiently than that of the average man. But with every year his training reaped diminishing returns: the capacities of lungs, heart, and muscles were almost fully extended. To improve his mile time even more, he needed to focus his training exclusively on the demands of running one mile and no more. His Fartlek-like training had increased the stamina he needed for the distance, which was mostly a factor of aerobic capacity. At Paddington he worked on his endurance of speed, which at a certain point was about fighting against the body's anaerobic limits. Pushing through the tape in less than four minutes demanded balancing and utilizing both types of energy to their breaking points.

Bannister's understanding of this was incomplete. Many decades would pass before science showed how fast twitch muscles (those used for speed) operate on anaerobic energy and slow twitch muscles (those used for endurance) operate on aerobic energy, how both can be developed on the cellular level, and how the lungs, heart, blood, and capillaries are adapted into enhancing this whole process. From what Bannister understood—which was much more than most—the body could manage a four-minute mile. His physiological investigations had led him to this conclusion; with both this research and his experience as a miler, he was able to dissect the way the race needed to be run, not only in terms of training but also in manner and style. Although he hesitated to admit it, he had learned firsthand the punishment that his body could withstand by using himself as a guinea pig in his experiment. He too had shot out the back of the treadmill, as McWhirter had done, and so he understood about endurance. His friend explained, "Psychologically the rest of life is an anticlimax. People make a fuss about physical pain, but everything [after these experiments] was a breeze."

When Bannister finished his typical day by falling into bed—having crowded into a single day caring for his ward, puzzling over patient histories, taking notes during lectures, fitting two hours' worth of effort into a thirty-five-minute workout, boiling down two years of lab research into cogent results, serving as secretary of the Medical Society, and trying to sustain a social life that included inviting dates to dances like the Achilles Club Ball, acting as Lord Darlington in Oscar Wilde's *Lady Windermere's Fan*, and enjoying drinks out with friends to discuss politics and art—he was tired. This was the life that he had chosen, hectic as it was. He was nothing if not well rounded.

By March 1953 the British "experts" who had wanted to send Bannister to the gallows after Helsinki were already beginning to opine on the singleness of purpose required to break the mile barrier. A columnist at the *Athletic Review* warned that Landy had "his eyes firmly fixed" on the prize and had devoted his time to training over fifty miles per week. "Our own milers," he wrote, "who think a few fast quarters or halves, with an occasional 1½-to-2-mile over-distance spin, totaling around eight miles per week, should note what is required to bring back the bacon."

As with his Helsinki preparations, Bannister followed his own counsel and ran mostly alone. He refused to train for hours every day to the exclusion of everything else. At the first race of the season two months later, he planned to show that it was still possible to have a life—a full life—outside of sport and achieve one of its greatest ambitions at the same time.

8

You can't flirt with the track. You must marry it.

—BILL EASTON, quoted in James E. Gunn,
"Second Isn't Good Enough"

WHILE THE Third Infantry Division fought hand-to-hand combat in Korea, President Eisenhower made nice with Soviet officials after Stalin's recent death, and scientists detonated another atomic bomb in the Nevada desert, Des Moines, Iowa, was filled with floats, parades, dances, and young women hoping to be made queen of the 1953 Drake University Relays. Hotels were sold out, restaurants had patrons lined up out the door, and streets were congested with fresh-off-the-lot Fords and Chryslers. The weekend was centered on competitions between athletes from around the Midwest, both at the high school and college levels. These were happy, carefree days in an America insulated by a booming economy and a feeling of invincibility. Yes, there was the scare of communism, but optimism abounded. After all, Norman Vincent Peale's *The Power of Positive Thinking* was the country's top-selling book, and people were less concerned with politics and the world stage than with outfitting their new homes with Bendix automatic laundry machines and GE electric ranges.

On April 25, at the height of the relays, ten thousand people jammed the stands on both sides of the stadium, many carrying placards for their favorite athlete or team, including Wes Santee and his

Kansas Jayhawks. Instead of overalls and boots, the men dressed in slacks, pressed shirts, and loafers. The women wore spring dresses and had coifed their hair perfectly before donning wide-brimmed hats to shade the sun. Flags encircled the stadium, and the football field's wide swath of deep, evenly cut grass had been sunk several feet below the track itself, making the oval look as if it were elevated for the occasion.

At the moment, however, Wes Santee was oblivious to everything but his coach. In only a couple of minutes Santee would anchor the distance medley (440–880–1,320–mile), a race that had already begun. His teammates had fallen behind Georgetown, again.

"Coach, let's drop out," he shouted over the cheering fans.

"Oh, no, no," Bill Easton replied, clutching a clipboard to his chest. The words — *Property of Coach Bill Easton* — were stamped on the clipboard's top. He was a commanding presence during a track meet, looking like a general on the field of battle. Set behind glasses, his dark brown eyes were determined. "We can't do that. No way."

"I'm going to be too far behind. It's silly for me to just run."

Easton shook his head. "No, I don't want to drop out. We're at Drake."

Santee stepped away. He wanted to run the open mile race instead of anchoring his team in another losing bid. What was the sense of wasting the energy if they didn't have a chance to win? As he watched his team slip further back in the race, his frustration grew. He knew this was an important meet for Easton, who used to coach Drake's track team, but Santee was sick of taking the baton seventy or eighty yards back and trying to win. Yesterday's embarrassing loss in the four-mile relay against Georgetown had proven there was only so much he could do. This was his third race in nearly twenty-four hours, and he wanted to focus on the mile.

With the third leg of the medley in progress, Santee again approached Easton on the side of the track. "Come on, coach. Let's drop."

"No," Easton said, barely even glancing at him. "You're going to run."

Santee walked away and positioned himself for the handoff from Lloyd Koby. Georgetown's anchor, Charlie Capozzoli, had already sprinted off. Santee waited, waited, and waited. Finally Koby neared and Santee began running. They exchanged the baton, and Santee settled in for the mile. With Capozzoli over half a lap in the lead and striding well, there was no way to catch him. It was over before it started. The best Santee could do was claim second place, one hundred yards behind Georgetown. He stormed off the track, avoiding a repeat of the previous day's drubbing when Capozolli had shaken his hand and said, "Hi ya, ya bum."

When Santee marched past his coach, Easton called for him to stop.

"I don't want to talk to *you*," Santee said, turning briefly before continuing forward. His teammates and a host of others watched, astonished, as Santee kept walking. For the first time in three years he had disobeyed his coach and retreated to the locker room. That had been his final race of the meet, and he was fed up.

It was the height of the outdoor track season. Santee was in the best shape of his running career. At the Texas Relays in March he had run his fastest mile to date — 4:06.7 — in the anchor leg of the four-mile relay, setting a new record in the event. After leading his team to triumph in the sprint medley, the distance medley, and the two-mile relay, he was named the meet's outstanding performer. Whispers that Santee was the one to claim the mile record quickly strengthened into downright statements of fact. At twenty-one Santee was young for a middle-distance runner — most of whom peaked at twenty-four or twenty-five years of age — but he had tongues wagging about his potential. After the Texas Relays a *New York Herald Tribune* reporter wrote, "It was a season-launching performance that has never been surpassed. . . . Any day, now, they'll be expecting Santee to go for the four-minute mile." Another witness to his domination at the meet was impressed by Santee's confidence:

> The guy has a lot of poise, a lot of self-assurance. He'll tell you what he can do, and you think maybe he's bragging a little, and then he goes right ahead and does it. You remember the old story about how Babe Ruth took two strikes and then pointed to the spot where he was going to sock a home run on the next pitch? And you remember the Babe went ahead and did it? Well, that's the way Santee is.

Weekend after weekend, however, his coach neglected to give Santee the opportunity to step up to the plate. Santee understood that winning meets wasn't an individual affair. Usually he was the loudest supporter on the side of the track, rooting for his Jayhawks. He certainly contributed to their success, running in nearly every distance event held to score points. But when was he going to be able to concentrate on the mile without being worn down from running four races every week?

He was churning this question around in his head, pacing the locker room, when his teammates entered. They told him that Easton had shuffled the mile relay roster and wanted Santee to put his spikes back on and race.

"I don't want to run with you guys, none of you want to do better," Santee said. "You're all out there just running."

His statement shocked them: Santee had never refused a race or complained about their performances before. They couldn't believe he was saying no to Easton. The coach's word was law. He set down strict rules, and his boys followed them or they were disciplined. Their teammate Bill Nieder once forgot to wear a tie for a meet, and Easton stopped him at the door of the bus. "Where's your tie?" Easton asked. "Oh, coach, I left it at home," Nieder replied. "Okay, get off the bus and get your tie," Easton said, then turned to the driver after his star shot putter had stepped out. "Okay, go on to Des Moines." The door closed and the bus rolled away.

If an athlete cursed, he had to contribute money to the "flower fund." If he was late to a training session, even by a couple of minutes, he paid in sweat. If anyone broke curfew on a trip away from Kansas, Easton sent him home immediately, whether or not it meant losing the meet. If a member of the team dishonored the team, the coach had the ability to yank his scholarship—and would. Track and field was serious business to him.

But Easton's athletes listened because they respected him, not because they feared punishment. As one teammate said, "When Easton told you something, you believed it was going to happen." Because usually it did. A disciple of the great Indiana University coach Bill Hayes, Easton was systematic about his approach to running. He loved his schedules and took detailed notes on his athletes, including how much they trained and the changes in their weight before and after a run. He gave written instructions on everything from how much sleep to get (solid eight hours) to what to eat before races (fruit, and definitely no fried eggs, sausages, or potatoes), to when to study (when not training or sleeping). He even told them which clothes to bring to meets (sport coat, white shirt, tie, and top hat), exhorting his team: "You are college men and are representing a university. . . . Don't be different!" Easton dedicated nearly every waking hour to his athletes. He earned the respect his athletes gave him—and he required it. His record spoke for itself: by 1953 he had claimed numerous dual meet, relay, and Big Seven championships—plus three NCAA titles.

And yet here was Santee, refusing him. Speechless, his teammates filed out of the locker room and returned to Easton to tell him the news.

He stuck his hands in his jacket pockets and with a no-nonsense expression said, "Go get him to run."

Only a few minutes before the mile relay was to begin, they rushed back to Santee and pleaded with him. "We think we can win . . . if you get off your ass and run with us."

Santee had cooled off enough to realize he was playing with fire by disobeying Easton. Not only was Easton more than a coach to him, but Santee had a strong sense of loyalty to his team. If they promised to start running with all their heart, he told them, he would run. They agreed. Back on the track Easton was cool with Santee. They barely looked at each other, and the coach's only words to him were that he was to run in the third leg. When Santee was handed the baton in the race, he channeled his frustration into a scorching 440-yard lap of 47.4 —fast enough to give his anchor Don Smith the lead to take home the win for the Kansas Jayhawks.

After the race Easton told Santee, "We need to talk."

At the University of Kansas Santee lived in a world defined by running and study, and Bill Easton was its ruler. Santee lived in the Acacia fraternity house. His small room overflowed with the newspaper clippings that he collected of his latest exploits. He woke early, usually at six o'clock, and was out of the house within a few minutes, taking a fast walk before the sun rose. The university was set on a steep hill called Mount Oread, and his hourlong stroll around the footpaths lined with trees and rustic stone buildings was a pleasant way to get his blood going. He then reported to the Pi Phi sorority house, where he laid out breakfast for the students. The job supplemented his athletic scholarship. By eight o'clock he was in class, fulfilling his requirements for his physical education degree, the major Easton had suggested during Santee's freshman year.

The coach had arranged his schedule and spoken to his professors before the start of each semester—as he did with his other athletes— to ensure that he was free to train at two o'clock and was not falling behind in his studies. If that occurred, the class's professor sent Easton a note. Once, when Santee was doing poorly in English, Easton told him he had two choices: improve his grade or miss the upcoming meet. "Do whatever it takes," Easton advised. Santee visited his professor, asked what was required to better his scores, and then worked day and night until he was finished. Easton never received another note.

At lunchtime Santee returned to the sorority house where he worked to bus dishes. Afterward he attended another class before heading down to Memorial Stadium to begin the day's training session. In the locker room he and the other athletes would undress and one by one sit on the examining table, where Easton checked their body alignment and adjusted their backs. Then each athlete weighed in and received the details for the day's session. They usually trained two to four hours a day.

In high school Santee had trained only forty-five minutes a day, usually during his library period, but since he had run two miles to his girlfriend's house and back nearly every night — not to mention the countless miles he ran on the ranch — it was hard to know how much distance work he used to do. When he was a senior in high school, the talk in Ashland was that he risked getting an enlarged (or "athletic") heart because of all his running. At the time this was considered dangerous. His heart was scoped and found to be very muscular, narrow, and long. This concerned him when he went to KU, but after he was given a physical and put through a step test by Phog Allen, the basketball coach and a certified osteopath, Allen assured him that he was perfectly healthy. From that moment forward he ran as much as Easton instructed. Santee felt like he had been given a license to get stronger with each day.

Easton's training sessions changed throughout the week. On Monday they warmed up with a five- to six-mile cross-country run along the dirt roads leading from Mount Oread. There was the occasional hill, but mostly it was flat land that stretched for miles, perfect for farming and long-distance running. The pace was about 50 percent of top effort. This pace was heated up by quarter- or half-mile dashes, usually prompted by Santee sprinting ahead of the others. During these faster portions of the run the team split off into packs based on ability.

Santee always ran with Art Dalzell, Lloyd Koby, and Dick Wilson, the "Four Horsemen" as they were called. They had arrived at the University of Kansas together as freshmen on scholarship and were the core of Easton's track and field team. Dalzell, who was well liked by the girls and could talk his way out of everything, was the second-fastest miler on the team. He and Santee roomed together on the road, and it was assumed that Dalzell would forget his track clothes before a meet and Santee would have to bring them in his bag. Lloyd Koby was the same kind of small-town farm boy as Santee when he arrived at KU. Dick Wilson was the "foreigner," the only one of the four not from Kansas. He and Koby were quiet, intelligent, and solid, but not extraordinary milers.

Throughout their cross-country runs the mood was light, and they bantered about the girls they were dating or how they were going to run the spikes off their opponents in the next week's meet. They often played practical jokes, like the time they lifted a Volkswagen parked outside someone's house and set it on his porch. By the time they returned to campus Easton had usually discovered what they had done. On that particular occasion he made them return the car to its proper spot—and repeat their run.

Normally when they returned to the stadium, they changed into fresh singlets and exchanged flat shoes for spikes. Then Easton immediately had them do a quarter-mile as fast as possible. Santee ran his against Dalzell and rarely lost. Easton believed that if a distance man had a good quarter-mile time, he could run any event. After a short rest they ran wind sprints barefoot on the grass infield, usually twenty 100-yard dashes. Once finished with these, they revisited the training table, where Easton examined them again and noted their weights. He kept his athletes under constant watch. He knew whether they had given a full effort for the day, if one of his boys had been out too late the night before, or if he'd eaten the wrong kind of meal (especially their favorite doughnuts from Joe's Bakery). "You're not running the way you should be running," he would say. Nothing got past him. When he asked what the problem was, it was wise to tell the truth.

On Tuesdays they warmed up with a two-mile cross-country run, then came back for track work that normally included step-downs from a mile to three-quarters, to half, to a quarter, and then back up again, jogging in between each. On Wednesday they ran two miles cross-country and then alternated between fast half-miles followed by sprints and doing step-downs again (but over shorter distances—from a half-mile to 600 yards to a quarter-mile to 220 yards). On Thursday they concentrated on speed work. This usually included eight quarter-miles or twelve to sixteen 220s. No matter how difficult the session, Easton told them at the start: "We're gonna have some fun today. Relax and enjoy it." They raced on Friday and Saturday. On Sunday the team got together for a ten- or fifteen-mile endurance workout, easing out the strains and tension from racing.

After a typical session Santee hightailed it back to the sorority house to serve formal dinner. He then grabbed some food for himself and came back to the stadium to clean the locker room, another scholarship obligation. By eight o'clock he returned to the Acacia house to study for two hours before bedtime. Opportunities to see his girlfriend, Danna Denning, were usually limited.

They had met the year before at the football stadium, where Santee was selling programs. Several of his fraternity brothers were dating her sorority sisters, and they urged the two to date. At the time Santee was still seeing his high school girlfriend, returning to Ashland on occasion for visits. After Helsinki he decided to take Danna out on a "Coke date" to test the waters. They went to the Rock Chalk Café, a block from his fraternity house, for a soda and a half-hour of conversation before she had to return to her sorority house by the time they flickered the lights for 10:30 P.M. curfew. Danna came from a wealthy, established family in Elkhart, Kansas—the hometown of Glenn Cunningham. She had entered KU at the early age of fifteen. She was attractive in a serious, bookish kind of way, and in many areas the two were polar opposites. Danna cared about her studies in accounting rather than sport. She was as much an introvert as he was an extrovert. While Santee had to work to scrape around for spending money, she had a generous allowance and drove around in an Austin Healey her father had given her. Yet they found that they worked together. One date turned into two and then many. They went to church on Sundays and attended formals together, and she would stop by the track to watch him train. By April 1953 talk of marriage and having children was on the table. As it was, his table was already fairly full.

Easton frowned on his athletes getting too serious with their girlfriends, but Santee had managed to get close to Danna without losing focus on his sport—not that he had much spare time to lose focus. In his sleep he had running dreams, many involving scenes where he surged past his competitors as he turned into the final bend of the last lap and then distanced himself from them to the finish line.

Only one month after his return from Helsinki Santee started the cross-country season. He traveled throughout the Midwest for dual meets and championships. The Jayhawks strung together six straight meet victories, including the Big Seven Championship in November. Easton motivated his team with speeches about "KU against the World," but his boys were far from underdogs with Santee winning every three-mile race he entered.

Before the holidays Easton sent each of his athletes a letter detailing how they should balance their training with study for final examinations. They were also advised to run every day at home over the break "so that you will be ready for hard workouts upon your return to the campus." The letter was headlined "Merry Christmas!"

The indoor season began in January, and Santee was equally dominant there. The papers called him the "1-man record demolisher" and the "Mincing Menace of Mount Oread." In late February this "running machine" led his team to another Big Seven title. There was hardly a break before the outdoor season, which saw him running in races every single weekend from March until late May.

This was his life. Even when he ran for fun—his version of fun—Easton was there to lead him along. In the winter Santee had challenged his Acacia brothers to a race after being razzed for all the press attention he had received: he would run the thirteen and a half miles from Tonganoxie to Lawrence, Kansas, against twenty-seven of his fraternity brothers, each one taking a half-mile of the course. He claimed he'd beat them all to the finish line. What started out as a fraternity stunt quickly captured the imagination of the town. Before the race Easton told reporters, "Knowing how determined he can be, I'll wager he makes it. Matter of fact, I think I'll go out and ride along the road just to time him for each mile. Might as well get some good out of this, you know." Santee's fraternity brothers were confident as well. The Acacia president was quoted as saying, "We can take him if we can get a three-minute or better half-mile out of every guy who runs in the race—and we're practicing."

On a frigid, twenty-two-degree December morning, with highway patrol cars and fans lining the highway, Santee, wearing a heavy blue sweatsuit and using wool gym socks to protect his hands from the cold, quickly went into the lead over freshman football player Ralph Moody. He finished his first mile in 4:41, then eased into a 5:36 average mile pace. When he was halfway finished, his opponents far behind him, he ribbed one of his waiting fraternity brothers, "I'm more than halfway there, how about you guys?" At three miles outside Lawrence, a north-west wind bit into Santee. His muscles tightened, his side hurt, and he feared that he might not be able to continue. When he turned back south, though, his body warmed, and he continued on pace to whip his fraternity brothers by over four hundred yards. Throughout the race Easton was positioned in the back of a station wagon driven by his wife, calling out his mile times on a jerry-rigged public-address system and heckling the waiting runners as Santee passed them.

Stunts aside, Easton told Santee—and the press, who gobbled up the coach's every word—that he was on course to become the best miler in the United States, and perhaps the world. He just needed more time to develop. Santee knew, however, that time wasn't on his side. The Australian John Landy had demonstrated that the four-minute mile was in serious contention, and with European milers like Roger Bannister and Gaston Reiff starting their seasons soon, the barrier might fall within months. Training to win meets for the University of Kansas was great, but it shouldn't have to mean the sacrifice of his greater ambition: to run the four-minute mile first.

When the University of Kansas team returned from the Drake Relays, Easton summoned Santee. At three o'clock Santee made his way across campus to Robinson Gym, where Easton had his office. Santee was the only student on campus who wore jeans, cowboy boots and western-style shirts. He always walked quickly and with purpose, passing other students before they even knew he was coming.

Of the many top athletes in America, Santee embodied better than most sport's changing landscape. Playing to the spectators and generating excitement was the name of the game, and he loved doing that. The days of quiet achievement and quieter heroes were over. People wanted athletes who were confident and colorful. And they wanted to see records broken. In the 1950s sportswriter Gerald Holland heralded this sea change:

> For world-wide interest and participation, for huge crowds and vast audiences, for smashed records and astonishing performances by outsiders and underdogs, this new golden age in scores of ways outstrips and outdazzles them all. As if no other world existed, the world of sport is crowded with action and excitement and filled with high sports spirits.

The exuberance in American sport reflected the age, a time that brought big Cadillacs with swooping tail fins, the "New Colorama Styling" of Frigidaire ranges, bright pink dresses and button-downs, hi-fis, Disneyland, Dean Martin and Jerry Lewis, and the hope of a television in every new home. Americans had money in their pockets and time on their hands, and sport reached a fever pitch as a consequence.

Children flocked to baseball diamonds, golf courses, soccer and football fields, swimming pools, running tracks, tennis courts, and boxing rings, dreaming of becoming the next great star. Their parents encouraged these hopes, and schools boosted intramural sports programs to meet the demand. This rise in participation was dwarfed, however, by the skyrocketing number of spectators crowding stadiums and tracking every movement of their favorite athletes. The 1952 Olympics showed that sport had political ramifications, but who performed better, the United States or the Soviets, was a minor theme compared to the sheer amount of money that could be made from impassioned fans. With the rise of television, athletic competition was brought into living rooms across the country. New promise was bestowed in dollar signs. Families hurried to buy this new black box; perhaps at first they watched only Lucille Ball and Desi Arnaz in *I Love Lucy*, the antics of Milton Berle, or the news anchored by Walter Cronkite, but soon they found it enthralling to watch sports as well from the comfort of their couches. In their lamp-lit rooms they could root for Ben Hogan to continue his streak of golf major championships, marvel at Native Dancer thundering to victory in another stakes race, shudder at the punching power of Sugar Ray Robinson and Archie Moore, and love (or hate) to see Mickey Mantle lead the Yankees over the Brooklyn Dodgers on their way to five straight World Series titles. If radio in the 1920s had built a sporting economy out of gold leaf, television in the 1950s replaced it with solid gold.

As sport became serious business, its landscape was completely altered. Since hundreds of millions of dollars went into sponsorship deals, it paid to win. Naturally this changed the nature of professional sports: there was more pressure than ever to achieve results, and failure came at a much higher cost. But amateur sports were also fundamentally affected. High schools and colleges were fast becoming farm teams, producing players for professional leagues. Sporting success could well lead to a lucrative career upon graduation. Gradually commerce was moving amateur athletics away from its original vision.

Santee understood that the pursuit of the four-minute mile had the power to fire imaginations and pack stadiums. And if he were to achieve it, he knew he would win more than headlines. He enjoyed the attention he received just commenting about the possibility. "I don't know when it will be," he told a journalist, "but I'll run it, you can be sure of that. I'm as certain I can run the four-minute mile as you are that you can drive your car home. There's always the chance of an accident, but barring that, I'll do it." Santee bathed in the media's limelight, and comments like these only heightened its intensity.

As an amateur college athlete, Santee knew that the only ones getting rich from his efforts now were the race promoters urging him to attend their events. He could make a few dollars later as a professional, especially if he became the one to claim this Everest of sport. The money could wait, but the barrier would not last forever. Easton needed to grasp this and give Santee his chance.

Santee climbed to the gym's third floor, taking the steps two at a time, ready to face Easton and answer for what had happened at the Drake Relays. He also needed to convince his coach of the necessity of concentrating on the mile. Easton was waiting for him behind his old wooden schoolteacher's desk scattered with newspaper and magazine clippings. The small office was crowded with file cabinets, trophies, and pictures of his athletes and teams through the years.

Easton went straight to the point, as usual. "I didn't think you acted in a professional and appropriate way yesterday."

"Yes, sir," Santee said.

"You were insubordinate and rude."

"Those guys didn't hold up their end. I was mad."

"Well, I know that, Wes, but that's part of life. You can't always have what you want." Easton was calm, his voice even. "I didn't want to be a dropout from the race, even though you had to run like the Dickens to get second. Do you understand my position?"

Santee nodded. He knew that his coach took pride in his former success at Drake and that he wanted the same for his Jayhawk team. Easton led Santee outside, where they sat down on the steps on one of those brilliant Kansas afternoons when the blue sky seemed to stretch to the ends of the earth.

"We may have many days that they won't produce," Easton said.

"I don't mind running for the team," Santee urged. "But when do I get to run for myself?" He meant his shot at the four-minute mile.

"Well, I've been thinking about how we mesh these things together."

Since John Landy had run his breakthrough mile in December 1952, Easton had been tracking his progress. He clipped newspaper articles about the "No. 1 World Mile Runner" and broke down the lap times Landy was running directly onto the page, studying how the miler paced himself through the race and how difficult it was for him to maintain his speed in the final lap after leading throughout the race. Easton registered every detail and formulated what Santee needed to do. The scene at the Drake Relays had shown Easton that Santee couldn't be held back any longer.

"I want you to run for the team," Easton continued. "But when we get down to certain meets, I want you to enter the open mile event only."

These were the words Santee had been waiting to hear for months.

"You're the one to run the four-minute mile," Easton said confidently. "But you still need to improve. You're going to have to do different workouts than everybody else. You need to put more pressure on yourself."

Over the next two hours they talked about how Santee would ratchet up his training by reducing the interval he took between repeat 440s; they spoke of trying to arrange for a "rabbit" to pace him through at least the first three-quarters of his record mile attempts; they discussed Roger Bannister and John Landy and others who might have a chance at breaking the barrier. It was finally clear to Santee that Easton wanted it as much as he did. Of course, his coach was always looking to help his athletes achieve their best. Santee had seen this with Bill Nieder, the former high school football star who had hurt his knee during his first season at KU and given up on sports when Easton convinced him to master the shot put—and turned him into a world-record holder. Santee had seen it in the day-to-day adjustments Easton made in the training of his athletes; spending long hours at the track, he was always the first to arrive and the last to leave. But Santee was unconvinced until this afternoon that Easton would be there with him in an ambition that had nothing to do with the Jayhawks.

After they exhausted talk of running, Easton turned to Santee to discuss his future, namely, what kind of job he planned to do after graduating and finishing his ROTC stint with the Marines. (He had enrolled in ROTC on Easton's direction to avoid the draft for the Korean War.) Although Santee was studying physical education with an eye toward coaching, Easton suggested that he was better suited for another career.

"Why don't you do something in the business school?" Easton asked. "Your temperament is much better suited for the sales side of things."

"I was thinking the same," Santee said.

"You're going to have to make the change quickly." And then Easton told him he'd help. By the end of the meeting Santee felt protected and supported in a way that he had not felt since Mr. Molyneux died. It was the longest conversation Easton and Santee had ever had, and one that he never could have had with his own father. They shook hands, and then Easton put his arm around Santee.

Santee's first serious bid for the mile barrier would come in early June 1953 at the Compton Invitational in California. In the meantime, Easton planned on contacting Al Franken, the meet's promoter, about getting a pacemaker to help push Santee through the barrier. Santee couldn't wait for his chance.

9

Whatever you can do,
Or think you can, begin it.
Boldness has power, and genius,
And magic in it.

—GOETHE

T THE HEIGHT of Landy's athletic season in 1953, Percy Cerutty invited the *Melbourne Argus* sports columnist Max Crittenden into his cluttered South Yarra study. The coach loved the
press that Landy was earning him, and he was his usual bombastic self.

"Will man ever run the mile within four minutes?" Crittenden asked.

"I'll live to see it!" Cerutty declared authoritatively—because *his*
athlete John Landy was going to be the one to do it.

Statements like these were typical of Cerutty throughout the summer. He continued to assert that he was still the miler's coach. Landy
simply ignored him. Since his breakthrough 4:02.1 run, when Cerutty
had shot off at the mouth in front of his parents, Landy wanted nothing
to do with the man. By April 1953, autumn in Australia, he was finished
with "record" runs as well, at least for the next eight months. He looked
forward to escaping all this talk of a four-minute mile for a while.

He was hard at work in his final year at the University of Melbourne,
where thirty-four hours each week of lectures and practical work in
agricultural science took the lion's share of his days. He had only just
begun training for the next athletic season, and it was likely to be his

last, since he had to give consideration to his future career: he was still weighing the decision whether to go into farming or teaching. He had chosen agricultural science because there were no specific courses in entomology at his university, and in whatever career he chose he wanted to be able to travel and work outdoors. His father, a self-made man who by age twenty-five had already launched his own accountancy firm in Melbourne, advised that it was unwise to engage in sport at the sacrifice of one's career prospects, particularly past the age of twenty-four. John would turn twenty-four the following April. "There are more important things in life," he told his son, and John agreed. In eighteen months he planned to retire from athletics.

But that did not mean his focus waned. If anything, it increased because of the little time he had left. He had already reached the two goals he set after leaving Helsinki: beating Macmillan's record and winning the Australian Championships. Now he wanted to break the world mile record and claim victory at the British Empire Games mile in August 1954 before putting away his running spikes. Although by doing so he would win renown as the world's best miler, this was not his ambition. Running had become more of a competition to draw out the best that was in him, as if he were plumbing the depths of his will.

Nonetheless, since his stunning run the previous December he had become a public spectacle in Australia. He received attention normally reserved for his country's star cricketers and football players. He was photographed racing, eating lunch, studying at the university library, and jogging around local parks—everywhere "but having his morning shower," as one journalist wrote at the time. There could be no more underplaying his pursuit of running, as he had done before the Olympics. At that time a lecturer at the University of Melbourne had stopped him between classes.

"I say, John, do you run at all?" the lecturer asked.

"A bit," he said.

"You know, I saw a fella who looked just like you with a mob of blokes with bloody spears or something, running down St. Kilda Road last Saturday."

"No," Landy replied, his face flushing with color, "couldn't have been me."

No doubt most of his embarrassment had to do with his association with Cerutty at the time. Landy was proud of what he had been able to accomplish on his own since Helsinki. He had dominated every mile race, leading from the front and dictating the pace throughout by running flat out from the start. World record or not, he had run the fastest mile in seven years. He had taken affront to the claim by Arthur Daley in the *New York Times* that there was no way an unknown from Australia could have increased his speed so dramatically. Some joked that his mile was timed by the big Bryant & May clock seen in the distance from Olympic Park. But when a *New York Times* correspondent attended his next mile race on January 3, Landy delivered another fast time, earning a welcome apology from Daley that read: "Maybe too much salt was taken here. . . . When this old-timer started to attend track meets, the 4-minute mile was considered an utter impossibility. It is that no longer."

Soon every race Landy entered came with the expectation that he would break a record—and it was the four-minute mile that most people had in mind. In the *Sydney Morning Herald* on January 18, athletics writer Frank Tierney delivered an itemized list of conditions that Landy needed to go about it:

- A relaxed mental outlook towards the race.
- A certain amount of nervous energy to be released.
- Skillful pacing, assistance.
- A level track with "life" in it.
- A temperature not more than 80 degrees.
- Atmosphere free of humidity.
- No winds.

These were the conditions that Gundar Haegg enjoyed when he set his world mile record of 4:01.4 in 1945. The tracks and weather in Malmo, Sweden, were ideal, and Haegg benefited from prearranged pacing by Lennart Strand.

Landy was not as fortunate when he showed for his Australian Championships mile in Perth on Saturday, January 22. The day before he had withdrawn into a 1,000-acre park near the city, his butterfly net in tow. He needed to escape the intense scrutiny he was under to run a good time. Winning the event was already a foregone conclusion. When reporters cornered Les Perry to ask when the miler might return, Perry simply said, "If he feels hungry." On race day the temperature was nearly eighty degrees and the humidity was high. Landy had raced each of the previous three weekends; he was not particularly relaxed—owing to the enormous pressure from the press—and though Les Perry would have loved to help his friend, he was not fast enough to set the pace. Finally, track officials had neglected to arrange for the calling of lap times, which was usually standard, so Landy was running blind in terms of his pace. Despite these factors, he finished seventy yards ahead of the closest runner in an impressive 4:04.2. But the crowd greeted the announced time with silence, shrugs, and a disappointed early departure. It was the disheartening response that Landy was beginning to expect. Before the race he had told a local reporter, "I'll do my best. If it comes, it comes; but, if it doesn't, for Hec's sake, have the gate open. This crowd will lynch me."

Landy continued to compete every weekend through the summer, though at times he could barely see the track from the perspiration stinging his eyes. Blunders by officials continued to plague him as well. In late February he was predicted to break the 1,500-meter record on an oval track in Melbourne. The track was roughly 330 meters around, which meant that it would take four and a half laps to complete the distance. Feeling good, Landy set out at a fast clip. At the finish of the first half-lap an official called out, "Three to go." As Landy ran past he knew that was wrong and yelled out, "You mean four." He circled the track again, and the official said, "Two to go," when it should have been three laps more. It couldn't be right, Landy thought, but continued to run. Maybe the track was longer than he had figured. Landy completed two more laps and broke through the tape. He was told he had run 3:55.4, which again he doubted, since the fast pace he was running would have at least given him a time of 3:45 in the 1,500 meter. Landy returned to the dressing room, thought through the situation, and then figured out he had indeed run a lap short. He stormed onto the track to confront the official. His elapsed time was actually 2:55.4, and the official had been mistaken.

At another mile race he so dazzled officials with his speed that they failed to stretch the tape completely across the finish in time. As they were uncoiling the wool string from its stick, Landy dashed across the line, having to angle to catch the four feet of string that they had managed to unwind. With little tension on the string, it did not break, and the official lost his grip on the stick. Showing the agility of his former football days, the miler caught the stick in midair and held it over his head for the photographers. Landy may have been ready for world-record miles, but the atmosphere in which he was running was hardly conducive.

By the conclusion of the track and field season in mid-March 1953, he was exhausted. In his last seven mile races, he had averaged 4:11. "About this four minute mile business—I guess I'll need another 10 years. For the present, I have had it," he said after one of the runs. If he was going to break any records in the next Australian season, he would have to do so without the ideal conditions Tierney had outlined in the *Sydney Morning Herald.* At least until then, he would not have to suffer the glare of publicity. He could study and train without distraction.

On May 2, with Landy starting his workouts for his next athletic season, Roger Bannister crossed Magdalen Bridge in Oxford, the waters of the Isis flowing below. He was headed toward the Iffley Road track. The university was in spring's full bloom, a time of year when the trees shaded the narrow, meandering streets and the scent of blossoms filled the air. Hauling stacks of books, students filed in and out of the gateways of their colleges. Generations of England's privileged had lived and studied behind the Cotswold stone walls of the colleges. Bannister had fond memories of his time at Exeter—its garret rooms, the dining hall lined with stained-glass windows and oil paintings, and the quadrangle where students lounged on the grass or pored over lecture notes. His university days were over, but he still felt a strong attachment to Oxford—particularly to its track, where he hoped to make history.

In 1946, as a freshman student, Bannister had found the track in shameful disrepair. At roughly six hundred yards per lap (three laps to a mile), the oval was misshapen and suffering from poor drainage. Rounding one bend, runners used to vanish down a steep bank behind some tall grass, only to reappear some moments later before heading to the finish. In some places old brick was exposed, a hazard for those in spikes. This was where former British middle-distance champions like Colonel Strode Jackson and Jack Lovelock had made their names, running *clockwise* around the track. "It was just a clinker," said Norris McWhirter of the track before Bannister was elected president of the Oxford University Athletic Club in 1948. Bannister decided to have it bulldozed and replaced with a new cinder track, 440 yards around and six lanes wide to meet international specifications. Bannister raised the money to hire contractors, and during the two years of headaches and near-disasters to see it completed he promised himself that the Iffley Road track would be the site of his greatest efforts.

He wanted to break the four-minute mile in Oxford not only because he had helped build the track but also because his university was deeply steeped in the approach to sport he considered his own. Early in the nineteenth century Oxford dons began organizing athletic competitions in an effort to match strong minds with strong bodies. These efforts gathered momentum when Victoria became queen of England in 1838. This began a new era in which the country set about curing the ills of the years before, when loose morals, corruption, idleness, and political scandal had reigned. Pursuing a strong education and an appreciation for the arts, England's youth learned the Victorian values of clean and purposeful living, independence, self-control, and strenuous effort through sport. In part this was an amateur ideal, as historian Allen Guttmann contended, that "traced back to the Renaissance, to the world of Baldassare Castiglione's *Il Cortegiano*, to the courtier who danced, wrote sonnets, played the lute, and commanded armies on the field of battle, who was, however, neither a dancer nor a poet nor a musician nor a soldier."

During this period of Victorian reform, athletic clubs began to form in London, Oxford, and Cambridge. They restricted members from competing in professional running events because they had been brought up to believe that sport was an ennobling effort — that it was not to be pursued for something as mundane as cash. In 1879 three Oxford students brought together the leaders from the disparate clubs for a meeting, followed by dinner at the Randolph. There they decided to create the Amateur Athletic Association, a governing body for the country's amateur athletics. Its purpose, as Montague Sherman, one of those three Oxford students, wrote a few years later, was to assure the true amateur that "wherever he goes to run under AAA laws he will find competent management and fair play — a fair field and no favour." It proved the example that the world would follow.

By 1953, however, Bannister knew that the gentleman amateur was fast becoming a dinosaur. The Helsinki Olympics had shown that high-minded ideas about how and why one participated in sport were losing their luster. Victory at any price was becoming the new ruling principle of sport. In many respects the Americans were leading the way. Their athletes were exciting, brash, well trained, and hell-bent on success. In a post–World War II world the United States reigned as the preeminent power and expected England and the rest of the world to follow in its path. This included the U.S. approach to sport. But Bannister was not ready to relinquish the values he had learned at Oxford. As Winston

Churchill said, "We have not journeyed all this way across the centuries, across the oceans, across the mountains, across the prairies, because we are made of sugar candy."

Because of his medical studies, Bannister didn't have the time to devote three or four hours a day to training. If he had been able to, he probably could have raced every week, since his body would have recovered faster from the strain. But instead of racing every week, the four-minute mile was his goal. Unfortunately, this made him appear distant and aloof to some athletes and newspaper editorial writers. For Bannister, breaking the barrier would be the best affirmation that the gentleman amateur was still capable of realizing athletics' most coveted prize. And for him to do so in the place where this ideal was in part forged would make the victory even sweeter.

The annual AAA versus Oxford University meet was the first opportunity of the 1953 season for athletes to make their mark after months of training. Given the limited number of runners in the mile race, there would be none of the jostling and elbow work that characterized larger competitions. In other words, it was a fine setup for breaking records. Only a few knew of Bannister's intention as he walked into the grounds and made his way alongside the track toward the stands where the locker room was located.

Those in the know included Chris Chataway, who had succeeded Bannister as president of the Oxford University Athletic Club. The stocky, redheaded runner was two and a half years Bannister's junior. They had met when Bannister was doing his postgraduate work at Merton College. Chataway had considered the miler a distant, senior figure and viewed him much as one does an Oxford don. Bannister was not known for often visiting the Iffley Road track, and he first gave Chataway the impression that he never trained, despite rumors that Bannister was often seen running on distant playing fields around Oxford. Only after Chataway roomed with the miler in Helsinki did he become friends with Bannister and learn how seriously he took his running efforts.

Chataway had agreed to pace Bannister through to the three-quarter-mile mark, regardless of the headlines of the previous few days' newspapers, which had exhorted: "Chataway Should Avenge Mile Defeat by Bannister." Chataway was better suited for three miles, and having recently traveled to Morocco with Bannister for a series of races, he knew that Bannister was in better shape. Victory was not in the cards for Chataway, so he chose to help. Plus, there was nobody else in the field who had the ability to push Bannister through the entire race, particularly the critical last lap. He knew it. Bannister knew it. Pacing him through the first three laps was the only way Bannister had a chance at the four-minute mile. There was precedent for the plan: in 1937 Sydney Wooderson had claimed his mile record of 4:06.4 when R. H. Thomas paced him through the first three-quarters at Motspur Park. If it worked then, it should work now. There was no time to spare with the likes of John Landy running such good miles.

In the two months since Bannister had begun his intense track work, his fitness had improved dramatically, despite a rough period of irregular hours caused by midwife duties at St. Mary's. After an Easter break spent hiking in Wales, where he drank from fresh mountain streams and dashed down steep screes as fast as his legs could carry him, he ran a three-quarter-mile trial in one second over three minutes. More important, his pacing for each quarter was even. Two weeks later, on April 13, he ran an 880-yard trial in 1:52.1, showing how well tuned his speed was. He had reached his peak, just at the right moment.

On May 2 the stands and surrounding banks of grass around the Iffley Road track were filled by three o'clock, fifteen minutes before the mile race was to start. The AAA versus Oxford University match always drew a crowd, and the press increased the turnout by announcing that the meet would prove the "most intensive start [to the athletic season] in sport's history." Having consumed only a glass of orange juice mixed with glucose for lunch (his own special concoction), Bannister took his usual twenty-minute warm-up jog in his sweatsuit and readied himself for the race. His focus on an all-out attempt was clear. Over the last week he had gradually become more and more excited about this day. Soon he would channel this focus and excitement, as he later said, "to release every ounce of mental and physical energy I possessed over four minutes."

After the race was called, the field, including Olympic steeplechasers Chris Brasher and John Disley and milers Derek Burfitt and John Bryant, lined up at the starting line to the left of the stands. They tensed as the starter raised the gun. *Bang!* They were off. Chataway jumped into the lead within a few strides. It was an unusually fast early pace and left the rest of the field trying to keep up. Chataway finished the first lap in 62.1 seconds, with Bannister a few yards behind him.

Chataway increased his pace, unsure of how fast he had run the first lap and getting no information from the timekeepers, despite shouting at them. Bannister remained second, sure in his rhythm. Disley moved into third place. The rest of the field was left behind. Chataway crossed the half-mile mark in 2:04.1, too slow. Battling against a strong wind, he spent himself completely in the third lap, struggling to finish it in 60.9 seconds, for a three-quarter-mile time of 3:05. Only a few strides later he bowed out of the race, almost veering into the long-jump pit, dizzy from fatigue.

"Only the silky-striding Bannister was still in contention," Norris McWhirter wrote in his *Athletics World* account of the race. "Serene and now alone Bannister sailed on. Wearing the sad relaxed mask reminiscent of the great Manelote as he delivered the *coup de grâce* in the bull ring."

Into the last lap, Bannister still had speed in reserve. His training had given him the endurance to follow Chataway at a harsh pace without exhausting his final kick. He delivered it now, pushing past the pain that was beginning to seize his legs. At the 1,500-meter mark, Bannister registered 3:47, only 1.8 seconds slower than his Olympic final time against the best in the world. The remaining 120 yards he sprinted, using everything he had to complete the mile in 4:03.6. It was his best time by over four seconds; it was also a new British record, and the fifth-fastest mile ever recorded. He finished seventy yards ahead of Disley, who came second, followed by Bryant and then Brasher. A crowd circled around Bannister to congratulate him. A few hours later he boarded a train to London, knowing he needed to get back to his studies.

By the next morning he was the talk of the town again. "Roger Made It Look Easy" headlined the *News of the World* after the race. "Amazing Mile by Bannister" read another. The *Daily Telegraph* praised him as "a hard-working medical student who between writing theses and delivering babies, turns his brain to the technique and theory of running. Bannister has a fine, though by no means an inordinately strong physique. Many others must have been as richly blessed as he. His running is a triumph of technique . . . and his success is the result of applying his intellect to the job." The British press followed with predictions of when, not if, Bannister would break the mile record. In the *Athletic Review*, Bannister was placed side by side with the British mountaineers who at that moment were "poised high up on the frozen, precipitous slopes of Everest ready for the final assault on the world's hitherto unconquerable high mountain."

Bannister expected the media frenzy. His 4:03.6 may have put him back in the good graces of the press, but he cared little for their forecasts. He knew for certain after this race that "the four-minute mile was not out of reach. It was only a question of time." But he also recognized that he would need two pacemakers to help him make the attempt: the first to carry him to the half-mile mark in under two minutes and the second to lead him through the third lap in roughly sixty seconds. He had diagnosed what was needed like it was a medical case study. Summoning will or emotion did not seem important.

Until he could arrange these pacemakers and further improve his speed, Bannister would have to wait helplessly to see whether another miler got the record before him.

In mid-May, at Bill Easton's two-story house in Lawrence, Kansas, Wes Santee and his coach sat on the couch in front of a grainy black-and-white television set. While they waited for the replay of an interview with Finnish miler Denis Johansson, Easton ran his small terrier mutt through a series of tricks, like balancing a biscuit on his nose before tossing it back and catching it. Looking on, Santee thought Easton's dog was as disciplined as his athletes. Finally Johansson appeared on the screen. Reports had it that the miler, who smoked twenty-five cigarettes a day and was known as much for his good looks and ease with women as his skill on the track, was shooting his mouth off about his upcoming race against Santee and the Belgian Gaston Reiff at the Compton Invitational in June. Wes and his coach wanted to hear it for themselves.

"I think Santee will someday be a great miler," Johansson said to the camera. "But he still has to develop more physically and mentally. He's too unstable, flighty and cocky."

Santee could hardly believe his ears. Who was this guy? His best time in the mile was 4:08.3, and Santee had bettered that on an indoor track this year. Sure Johansson had seen him fail miserably in the 5,000 meter in Helsinki, but that was some time ago.

Johansson continued: "It may be some years yet before he really blossoms, and his mental attitude could do more to hold him back than his physical development, which hasn't far to go. I think that Santee is good enough to set a fast pace, but lack of experience in big-time competition is against him." Johansson finished by saying that the thirty-one-year-old Reiff was the man to beat given his world records in the two-mile, 2,000 meter, and 3,000 meter.

Santee boiled over. "I'll get you," he shouted, shaking his fist at the television. Easton tried to calm him down, but he didn't try very hard. He *wanted* Santee fired up for the race, and Johansson was stoking the flames nicely. The Compton Invitational was Santee's best chance at the four-minute mile this season. The clay track was fast, the weather typically good, and the competition the best he would see that year. This competition was important, since Easton's attempt at getting a rabbit to pace Santee at Compton had hit a brick wall with the Amateur Athletic Union, the same group that kept him from representing the United States in the 1,500 meter at Helsinki.

The AAU was founded in 1888 by a group of private athletic clubs led by the New York Athletic Club. Its mission was to help promote and codify the rules of amateur sports, as had been done in England ten years before. By 1912 the AAU ruled U.S. track and field, most significantly by controlling eligibility for the Olympics. Since then, the organization had carefully tended to its power, working under the fiat that "since it was a voluntary organization, athletes had no rights . . . only privileges."

Its leader was Avery Brundage, albeit more in influence than title by 1953. A former decathlon athlete who had often lost to Jim Thorpe, Brundage retired from competition in 1912, worked as an engineer, and eventually became a millionaire in the construction business. His first love was amateur sports. At one time or another he had held almost every position in the administration of amateur athletics, and in 1952 he was elected the first American president of the International Olympic Committee (IOC). He believed devoutly in sport as recreation, not work. In his opinion, professional athletes were "a troop of trained seals," while amateurs lived up to the "highest moral laws." There was no doubt that he believed this view. The Olympics became his particular obsession, so much so that when Jewish groups tried to get the United States to boycott the 1936 Berlin games, Brundage became a vocal anti-Semite. Nobody dared mess with his Olympic movement—or his hold on the reins of power.

Brundage refused to accept the changing face of sport by the 1950s, particularly the rise of sports stars, the increase in commercialism, and the pursuit of records. He was aided in his fight against these changes by Dan Ferris, the secretary-treasurer of the AAU, who had held tightly to his administrative job for forty years. Ferris was a short, fleshy-faced man with the demeanor of a school principal whose first instinct was to punish, not help. Any decisions made by the AAU crossed his desk first, and although he knew the pursuit of the mile record could draw enormous attention to U.S. amateur athletics, it did not deserve any rule-bending. Ferris made it clear to Easton that if pacemaking was even suspected to have occurred at Compton, or at any other meet for that matter, Santee's time would be disqualified. Since the AAU provided no avenue for appeal, the decision was final, just as it had been when Santee was removed from his Olympic trial the year before. These AAU officials — or as Santee called them, the "Transatlantic Oceanic Hitchhikers," for their tendency to travel around Europe and the United States eating fine dinners and staying at nice hotels on the backs of their athletes — were increasingly looking like they had it out for him.

Though they had blocked any plan of a paced attempt, competition from the likes of Denis Johansson, particularly after his remarks on Santee's maturity, was the next best thing. Bannister had just recently posted a 4:03.6 mile, which Easton had broken down into split times the moment he saw the Associated Press article. Meanwhile, Landy was already training hard for his next season, according to the bible *Track and Field News*. Santee had to make a go at the four-minute mile now, and Compton was his best shot. Even though Johansson would be striving to win the race on his own, he would make almost as good a pacer for Santee as a rabbit. If Johansson was near enough to Santee in the final lap, he would provide Santee with the inspiration to push harder.

On Sunday, May 24, Santee gave the Finnish miler a preview of what he could expect in California. At the Big Seven conference championships in Ames, Iowa, Santee blazed the mile in 4:06.3, taking the national collegiate mile record from Glenn Cunningham, who had held it for eighteen years. After the run Santee said, "I caught my quarters right on time and the race went exactly as Uncle Bill and I had planned." Forty minutes later he won the half-mile in 1:50.8, prompting the crowd to shout, "Break up Kansas," as his team romped home to an overall victory. A week later he ran a 4:07.4.

"Nuts to Denis. We'll see who's immature Friday night," Santee said to reporters before he left for California. "I hope he read what I did at Ames and in the Valley AAU and choked on it. I'm going to have a score to settle with that guy." Easton was only slightly more diplomatic when told by the press that his runner was the favorite to win. "That's okay by us. We never run a race we don't figure we can win. If you don't feel that way, why run?"

At the Kansas City airport, Santee and his coach were ushered into the first-class cabin of the TWA Super Constellation airplane, the Waldorf-Astoria of comfort travel at the time. The pilot came back to say hello and wish Santee luck in California. Drinks and a gourmet meal were then served. The young miler was fast learning that when he competed in a meet promoted by Al Franken, everything was first-class. The AAU might not allow its amateur athletes to get paid, but no rules forbade Franken from treating his star attraction well. After all, Santee was the reason people were buying tickets and companies had enlisted as sponsors to the meet. It was this influence, however, that the AAU was beginning to fear, whether Franken or Santee knew it yet or not.

When Easton and Santee arrived in Los Angeles on Thursday, June 4, Al Franken picked them up in his Ford convertible. The day was all sunshine. Franken was six foot two and rail-thin, no doubt owing to the energetic excitement that punctuated his every move. He had the salesman's touch of making one feel he was the most important person in the world, and after he checked Easton and Santee into the posh Beverly Hills Hotel, Franken went to work. He escorted Santee around town for a series of television and radio appearances. He arranged for the gab-about-town Hedda Hopper to interview him. He drove the miler to Hollywood movie sets, where he met Katherine Grayson and Howard Keel, two of Hollywood's biggest stars. In the middle of a shoot Howard spotted Santee and called "Cut!" The actor shot toward Santee and told him what a big fan he was. There was even a brief encounter with Marilyn Monroe. Franken appeared to know everybody, and Santee was dazzled by the attention and glamour of it all. "I was all eyes," he later said. Afterward, when Santee went out to train, Franken arranged for the press to watch, fueling even more excitement for the next day's race. Santee was the promoter's dream. He saddled up to reporters to declare his confidence in winning—and yes, breaking the four-minute mile barrier was decidedly a possibility as well.

Over the previous week Santee had refined his speed, doing fast quarters instead of long runs in training. He and Easton had already gone over their tactics on a blackboard back in Kansas. The plan was for Santee to hold back in the first two laps, then to take over in the third.

Reiff and Johansson wouldn't see him coming. Santee was ready to show what he was made of.

On Friday morning, while Santee went for a walk after his pre-race breakfast of oatmeal, hot tea, and honey, Easton read the morning papers back at the hotel. "Santee Set to Teach Finnish Runner Lesson," predicted one. "Santee Choice in 'Miracle Mile,'" said another. The *Los Angeles Herald and Express* published a large cartoon showing Santee racing around a clock with Reiff and Johansson pushing him ahead. The quote read: "The Kansas Cyclone, Wes Santee, prodded by Reiff and Johansson, could well be the boy to break through the 4 minute barrier!" Easton knew his runner had the confidence and ability to rise to the occasion of the biggest race of his life. Franken had obviously done his job in drumming up attention.

Easton and his athlete arrived at the stadium in the early evening. The race was scheduled for ten minutes after nine o'clock. The Compton Invitational program, written by Franken, featured the mile event as "the greatest ever to run on the West Coast. That is not a publicity man's pitch but a statement of fact." Each of the five milers was briefly profiled: Gaston Reiff—"one of the world's all-time distance stars"; Denis Johansson—"He's loaded with class, and is the favorite of many in tonight's chase"; Bob McMillen—"he is the mystery man in the field"; Russ Bonham—"the longshot in the class"; and Wes Santee—"America's greatest four lapper of all-time."

While Santee prepared for the race, he put all the hype aside. Four hours earlier he had had some toast and more hot tea and honey. This was his ritual, and before a race he never deviated from it. An hour before the mile he put on his "Kansas Olympic Team" sweatsuit top and went outside the stadium to do some light running and stretching. Then he returned to the infield. While the crowd of nearly nine thousand was preoccupied by the 880-yard relay, he ran wind sprints, working up a sweat. He finished by running at race speed for the last bit. Afterward he returned to the locker room, changed into a dry singlet and shorts, and lay down on the training table for fifteen minutes, hands on his stomach, eyes closed. Fifteen minutes before the race he rubbed his lips and gums with Mentholatum to prevent cotton mouth from nerves. He left the locker room with a towel draped over his head like a boxer and wearing his specially made Japanese track shoes. Whenever he needed a new pair, he sent an outline of each foot on a piece of paper to a shoemaker he had met while competing in Japan after his freshman year. They were particularly light.

Santee spoke to nobody before the race, not to his competitors, not even to Easton. They had already worked everything out between them. It was up to Santee now. Only moments before the gun was set to go off, Santee stepped to the starting line. His one thought was of crushing Johansson. The packed stands were edged up very close to the track, giving the stadium more of an indoor than outdoor feel. Santee faced straight ahead as he waited for the gun. He was oblivious to the noise around him, but he knew the fans would inspire him during the race. They were the equivalent of another runner breathing down his neck.

Reiff went to an early lead. His best mile time was 4:02.8, but a foot injury had disrupted his normally smooth gait. Still, he finished the first lap in first, followed within a few yards by Santee, then Johansson, McMillen, and Bonham. When Santee heard the lap time — 62.7 — he knew it was slow, but his moment to strike had to wait. Reiff continued to set the pace for the field through the second lap, registering a half-mile time of 2:05.2. The crowd sighed, resigned to a slow race. Franken yanked on his hair; he hadn't brought all these mile stars together to run a mediocre race. One official standing next to a *Track and Field News* reporter sighed: "It's going to be a 4:10."

Santee was equally anxious; the first half-mile was too slow for a record time. He had to do something soon. In the third lap Johansson sped quickly past Reiff, and Santee followed. As they rounded out of the turn, the pace was still not fast enough for him. The crowd continued to groan and boo. Into the back straight Santee lost his patience. He charged, nearly into a sprint, fueled by pure emotion. He swept by Johansson before the end of the straight. The Finnish miler couldn't believe it. What was this kid doing going into a sprint seven hundred yards from the finish? He had made his move too early. Santee didn't think so. He had to "go for broke" if he was to have a shot at the four-minute mile. The crowd loved him for his boldness as he opened a five-yard spread. Johansson increased his tempo, knowing that if Santee put too much distance between them the race was over. Reiff followed suit. By the end of the third lap the Finn had won back a yard from Santee, with the Belgian miler six yards back from the lead. Santee had run an incredible 58.2 third lap, and the scoreboard read an elapsed time of 3:03.5. Cheers erupted from the stands. This might be a fast race after all.

McMillen and Bonham had all but thrown in the towel. This was a three-man race. Santee continued driving furiously, somehow maintaining his pace, to the bewilderment of Johansson. Reiff passed the slowing Finn. By the start of the back straight Santee boasted a lead of fifteen yards over Reiff. Santee's last 440 yards, from the middle of the backstretch in the third lap to the middle of the backstretch in the fourth, was run in a heart-stopping fifty-five seconds. He was tiring, though. Johansson began to regain ground while Reiff slowed. As the three strode into the bend the Finn passed Reiff. Santee struggled to maintain pace. It was obvious that his legs were giving out, but his lead was too great. He couldn't hear Reiff's or Johansson's breath behind him, a sure sign that he was far in the lead. Johansson couldn't catch him. The crowd roared again as Santee approached the tape. Drive to the finish line, he told himself. Don't let up. He leaned forward into the tape, breasting it twelve yards ahead of Johansson in 4:02.4—the fastest mile ever run by an American. The crowd chanted his name as he slowed into a walk.

The Finn came up to Santee. Easton was already by his side. "You guys are crazy," Johansson said, barely able to talk. "I never had anyone sprint seven hundred yards before the finish."

Santee smiled and shook Johansson's hand, as he often did with his competitors after a race. He could always tell how tired they were by the strength of their handshake. Johansson was exhausted. In a rare display of humility, the young Kansan had to be pulled back onto the track by the meet director for a victory lap, and Santee agreed to do it only after the public-address system urged him on. He took the lap barefoot, holding his shoes in his hand to wave at the crowd. They had served him well.

Afterward he autographed race programs pushed into his hands by kids pressing against the railings at the bottom of the stands. It was a moment of a lifetime. His immodesty returned when he responded to a reporter about how he ran: "I didn't think it was so fast," Santee said. When Easton was asked what he thought of the race, he simply said, "We're getting closer." Everyone knew what he was talking about.

News of the race made headlines from Los Angeles to New York to London to Melbourne. Johansson was the first to express how great Santee was, followed by something of an apology: "He taught me not to pop off so much." Gaston Reiff predicted that if Santee were to go head to head with Bannister, Santee would win: "Santee runs the last 500 or

600 too fast." Most reports, however, talked of the four-minute mile. Easton was quoted as saying, "This was the ultimate. We'll wait a while for the next ultimate. . . . But if that first half had just been faster. . . ." The banner headlines spoke for themselves: "Santee Sees Magic Mile"; "4-Minute Mile? Santee Vows He'll Run It Faster"; "Santee Admits Getting Closer to Phantom Four-Minute Mile"; and "Jet-Propelled Santee Flirts with 4:00 Mile." If some people had yet to hear that Santee was out to break the barrier, they most certainly knew now.

10

Still as they run they look behind,
They hear a voice in every wind,
And snatch a fearful joy.

—THOMAS GRAY, "Ode on a Distant
Prospect of Eton College" (1742)

IN THE SMALL COMMUNITY of Melbourne's athletes, news of the
latest exploits by international milers was traded like good gossip.
The local papers carried only the sparest of reports, so those few
who subscribed to magazines like *Track and Field News* and the *Athletic
Review* were sought-after purveyors of information. Les Perry was one
of those who shared his magazines with his friends, including Landy.
Occasionally the two would get together for a lunch of meat pies at a
restaurant overlooking the railway station near the Water Board, where
Perry worked as a clerical officer. Perry, having already devoured the issues, would give them to Landy to read. It was understood that they
would be passed around to Geoff Warren and others. Somehow the
dog-eared copies eventually found their way back to Perry.

The recent headlines were startling: "Oh, That Compton Meet!" and
"Bannister Runs 4:03.6!" topped the most recent issues. The write-ups
told of how Bannister and Santee were nearing Haegg's record and setting their sights on the four-minute mile itself. Landy had to wait out
their seasons, despite receiving invitations to compete in the United

States and England. Their summer was his winter, and he was in the middle of his studies. This was a great disappointment to track promoters, who were conspiring to bring these three milers together. The closest Landy came to being on the track with them was when he saw a brief segment of a race in the United States or England among the hourlong mix of cartoons, newsreels, and short movies shown at one of the theaterettes around town. Geoff Warren, with whom he had roomed in Portsea, had an inside connection with one of the theater owners and was alerted whenever there was a new clip of athletics, but they were always a couple of months behind. Although eager to see or hear news of Bannister's and Santee's runs, Landy felt that their progress was almost inconsequential: he had his own course to follow, and he wouldn't let himself be rushed by others. The pursuit of the mile record was about proving how good *he* was, not about being the one to cross the four-minute threshold first. He was running for himself, not for national honor.

At the end of his 1953 season Landy had made it clear that he wouldn't be taking much of a rest. "It won't be any good my dropping training until next spring, if I want to run fast miles [next] December and after," he told reporter Joseph Galli. "My idea is to carry through this heavy training program right through the winter." The details of his program were listed on a sheet of paper tacked to his wardrobe door. His theory of training was a rather simple adaptation of the previous year: he planned on working one and a half times harder. To see that he did, he marked down each session. The listings from the previous three months read like a diary of torture.

Between March 18 and May 24 he ran over three hundred miles, primarily endurance runs on roads leading out of Melbourne. The previous year he had not timed his runs, but this year he did, so that the effort he expended in each session was more stringently defined. On May 25, 27, and 30 he ran seven miles in forty minutes, followed by half an hour of weightlifting to strengthen his upper body; on June 1 he ran six miles in five minutes for each mile, three miles in sixteen minutes, and finished with thirty minutes of weightlifting; on June 3 he alternated 880 yards of "fast striding" with 880 yards of jogging for a total of eight miles. He spent so much time training in Central Park that he joked that he knew every magpie in the surrounding trees, particularly the ones that "bombed" him.

Instead of listening to Cerutty's thoughts on what it took to run a

3:53 mile, which his former coach was propagating widely in the athletics press—including advice on how to run "OVER THE GROUND" and when to abandon racing conditioning to "go to the hills, the sand track or the bog lands and do steady running up to 10 miles every day"— Landy felt convinced that a more intense regime would produce better times than before, regardless of the slow tracks and lack of competition in Australia.

In late June 1953, with frost on the ground, as well as the leaves of the transplanted oak and elm trees, he stuck to this approach, not giving in to the urge to take a rest and put off his training. On his long runs along the Dandenong Road, which is the start of the coastal road that links Melbourne to Sydney, he listened to the sound of his footfalls, sinking into a near-trance from their rhythm. He knew that come his first race in December, when the nervous energy had expired after the first lap and the momentum from that first lap had carried him only as far as the half-mile point, he would need the conditioning from these training runs to sustain his speed to the very end. To run a record time, every mile of the seven he ran that day, and the day after, and the day after that, was necessary.

Although his studies and training limited his social life to time spent mostly with his family, at home or at their South Gippsland property on weekends, planting trees or walking around the farm, he didn't see his running as a sacrifice. He liked the discipline it required. He liked the feeling of his body learning to tolerate ever-increasing levels of stress. And he was comfortable being alone to test how far he could push himself.

In the third week of that same June, Australian miler Don Macmillan was studying quietly in his London student hostel when someone down the hall shouted, "Hey, Don, you're wanted on the phone." It was surprising for him to get a call, so he hurried downstairs. After Helsinki, Macmillan had decided to attend a teachers' college in Britain for a year while continuing to run competitively. He would have preferred to be in Australia, racing against his good friend Landy, each pushing the other to faster times, as Haegg and Andersson had done.

He picked up the phone quizzically.

"Roger here. Roger Bannister."

It took Macmillan a moment to register that it was really Bannister on the other end. "G'day, Roger."

"Jolly good news about the climbing of Everest, isn't it?"

Strange that he would be calling to talk about the news. "Yeah, it is, isn't it?"

"Great Empire effort," Bannister continued.

"I suppose it was." Macmillan couldn't understand why Bannister had phoned him. They hadn't spoken in a while. "Marvelous," he finally added.

"Did you enjoy the Coronation?"

"Oh, yes."

"How are you running?"

"Not too good at the moment. I have a sore leg. How are you?"

"I'm going very well. What do you think about Wes Santee?" Bannister asked.

News of the American's Compton Invitational win and his proximity to the mile barrier would have been hard to miss. The British papers covered the event as well as Santee's announcement that he would make another attempt on June 27. Gundar Haegg had even written the young Kansan, urging him on in a widely publicized letter: "I think you can be the first man under four minutes, but you must hurry on." Bannister was cited as the reason to hurry.

"Do you think he could do it?" Macmillan asked.

"I think he might be able to, but I want to beat him to it." There was a pause. "Would you be prepared to help me?"

"I'll do what I can, but I'm not very fit."

"The idea is, we go down to Motspur Park on Saturday morning [June 27]. Wes is running on the same day." Bannister explained that he could beat Santee to the punch because of the six-hour time difference. It had to be that weekend, though. Norris McWhirter had convinced the director of a schoolboys' meet (the Surrey Schools AAA Championships) to include a special invitation mile in their schedule. "I'd like you to run as far as you can at sixty seconds a lap. Chris Brasher will be there, and he will drop back and time it so when we're starting the last lap Chris will have been jogging around and he'll be a lap behind us. He'll then be fit to take me around the last lap."

"All right, I'll do my best. I'll go as far as I can," Macmillan said. If he could not push Landy to a four-minute mile, it was better to have Bannister, an Empire man, run it than an American, he thought.

"On Saturday morning you'll be picked up in a black car by one of the McWhirter brothers." Bannister's tone indicated that this was to be kept quiet. "He'll meet you at the corner of Tottenham Court Road and take you to Motspur Park."

Macmillan agreed, and they exchanged good-byes. Bannister had his hare.

Since the 4:03.6 mile highlighting Bannister's potential as the first four-minute miler, the pressure to do so had intensified. Obviously he was in good form. He had performed well in a series of races during the early summer, and as a result the press hounded him at every turn, asking whether this day would be *the* day. "It's becoming quite a tyranny," he chided a reporter. On May 23 at White City Stadium he had run a slow race, and a group of fans booed and harassed him for not breaking the barrier, though he easily beat the rest of the field. The next day the newspapers had Bannister "disappointing a big crowd" and "scarcely fulfilling the expectations of the 20,000 people present." When he then ran a record-breaking 1:51.9 half-mile on May 30, through a blustery wind, he barely warranted mention in the papers. The British public wanted another big achievement—four-minute-mile big—to match the recent conquest of Everest and the coronation of Queen Elizabeth. Anything less wasn't enough.

"We know the race might not be the way you would wish, but I can organize it," Norris McWhirter had told him in mid-June after a training session at the Paddington track when the McWhirter twins began putting together the Motspur Park race. The clandestine nature and overt pacing of the race were not optimal. Plus, Bannister had torn his left thigh muscle in a quarter-mile race the same day Santee ran his 4:02.4 at Compton. For a few days afterward Bannister felt like he had been kicked by a horse in the back of his leg, and he was still not confident that it could take the punishment of a fast mile attempt. Nonetheless, Norris urged him onward. "Santee's going to do it. . . . And you simply wouldn't want to let him do it."

Bannister was as swept up as anyone by the exuberance his country was experiencing. Throughout May the country could talk of little else besides the details of Queen Elizabeth's ceremony in Westminster Abbey and the progress of the British expedition on Everest. Himalayan weather reports and procession routes were pored over. On June 2, Coronation Day, he and his fellow Britons were swelled with a pride they hadn't felt in almost a decade. The celebrations reminded the world of Britain's reputation for grandeur and greatness. That day news reached London that a member of the British expedition team, Edmund Hillary, along with Sherpa Tenzing Norgay, had reached the summit of Everest, the rooftop of the world. The *Times* said the achievement matched Sir Francis Drake's circumnavigating the globe in terms of historical greatness. Historian Richard Holt explained the significance: "It was the manner of this triumph as much as anything else that pleased the British. There was a charming amateurism and eccentricity about the expedition. Umbrellas had been carried up to 13,000 feet. [Colonel] John Hunt played the part of the cultured, competent, phlegmatic Englishman reading the *Oxford Book of Greek Verse* while organizing supplies and technical support with a minimum of fuss. There was still hope for Britain." Editorial writers and historians aside, the feeling that overwhelmed the country on June 2 was best summed up by an English father telling his son that day, "The British are the best in the world. We are the only ones who could have done it."

Bannister had closely followed the Everest expedition both in the papers and on the radio. He knew several of its members from his physiology experiments, and he had even compared his progress with the mile that summer as being at "Camp Six." With Santee fast approaching the record, it was critical for Bannister to get there first and to claim the same honor that Hillary had when staking the Union Jack on the world's tallest peak. Compared to Landy, Bannister had a greater appreciation of the historical significance of being the first to run under four minutes, and he was not going to let anything stop him.

By the morning of June 27 everything was organized for the attempt. From London, Norris McWhirter drove Bannister, Macmillan, and steeplechaser Chris Brasher, an Achilles Club member who had recently started training under the Austrian coach Franz Stampfl, to Motspur Park. Brasher was not a particularly fast mile runner, but he wouldn't have to be, given their pacemaking arrangements. Chris Chataway could not participate because he was studying for his Oxford finals in politics. They arrived at 1:15 P.M., half an hour before the race was to start. The two official timekeepers whom the McWhirter twins had arranged were on hand to validate the time—if it was record fast. Norris himself would serve as the third timekeeper. AAA officials Jack Crump and Harold Abrahams were also present. There were few others, apart from the one thousand schoolboys in attendance for the meet.

While the schoolboys broke for lunch and the three runners warmed up on the adjacent cricket field, head groundsman J. McTaggart rolled and then lightly watered the cinders in preparation for the race. At 1:50 P.M., with the sky clear, the temperature fair, and only a slight breeze blowing into the finishing straight, the three runners lined up at the start. Bannister was wearing a new pair of German spikes, and his pulled muscle felt completely healed. The 190-pound, six-foot-four-inch Macmillan, whose best mile time was 4:08.8, turned to Bannister and said he would try to run a 4:05. Brasher was silent, knowing exactly what he needed to do, and typically enthusiastic about getting started.

"Hope for the best," Bannister said, and the race was on.

As planned, the Australian led from the beginning, Bannister tethered closely behind him. Brasher, who wore thick dark glasses and had an unnatural gait on his best of days, moved purposefully slow, since his job didn't come until the end of the third lap. Although he looked like "an amputee getting used to a new limb," as McWhirter described it, his minute-and-a-half laps would keep him fresh for the end. In comparison, Bannister and Macmillan were flying. The Australian proved a superbly even pacemaker for the first two laps. He crossed the 220-yard mark in 29.5 seconds, the first 440 in 59.6, the 660 in 1:28.8, and the 880 in 1:59.7. Perfect. Brasher was over half a lap back at the halfway point. Macmillan didn't have the legs to maintain his speed. His thighs burned, and his bruised heel shot pain up his leg as he struggled to finish the next 220 at a good clip. When Bannister yelled, "Wide open, Don"—meaning full throttle—Macmillan stalled. He was exhausted. Bannister hesitated, losing a precious second, before shifting past the Australian to finish the third lap in 3:01.8. From track side McWhirter called out the time. The schoolboys in attendance chewed quietly on their sandwiches, not sure why these men were running in the middle of their meet.

At the ringing of the bell Brasher, having run only two laps, was in position to bring Bannister around the last 440 yards. Over his shoulder Brasher yelled "a stream of expletives" at his friend to hurry. Bannister crossed the 1,500-meter mark in 3:44.8—a time that would have earned him gold in Helsinki. In the last 120 yards he started to "climb the ladder," as Macmillan described the moment when exhaustion takes over and the head tilts up, the knees lift, and the arms swing higher and higher to get every inch out of the stride. Brasher shouted back again, "Come on, Roger." Bannister fought mightily to the tape, but it was not fast enough. He clocked a 4:02. The one thousand schoolboys finally erupted in cheers, more from believing that Bannister had caught

Brasher in the last straight to win than from realizing that the third-fastest mile in history had been run.

Although Bannister had clocked an incredible time, the mood was somber afterward. It had taken a lot to arrange this event, yet it had been for nothing, and there was now a sense of helplessness in having to wait to hear about Santee's performance in six hours. In the locker room Bannister thanked Brasher and Macmillan for their help, despite the failed attempt. Everyone had given their best.

"Only five yards outside the world record," Bannister said, though he was still fourteen or fifteen yards from the four-minute mile, a distance that seemed much longer than the few strides it would take him to span it.

The three quickly changed and headed to the cars. Macmillan was off to Wimbledon, courtesy of tickets provided by the McWhirters. Bannister and Brasher crammed into an Aston Martin driven by Dr. John More, ready for a weekend's climbing in North Wales. They would have to wait until after they arrived in Snowdonia to learn that Wes Santee had also failed in his bid. They heard from McWhirter by telephone that he had run 4:07.6 in Dayton. That night, as Bannister rested in a hayloft before the following day's climbing, he knew that he wouldn't be able to summon the energy to make another attempt against the clock that summer. He desperately hoped that Santee would not either. Regardless of his competitors, however, Bannister was concerned about what it would take for him to cut two more seconds off his time considering how much he had improved, the sacrifices involved, and the limited time he had left in his running career.

"Maybe I could run a Four-Minute Mile behind one of my father's ranch horses," Santee replied when asked what he thought of the Motspur Park paced race. "If that's what you want." By the time Santee reached Europe on July 1 for a summer tour sponsored by the AAU, there was a groundswell of reaction to Bannister's 4:02. Some called the race "fixed" and "unsporting." Jesse Abramson in the New York Herald Tribune opined: "The world obviously would like to see a 4:00 mile, but let's keep it kosher in a regularly fixed race." Many in the British press felt the same: the Daily Mail declared the race not "bona fide," and the Daily Mirror called the miler a "clock-runner" who was "brilliant at running against that rhythmically moving second hand on the clock face, but has little relish for the cut-and-thrust of flying spikes and jolting elbows." Further, British amateur officials were considering whether or not the record time should be ratified. Given the AAU's stance on paced races, Wes Santee thought the barrier should fall in a real race—preferably one won by him.

His European trip was supposed to provide the opportunity. The fast tracks and top-class competition had many thinking that during his travels Santee would "beat the rest of the world to the Mount Everest of trackdom," as Abramson wrote in the same article in which he derided Bannister. The last month had brought many things to Santee—little rest, a lot of travel, bad food, disgruntled track officials, meager prizes, and day after day of racing—but not a mile record. The tour started in Finland, where Santee lost a 1,500-meter race to the hometown boy, Denis Johansson. Afterward Johansson took Santee to a sauna, where it was so hot that the Kansan had to use his towel as a mask to breathe before the Finn led him unsuspectingly into a pool of ice-cold water. And that was the peak of hospitality shown to Santee during his trip.

After a grinding schedule of races across Finland, he and his AAU teammates, including close friend Mal Whitfield, flew to Sweden, where Santee managed to break the American 1,500-meter record. Two days later he was entered in an 800-meter event, which he also won, before flying to continental Europe for more races. In total his two-month tour schedule had him running in twenty-two races. Santee was either at the track or in transit the entire time he was away. He missed Coach Easton, and he particularly missed Danna, to whom he had given his fraternity pin in a sure prelude to a marriage proposal. In his suitcase he had packed an eight-by-ten photograph of her. He removed it at each hotel and stared at it as he wrote to her almost every day. At one point in the tour he wanted to cut short his trip and go back to Kansas to be with her, but AAU officials demanded that he stay.

In Berlin on August 3 Santee decided he was through with being treated like a one-man dog-and-pony show. For weeks he had packed stadiums with tens of thousands of fans. Meanwhile, amateur officials in each country (who worked closely with the track promoters selling tickets) were providing him and his American teammates with spartan meals. If they wanted dessert or a second cup of coffee, they had to pay. Expense money was almost nonexistent, and if one of them didn't perform to standard, reprimands were handed out. When Santee came first in a race—a common occurrence—he was given a plaque, a mechanical pencil, or an inexpensive watch for a prize. What he should have been doing was conserving his strength for one or two good races, like the British Games a few days later, but instead he was working day in and day out for no reward. "It was work," he later said. Having labored many long hours for his father on the ranch without pay, he knew when someone was taking advantage of him.

A few days before, he had approached a German official to ask if he could pool several of his prizes for an Agfa camera. At the time it was the Rolls-Royce of cameras, and before Santee had left Kansas, Easton had even suggested that he should try to get his hands on one when he was in Europe. The official told Santee that he would take care of it. On the morning of August 3 Santee called the official at his house to ask whether he had arranged for the camera. The official put Santee off, saying that he was looking into the matter. At lunch Santee handed his unopened prizes to the official and asked for his camera. The official said that the camera was more expensive than the amateur rules allowed and that "they could not consider any such demands." This sent Santee off. After all the money they had made on him—and the sacrifice involved on his part—they could at least provide him with a camera. Santee pounded his fist on the table and yelled, "You're a damn liar."

The official said there was nothing he could do, but regardless, "We want you to stay on and run another race."

"To hell with you. I'm not staying here." Santee stormed from the room, slamming the door behind him. He was finished with this kind of treatment. He left Germany immediately for his next race in Finland. The rest of the team followed him there after they finished competing. Little was said of the affair, but everyone knew Santee would have to pay for his outburst one way or another. Amateur officials did not suffer this kind of action from their athletes.

From Finland Santee went to London for the British Games, hoping to compete against Roger Bannister. On his arrival he learned that Bannister was busy with his medical exams and had backed out of the international mile event. Still, the race was a big affair; Gundar Haegg, Sydney Wooderson, and Paavo Nurmi were paraded around the track before it was held. With Johansson and several of Britain's best middle-distance men in the event, including Chris Chataway, Bill Nankeville, and Gordon Pirie, this would have been a prime chance for Santee to get the competition he needed for a record attempt, but he was simply exhausted from the traveling and the constant competition. By the fourth lap, when most expected Santee to explode to the finish line, he had nothing left to give. Pirie sprinted past him in the back straight to win by three yards in 4:06.8.

"I've run seven races—one every other day," Santee told reporters afterward. "I'm more than a bit tired."

When he returned to the United States, news of his defeat caused the pundits to declare that Santee risked burning out before he reached his prime if he continued to compete so often. Santee discounted the claims, but privately he knew he wasn't being given the support necessary to break the mile barrier. Like his counterparts, he needed the ability to enlist pacemakers, events featuring the top-class competition, and enough breathing room beforehand to prepare and focus properly. His confrontation with amateur officials in Berlin had ignited a firestorm, so his chances of receiving this support were almost nonexistent. Plus, his cross-country season loomed. Nonetheless, he felt that the four-minute mile was his to run first.

11

We must wake up to the fact that athletics is not, nor ever can be perfected; there will always be more to learn.

—ARTHUR "GREATHEART" NEWTON,
legendary long-distance runner (1949)

WEARING JACKETS AND TIES, Roger Bannister and Norris McWhirter exited the subway car at the Holborn tube station in central London on their way home from a late dinner party. It was eleven o'clock, and the station was nearly deserted as they made their way through the labyrinthine tunnel toward the escalators. At the base of the escalators they decided to attempt to run up the one that led down. Holborn was one of the city's deepest stations, and it would require some effort to reach the top. Both knew the attempt was childish, but they found it no less compelling—nothing wrong with a little harmless fun. Halfway up, the attempt proved less simple than either had imagined. It was a long way, and to ease off only an instant doubled the effort required. They couldn't let up now. To the few subway riders ascending on the proper escalator, they looked like lunatics. Still, they continued to drive up the steps, urged on by the embarrassment they would suffer at being shot back down to the bottom. At the top, winded and legs burning, they reveled in their triumph.

Neither young man drew much of a lesson from the late evening escapade, but if Bannister was ever to achieve the four-minute mile, he knew he couldn't let up with his training. It was unlikely that Landy or

Santee would slack off. But by September 1953 Bannister needed a change from pursuing this uphill battle on his own. He had started his final year at St. Mary's and was to take his medical board exams the following summer. He would have to hang up his spikes in August 1954 after the Empire Games in Vancouver and the European Games in Berne. Bannister wanted to finish his running career on a high by winning these two championships and breaking the mile barrier. For the first time, though, he wasn't sure he could do it alone.

The previous season had ended badly. On his return from his North Wales hiking trip, he suffered a terrible thrashing by the press for the secret Motspur Park attempt, followed by an embarrassing decision from the British Amateur Athletic Board to reject his 4:02 mile at Motspur Park as a British record. The board announced that it

> has been compelled to take this action because it does not consider the event was a *bona fide* competition according to the rules. The Board wishes it to be known that whilst appreciating the public enthusiasm for record performances, and the natural and commendable desire of athletes to accomplish them, it does not regard individual record attempts as in the best interest of athletics as a whole.

The decision was based on the failure of the two other runners to complete the race and the lack of prior advertising for the event. Bannister accepted this decision without appeal, though the rebuke from amateur officials stung. In hindsight, he knew it was wrong to have attempted the record in conditions so far outside those of a normal race, but at the time there seemed to be no other choice if he was to be the first to break the mile record.

In the AAA Championships mile, Bannister ran a 4:05.2 but was overshadowed by Gordon Pirie, who broke the world record in the six-mile race. Pirie was unabashed about training for hours each day. Many considered him the future ideal of British athletics, though it was rumored that he was almost a professional given that his employers at a paint sales company allowed him as much time off as he needed to train and race—his name association with the company presumably providing all the benefit of their arrangement. In August Bannister managed to participate in a world record 4 x 1 mile relay event and ran his best half-mile time, but Pirie was the man of the hour, particularly after beating Santee at the British Games.

Bannister appreciated having the limelight shift to another runner, but he had to wonder whether Pirie, who boasted that the mile barrier was in his sights, might be more fit to go for the record. After all, Joseph Binks, a longtime Bannister supporter, had declared after the British Games that "Pirie is the most extraordinary runner the world has known, bearing in mind his amazing type of training and the distances over which he seems to be able to beat records."

For seven years Bannister had followed his own advice and methodically improved his times. He hadn't relied on others to help him train or to sustain his level of commitment. Although his list of race championships and record times was pages long, he found himself coming up short when it came to his greatest athletic ambitions. In the fall of 1953 he took his first step away from his press-decreed "lone wolf" approach by running with Chris Brasher at the Paddington track during lunchtime.

Born in British Guinea into a family at the top end of the social ladder, Brasher had been educated at the esteemed Rugby public school and at St. John's College, Cambridge. He took nothing in life for granted, however; his achievements were won with a fierce drive, great energy, and a never-say-die attitude. When Brasher discovered that he did not have the natural talent to be a miler (an asthmatic, he wheezed around the track), he took to the steeplechase, which required more strength and determination than anything else. He intended to make it to the 1956 Olympics. Outside athletics, Brasher was an avid climber and just missed the 1953 British expedition to Everest. What he lacked in technical skills as a climber he made up for by demanding the impossible from himself—and others. "Enthusiasm was the feature you noticed about him right away," said one friend. "He was a thrusting sort of person. . . . You had the feeling that he wanted to master what he was doing and literally forced himself to do it," said another. By the fall of 1953 Brasher was balancing his athletics and climbing while working for Mobil Oil in a management trainee program.

For the past year Brasher had trained with Franz Stampfl, a man of equal immoderation who coached athletes on the grounds of the Duke of York's Barracks in Chelsea on Friday evenings and in Battersea Park over the weekend. Stampfl had given Brasher a training schedule, and part of it he fulfilled by running with Bannister at the Paddington track. On occasion they were joined by Chris Chataway, who had lately started training with the Austrian coach as well.

Like Brasher, Chataway wasn't the type one would immediately identify as a runner. His stout build was better suited for rugby than fast miles, and he enjoyed a less than healthy admiration for smoking and drinking, particularly after a good hard race. Furthermore, he never seemed to like running very much, particularly when it came to hard training, which he abhorred. Of the regimes endured by the likes of Landy and Zatopek, he said, "For me and many others, it is simply more than we could stand." That said, Chataway had always excelled at running, loving the thrill of competition. At eighteen he clocked a 4:27.2 mile; in 1950, while performing his National Service as an officer cadet, he set an inter-Services record with a 4:15.6 mile; and at the 1952 Olympics he might have won the 5,000-meter event (his best distance) except for falling at the last turn. It was the mettle he showed by finishing the race that distinguished him as a runner. Norris McWhirter wrote that he was "a man of spirit — the right spirit."

Two years younger than Bannister, Chataway was the oldest of four children whose father was slowly dying from angina. He had graduated from Oxford that summer and had since taken a job as an under-brewer with Guinness. He had all but given up on running in order to earn a living when Stampfl got hold of him. "He invested with magic this whole painful business of trying to run fast," said Chataway of his new coach. "He made you feel that this would be the most wonderful thing. It would put you along with Michelangelo, Leonardo da Vinci, if you could do it, and he was quite convinced you *could* do it."

After a few weeks of running with Bannister, Brasher and Chataway convinced their friend to meet with Stampfl. "Come and join us, because it's fun," they said at first. Bannister resisted. It had been a long time since he had taken a coach (or "rubber," as they were called, from Victorian times when masseurs used to be the ones who gave advice). Training for distance events was about getting the best out of oneself by making minor adjustments in how much to push the body. How could a coach read this better than the athlete himself? Although Bannister was finding training with others helpful and he liked the companionship, this was taking it too far. Surely Stampfl could help him, Brasher and Chataway pressed, just as he had helped them. Brasher was most insistent. He believed that taking a coach was essential. "It is absolutely necessary to have someone to whom you can turn, who is entirely honest with you," he said. "Who you know will not give spurious advice. This for me was my coach, which wasn't so much how to lift my arms or legs up, but when I felt that I have had it, he came on reassured, showed me the goals ahead. . . . I don't think anyone can be so self-sufficient that they don't feel the need for somebody else."

For a very long time Bannister had admittedly followed a solitary path, one that did not allow him the comfort or insight of others. His failure to break the mile record the previous season had finally brought him to the point where he decided to open himself up to others. He had come as far as he could on his own. In October, after a day at the hospital, he went to meet Stampfl at the Duke of York's Barracks to listen to what he had to say. Chataway and Brasher were with him. The training ground was just off Sloane Square, an upmarket area in west London. Adjacent to the barracks housing Territorial Army soldiers was a cinder track. It was in poor shape and smaller than standard — roughly five laps to a mile. In the early evening the track and a drill hall in the barracks were not used, and Stampfl had arranged with the army to use the facilities to coach athletes. He charged one shilling per session.

When Bannister entered the large hall, Stampfl was leading a group of forty athletes through warm-up exercises, mostly pushups and calisthenics. His thick Austrian accent echoed throughout the large room as he urged his athletes onward. Stampfl was barrel-chested and almost six feet tall. As he approached Bannister and his companions, he looked even bigger, his stride strong, features sharp, and eyes alight with power. Despite being in a room full of athletes in sweats and shorts, he wore a Savile Row blazer, corduroy pants, and polished shoes. He looked more like an intellectual, albeit a massive one, than a coach.

Born in Vienna, Austria, in 1913, Stampfl was the son of an Austrian general and had studied writing and painting in his native city. A talented skier and javelin thrower, he had always had sport in his life, and he participated in the 1932 Olympics in the javelin. In 1936, sensing the inevitable rise of Hitler, he moved to England to study at Cambridge University. Two years later, when Hitler marched into Austria, the British government demanded that Stampfl leave the country unless he could show a unique, necessary skill. Having taught skiing back in his homeland, Stampfl pitched AAA officials to coach their athletes in the latest training methods. His overpowering presence won him a job in Northern Ireland. When Britain declared war on Germany, Stampfl returned to England to join up with the RAF but was interned immediately as an "enemy alien."

He went on a hunger strike to protest his confinement. Early one

July morning in 1940 he was shipped to Australia on the liner ship *Arandora Star* with a host of other prisoners of war. In the middle of the North Sea a German U-boat torpedoed the ship. Explosions ripped through the *Arandora Star*. Within thirty minutes, amid screams of fear and dying, the ship flooded with water and eventually sank to the bottom of the Atlantic. To survive, Stampfl forced a steel plate aside to get to the surface of the ship and then jumped into the cold, oil-slicked sea. For eight hours he swam, warding off shock from the cold and struggling to keep his head above the water before a rescue boat sighted him. Hundreds died in the disaster, but those who survived were interned and shipped once again to Australia. There Stampfl was sent to an internment camp in Hay, and to ease the desperation plaguing the prisoners he organized athletics—boxing, wrestling, and football matches. "It was not just a job for me," he said. "It was an inner desire to survive and remain sane for myself and my friends in camp."

When the war ended, Stampfl married an Australian woman he met in Melbourne and moved back to London. Although he had suffered terribly over the previous years and still had trouble sleeping under linens or far from an open window because of his long confinement, he still admired the English, particularly their love for amateur sport, and felt that their athletes could use his help. He reconnected with amateur officials and found a number of coaching posts, including part-time ones at Cambridge and Oxford Universities. Still, he was not asked to aid the British Olympic team in 1952, evidence that amateur officials never brought him fully into their fold because he was an outsider. Instead, he assisted the Pakistani team.

Coaching was not a well-paid profession, and on occasion he needed to work in a sports shop for additional income, but he loved helping athletes, whether they were talented or otherwise. By the fall of 1953 he was training athletes in everything from field events (including javelin, hammer throw, and discus) to distance running. Although he knew a great deal about interval methods and racing techniques, his most valuable insights came from an understanding of what it took to get the most out of an athlete. His experiences during the war, many too terrible to recall, had taught him a lot about willpower. In his opinion, the best coaches had "the ability to make a man go beyond the point at which he thinks he is going to die." Any effort short of this neglected an athlete's full potential.

Stampfl was unlike anyone Bannister had ever met. Partly aware of his history, the miler sensed that this coach truly knew about courage and determination. They had not been talking for very long when Stampfl said quite simply, "You have to train harder." When Bannister said he had medical school to think about, Stampfl replied, "Do both." In his opinion, nothing was impossible. An athlete was restricted only by what he thought he was unable to do. The four-minute mile? Easy. One could run a 3:52 or faster if one truly wanted. It was not about spending endless hours in training—an option not available to Bannister given medical school—but rather the quality of the effort.

Stampfl's certainty and passion fascinated Bannister. By the meeting's end he had agreed to come by the following Friday to run. No other commitment was made.

One September night, at 2:00 A.M., John Landy was running alone along the Dandenong Road. The sodium vapor lights above the road were nearly lost in the fog and cast an eerie orange glow onto the pavement. Landy was ascending a straight uphill stretch on the road when he saw a pair of headlights coming toward him. The car was swerving left and right, the driver obviously drunk. Landy slowed a little and waited for the car to pass, when suddenly it stopped a few feet ahead of him. Although Landy made a habit of running this road, he understood that most people would be suspicious seeing someone along the road in the middle of the night. Apparently this driver was one of them. He rolled down the window, and Landy stepped up to the side of the car.

"Who do you think you are, mate?" the inebriated driver asked. "Bloody Landy?"

Better than admit he was indeed Landy, the miler headed off down the road. Although not every Australian could recognize him, they had most certainly heard of him. Most of the time the reports spoke of his rigorous training. "While you were at the pictures, or square dancing, last Saturday night," wrote Harry Hopman in the *Melbourne Herald*, "John Landy was doing a 10-mile training run." Word was that the miler had missed only two training sessions since the previous May. Few had any idea of the nature of these sessions, and only those closest to Landy would have believed how rigorous they were if they had known.

From July 21 to September 30, Landy averaged ten 600-yard fast runs daily, at roughly a sixty-six-second quarter-mile pace. In between each run he jogged 600 yards. Since he was studying for his final exams in October and November, he decided to train double his normal session on alternate days. On the off-days he jogged at a five- to six-minute-a-mile pace for half an hour so that he would have more time to study. On the hard days in October he ran twenty 600-yard fast laps with a jog in between each (approximately fourteen miles a night). Every other day in November, having measured out a quarter-mile grass lap on the inside of the Central Park gravel path, he ran twenty 440-yard laps at a sixty-two-second pace, further developing his stamina. Night after night he pushed himself a little bit harder. If his body was a rubber band, he was stretching it just to the point before it snapped. Sometimes he even amazed himself with what he put himself through in a session.

Throughout this training he received letters from Cerutty, advising him on how he should train. Landy refused to answer, let alone listen to his former coach's advice. The outburst the previous year had completely severed their relationship, but still Cerutty wouldn't let it go. He showed up at Central Park, running behind the miler as he trained, shouting that he was an "impostor" and didn't have the "killer instinct" to go anywhere. Landy laughed off the remarks and sped away. Cerutty was having difficulties. His marriage was deteriorating, and his Stotans had left him one by one, many because of his behavior at the Olympics and his attitude toward Landy. Cerutty still hoped his former Stotan would claim the mile record. At the start of the new season Cerutty wrote in his diary that his coaching method would be in great demand if Landy succeeded.

Landy's former coach wasn't the only one with expectations of him. Before his first race on November 21, the headlines cried out, "Landy Back for Big Mile Series" and "Crack Miler Resumes at Olympic Park." In Landy's mind, this race was only an early season tune-up run, and he had to repeatedly deny claims that he was gunning for the "magic mile." Regardless, when he ran a 4:09.2, over seven seconds faster than his first race the previous year, the public smelled the blood of a four-minute mile. Of these expectations Landy said, "The only thing of which I am certain is that I have a greater capacity for punishment this season." A few days later he received a call from Ken Moses at the *Argus*, informing him that he had been selected as a 1953 winner of the Helms Trophy, an award given to the best athlete from each of the six continents (not including Antarctica). Of the honor, also awarded that year to Gordon Pirie of Europe and Mal Whitfield of North America, Landy said, "Gee, is that true? That's great news," before quickly escaping for a training session. The constant attention, acclaim or not, was beginning to get to him.

After the completion of his finals and two more tune-ups at Olympic Park, Landy was ready to make his season's first fast run. He was in self-described "top condition," and it was exactly one year to the day since he had surprised the world with his first spectacular mile. News of his expected challenge to the four-minute barrier reached Bannister with the *Athletics World* headline "Landy's 'D' Day" and Santee with a *Track and Field News* report: "Landy has the best chance of all men today, because he is not dependent on pacemaking. He makes his own, which gives John an advantage over U.S., British and European milers."

For his December 12 race there was a world of difference at Olympic Park over the previous year. The prime minister of Australia was in attendance, and all that week the papers had drum-rolled the event. The *Age* published a cartoon with Landy racing toward the finish while carrying on his back a man with the face of a clock who was shouting, "4 Min Mile — Faster!" The immense pressure was palpable, and Landy knew that if he felt too tense, he wouldn't run well. He had trained for this day, though, and understood that he had the speed — as long as he didn't force it.

At 3:00 p.m., Landy lined up with three other runners. As he looked out at the crowd and then down at the track, those who knew him could see that he was obviously edgy. But with the limited field and track in perfect condition (the inside lane had been especially reserved for the race), he still had a good shot.

From the start, Landy raced into the lead. Within two hundred yards, it was clear that he was out for the record. John Marks tried to push him through the first half-mile, hanging as near as he could to Landy's shoulders as the "Meteor Miler" clocked a 58.2 first lap and a 60.4 second lap. At that point Marks dropped out of the race, unable to continue, and Les Perry then struggled through the next lap behind Landy, doing what he could to force competition on him. But it was no use. Landy might as well have been in the race alone. In his mind, he was. The clock was his only competition.

Perry stumbled off the track at the three-quarter mark. The bell rang at 3:00.2. Having heard the time, Landy thought he could at least beat Haegg's world record of 4:01.4. It was in the last lap that his hard training would bear its fruit. The crowd was on its feet, clapping loudly. Landy felt pulled along.

Those unofficially clocking him—and there were quite a few who had brought their own watches to the meet—took his split time at the end of the first furlong of the last lap. He had run it in 29.2 seconds, which meant that he only needed to run the last 220 yards in less than 30.6 seconds to break the four-minute mile—and if not that, less than 32 seconds to break the world record.

He continued to run well, maintaining his pace through the back straight and into the last turn. But when he came into the straight, he suddenly felt like the finish line was miles away. A cruel gust of wind seemed to stop him flat, though his legs kept moving. The wind ruined the rhythm of his stride, making it uneven. Within five yards of the tape he slowed noticeably, and when he crossed the line, he had to lean against a Victorian AAA official to keep from falling. His time was 4:02, only one-tenth of a second faster than his best mile the previous year, despite his increased training. His last furlong was run in a slow 32.6 seconds.

Landy shook hands with the prime minister, smiled for a few photographs, and then retreated to the locker room, where he became physically sick. But he quickly came out to speak with the reporters, and his frustration was clear in his words:

> No one outside of sport can imagine the grind of years of continuous training. I feel I could go on for 10 years, but I don't think it's worth it. Frankly, I think the four-minute mile is beyond my capabilities. Two seconds may not sound much, but to me it's like trying to break through a brick wall.
>
> Someone may achieve the four-minute mile the world is wanting so desperately, but I don't think I can.

No doubt some of this statement was made to reduce the pressure on him. Privately Landy felt that he still could lower his time in subsequent races. He had finished his exams only two weeks before, and with some more race preparation, he was sure he could run faster.

The next day Landy left for the bush in Tallarook, an area sixty miles northeast of Melbourne, to forget about running for a while. He and several others devoted to butterfly collecting were interested in finding a stenciled hairstreak (*Jalmenus ictinus*), a butterfly that had not been captured in Victoria in more than half a century. They had a museum record of its presence in Tallarook. Landy savored these trips, net in hand, spying for a particular wing pattern and color. It was a solitary, fulfilling pursuit, one that running had taken him away from more and more.

When reporters asked him about his hobby, he was spare in his answers. Their stories usually characterized him as running hell-bent through the trees swinging a net. In reality collecting butterflies was a much slower, more deliberate process. It was his passion, something separate from running, and he preferred to keep it private. Landy rarely spoke about his hobby with his friends in athletics either. The most that Les Perry knew of his interest was when Landy came into his room to find a butterfly framed in a glass case. Perry had served in New Guinea during World War II and brought back the butterfly because he thought it beautiful. Amazingly to Perry, Landy immediately identified its taxonomical classification.

On his trip to Tallarook Landy managed to find a stenciled hair-streak, with its dark brown wings that had a patch of metallic blue in the middle. It was a triumph that gave him, as he later said, "equal pleasure as running 4:02 for the mile."

A blanket of snow lay over the ground and hung heavy on the trees throughout Mount Oread at the University of Kansas. The campus was quiet; most students had not yet returned after the winter break, and only a few footprints disturbed the snow-laden paths threading through the campus. On the path leading to Memorial Stadium the falling white flakes were just beginning to cover the tracks made by Santee and his coach. From the stadium there was the muffled sound of a foghorn.

Underneath the concrete stadium stands, in a half-lit corridor only a few feet wide, the miler burst down the home straight. He ran at full speed on a dirt track that was twelve laps to a mile and banked around the corners. The corridor was cold and dank with condensation. Easton timed his laps in the middle of the straight. When Santee ran past him and disappeared around the corner, heading toward the backstretch on the far side, Easton readied his foghorn. Along the far side several doors, behind which students lived, opened on to the tracks. If anyone had stayed for the holiday, Santee risked a collision. He was going too fast to react in time.

The horn's cry cut through space, the sound reverberating under the low concrete ceilings. Santee ran unconcerned, feeling strong as he took each stride. One lap to go in his three-quarter-mile trial. He passed Easton at the starting line, where the track was four lanes wide. Santee sensed the time was good. Usually he could judge his pace over a quarter-mile within a second of the stopwatch. When he went out of sight around the corner, the horn sounded again, drowning out the patter of his feet on the dirt. Seconds later he reappeared, sprinting to the finish line, strong, very strong.

After crossing, he slowed and turned back to Easton, who held out his stopwatch. The miler's face was flushed, and the electric heaters placed around the track only made the sweat sear his skin.

"Man, look at this. You're ready. You're ready," Easton said. "If you can run 2:58 in this rat hole, you could have walked it on a real track."

Santee knew he was right. It was early January 1954, two weeks before his four-minute mile attempt during the halftime break in the Pro Bowl, to be held in the Los Angeles Coliseum. He was hot and ready to roll, and Al Franken, who had organized the race for Santee, was expecting great things.

Easton had ratcheted up Santee's training yet again. The goal was for Santee to accustom himself to running a 4:04 to 4:06 mile, so that doing so was more a matter of habit than of strenuous effort. The year before Easton had Santee regularly running a 4:08 to 4:10 mile. He explained to reporters, "The process of running a lot of miles between 4:04 and 4:06 will put Wes in the proper mental state for his major efforts outdoors. A great miler has to feel himself capable of cutting two or three seconds off his time, should the necessity arise." Given the right factors — namely, good competition and fine track conditions — Santee would have a shot at four laps in the record time.

Over the past months, in addition to his training with the team, Santee had included numerous extra quarter-mile runs throughout the week. Some days he ran five quarter-miles in fifty-two seconds each. The type of break he took between quarters made these workouts particularly tough, but Santee knew from hard work. "This was chicken feed," he later said of training compared to the backbreaking labor of his youth. "This background was the difference that I had from all the other athletes in the world at that time."

Instead of slowly jogging a lap before the next fast quarter-mile, Santee finished the quarter, jogged the 110 yards around the curve, sprinted the 110 yards back straight, and then started another fast quarter. "My break between quarters," Santee said, "was no break." After these he did wind sprints from sideline to sideline on the field, putting to shame any workout by the Jayhawk football team. Other times he ran eight to ten quarters in a session, starting the first two at sixty seconds each, and then increasing the speed for the second two to fifty-eight seconds each, then the fifth at fifty-five seconds. If he had trouble getting down to this last time, he shortened the distance run, usually to 220 yards and speeded up. "This keeps you going harder," he said. "Otherwise, you can get slower, slower, and slower—all your life." As the weather worsened through the fall and into the winter, he held many of these sessions alone inside the stadium on the makeshift track. This was in stark contrast to Santee's cross-country sessions, which he ran regardless of the weather. Lately he had been accompanied by Sarge, a reddish-brown German shepherd he had befriended, who met him on the track and followed him along the roads leading from campus.

The payoff from all this training was obvious. In November Santee led his Jayhawk team to victory by placing first in the Big Seven and NCAA cross-country championships. On the last day of 1953, at the Sugar Bowl in New Orleans, he dashed to a 4:04.2 mile, which was amazing not only because the track was soggy from rain but also because he ran the final lap in a stupefying fifty-five seconds. After the race an Associated Press reporter hit the wires with the following question: "Wes Santee . . . John Landy . . . Roger Bannister . . . Who is going to be the first to reach the end of the rainbow and run the fabled four-minute mile?"

According to the press, the only person able to catch Wes Santee was Danna Denning, his newly announced fiancée. Their picture together, wearing matching cowboy shirts, was plastered across papers under the headline "The Girl That Finally Caught Wes." She had traveled down to New Orleans with him, making for the uncomfortable arrangement of Santee sleeping in a room with Easton and Danna with Easton's wife Ada. But it was wonderful to have her watch him race. Danna gave him all the more incentive to do well.

Now, with this fast time trial under his belt, Santee was set for the Pro Bowl run. Just as he was about to leave for Los Angeles, however, Dan Ferris hit him with two major pieces of bad news. First, the AAU had ruled him ineligible for the 1954 National Collegiate Athletic Association track championships because Easton had mistakenly included

Santee as a member of the "varsity squad" at the NCAA Championships his freshman year. It was a technicality, since Santee had the right to participate as a member of the University of Kansas "K-Club." Easton had been fighting this judgment for the last two and a half years; it was literally a matter of having ticked the wrong box on the form, but Ferris was not to be swayed, not now. Second, Ferris had decided to continue his investigation into Santee's European trip, and reports had it that Santee risked losing his amateur status as a result. The investigation had already cost him the Sullivan Award, the prize for the year's best amateur athlete, though no evidence of his misdeeds was presented. Ferris simply explained to reporters: "Something is hanging over [Santee's] head. . . . This award is based on sportsmanship and character as well as ability." The situation looked to be getting worse. It was a constant item on the sports pages, equal in coverage to his mile attempts.

Santee and the AAU were heading toward a collision. Increasingly Santee was a threat to the organization's hold on power. Because he sold out the meets in which he participated, particularly with his penchant for publicity and the mile barrier looming ever nearer on the horizon, he had power. The confrontation in Germany had scared AAU officials. Santee might be out of control. Then the *Saturday Evening Post* published a profile of Santee called "Sure I'll Run the Four-Minute Mile" by Bob Hurt. In the article Santee was quoted as saying, "I'd like to run for about ten more years. But I'm not going to run unless I can make it pay. I wouldn't want to waste ten years." Hurt also wrote that Santee was hoping to earn enough "expenses" from his track meets to buy a farm. Brundage must have read the article and gone ballistic. No amateur under his watch would boast of such a thing. Ferris approached Santee after the article hit newsstands, and the miler denied saying these things. Regardless, the AAU appeared bent on bringing the miler down, at least by a notch or two.

When Santee arrived in Los Angeles and met Franken, he was weighed down by concerns over the AAU probe. But with some of the best American milers set to race against him, including Charlie Capozzoli and Bob McMillen, he had a great chance at the record, AAU investigation or not. Franken was upbeat. "I hope we've set it up so you can do it here," he said.

Early on January 17, the day of the Pro Bowl, Santee left the Ambassador Hotel to take his morning walk. When he stepped out on the grass, his foot sank into six inches of water. It had rained through the night. A few hours later Franken came by to take him to the stadium. He was shaking his head, obviously distraught. "I'm really sorry, Wes. It hasn't rained like this in five years. The track is flooded."

As they drove to the Coliseum, the sun finally appeared in the sky, but it was too late. The track was standing under water. The race was canceled. Santee was devastated. He was in perfect form now. Landy was at the height of his season, and Bannister was sure to run well as soon as he started. Santee's outdoor season didn't begin for several months, and if the AAU had its way, his prospects for competing in any top-flight races then were in serious jeopardy. During halftime he ran a few laps around the football field with Capozzoli and McMillen, waving at the packed stands. If only the AAU officials shared in the enthusiasm for what he was trying to accomplish. Some good luck wouldn't have hurt either.

12

Yet that man is happy and poets sing of him who
conquers with hand and swift foot and strength.

— PINDAR

A T FOUR O'CLOCK in the afternoon, on Thursday, January 21,
1954, a clear, windless summer day in Melbourne, they started
to come — first pairs, then dozens, then hundreds — to Olympic Park. Men in suits and hats left work early to attend, crowding the trams and streets. Women in seersucker dresses joined their husbands, and schoolchildren their parents. Bars emptied of their patrons, and shopkeepers shuttered their doors to get to the track on time. The whole city looked to be descending on the stadium for the special twilight meet featuring miler John Landy. This was to be the race.

"A Perfect Night for John's Mile" headlined the *Melbourne Sun*. "Flat-out Attempt on 4.0 Mile," said the *Melbourne Age*. Landy was on the front or back page of every city newspaper, taking up inches of column space. Reporters consulted the Weather Bureau and pronounced the season's weather "hoodoo" — no longer a threat to Landy. Dick Crossley, the venerated groundsman at Olympic Park, had personally rolled the track and declared it in perfect condition. As for Landy himself, he felt good to go. Since his 4:02 mile six weeks before, he had run in two mile races, and in neither did he make a record attempt. Surely, people felt, he was saving himself for a specially arranged event.

With his university exams completed, he now trained during the day in Central Park. He was doing a lot of speed work on the 440-yard grass path inside the gravel path. On weekends half-miler Len McRae, who was now teaching at a school outside Melbourne, ran quarters with him. They trained for an hour and a half in the ninety-degree heat, rarely speaking. Landy timed himself, and McRae felt that his friend would have been just as happy to have been training alone. Occasionally runners who competed in professional sprint races like the Stawell Gift came by the park to watch Landy run. Their response was generally, "Why would you train like this?" and, "You're going to kill yourself." After they left, Landy and McRae used to joke about how much more advanced the professionals were, what with their rating of trivial matters of style, such as holding your hands out flat to reduce wind resistance, as more important than conditioning. Short of these moments, however, Landy was serious and purposeful in his training. This twilight race was to be his judgment day.

Three days before the race Landy went to Gippsland, taking a needed break from his training by stalking through the bush for butterflies that he had yet to add to his collection. The night before the race he slept for twelve hours, and throughout the big day he relaxed by reading Nehru's *Discovery of India* at his East Malvern home. His only interruptions were calls from reporters and a batch of telegrams delivered to his door, wishing him good luck.

Of his attempt on the mile record he told the press, "I'm not a bit worried. It's just a big gamble. It might come off and it might not. . . . This four-minute mile business is more than just beating opponents. It is trying to achieve something that nobody else has ever done." Story after story praised the miler for his intelligence, work ethic, charm, and modesty. One reporter described Landy as the "most retiring world-class performer" he had ever met, yet he also found the miler a good talker, with "boyish laughter" and a "studious analytical mind."

By six o'clock the ticket sellers had run out of the specially made programs. The police transmitted an SOS to headquarters, requesting reinforcements to handle the unexpected snarl of traffic. Over one thousand cars sat bumper to bumper on Batman Avenue, some not having moved in over an hour. More and more people poured into the stadium. Tickets could not be sold fast enough. Lines formed hundreds of yards long behind the booths.

Landy arrived at the stadium near the height of this bedlam with

Len McRae and quarter-miler Ian Ormsby. McRae had picked up Landy at his house in his red Singer Six convertible, but because of the traffic they had to park the car on a nearby hill. Landy was astonished at the mass of people in attendance—ten thousand, maybe twenty. The atmosphere seemed more appropriate for a football match than a track event, which typically drew three or four hundred fans at best. The three athletes forced their way through the crowd, but it looked impossible to get to the front. They worried that they might miss their races.

"How are we going to get in?" McRae asked. The crowd was becoming rowdy, anxious to get inside.

The three spotted the eight-foot-high wire fence surrounding Olympic Park and, after a brief conversation, decided to scale it. They tossed their gym bags over the fence. Then they climbed the pickets, making sure not to get stuck on the sharp points at the top.

As they cleared the fence a highly regarded South Yarra doctor, waiting with his son at the back of the line, shouted, "Look at those louts, getting over the fence and not paying. They're trying to gate-crash."

"Dad," the boy said, "that is John Landy."

By the time the miler had changed and begun to warm up, the crowd had swelled to such proportions that they knocked down the fence and rushed inside the stadium. Some climbed on top of the tin roof over the grandstand. Others threaded their way through the bushes and tall grass on the surrounding hills until they found a clear vantage point. By race time a wall of people had encircled the track, and many were standing on the outside lane. At one point a chicken found its way into the grounds, and a melee of men chased it around until one of them caught his dinner. The place was total chaos.

When Landy took to the track minutes before the race at 7:30 P.M., the fans cheered wildly. Newsreel cameras spun, and the runners were momentarily blinded by camera flashes. A horse-caller had been brought in to announce the race on radio. More than ever, Landy felt obligated to deliver a record or risk letting everybody down. The pressure was intense. At the starting line he shook the hands of his competitors and then settled down in a crouch in the third lane from the inside, waiting for the gun. Les Perry and Geoff Warren were by his side, hoping this was the day for their friend. But there was little they could do to help. For a moment the crowd silenced as twenty thousand pairs of eyes stared at Landy, eager to see him break the barrier for the glory of Australia.

As usual, Landy went into the lead by the first turn and never looked back. Nobody could keep up with him. He had refused pacing before the race, telling the other runners that if he suspected they weren't running to win, he would step off the track. If he broke the mile record, he wanted to have done it on his own. Landy ran the first lap in 59 seconds and the second in 61.3, but because of the crowd he couldn't hear his times called. He had a good sense of his pace, much as a seasoned golfer knows how far he will hit a ball by the force he applies to his swing. Yet it wasn't an exact science. Landy knew there were conditions—his level of relaxation, wind, temperature, track condition, pressure of competition, and a favorable crowd—that affected his speed. It was impossible to know the difference between running a 59.5- and a 60-second lap, just as the crowd could not tell simply by watching him. The only thing Landy could do was run at 100 percent effort and hope that it was enough. If the other factors aligned, he might break the record.

When the bell for the fourth lap clanged, the timekeepers read 3:02.1 on their watches. Landy was far in the lead. The crowd urged him forward. They were on their feet, their applause deafening. Landy responded, looking to push faster—harder—around the track. At two hundred yards from the finish, however, Landy felt as if someone had pulled the "master power switch," draining the electricity from his legs. He willed himself onward nonetheless, fighting against the fatigue to keep driving to the finish line, trying to refuse the temptation to slow down. It was difficult. He had run alone from the beginning, unaware of his times and without the push of competition.

Not long now. The tape was in sight. He stretched to the finish, hoping it was enough. As he broke through the tape, the spectators threw programs, handkerchiefs, and hats into the air. They followed with a standing ovation. Landy waited for his time, uncertain if he had broken the record or turned in another 4:02 performance. He rolled his head around, as if working out a kink in his neck. Finally the official time was announced on the loudspeakers: 4:02.4.

Roiled with disappointment but unwilling to show it, he jogged forward, waving at the crowd who continued to clap.

"I thought I had it," he told the *Sun*'s Jack Dunn.

Later, after he had recovered from the effort, he explained to reporters that he couldn't hear his lap times because of the cheering crowd, but that was not the true problem: "I am convinced I must have

someone to grind record figures out of me. I must have someone behind me to push me out." That was the condition that would make all
the difference.

When he returned to East Malvern with McRae and Ormsby, his
mother had organized a party for him. Although he had not broken the
mile record, none of his friends or family bemoaned the fact. After all,
he had won the race. McRae knew Landy was frustrated with not having brought his time down again, but they shared a few beers instead of
talking about it. Landy was ever reluctant to open up to anyone about
his disappointment. That evening Landy suspected that he would never
be able to run faster unless he went overseas, where the tracks and competition were better.

The next day his run was characterized on the front pages as a "Magnificent Failure!" The Finnish miler Denis Johansson, who was in attendance in preparation for a race against Landy the following month, had
a different viewpoint: "Landy is magnificent — the greatest mile runner
I have seen. On a first-class cinder track with solid opposition he'll run
3:55 for the mile." Johansson promised to help him see it happen, rais-
ing the possibility of Landy traveling to Scandinavia at the end of the
Australian season.

On February 10, Coach Easton and Santee made one last effort to stop
the AAU from punishing the miler. Santee's amateur status was at stake,
and they had little recourse to overturn any judgment the AAU sent
down from its New York offices. So they sent letters to Lloyd Olds, the
chairman of the Track and Field Committee. They vehemently denied
reports from Germany that Santee had thrown a chair at the foreign
official who refused to give the miler the Agfa camera. They also made
it clear that Bob Hurt from the *Saturday Evening Post* had misquoted
Santee about trying to make money from his running. In his letter to
Olds, Santee included the two notes he had previously written to Dan
Ferris explaining these matters. Neither had stopped the AAU official
from continuing the investigation. Easton discounted each of the allegations in a typed letter to Olds and then appealed personally to the
AAU official in a handwritten note on the last page that said, "This
boy is a worker and not looking for a soft job. Also, he's had to work his
way in college because his Dad is not for higher education, so won't
help Wes."

A week later Hurt wrote to Ferris saying that he had inferred Santee's meaning rather than directly quoted him in his article. Further, Ferris had no evidence that Santee had broken any amateur rules in Germany and had scant corroborating proof that the miler had done anything more than raise his voice to the foreign official and slam his fist on the table. Still, the AAU issued an edict that banned Santee from competing internationally for one year. The only explanation they released to the public was that the miler had broken training while in Europe the previous summer. Bitter at the AAU's decision, Santee declared to reporters:

> The restriction is nothing—absolutely nothing—and Bill and I take it for exactly what it is, a token action to satisfy some higher-ups. . . . It's why they imposed the ban, or the reason they gave, that makes us so mad. Breaking training, my foot! I no more broke training than I flew the Atlantic without an airplane.
>
> Why don't they show some courage and nail me, if they have to nail me, for what they're really sore about—the fact I told off some of their foreign officials . . . but instead of saying so they tab me with this "breaking training" deal. That's what makes me mad, not the restriction. That's a pretty nasty way to go about it, I'd say.

Soon after, Santee told reporters that he didn't need any competition to push him to run the mile record. He could do it anywhere, track and weather permitting, as long as his legs felt all right. But privately he later admitted, "For me to drive myself . . . I could do it up to a point, but there was something about competition that raised the bar. . . . It's like someone pulls you along. I loved to be behind. . . . I judge my pace against his pace, and I'm coming on him. When I catch up and pass, it's great." With this ban in place, good competition was going to be hard to find.

On Friday, February 26, 1954, Bannister finished his last round in his hospital ward, done for the day with reviewing charts, checking on blood tests, and inquiring how his patients were doing. After hanging his half-length white coat in his locker down in the underground pass between the medical school and the hospital, he grabbed his gym bag and left St. Mary's, heading toward Sloane Square. He was to meet with Chataway and Brasher at the Duke of York's Barracks. The weather was no better than it had been during the past two weeks. A bitter wind from the west threatened more heavy showers, the occasional bit of hail, and a deep, pipe-bursting frost that night.

Throughout the winter, regardless of the weather, the three had trained together every week since Bannister first met with Stampfl. They started with calisthenics in the drill hall, working alongside scores of other athletes, including shot putters and discus and javelin throwers. Stampfl ran them through a series of press-ups, stretching, and resistance exercises, increasing their upper body strength but also fostering a sense of belonging to a much larger group. On occasion, he even had them wrestle one another. After twenty minutes they took a brief rest and then hit the track.

While training his other athletes, Stampfl kept his eye on the three runners as they went through their interval training together. He yelled out to them from time to time: "Do it again!" "Harder!" and "Faster— it is only pain!" The program they had worked out was only a slight variation of what Bannister had been doing on his own. It was simply more regimented. In December 1953 they had commenced with ten quarter-miles in sixty-six seconds, with a two-and-a-half- to three-minute recovery lap in between each one. The aim was to increase the lap speed gradually over several months. They carried their own stopwatches to ensure they were running to pace. They often ran through fog, rain, and cold, and after three months they were down to a sixty-three-second average. Although they exercised throughout the week, doing either the same kind of interval work, repetition half-miles, or Fartlek sessions, Friday at the Duke of York's provided "the focus of the week," Bannister said. There they measured their progress to date, strengthened their sense of working together, and soaked up Stampfl's enthusiasm.

The Austrian coach had eased his way into Bannister's confidence slowly, knowing that the miler was uncomfortable taking direction from a coach. Instead of imposing a regimen, Stampfl offered suggestions and guidance. He tried never to push too hard. From the start, he knew that Bannister needed three things if he was to run the four-minute mile: pacemakers to carry him through the first three laps; more strength in his legs; and complete belief in himself. Over the past three months Stampfl had worked hard to realize these goals for the miler, not only because he had a passion for helping an athlete who was impassioned himself ("They've got to love it," he always said), but also because if Bannister broke the barrier under his guidance, no matter how overt that guidance was, more athletes would come to him for coaching.

Pacemaking was an obvious factor, but the question was how best to arrange it. Stampfl had seen Bannister at the Olympics and had watched him compete in England innumerable times. Like many milers, particularly British milers, Bannister stayed in the pack for most of a race and then delivered a lightning-fast finishing kick at the end. Stampfl knew that Bannister would have trouble running alone through the first three laps at a fast pace. Two pacemakers were necessary, as the Motspur Park race had shown: one to take Bannister through the first half-mile, the second to the three-quarter mark. They had to be able to maintain even sixty-second laps as well as finish the race. This was the only way to comply with amateur rules.

From the beginning, Bannister made it clear that he wanted there to be no possibility for dispute as to whether his next attempt was bona fide. The arrangement could not be made on the spur of the moment either. Bannister needed to be able to rely on his pacemakers, to know that they would deliver the goods. Chataway and Brasher had already enlisted the previous November. Their contribution was not entirely selfless: the sessions were good training for their events, the steeplechase (Brasher) and the three-mile (Chataway), and they wanted to be part of the potentially historic feat. Stampfl made sure that the team was cohesive and that Chataway and Brasher were ready.

Physically Bannister was already very close to being capable of the achievement when they met. Stampfl just needed to push him a little further. The systematic, gradual increases of speed in running the 440 laps over several months promised to better adapt Bannister's body to the stress. It was a plan that appealed to the miler's methodical approach to running. At his level improvement was difficult to discern. Running with Chataway and Brasher relieved the monotony, and Stampfl encouraged him week after week to keep at it. Ultimately, though, it was up to the miler. As the coach wrote, "Training is principally an act of faith. The athlete must believe in its efficacy: he must believe that through training he will become fitter and stronger. . . . He must believe that through training his performance will improve and continue to improve indefinitely for as long as he continues to train to progressively stiff standards." Stampfl simply helped to set these standards.

But Stampfl's greatest contribution to Bannister's attempt to make history was his ability to inspire the miler. Although Bannister had the scientific understanding to refute the notion that the mile barrier couldn't be broken, believing you were the one to do it was altogether different. "The great hurdle was the mental barrier," Stampfl said. The Austrian's experiences as a coach and survivor of great hardship had proved to him that no obstacle was insurmountable. His unwavering belief in this was infectious. He loved sports and what they symbolized in life as a whole: the ability to overcome. Stampfl invested their efforts with a degree of heroic struggle. In a very real sense, he made running fun again.

After their sessions at the Duke of York's track, Stampfl joined the three for dinner near Sloane Square, where they took refuge from the cold, enjoyed a bottle of wine, and relaxed. Stampfl dominated the conversations, which usually started with a discussion of their training and how they were advancing. They spoke of Landy and Santee and how close they were coming to the four-minute mile. But as the dinner progressed the conversation shifted to politics, art, philosophy, whatever. The Austrian coach read widely, and he could take every side of an argument, making for lively dinners that the three runners looked forward to after an exhausting session.

At dinner in the last week of February, aside from potential discussions of a new Tate Gallery exhibit of French impressionist paintings and Churchill's stance on the "Sovietization" of a divided Germany, they talked more than usual about their pursuit of the four-minute mile. Week after week they had nervously waited for the latest news from the United States and Australia. The McWhirter twins continued to be their main source of information. Ross and Norris drove over to see Bannister when he trained in Paddington. They brought a watch, timed his laps, and then delivered updates on Landy's and Santee's progress over lunch at a nearby café before driving their busy doctor friend back to St. Mary's. Only three days before, the twins had brought news that Landy had run another sub-4:03 mile, the fifth in his career. They knew about the kind of training sessions that Landy was running, and yet the Australian miler was coming up short again and again. Somehow he was stuck, but with reports confirming that Johansson was bringing him to compete on Finland's fast tracks, anything was possible. As for Santee, his threat was obvious. He had recently clocked a 4:02.6 mile on an indoor, eight-lap-to-a-mile track. A meager forty-one minutes later he ran a 1:51.8 half-mile. It was the "greatest double in American track history," exclaimed the latest issue of *Track and Field News*, and evidence that "the honor of running the first four-minute mile will be lodged in the USA." Santee was likely to better his time once the outdoor season began. As the McWhirters had reminded Bannister, the mile barrier was becoming "an almost uninsurable risk," and "obituary notices" about it were being prepared by newspapers around the world.

Their earliest opportunity to make a bid was at the AAA versus Oxford University match in early May. Bannister understood that, like scaling Everest, his goal would require not just ability and hard work but also luck, teamwork, and a dose of inspiration. This had not always been so clear to him. When he invited Edmund Hillary to take his treadmill test a few months after he returned to England from his Everest climb, Bannister discovered that the mountaineer wasn't in the kind of otherworldly shape he had expected. After the tests he approached Hillary, shaking his head, and exclaimed, "I don't know how you did it."

Over the past sixteen months the mile barrier had withstood the greatest assaults ever. Bannister knew he needed to throw every advantage he had at the "brick wall" to have a chance of breaking through it. Two seconds had never seemed so long a time, but at least now he was part of a team, one that encouraged him when the training became tedious or his confidence faltered. It was making all the difference.

Most weekend mornings at the University of Kansas passed in a tranquil calm: students slept late, streets were empty of cars, and shops kept their doors closed. Every spring, though, the university played host to athletes from around the country for the Kansas Relays. It was a great excuse for a party.

On Saturday morning, April 17, preparations were in full gear. Since dawn, fraternity and sorority members had been finishing the construction of their floats for a grand parade. The sound of hammers banging, saws cutting, chicken wire being stretched, and paint sloshing drowned out the songs of Glenn Miller and Johnny Ray playing on the radio. High school students, many of whom had never been out of their hometowns, ran about the campus, wearing varsity letter sweaters and feeling the rush of college life. Cars jammed the streets around Mount Oread, and hundreds began to line the sidewalks for the big show. From Memorial Stadium, tinny loudspeakers announced the start of the discus event for the decathlon. A few spectators dotted the stands for the morning field events, but this was nothing compared to the thousands that would arrive for the 3:05 P.M. start of the Glenn Cunningham Mile. The sun shone brightly, and it looked as though the Kansas Relays would be staged on "one of those first-day-of-spring, glad-to-be-alive" days.

Wes Santee didn't let the beehive of activities disturb his pre-race ritual. He had his breakfast of oatmeal, hot tea, and honey, and then a few hours later he walked down to the stadium to warm up. His calm exterior belied the fact that this was a big weekend, perhaps the biggest of his life. He intended to claim the four-minute mile on Saturday and then marry Danna on Sunday.

Three months to the day had passed since his disappointment at the Pro Bowl, where the only running he did was around the stadium to burn off some nervous energy while the Eastern All-Stars football team led by Paul Brown beat Buddy Parker's Western team 20–9. Since then, he had scorched up the tracks week after week, keeping fit while fueling the four-minute fever with every stunning performance. His team waltzed away with the Big Seven indoor championship for another year, thanks in large part to Santee. At the first outdoor meet of the season in Austin, Texas, Santee arrived wearing a royal blue suit, copper tie, and orange boots. He equally dazzled with his running that day, earning his team a world record in the sprint medley with an anchor half-mile of 1:48.3 and leading the Jayhawks in the distance medley as well as the two- and four-mile relays. Santee was earning so much press that it was almost a chore for him to stay up to date with pasting the clippings that fans sent him from around the country into his scrapbooks.

A herd of reporters attended his every race, some from local papers, but many also from major national publications like *Time, Newsweek,* the *Saturday Evening Post,* the *New York Times,* and the *New York Herald Tribune.* Santee liked their headlines: "Super Sonic Santee," "Santee the Lure—May Hit Magic Number," "Mile King in Relays Here," and "Santee Is Star." The stories read even better: "Some night Santee's going to travel around that course like the wind and then he'll not only run the four-minute mile but he'll cut three or four seconds off that goal."

Despite the flood of prognostication, Santee was yet to have a good chance at the mile record because of his team obligations. At the Kansas Relays, however, Easton had set those obligations aside to give Santee a shot at a fast mile. Throughout his senior year Easton had treated his athlete almost as an assistant coach. They sat in the stadium stands after a workout, discussing how his younger teammates were running or who they were competing against in the next meet and which Jayhawk runner should compete in which events. Together they had decided that the team was in a strong enough position to risk Santee competing in the open mile rather than in four team events, as he usually did.

With Landy heading to Finland and reports that Bannister was preparing for a paced attempt in early May, it was critical that they go for the four-minute mile straight away. Santee was also running out of time because his Marine officer training began in July. He was supposed to have done his twelve weeks of boot camp during his sophomore year, but he went to the Olympics instead. After his junior year the AAU arranged for another year's reprieve because it wanted him running in Europe. Further delay, however, appeared impossible. It did not help that the AAU had banned him from competing internationally. With that restriction in place and the Marines demanding that he report for duty, the Compton Invitational was the best competition he would get for the four-minute mile. Apart from that meet, his home-field advantage at the Kansas Relays was the next best thing.

By two o'clock on Saturday afternoon the parade was over, and the floats (bearing themes that included the "Easton–Wes Express" and "Joy Through Effort") idled outside Memorial Stadium, where over sixteen thousand people were crowded. It was hot and sultry, and the concessions stands quickly sold out of soda, followed by ice, and then by cups. Spectators sheltered themselves from the sun with umbrellas and fanned themselves with Kansas Relays programs that featured a picture of "The Kansas Flyer — Wes Santee" on the cover. He was the star attraction, and many had filed into the stadium early to get the best seat for the show.

As part of his ritual preparations, an hour before the race Santee jogged outside the stadium and then came onto the infield for a few wind sprints. Back in the locker room he changed and the trainer rubbed him down. Easton was outside watching the two-mile relay, a race Santee normally would have entered. The two had said everything they needed to say to each other the night before.

"Let's try to break it," Easton said down at the track after a brief workout. "Do you have any questions?"

"No," Santee replied, and they were done. After nearly two years of planning and dreaming about how to run the mile in less than four minutes, there was no new territory to cover.

Fifteen minutes before race time Santee taped a four-inch square of cotton dipped in Kramer's analgesic hot rub to the base of his spine. It was believed to stimulate the nerves and stir the legs. Then he left the locker room with a towel draped over his head. Underneath, his face was a mask of cool determination. Outside, a bank of dark clouds hung in the sky—and then suddenly erupted in a torrent of rain. Umbrellas—used moments before to shield the sun—were now deflecting pelts of rain—then hail—from a flash storm. Gusts of wind blew across the field. Those exposed ducked for cover. As suddenly as the storm came it passed. The clouds broke, and the sun returned. Short of a few upended umbrellas, everything was just as it was—except for the track. Puddles covered the track, and there were divots in the cinders from the hail.

Santee was stunned. The track was wrecked, and it seemed that so were his hopes of a fast mile. It was hard not to think that the world was conspiring against him, that nothing was on his side. Then Coach Easton went into action. Hands buried deep in his pockets, a sure sign that he meant business, he called a group of his athletes together and told them they needed to get the track ready for the open mile. With military precision, he organized a crew of freshman athletes to shovel off the water. Then he had one of his boys go over the track twice with a power-driven roller to level it off. Easton also arranged for what amounted to a rolling propane-fueled flamethrower to further dry out the track.

Jogging off to the side, Santee tried to keep warm as his coach and teammates did everything they could to give him a shot. The largest crowd in the Kansas Relays history was waiting in silence, holding their collective breath with the hope that enough could be done to make the difference for Santee. As the young Kansas miler looked around him—Easton pointing to one section, then another, guiding Santee's teammates around frantically to the areas of the track that needed attention—he felt how much he was supported. Of course, he had made sacrifices in his efforts at the mile record for them, but he now realized what kinds of friendships he had earned in the process. Those friends were still working on the surface seconds before the race was to begin.

When Santee moved to the starting line, the track was still heavy underfoot, but at least Easton's efforts had given him a shot at a good time. Santee planned on making the best of it. Opposing him in the race were Oklahoma A&M's Bjorr Bogerud, a freshman who had placed third in the Texas Relays; Drake's Ray McConnell, winner of the Drake Relays open mile the previous year; and Oklahoma's Bruce Drummond, a graduate student and defending champion in the Cunningham Mile. None in the small field could challenge Santee, he knew that, and with the crowd already on their feet and shouting his name, he felt charged up. He just needed to stick to the pacing that he and Easton had carefully calculated. First lap — fifty-nine seconds. Second lap — sixty seconds. Third lap — sixty-one seconds. Fourth lap — go for it. His strong kick would carry him under the wire. Watching from the stands was his bride-to-be. She had wished him luck before the start of the race and now simply had to hope for the best. She knew how important this day was for Wes. These big races were difficult for her. "I just can't talk," she explained. "There's no use trying to be objective, because I can't. I get all tied in knots."

Right before the gun sounded, Santee drew in a breath and held it. The gun fired, and he burst forward. Bogerud started slightly quicker, but by the end of the first turn Santee took the lead. Bogerud tried to catch up, but there was nothing he could do — and he knew it. By the start of the second lap Santee was only a half-second off pace. Easton was calling out his times, and despite the cacophony from the stands, Santee heard him. No matter how noisy it was, he always heard his coach. His ear was tuned in to Easton's voice.

The miler was still uneasy, though. The track was soft and wet in patches, and when he drove forward, he lacked traction. There was also a strong crosswind. Nonetheless, he continued to push, extending his fifteen-yard lead over the others. The crowd spurred him forward. In the second lap he ran a second and a half over pace, and for the half-mile, he clocked 2:01. It was very good, given the conditions. Better than he thought. He began to settle into his stride. To keep his arms relaxed, he kept his index finger on his thumb in each hand, making sure not to make a fist. The crowd shouted, "Go, Wes! Go!" when he passed the stands. They knew he was close too. Into the third lap Santee was gripped by the desire to run the mile record. To do it this day in front of Danna and his home crowd.

At the bell Santee was a hundred yards ahead of Bogerud. His three competitors looked to be running in an altogether different race. The third lap was slow, much slower than he wanted: sixty-three seconds.

The wind and traction might have affected him more than in the two previous laps. It was hard to say what caused the slowdown—not a lack of desire. He could still do it, though. He had run a fifty-five-second final lap in the mile before. That would give him a 3:59 mile. The four-minute mile would be his.

Easton yelled from the side of the track, "Go! Go! Go!" The crowd cheered. They want it, Santee thought to himself. Everyone wanted him to be the one. The last lap was always the hardest. He stepped up his pace. With 220 yards to go, he felt the charge from inside in his chest to keep going. He was fighting against the pain and exertion. He was running with all his heart.

"Go, Wes! Go!" boomed the crowd.

His training had prepared him for this finishing burst. He increased his arm action, looking to almost strike the air like one would a punching bag. His legs followed his arms. His exhale was heavy. By the last one hundred yards, he was working on sheer emotion and the enthusiasm of the crowd. The timekeepers waited at the finish line. A mass of athletes on the infield pressed forward at the edge of the track to get a better look. Many held their breath in suspense.

Santee took one last stride, driving with his right leg as he broke through the tape, mouth wide. It was a remarkable last lap given the conditions, but not remarkable enough: 58.6. The time flashed on the scoreboard: 4:03.1. He had come up short again. The brief downpour had stripped him of confidence in his chances, and the competition was not able to provide the jolt of adrenaline he needed.

After seeing the time, the crowd deflated for a moment and then shifted to applause, followed by chanting, "Santee. Santee. Santee." The disappointed miler accepted his trophy from Glenn Cunningham, who offered to hold the trophy until Santee had finished his distance medley relay. Santee politely declined. He passed the trophy to a policeman, who walked it up to Danna. If the weather had been better, Santee was sure he could have presented her the gift of the four-minute mile instead.

At two o'clock the next afternoon, Easter Sunday, he and Danna were married in a quiet ceremony in Lawrence. Easton and his wife stood in for Santee's parents, who had not been invited. After the ceremony a small party was thrown in their honor at a friend's apartment, and then Danna's parents and the newlywed couple drove to Kansas City. Santee honeymooned for less than twenty-four hours. By Monday afternoon he was back at the track for training. Bets had been made that he wouldn't show, and those who doubted his commitment to breaking the barrier first were the ones who lost. In any event, Easton would not have permitted Santee to miss practice. The *Kansas City Star* was there to report to their readers that "Wes Santee isn't going to let a little old thing like matrimony disrupt his plans for fast running. . . . Santee still eyes the mile in four minutes."

13

Care I for the limb, the thews, the stature, bulk and big assemblence of a man? Give me his *spirit*.

—SHAKESPEARE, *Henry IV, Part 2*

T HE STOPWATCH told the whole story. By mid-April 1954, Roger Bannister felt drawn out and spent. After four months of the most difficult training he had experienced in his running career, coupled with the intensity of his last days at St. Mary's before taking the medical board's exam, he was in need of a break. Chataway and Brasher needed the same. All three were tired and feeling as though their efforts on the track, no matter how strenuous, had stopped returning gains.

Since December 1953 they had improved their lap times in their typical workout—ten 440s with a two-minute rest interval—from sixty-six seconds to sixty-one seconds. But in the past several weeks they had not been able to get down to the magical sixty-second mark, the point where they could feel confident that the mile barrier was within range. Each attempt brought failure, and each failure a sense that they had reached their bodies' limits. Perhaps sixty-one seconds was indeed the best that they could do. They tried again and again, but their time never improved. As Chris Brasher said, they were "bogged down."

Bannister had always been afraid that by overtraining he would become stale and reach a state where more running would only bring worse results and he would be overcome by a sense of listlessness. This was how his hero Lovelock had described the condition of staleness. Its cause was unknown. Some thought it entirely physical: the muscles were worn out and overstrained, incapable of taking any more punishment. Others thought it entirely mental: the mind, tired of willing the body to work hard day after day, could not translate the desire for more speed into action. Whatever the cause, the effects of staleness were very real. An athlete experienced appetite loss and overwhelming physical and mental lethargy. It was as if one were living in a kind of waking sleep.

Stampfl didn't believe that overtraining led to staleness. He wrote: "It is a belief that finds no support in other fields of endeavor. The child learning to write, the pianist who practices for six hours a day, the bricklayer laying bricks — the work of these people does not deteriorate as a result of constant repetition of the same movements." In his view, staleness resulted from having no competition and losing sight of one's objective.

Whatever the reason, the three athletes risked sinking into lethargy if they continued to run sixty-one-second laps in their interval training. The Oxford versus AAA meet was fast approaching, and Bannister knew that feeling jaded about his running was no way to approach the four-minute mile. Stampfl advised the three to relax by getting away from training for a few days. Brasher suggested rock climbing. "I'll get my friend to drive us," he said confidently. Most coaches would have cringed at the idea of their athletes taking such a trip, but Stampfl thought it a fine suggestion. Chataway declined the offer, choosing to take his rest in the comforts of London. Soon enough, Bannister was crouched in the luggage space behind the seats of an ex-Le Mans Aston Martin, speeding toward the Scottish highlands. Brasher and his friend Dr. More (whom Bannister described simply as a "risk-taker") shared the driving. Legs wedged against his chest, Bannister listened to the hum of the engine as they drove for ten hours, through the night, to reach Glencoe, a small Scottish town nestled in the hills.

Several times before, Bannister had escaped from running in order to return to it. He found that he needed to breathe different air to refresh himself. Throughout the summer and early fall of 1950 he had lost a series of races — and was so tired of traveling and competing that he had begun to think that losing was okay. One time after a meet in Paris he had decided suddenly to leave the city to go hiking. He purchased a pair of boots at a local shop, jotted a note to friends, and took the earliest train to the countryside. He hitchhiked across the south of France, then into Switzerland and Italy, loving the freedom and the sense of not quite knowing where each driver's destination would be. Some nights he spent in fields, others in barns, and many, like the one on Friday, April 16, 1954, on a dark highway, trying to catch a few minutes of sleep between stops for gas. The entire experience was like a shot of adrenaline.

At dawn on Saturday morning the Aston Martin cut through the Pass of Glencoe. Light began to edge over the horizon, softly at first. Slowly but inexorably the night lost its hold, and colors spread across the sky. As the sun rose the thick mist that had settled over the land gave way, and the mountains that Bannister knew were surrounding them finally appeared. With the windows rolled down, he felt the cool, crisp air on his face and felt renewed.

They got into the adventure straight away. Brasher and More were experienced climbers; before they started a particular ascent, they would tell Bannister, "We'll go up this first." That was little comfort, since Bannister knew that he would have to follow. They were roped together, and the climbs took a fair bit of skill. On occasion Brasher helped Bannister up with the rope, but the miler was strong and limber enough to handle most of the faces himself. It was stressful, muscle-numbing activity that required the kind of jerking and pulling that his body wasn't used to handling. A couple of times they ascended routes with mountain streams pouring down on them; water soaked their shirts and spilled out of their trousers, often leaving them frozen to the bone. For three days they climbed, sustained by little more than fish cakes and a few hours of sleep in a local inn while their boots and wool sweaters dried out. There was little time to talk of record miles—or of anything at all except the next day's route.

On Monday morning Brasher slipped as he led the ascent up a steep face called Jericho Wall. Before he could catch his grip, he was falling. He was saved from the twenty-five-foot fall by the belay of his nylon rope, which took most of the speed out of his fall before breaking. Before their luck ran out, they decided to call it quits, realizing that at the very least they risked spraining an ankle by continuing with the adventure. Ten hours later they were back in London, uncertain whether the long strenuous weekend had left them worse for wear. At least it had taken their minds off running for a while.

After three more days' rest from the track, the three runners met

Stampfl at the Duke of York's Barracks on April 22. It was time to make another go at reducing their lap times to sixty seconds in their repeat 10 x 440 interval regime. They all knew that achieving this would prove their readiness. After warming up, they ran the first 440 in 56.3 seconds. A very good pace. They jogged around the unmarked cinder track in two minutes and started the next 440, then the next. Bannister ran the tenth lap in exactly the same time in which he had run the first, making the average for the entire session 58.9 seconds. They had knocked two seconds off what had earlier seemed like a wall. It was a moment of exultation after months of training, and it almost felt as if they had run the four-minute mile itself. The team was finally ready.

Later they gathered at the Lyons Teashop in Sloane Square. The four men stood out among the host of women who congregated in the simple teashop for a decent cup of tea and a gossip. In the upstairs section they talked quietly of the race to come. Stampfl drew an oval on a scrap of paper to illustrate his plan.

"You, Chris"—he looked toward Brasher—"should take the first two laps. Fifty-seven or fifty-eight seconds for the first lap, sixty seconds for the second lap. No faster—but no slower, mind you. Can you do that?"

"Yes, I think I can guarantee that," Brasher replied confidently. His speed had improved dramatically under Stampfl's watch. In his own mind he had always felt that his coach saw him as the weakest link in their pacing plan. Brasher respected Stampfl so much that he felt it necessary to prove him wrong—and he had.

"And you, Chris"—Stampfl turned toward Chataway—"must take over and complete the third lap also in sixty seconds."

Chataway nodded.

"And after that it's up to you, Roger," Stampfl said. "You're on your own for the last lap."

It was agreed. The attempt on Thursday, May 6, was to go ahead. Bannister had less than three weeks to fine-tune his speed for the big day. The McWhirters had made him painfully aware that Landy was competing in Scandinavia as early as May and Santee was looking toward the Compton Invitational in early June—and so the race at the Iffley Road track might be his last chance.

On the tarmac of an airport outside Melbourne, John Landy ascended the steps of the four-engine Qantas Constellation that would take him first to Sydney, then by connection to Singapore, and onward to Helsinki. It was April 28, and he was looking forward to leaving Australia. He could run 4:02 miles in his sleep, but he couldn't seem to improve on that time. Scandinavia promised the best tracks in the world, as well as a release from the weight of expectation. He was excited about the prospect. After reaching the top of the stairs, he turned and allowed a bank of photographers to snap his picture while he waved down to his father, who had driven him to the airport. His parents' support throughout these many months of training and racing had been unwavering, and his mother's last words to him before he left were simply, "Enjoy yourself."

Expectations were still high. The trip to Scandinavia was supposed to bring him the four-minute mile. His sendoff had been quite an affair. A few nights before, a dinner was held in his honor at the Danish Club. It was hosted by the former chief justice of the High Court, and Landy was given a gold watch for his athletic achievements—and perhaps good luck as well. Before ducking into the airplane, Landy smiled again for the photographers and then disappeared inside. As the door closed behind him, he settled back in his seat for the long series of flights ahead. His countrymen wanted him to break the barrier on this trip, but Landy simply hoped that he would be able to knock off Haegg's record.

His times since the late January twilight meet at Olympic Park, even though disappointing, had nonetheless qualified him—in the opinion of *New York Times* columnist Arthur Daley, a former skeptic—as the world's strongest miler. On February 11, in Sydney, while suffering from strained ligaments in his left ankle, not to mention battling fifteen-mile-per-hour gusts and a spongy track, he had beaten Denis Johansson with a time of 4:05.6. Two weeks later he ran 4:02.6 through semidarkness and a slight rain in Melbourne. On March 5, he clocked a 4:05.9 mile. And just the previous week, the day after Santee competed in the Kansas Relays, Landy made a devastatingly courageous effort at the mile record on a grass track, despite getting a leather football spike stuck on his right shoe during the first lap. Though his stride was affected because the spike made each footfall awkward, Landy tore around the Bendigo Showgrounds in a time of 4:02.6.

Throughout the first half of 1954 the Australian and international press were relentless in their coverage of Landy. They heralded every one of his races as a historic attempt. "Landy Likely to Achieve Impossible" and "Landy Should Do It Tonight" were only two of many such headlines. Landy had to bear the cross of these expectations knowing that the four-minute mile had become bigger than athletics—that his attainment of it was increasingly a matter of Australian pride in the world arena. In the days before a race he read the papers to see what was expected of him. "I had an obligation to perform," he said. He would have preferred to make his record-breaking attempt in a stadium empty of everyone save some timekeepers and officials.

Whenever he had failed to break the barrier in front of a cheering crowd, it was never held to be his fault. Instead, the Australian press floated a variety of reasons: the blinding rain, the sweltering heat, the gale-force winds, a loose track, the pathetic competition—and on occasion all of the above.

Landy rarely uttered a word about why he had failed in a particular race. In his mind, if he were capable of running under four minutes, he would already have done so. As time went on, however, he was accused of being an "alibi-artist" because of the excuses constantly put forward by his native press, which set off a firestorm of attacks elsewhere. The New York Post asked, "Do the winds blow differently 'Down Under' than they do here?" United Press took up this refrain: "A great runner, the young Australian unfortunately has proven even faster to date when it comes to second guessing the results recorded on the stopwatch. . . . You can take it from John that his failures were not due to the lack of four-minute muscles, but because it was too hot or too cold, his feet hurt, the crowd applauded so loud that he could not hear his lap times."

The tour in Finland was to provide an escape from this madness. But more than anything, Landy just wanted to improve on his fastest time. He hated the thought of continuing to run the same times, and if it took traveling to and running on two continents to make a difference, so be it. He deserved at least to better Haegg's world record. The plan was to spend two and a half months racing in Scandinavia, enjoying the fast tracks and crisp weather, and then to travel to Vancouver for the Empire Games. After that, he had decided, he would call an end to his running career. He hoped that Johansson was right when he said that if Landy could run 4:02 consistently at home, he could easily run a couple of seconds faster in Finland and break the record there. It could well be his last chance.

Nearly a day later, when the plane arrived in Singapore after his connection in Sydney, Landy went out for a training session, not wanting to lose any of his fitness during the long series of flights. Through the sweltering heat he ran for an hour and a half, burning off several pounds in the process. Meanwhile, back in Melbourne, newspapers rolled off the presses with pictures of Landy at the airport and stories about how "in one slimly built young Victorian lies the world's best prospect to conquer athletics' Mount Everest." At last Landy was far enough away to be free of this constant bombardment, left to focus on training and running fast times. In a few days' time he would finally arrive in the place where he stood a chance to get the best out of himself, which was the only thing he had ever wanted when he first began to aim for the world's record in the mile.

On Saturday, May 1, Santee, accompanied by his bride, descended out of a thunderstorm in a single-engine plane to land on a thin ribbon of runway in Ashland, Kansas. As the plane taxied, the local high school band fired up its march for "Wes Santee Day." Ashland's most famous son had come home.

The previous weekend Santee had been in Des Moines for the Drake Relays, the scene of his first coming-out as a world-class runner three years before. The meet was business as usual, with Santee participating in four events to lead his Jayhawks to unchallenged victory. In the 4 x 1 mile relay, Santee was almost lackadaisical about his role as the anchor. When his teammate Art Dalzell was running the third leg of the relay, Santee visited his wife in the stands for a brief chat, still wearing his sweats. Then he ran over to speak to Easton as Dalzell began his fourth lap. Some in the stands worried about whether Santee was even going to run. He looked unconcerned. Finally, when Dalzell neared the finish, Santee jogged back to his starting position, peeled off his sweatsuit, and collected the baton just in time. He strolled a 4:24 mile, just fast enough to win the race.

The next day Santee exerted himself a bit more in the distance medley, reeling in a 4:07.4 mile to top off the fine quarter-, half-, and three-quarter-miles by his teammates and setting a new world record of 9:50.4, six seconds faster than the previous mark. Fifty-five minutes later Santee anchored the two-mile relay in 1:51.6, giving his Jayhawks another crown. The journalists covering the Drake Relays focused mostly on the fact that Easton had benched five athletes for breaking curfew. The coach explained his decision: "Under our system, the team comes first. Any man—any man—is expendable. If he doesn't put the team and its goal above himself we'd just as soon not have him in a KU uniform." He might as well have been speaking of Santee, whom many would have preferred to see run in the open mile to break the four-minute barrier.

His Ashland hometown fans, however, could not have honored him more fervently, even if he had claimed one of sport's greatest prizes the weekend before. The local newspaper was awash with well-wishing. The Stockgrowers State Bank took out an advertisement welcoming him home while plugging its services: "Pay by Check. It will travel as swiftly and as tirelessly as our great miler!" The Heat 160 Highway Café, the Crosby Oil Company, Earl Haelsig Clothier, and a host of others also paid for ads congratulating him on his success. The mayor gave him the town keys, a parade led him down Main Street, and a dinner was held in his honor. It was joked that since his arrival had brought nearly an inch of rain—the "best soaker" in two years—the town planned on holding a "Wes Santee Day" every weekend.

His old coach, J. Allen Murray, was on hand, recounting how the first time he saw Santee he thought, that boy is a runner! His first-grade teacher told of the day the fire alarm rang by accident: by the time the classroom cleared she found Wes halfway down the street and up a windmill ladder. Though not mentioned, everyone in the room understood what kind of hardship Santee had endured at the hands of his father, and it made the evening that much sweeter that he had achieved so much nonetheless. Santee's parents and siblings were there, but remained quiet. Wes could hardly stand to spend more than a couple of hours around his father, and Danna, knowing more than most about what David Santee had wrought upon his son, had little time for him too.

At the end of the night Wes Santee thanked those who had helped him throughout his childhood, particularly his coach, and he promised that one day soon he would break the four-minute barrier. For the five hundred people in the grade school auditorium who had just finished watching a twenty-five-minute newsreel of his best races, one after the other evidencing his breakneck speed and dominance on the track, this promise must have seemed as good as delivered.

In the two weeks before May 6, Bannister trained for speed and nothing else. He had to tune up his body so that in the space of four minutes he could spend the same amount of energy that he typically used during a long interval training session. At Motspur Park, on April 24, he ran a three-quarter-mile time trial with Chataway. As had happened at the trial in anticipation of the Helsinki Olympics nearly two years before, only a few people were there to watch. Two of them were English miler Bill Nankeville and AAA national coach Geoffrey Dyson.

From the start, Bannister took the lead, and throughout the trial he sensed how keenly tuned he was. His running had reached a kind of apotheosis. He felt strong and full of energy. As he described it, "There was no longer any need for my mind to force my limbs to run faster." Every muscle and fiber of his lean six-foot-one-inch frame was attuned to an effortless stride. He did not have to think about how best to move his arms or kick out his legs to economize energy. It was as natural for him to shoot around the track with seven-foot strides at Motspur Park as to cross the length of a room. His judgment of pace was deadly accurate as well. "It was as if all my muscles were a part of a perfectly tuned machine." When he crossed the three-quarter-mile mark in three minutes flat, Chataway at his side, Bannister was delighted. They had run an even pace, and he still felt energetic. It was a far cry from his 2:52.9 in July 1952, but he knew how much more strength he had in his legs now—enough to go the full distance of a mile with the same kind of speed.

After watching the trial, Nankeville was shaken by how well Bannister was running. Dyson, also amazed by the ease with which Bannister and his companions ran, left the track soon thereafter to get to White City Stadium for a London Athletic Club meet. There he ran into George Smith, an AAA staff member. Bubbling with excitement, Dyson said, "The world's one-mile record is doomed. I have just come from Motspur Park; Bannister and Chataway, finishing together, ran a three-quarter mile in three minutes dead, and both were as fresh as paint at the finish. Believe me, my friend, great things are about to happen in the near future."

Bannister would probably have discounted the claim, but one thing was certain: in his many years of athletics he had never experienced such freshness and pleasure in his running. On April 28 he went to the Paddington track at lunchtime for another trial, this one to be run alone. Norris McWhirter met him there with his stopwatch. This was the critical test. If Bannister could get in just under three minutes, then he felt strongly that he had a 3:59.9 mile in him. If not, if he was over three minutes by even a second, his mile time would probably translate into a 4:01. This was how close to the razor's edge his training had brought him.

The strong wind made Bannister hesitate at the start. He would have preferred to have the best conditions possible for this trial. If he failed to run the first three laps under three minutes, it might shake his confidence. Finally he decided to go for it, and when McWhirter stopped his watch as Bannister crossed the line, the time showed 2:59.9. For a moment Bannister was overwhelmed with nerves. His mouth went dry. The time meant that he had a good shot come May 6. McWhirter believed the same. The next day the publisher gathered his *Athletics World* staff in their garret office at 15 Great James Street to make their predictions for Bannister's mile. On his office door, three times were written: 4:01.8, 4:01.2, and 3:59.5. The last prognostication was from Norris himself. He knew his friend was in four-minute-mile shape—and just in time. Landy was due to arrive in Helsinki on May 3, and Santee was preparing for the international competition and fast tracks at the Compton Invitational. It was now or never. As McWhirter would write in the May edition of his track and field magazine, "It is not the doing of it that really counts, but doing it FIRST." He had continued to make this clear to his friend.

On April 30 Bannister ran a half-mile to polish his speed one last time and then put away his running spikes until the AAA versus Oxford race. He and Stampfl agreed that the best thing the miler could do now was build up his nervous energy. This had the unfortunate consequence of leaving Bannister with nothing to do with his surfeit of anxiety about the approaching day, the culmination of two years of effort and focus. He was a well of emotion with no way to sweat it out.

For the next five days he worried that he was getting sick or that hurricane winds were certain to descend on Oxford on May 6. Every night he envisioned himself at the starting line, waiting for the sound of the gun. Picturing the race in this way, he literally shook, and it took him a while to relax enough for sleep. Only twenty-four hours before the big day, he lost his footing on the polished, ice-like hospital floor and hobbled around the wards for the remainder of his shift. A long night of restful sleep was hardly a possibility either. All in all, he was a bit of a wreck.

As for Brasher and Chataway, in the days before the race they were busy with their jobs. Still, they spent long hours on the telephone with Bannister, who was convinced that there was no way the attempt was going to come off. They let him vent his concerns and tried to reassure him. As Chataway told him one evening, "You can do it. If you've done 4:02 and 4:03, the training you've done has been better this time. There's absolutely no reason you shouldn't do it."

Of course, they had their own worries. The week before, Stampfl had approached the two, over tea at Lyons, about changing the pace-making. Instead of Brasher leading for the first two laps, Stampfl thought it better that he try to make it two and a half laps around, at which point Chataway would take over to the three-and-a-half-lap mark. This way Bannister would only have to take the final half-lap alone, instead of a full 440, as earlier planned. That was fine and well, but the two doubted that they were in good enough shape to hold fast through another half-lap. As Brasher explained, however, "Stampfl had a way of exorcizing such doubts from the mind of an athlete." Their coach had them so fired up that each runner daydreamed that not only would he manage the extra effort but also that he would somehow find a way to kick past Bannister in the final turn and seize the record himself.

The evening before the Oxford meet, Franz Stampfl was in his one-bedroom apartment off King's Road, as nervous as his athletes. He felt certain that Bannister could do it, but as he told his wife, Pat, "It's going to be a big day. I think we can do it, but you have to have luck in everything." His small apartment was littered with athletic journals detailing the latest exploits of the world's great milers. Stampfl believed that someone was going to run the four-minute mile soon, so Bannister needed to do it straight away. If he didn't, Stampfl was certain that the British athletic community would blame the coach.

Across town in North London, Norris McWhirter was practicing for his role as public-address announcer at the Oxford versus AAA match. He had spent a hectic day fielding phone calls and making sure that everything was ready for Bannister's attempt, including good media coverage. To this end he had written a May 5 story in the *Star* headlined "Aim May Be Four Min Mile." Yet when he called Peter Dimmock of the BBC, McWhirter learned that the BBC wasn't even planning on attending.

"It's not a very important match, and it's not really international," Dimmock had said. "Can't spare the camera or crews."

"Well, I'm just merely warning you that you'd be extremely unwise to miss it," McWhirter said plainly.

"Are you telling me something?"

"I'm not telling you anything really, but if the weather is propitious. . . . Bannister is understandably anxious about the priority of Landy and Santee."

"Oh, right," Dimmock replied. He agreed to have someone there for the event and then hung up.

In the bath that evening McWhirter, who was more concerned about his announcing responsibilities than his expected participation in the 4 x 110 sprint relays, decided what he would say if Bannister successfully broke four minutes. He wanted his tone to be measured but his words full of suspense. It would start with something like this: "Ladies and gentlemen, here is the result of event number nine, the one mile. . . ."

July 26, 1952, Helsinki. Josey Barthel seizes the gold in the 1,500-meter Olympic final. Roger Bannister comes in fourth. *Bettmann/Corbis*

Bannister balances his work as a medical student with his ambition to be the world's first sub-four-minute miler. *Larry Burrows*

John Landy relaxing at his East Malvern home. *Fairfax Photos*

above Wes Santee, grinning at the finish at the 1952 National Championships in California, earns the right to qualify for the 1,500-meter Olympic trials. *Bettmann/Corbis*

left The "human locomotive," Emil Zatopek, grimaces his way to another Olympic gold medal. *Frank Scherschel/Time Life Pictures/ Getty Images*

above At Portsea, Percy Cerutty times his two fastest milers, Don Macmillan (left) and John Landy. *Courtesy of the Herald & Weekly Times, Ltd.*

right Percy Cerutty, in typical attire, holding forth on his running theories. *Leonard McCombe/Time Life Pictures/ Getty Images*

left Coach Bill Easton holds the stopwatch for Wes Santee in a time trial. *Photo by Duke D'Ambra, courtesy of Wes Santee*

below Santee (right) and his teammates on their way to class at the University of Kansas. *Photo by Duke D'Ambra, courtesy of Wes Santee*

On a cold winter afternoon in Kansas, Santee challenges his fraternity brothers in a fourteen-mile race. *Photo by Duke D'Ambra, courtesy of Wes Santee*

May 6, 1954. Chris Brasher sets the pace for Bannister in his attempt at the four-minute mile at Iffley Road, Oxford. *Hulton Archive/Getty Images*

above Bannister's coach, Franz Stampfl (left), speaking with the famed British journalist John Macadam. *Hulton Archive/Getty Images*

right Bannister in a state of collapse after his historic run. *AP*

May 7, 1954. The day after the four-minute-mile run, fellow students at St. Mary's Hospital School in London celebrate Bannister's victory with him. *Jimmy Sime/Central Press/Hulton Archive/Getty Images*

Santee signs an autograph for a young fan. *Lisa Larsen/Time Life Pictures/Getty Images*

June 21, 1954. In Turku, Finland, John Landy (second from left) bursts ahead in his bid for the world record. Chris Chataway is at the far left. Denis Johansson is at the rear of the pack. *AP*

July 26, 1954. Chris Brasher, Roger Bannister, and Chris Chataway arrive in Vancouver for the Empire Games. A herd of journalists is there to greet them. *Bettmann/Corbis*

John Landy (pole position) and Roger Bannister (fifth position) at the starting line for their great race at the Empire Games. *Silk/Time Life Pictures/Getty Images*

A packed stadium watches Landy dominate the early stages of the race in Vancouver. *Ralph Morse/Time Life Pictures/Getty Images*

Bannister approaches the finish line in Vancouver, with Landy nowhere in the picture. *George Silk/ Time Life Pictures/Getty Images*

Roger Bannister wins the Mile of the Century. *Ralph Morse/Time Life Pictures/Getty Images*

14

I felt at that moment that it was my chance to do one
thing supremely well.   —ROGER BANNISTER

ON THURSDAY, May 6, Bannister woke in his Earl's Court apartment. When he glanced outside, his hope of a nice day disappeared. The wind swayed the treetops violently, and clouds of slate gray promised rain. Swallowing the fear of having to reschedule the attempt, he got ready to go to the hospital for the morning. After breakfast he went outside, and the wind buffeted his shirt like a sail. Trying for the mile record in these gales was certain to be futile. If they did go ahead and he failed—and he would most certainly fail on a day like this—then he would waste his nervous energy and find psyching himself up another time doubly difficult. Putting off the attempt until the next opportunity, May 17 at White City Stadium, would mean bearing over a week more of anxiety and strain. Neither option was very appealing.

With these thoughts in his mind, Bannister arrived at the hospital. Distraught, he had nothing to do but continue with the day as if the attempt would go ahead, all the time feeling certain that it was hopeless. At eleven o'clock he went down to the hospital laboratory to grind his spikes and rub them with graphite. Given the likely conditions, this would keep the cinder ash from clumping to the bottoms of his shoes, which could mean a few yards over the mile. When someone peered into the laboratory, found him at the grindstone, and asked, "You don't really think that's going to make any difference, do you?" Bannister knew very well that in the battle over tenths of seconds and half-seconds it would indeed make a difference. In addition, the shoes he planned on running in had been ordered from a specialist London cobbler. "They should be light," Bannister had said to the man who once supplied Jack Lovelock with his shoes. "I need them only for three races, for twelve laps." The resulting pair weighed four ounces, two less than his normal shoes. He factored this into his carefully calculated plan. Every advantage counted.

Once finished with his spikes, Bannister decided to take an early train alone to Oxford so that he could gather his thoughts and come to some resolution about whether the attempt was worth making. The mile event was not scheduled until six o'clock, which left plenty of time for the weather to change, but Bannister was already leaning toward putting off the attempt altogether. Walking to nearby Paddington Station, he waded through the sidewalks full of people wearing raincoats and carrying umbrellas. The station was dark and noisy and left one choking for breath. With the sun absent from the sky, the soot veneer on the arched glass ceiling let in very little light. Whistles blew, and "all aboard" announcements were shouted down the platforms, while smoke coughed out from train engines. After finding his platform on the information board, Bannister hurried to his train, ready to settle in for the sixty-three-mile journey he had taken so many times before. While looking for an empty seat, he unexpectedly spotted Franz Stampfl sitting in one of the compartments. Bannister pulled the door open, surprised at how glad he was to see his coach. He needed to lay bare his fears, and there was nobody better than Stampfl to help him deal with them.

Bannister wasn't alone in his worries over the weather. Stampfl too had looked out the window that morning in despair. His wife Pat, a short, kind-spirited woman who helped support them by working as a bookkeeper, sensed his concern, but Stampfl told her that he believed everything would be all right. He barely spoke through breakfast and left early to take the Underground to Paddington. Nonetheless, when Bannister found him, Stampfl conveyed nothing but complete confidence. To have shown anything else would have been disastrous to his athlete.

The doors slammed closed, and the train jarred into movement. The dull tremor of the engine reverberated through the compartment as the two sat opposite one another, not speaking of the race to come. When they cleared the cover of the station, rain slapped against the windows, and as the train gathered momentum, cutting north out of London past rows of dilapidated Victorian houses with laundry lines strung out behind them, Bannister hesitated to ask for Stampfl's advice. At this critical moment in his athletic career he disliked the idea of needing to depend on a coach.

The train sped past warehouses and factory smokestacks under the gloomy sky. As Bannister watched the trees buffeted by the gale-force winds, he finally began to talk about his concerns. He explained to Stampfl that the weather might ruin any chance of breaking four minutes. The wind would add a second to each of his four laps. This meant he would have to run the equivalent of a 3:56 mile in ideal conditions. A 3:56 mile. Given how much he had invested in today being *the* day, future attempts looked less hopeful. He was at his best *now*, mentally and physically. It was too difficult to keep himself at this peak, whether for the race at White City in ten days' time or for even later ones.

Stampfl knew the damage that doubt could do to an athlete. He assured Bannister that on a calm day he could run four seconds under the barrier. He had the legs for it. "With the proper motivation, that is, a good reason for wanting to do it," Stampfl said in his usual bellowing Austrian voice, "your mind can overcome any sort of adversity. In any case, the wind might drop. I remember J. J. Barry in Ireland. He ran a 4:08 mile without any training or even proper food—simply because he had the will to run. . . . In any case, what if this were your only chance? Sure it'll be painful, but what's pain?" Bannister considered the question, knowing well what Stampfl had endured. Stampfl continued, absolutely convinced in his own mind that the miler was capable of the effort, no matter the weather. "If you forgo this chance, would you ever forgive yourself? Nobody knows what the future holds. Wes Santee or John Landy may do it first. You might pull a muscle. You might fall under a bus. There may never be another opportunity."

While the train rumbled over the rails toward the black cinder track at Iffley Road, Oxford, Stampfl continued to speak of other runners and their times, but Bannister scarcely heard his words. He stared out the window as they wound their way across the rolling green hills of the countryside, past the blurred trees. The miler steeled himself to the realization that despite the weather, this was his best opportunity. Stampfl had faith in him. His running partners, Chris Brasher and

Chris Chataway, had faith in him. And somewhere underneath the fear and doubt, Bannister had faith in himself.

When they finally arrived at the Oxford station, coach and miler went their separate ways. Bannister's close friend Charles Wenden was waiting for him, and they drove together to the Iffley Road track so that Bannister could test his spikes on the cinders. He needed to see how well the graphite-rubbed spikes entered and released from the track's sticky ash. Wind blew in gusts across the wet track, and once again he lost hope in the attempt. His friend invited him for lunch with his family, and Bannister accepted, knowing that it would be a good place to relax and get away from his thoughts.

Wenden was an Oxford lecturer in education studies and had won the Military Cross during the war. The two young men had first met at an Oxford cross-country race years before. Bannister had turned to Wenden after the other competitors had shot quickly off the mark and asked, "Are they going to run like this?," implying that he was not capable of the pace. Wenden replied, "Well, they are, but we don't have to." Bannister was close to Wenden's family, his wife and two daughters, having stayed with them during his postgraduate research, and his friend knew him well enough not to ask any questions about that afternoon's record attempt. For several hours the miler lost himself in the domestic routine, enjoying a lunch of ham salad and prunes with custard and playing with the children.

Bannister left the Wendens in the late afternoon to visit Chris Chataway, who had arrived in Oxford early as well. At Magdalen College Bannister found his running partner reclining by a window, calm and cheerful as ever. Magically, the sun had appeared in the sky at last. Chataway said, "The day could be a lot worse, couldn't it? Just now it's fine. The forecast says the wind may drop towards evening. Let's not decide until five o'clock." Until that time, Bannister stared out the window, praying the wind would stop rustling through the treetops.

When they finally went down to the track, Bannister bumped into reporter Joseph Binks on the way. "The wind's hopeless," Binks said. They found Brasher in the wood-paneled changing rooms under the stands. There they debated whether to go ahead with the attempt. Through the narrow slit of the window Bannister stared at the red-crossed flag of St. George over the square tower of a church on Iffley Road. It whipped strongly in the wind.

Stampfl suggested that they decide nothing until closer to race time.

So forty-five minutes before the race was due to start, the three runners went out to the rugby fields adjacent to the track to warm up. While they jogged on the grass, a bank of dark clouds rolled across the sky. A few minutes later a quick shower burst over them. They scrambled back to the locker room. The capricious English weather had struck again.

But precisely at 5:45 P.M., the clouds cleared and a rainbow arced over the square tower where St. George's flag flew. Stampfl approached the three runners to see whether they would try for the mile record. The first vote was: no (Bannister), neutral (Chataway), and yes (Brasher— always one to say yes to anything). As it was unlikely they would go ahead, Brasher tracked down Leslie Truelove, the AAA team manager, who was dressed as if he had come straight from a business meeting, to see whether he could switch to the two-mile event. Truelove declined, saying that it was too late. With five minutes until the start, Stampfl noticed that the wind was dying down and told the three runners, "There's nothing a man can't do if the spirit's there." Brasher agreed, saying, "We've done all this bloody work, we might as well go." They took a second vote: no (Bannister), yes (Chataway), yes (Brasher). Bannister took another 150-yard warm-up sprint, moved to the starting line, and then saw the flag over the church go slack. This was the only sign he needed. "Yes," he told Brasher and Chataway. They were going for it.

The crowd of 1,200, many of whom were undergraduates who had just arrived on their bicycles, waited anxiously for the start. Although the meet had been under way for over an hour, most had come to see the mile race. Many wore heavy coats and scarves wrapped around their necks, despite the fact that it was May. Only a few days before, the *Oxford Mail* had headlined: "Bannister at Oxford—May Make Attempt at 4-Minute Mile." In the center infield two men from the BBC's *Sportsview* had set up a 35mm camera on top of its leather-box case. They planned to shoot the race in a continuous take, 360 degrees around. Norris McWhirter, who had arranged for their appearance, had also convinced American journalist Milton Marmor to be on hand, saying he would be "ill advised" not to attend, since he would be the only one of his countrymen there. Begrudgingly, Marmor agreed. Unbeknownst to Bannister, his parents had also arrived in Oxford to watch the race. They did not tell him to avoid adding any more pressure than he already felt. Regretfully, his older sister Joyce couldn't come from Bristol, though he had written in a letter to her a few weeks before, "By the way, I may be trying for the four-minute mile at Oxford soon."

The moment had arrived. The six runners approached the starting line for event number nine, the mile. Alan Gordon and George Dole, an American studying theology at Oxford, represented the university. Brasher, Chataway, Bannister, and William Hulatt represented the AAA. As they settled at the mark, the sun reappeared in the sky. Bannister, wearing a green, gold, and blue striped singlet and the number 41 pinned to his chest, looked down at the track, arms loose by his side, his right foot slightly forward. The air was wet and cold on his skin. He was fourth from the inside, with Chataway directly to his right and Brasher a man away to his left. The crowd grew silent. Bannister coiled and readied to spring. Before the starter gun shot, Brasher jumped—a false start. After he received an official warning from the starter, the runners returned to the mark, with Bannister upset that they might have wasted valuable seconds of the pause in the wind, which could pick up again at any moment.

Again the crowd went silent. Bannister waited, shifting his spikes on the cinders to get better traction. He took a long breath. This might be his last chance to be the first through the barrier. His pacemakers were ready. The plan was set. Thanks to his training, he had the endurance and speed to manage the pace. And thanks to Stampfl, he had more than just the knowledge that a sub-four-minute mile could be run— Bannister *believed* he was able to do it, no matter the conditions. He was as prepared as he would ever be for the attempt.

The gun banged, and Brasher shot forward as arranged, quickly passing Dole, who was on the inside lane from the start. Bannister followed closely behind Brasher, and Chataway moved up steadily through the field as they made their way around the turn. Finally Bannister was free of the thoughts that had plagued him throughout the previous week, free at last to run, and run fast. His whole body felt electrified, as if he could move around the track without expending any effort. Five days of not running had left him with a bundle of energy. And here, at last, he could put that energy to use.

As they neared the first half-lap marker, Norris McWhirter read off the time on his stopwatch into the microphone: "Twenty-six . . . twenty-seven . . . twenty-eight." He had hired an electrician to wire two speakers to the microphone, one pointing down the home straight and the other on the back straight. Since he was the public-address announcer, it was entirely permissible (albeit seldom arranged) for him to give the half-lap time. This would help with the pacemaking. Bannister didn't hear him correctly and felt so fired with energy in that early part of the race that he thought Brasher was setting too slow a pace. In the back straight Bannister yelled, "Faster, Chris! Faster!"

Brasher heard the call but refused to react. He was running smartly and believed the pace was right. Plus, he was going as fast as he could without getting up on his toes and sprinting, which would have meant the end of him by the start of the second lap. He maintained his speed, and Bannister, despite remaining anxious over the pace, was forced to hold steady behind him. Bannister was so restless that he was unaware of how fast he was running. As they reached the end of the first lap McWhirter's voice boomed out of the loudspeaker, "Fifty-four . . . fifty-five . . . fifty-six . . . fifty-seven." Brasher crossed the line first, Bannister a half-second behind him in 57.5, and Chataway third. The three were evenly spaced and already well ahead of the rest of the field. The crowd began to sense that something very special was afoot, particularly given how quickly and purposefully the three runners were striding.

Into the second lap, Brasher sustained the pace. Bannister continued to run on his nerves and had not yet settled into an easy stride. When they turned into the back straight, Stampfl shouted, "Relax! Relax!" Bannister was wasting energy by running so stiffly. Whether consciously or unconsciously, Bannister heard Stampfl and began to get into his rhythm. If they were running too slow, it was too late in the race to adjust. Calm descended over him, and his legs began to move as if on their own. He felt free of exertion.

"One-twenty-five . . . one-twenty-six . . . one-twenty-seven."

Brasher passed the 660 mark and began to feel the strain. He was running less easily than the other two and starting to chug around the track like a freight train, arms coming across his chest as he ran. Behind him, Bannister strode smoothly, beating a steady cadence on the cinder track as they approached the half-mile mark. Chataway kept to the strong pace in third position.

"One-fifty-six . . . one-fifty-seven . . . one-fifty-eight."

Bannister scarcely heard the time. His body was running within the groove that he had trained many months to shape. He was in the zone. Brasher continued to lead, making a mighty effort to maintain the pace. To his mind, the bend lasted an interminable amount of time. Around the stadium the crowd clapped louder and louder. They whispered among themselves that this might be the big day. Athletes in the infield stopped their warm-ups to get to the side of the track for a better view. The time was fast for the half-mile, and the officials responsible for making sure everything went according to the rules began to realize they had a reason to be especially careful.

As they approached the two-and-a-half-lap mark, Brasher was struggling. His mouth was wide open, and he looked ready to fall over at any moment. Bannister sensed that his friend was about to stall and called for Chataway to take over. "Chris," Bannister yelled. Chataway was tired, but hearing Bannister, he found the strength to spring forward. With his short but powerful strides, he quickly overtook Bannister, then Brasher. The three other men in the race had been long forgotten.

"Two-twenty-seven . . . two-twenty-eight . . . two-twenty-nine."

Stampfl checked his own stopwatch, reassuring himself that they were on pace. Brasher had always been the question mark in the pace-making scheme because of his lack of natural speed, but he fought mightily through the first two and a half laps. They were on schedule. The steeplechaser had a giant heart. Now it was up to Chataway, then Bannister himself. Stampfl knew the moment would soon come for both when their fatigued legs and lack of oxygen would cry out for them to stop. The coach only hoped he had helped them enough to know they could push back this pain, convince their legs to keep striding, and will themselves onward.

Rounding the bend, Chataway focused on maintaining their speed, his lips pursed as he ran. Bannister still felt good. He allowed the motion of his arms and legs to almost lull him into a trance. It would be in the final lap that he would have to earn his chance at immortality.

"Two-fifty-eight . . . two-fifty-nine . . . three minutes."

At the sound of the bell for the final lap, Bannister had run a 3:00.4. The crowd had been steadily clapping with the occasional cheer, but they now stood to their feet and let loose. Their voices raised into an uproar — this might very well be it. Chataway made his way around the turn, his flushed cheeks swelling with breath. At 350 yards Bannister considered bursting past him, but he waited. He needed a fifty-nine-second last lap or the attempt would fail. It was too early to begin his finishing kick. Chataway turned into the back straight, even his world-class endurance finally giving out. From the sidelines Stampfl shouted, "Go all out!" Chataway tried to hold on as long as he could, but then at the 230-yard mark Bannister swept past him on the outside, his great stride devouring the track.

"Three-twenty-eight . . . three-twenty-nine . . . three-thirty . . . three-thirty—"

Bannister had to finish the final half-lap in less than thirty seconds. He forced himself faster, feeling as if his will to break through the tape in less than four minutes was outpacing his feet. He heard the crowd shouting his name, their support urging him forward, stronger, faster. His great stride lengthened. He accentuated the drive of his arms to keep balance. As he passed the 1,500-meter mark, his face drained of color and contorted with effort, Ross McWhirter took the time—3:43, world-record fast. He dashed over to his brother Norris and told him the time. The twins were convinced that Bannister was about to make history.

From over seventy yards back Brasher gasped, "Come on, Roger . . . Roger . . . Roger!"

But Bannister was beyond tired. At fifty yards from the finish he had exhausted himself completely. There was no pain. He was simply used up. Yet he forced himself ahead, drawing deep upon a reservoir of will only few ever discover. Twenty-five yards. Ten yards. Five yards. The distance from the tape appeared to lengthen. He began to push his chest forward. His legs were still moving. Two strides. His chin went up, his arms drove higher. Keep going. One stride. Keep going. He flung himself at the tape, a tortured yet glorious expression of abandon on his face.

When he crossed the finish line, his legs buckled and he collapsed into the arms of former Olympic sprinter Nicholas Stacey. Leslie Truelove stepped in and draped his arm around Bannister from the other side. The crowd spilled onto the track as the other runners finished their miles. After a few steps Bannister tried to stand again, but his legs gave out. He could barely understand what was going on around him.

"Give him air," someone shouted.

Stampfl moved forward and held Bannister up, his powerful shoulders a ballast. Meanwhile, Chataway and Brasher struggled for breath on the grass infield, unable to get to their friend because of the stampede of people surrounding him.

Bannister was barely conscious and was overwhelmed with pain. For a moment he could see only in black and white. His system was completely taxed from a lack of oxygen. His legs and arms felt as if someone were gripping them tightly. He felt certain that he had broken the barrier, although the time had yet to be announced. Chest swelling with deep breaths, he closed his eyes and rested his forehead in the crook of Stampfl's neck. The coach supported him as they took a few careful steps forward.

"Did I do it?" Bannister coughed out his first words, his face still pale.

"I think so," replied Stampfl, concerned for his runner.

Two minutes later the timekeepers handed Norris McWhirter the official time of the race. It was his responsibility to give the result. Trying to keep his voice from breaking, McWhirter spoke into the microphone, resolved to give his announcement the tone that he had practiced the previous night. The pandemonium on the track silenced as the words came over the loudspeakers:

> Ladies and gentlemen, here is the result of Event Number Nine, the One Mile: First, Number Forty-One, R. G. Bannister, of the Amateur Athletic Association and formerly of Exeter and Merton Colleges, with a time which is a new meeting and track record, and which subject to ratification will be a new English Native, British National, British All-Comers, European, British Empire and WORLD'S RECORD. The time is THREE . . .

The rest of the announcement was drowned out by the joyous cries of the 1,200 people who had witnessed history. Bannister had run the mile in 3:59.4 — at last the barrier was broken.

"Three cheers for Roger Bannister!" a young undergraduate shouted. The crowd responded. "Three cheers! Three cheers!"

Hundreds swarmed around Bannister, pressing closer and closer. His parents broke through the crowd and threaded their way to him. "I knew you would do it one day, Roger," his mother said, throwing her arms around him. He embraced her as newsreel cameramen, photographers, journalists, undergraduates, and children tried to get his attention.

Bannister finally recovered enough to stand on his own and raised his arms over his head in triumph, calling out for Chataway and Brasher. He hurried toward them. After so much effort spent together, he wanted to share the moment. He vigorously shook their hands, his usual reserve replaced by a warm smile. "Without them, I could not have done it," Bannister said to all around him. The three then took a victory trot around the track, a wake of well-wishers following them.

While officials tried to get the meet running again, Bannister signed autographs, spoke to the press, and thanked the head groundsman, Walter Morris. Meanwhile, Chris Brasher, who had a talent for getting straight to the point, told the *Daily Mail*'s Terry O'Connor what many were thinking: "Well, we did it," Brasher said. "That means Landy and Wes Santee can never break the four-minute mile first."

After a quick shower, Bannister went to the Vincent's for a glass of water mixed with table salt (chased with a shandy) and then was shuttled off in a waiting blue car to appear on BBC evening television. It was a far cry from how he had quietly come to Oxford earlier in the day. His great celebration was about to begin. With a covey of journalists fluttering about to file their stories, one finagling a desk and phone at the local police station, another bribing a pub owner to monopolize his phone, life promised never to be the same again for Roger Bannister.

It was a humid afternoon on May 6, one threatened by thunderstorms at the University of Kansas, when Bill Mayer, athletics writer for the *Lawrence Journal World*, read of the broken barrier. His office's ticker tape relayed the news amid word of a Willie Mays home run in Cincinnati and Sam Snead losing his lead in a golf tournament in New York. Before he knew it, Mayer was kicking the machine. The four-minute mile was supposed to have been for Wes Santee. Moments later Mayer left his office to find Santee. He had to move quickly since other local reporters were bound to be fast on the hunt for the miler. His reaction was sure to be flavorful. Mayer knew that at that time of the day the surest bet was to head for Memorial Stadium.

Santee was finishing his workout when the newsmen rushed toward him. He was sweating and still short of breath when he heard what Bannister had done. Instantly he went numb, feeling as he did physically when he lost a race. Easton, who was stunned as well, tried to shield Santee from the questions, but he would have had as much luck trying to hold back an avalanche.

"What do you think of the news?" one reporter asked.

"I am not exceptionally disappointed," Santee replied. "Of the milers capable of doing it, Bannister is the one I'd just as soon have seen break it. There still is the challenge to see who will be the first American to break the four-minute mile. The time is still not as low as it can be run."

"Why were you beaten to the punch?"

"Having to compete for the university, I've had to run everything from soup to nuts. I haven't been permitted to concentrate."

"Would you like to run against Bannister?" asked the *University Daily Kansan* reporter.

Santee was clear. "Yes, and I think I could beat him if I had the chance."

Once the reporters got their quotes, Easton talked with Santee alone. He knew Santee was stung by the news. "We tried," he said. "But we have to keep on. You still have more running to do."

Santee agreed, although it would be several days before he was convinced of it. More than anything, he wanted a chance to compete against Bannister in a real race, one man against the other without pacing. Then the world would see.

The young miler walked alone back to the locker room. He didn't want to talk about Bannister or running for a while.

At a restaurant in Turku, the ancient capital of Finland and a far cry from the shores of Melbourne, Denis Johansson strode toward Landy, holding a cable in his hand. They had been together since Landy arrived on May 3, and for the first day since his arrival the Australian had not trained, perhaps wanting to see first how Bannister ran in Oxford.

"Look at this," the Finn said, passing him the cable across the table.

Bannister had done it: a 3:59.4 mile. It was a surprising performance, Landy thought at first. He knew the English miler was about to make another attempt, but Landy had thought that Bannister would break Haegg's record at best. Unbelievable—Bannister had knocked two seconds from the record. At least this meant an end to all the talk of the barrier, and Landy would be able to run without the "four-minute mile" punctuating his every stride. Then the disappointment began to settle over him. After so much sweat and strain, he had been beaten to the record. Reporters would want his response, Johansson told him. Landy didn't feel up to it. Not now. He asked the Finn if he would reply to the cable and then told him, "Well, let's have a go [for the record] on May 31."

Johansson sent back the following quote to reporters: "It's great, great, great. He's a great runner. I think the brilliant achievement will be bettered."

The next day Landy planned two workouts, one in the morning and one in the afternoon. He still believed he had a good chance, on these beautiful Finnish tracks, of running faster than anyone before. If Bannister had been able to break four minutes, then Landy felt he should be able to do it as well. He had run many more miles under 4:05 than Bannister—or anyone else for that matter. His training was more intensive as well. It was just a matter of all the right elements coming together.

And fast times weren't everything either. He also had the Empire Games to look forward to, when he and the Englishman were likely to face off against one another. Landy had been waiting a long time to see how he would fare against the best in the world. In Australia, and even Finland, he was finding that nobody could test him in the mile.

PART III
THE PERFECT MILE

15

I see you stand like greyhounds in the slips, straining
upon the start.   —SHAKESPEARE, *Henry V*

S EVENING FELL on May 7, twenty-four hours after the triumph at Iffley Road, Bannister and his two pacemakers, Chataway and Brasher, climbed Harrow Hill, an isolated elevation of
land 345 feet high in the west of London. The sun had set, and a cool
breeze rustled the leaves in the trees overhead. At the top of the hill
stood St. Mary's Church, whose foundations dated back to A.D. 1087. In
the surrounding churchyard a weathered assembly of mossy tombstones sprang up from the landscape. The poet Lord Byron—who,
with Winston Churchill and Lord Shaftsbury, was one of the most famous Harrovians—had spent many hours as a young boy leaning on
these tombstones, dreaming of future adventures. The three runners
looked out on the view as Byron might have seen it. They could see
the proud stance of St. Paul's Cathedral and the twisting shape of the
Thames, a seam of darkness threading through the glittering cityscape.

None of the three had slept more than a few hours in the past two
days. After leaving Oxford, Bannister had been driven quickly to London by the BBC crew. In the car he sat quietly, the pride in his accomplishment overcoming him. "No words could be invented for such
supreme happiness," he later wrote. His Helsinki defeat was vindicated.
He had finally achieved a great athletic ambition. That evening on
Sportsview, he appeared on television screens across his country—

many of them bought only a year before to watch Queen Elizabeth's coronation. Bannister was later praised for his "adroit modesty" during the interview, despite his excitement. He explained how bewildered he felt to be sitting in front of a camera in London only a few hours after his run. When Peter Dimmock, the honored statesman of British broadcasting, asked him why it was they finally decided to make a go for the record, despite the bad weather, Bannister said, "There comes a moment when you can't go on waiting indefinitely. You just have to accept an all-out effort."

"And your plans for athletics?" Dimmock followed.

"Naturally we all wanted to achieve the honor of doing the four-minute mile. But it is in fact only a time. And in athletics, the main essence is races, races against opponents more than against the clock. . . . And those will be what I shall set my main sights on."

Dimmock neglected to pursue that answer by inquiring whether that meant Bannister intended to race against Landy and Santee. Instead, he concluded the interview, congratulating the miler for "putting Great Britain back on top of the sporting world again!" It was a time for celebration, not more questions.

Once Bannister left the studios in Lime Grove, he met Brasher and Chataway for dinner at Clement Freud's cabaret club over the Royal Court Theater in Sloane Square. They drank champagne, enjoyed four-minute steaks (appropriately), and danced with their dates—Bannister's "a tall fair girl in an off-the-shoulder green gown," as a *Daily Express* spy reported. The McWhirter twins stopped by the club to share in the celebrations.

In the booth Bannister turned to the twins. "I can't believe I did it."

"You gotta believe it. It will be in the papers tomorrow," Norris said.

At two-thirty in the morning, Bannister, Brasher, and Chataway wedged themselves into Chataway's prewar Austin 8 and tried to find the Sunset Club in Piccadilly Circus. When they pulled up alongside a policeman to get directions, he gave them the once-over and said, "You gentlemen are no gentlemen if you take these ladies to that club." He took out a notebook from his top, left-hand pocket, as if to write them a ticket, and then handed it to Bannister. "Perhaps I can have your autographs, gentlemen."

In the dark smoky basement club off Carnaby Street, news of the feat was announced, and Bannister was called to the front to say a few words. He pulled his two pacemakers into the light with him and said,

"I've got two better boys." Gesturing to Chataway, he said, "He's the one who makes me work—and keeps me amused. He will soon run a four-minute mile himself." After more champagne and dancing, Bannister took the microphone and sang "Time on My Hands."

At 4:30 A.M. the morning newspapers were delivered to the club's door. A photograph of Bannister breaking through the tape was plastered across the front pages: "The Triumph of R. G. Bannister" read the *Times;* "This Magnificent Man" swooned the *Daily Mail;* "Wonderful Bannister!" headlined the *Daily Mirror;* "At Last—The 4-Minute Mile" crooned the *Daily Express.* Amid details of the race, Bannister was praised for restoring honor to British sport after so many years of defeat and ignominy. He was heralded as a national treasure whose name would be on the lips of millions of people throughout the world once they read of his achievement on their front pages. "The Empire is saved," claimed one editorial. "Roar, Lion, Roar! There's been nothing to compare with this since the destruction of the Spanish Armada. Let the Aga Khan take such satisfaction as he may from his Epsom Derby winners. Let Ben Hogan have the British Open title and welcome. England has the four-minute mile."

As dawn neared the day's events began to take their toll on Bannister, and he finally called his celebration to an end. National hero or not, he had to show up at the hospital that morning and needed to catch at least a couple of hours of sleep. Chataway dropped him off at Brasher's house in Highgate. Brasher left his mother a note that the miler would be down for breakfast, and then he and Chataway quickly jumped back in the car with their dates and headed off to Beachy Head, two hours away, to watch the sunrise. When Bannister arrived at St. Mary's in the late morning, he was given a royal welcome. His fellow students paraded him through the front entrance on a chair and showered him with hundreds of telegrams sent to the hospital. In the afternoon he traveled to Oxford to escape the attention and spent some time with the Wendens. Then he returned to visit his parents in Harrow, carrying a suitcase full of congratulatory notes and telegrams. Press from around the world were cordoned around the front of his house. Reporters had been tracking his movements throughout the day. To avoid their flashbulbs and demands for more interviews, he climbed a series of fences leading to the back of his house.

Later, when he left to meet with Brasher and Chataway on top of Harrow Hill, he used the same route. With London unfolded before them, they had a moment of quiet together. They had not expected such an uproar. Bannister had won headlines in literally thousands of papers, and he was credited for demonstrating that in life "the impossible is no longer out of reach." Together they had achieved the ultimate in sport, but it was just that: sport. As amateurs, this was not supposed to be their defining achievement. There was much more to the world than running. There was real work with real consequences to be done.

"Now life in earnest was beginning," Bannister said, and there was much they wanted to do: Bannister in medicine, Brasher in business, and Chataway in politics. They believed that their pursuit of the four-minute mile had shown the way. Their single-minded focus was the reason Bannister had beaten Landy and Santee to the barrier. As Brasher said later of their conversation, "We honestly believed that, if you have a dream and you work to make it come true, then you really can change the world. There's just nothing you can't do."

As Bannister walked around the old graveyard with his friends, he realized that before he turned to medicine full-time, there was still one thing he needed to prove to himself as an athlete. Since the Helsinki debacle, he had been accused of being incapable of winning a race against the best in the world. Sure, he ran well against the clock. But did he have the ability to win in heated competition? He had yet to answer this question, not only for his critics but for himself. Until he did, he would not be content.

In Turku, Finland, on May 10, after a light half-hour jog in the morning, John Landy sat down in his hotel room to write to Len McRae. Of his many friends, McRae knew better than most how seriously Landy took his running and the pressure he had been under since he ran his 4:02.1 mile in December 1952. In the letter Landy described his trip to Scandinavia—the fellow passenger on his flight who'd had a bit too much "grog," the gift from his hosts, on his arrival, of a new track suit and spikes. Of Bannister's record, which his running mates back in Australia thought was a dishonest effort because of the pacemaking, Landy had only a few words to say: "Heard a rumour that Roger ran 3:59.4, which makes a guy look rather slow!!! However, I am not unduly pessimistic. In fact, I am reasonably confident of recording my best figures for one mile on 31st May."

Even to one of his closest friends, Landy didn't want to promise too much, but he was feeling very good about his chances in the days ahead. There was no better place in the world to train and race. Turku was a quiet old city at the mouth of the Aurajoki River. The surrounding seven hills had paths cut through them on which he could run. They were bedded with pine needles and banked with virgin forest, rivers, and lakes. The air was cool and had an inspiring freshness to it. Here in the hometown of Paavo Nurmi, whose feats were spoken about in the whispers of legend, running was revered, and the city stadium's track was cared for in the way a mother dotes on her dearest child.

When Landy arrived, the black cinder track was dimpled and uneven from the ice that was still frozen underneath. Over the intervening two weeks the ice had melted, and the groundsmen had rolled and smoothed out the cinders. Landy found it electrifyingly fast, though he had to shorten his stride a little because the bounce from the track tended to tire his legs out more quickly. When he adjusted to the bounce, however, he easily ran fifty-seven-second laps. Once he reached the proper pace, maintaining his speed required less effort than it did in Australia. He was so impressed with the track that he took a core sample of it to be examined back in Melbourne.

In the three weeks leading up to his first race in Turku, Landy trained every day, sometimes twice a day. The newspapers had detailed how Bannister's interval session of ten 440s at a 58.9-second average was a key marker that he was ready for his attempt. Landy was regularly running the same session over a second faster. On occasion he ran repeat 440s with only a half-lap interval jog in between and still came one-tenth of a second faster than Bannister averaged. If hard training sessions were the only factor, Landy was sure to beat the Englishman's time. Denis Johansson, who often trained with Landy and timed some of his trial runs, felt that it would take more than superior fitness, however. "Running is not only physical," he explained. "If it were, you could put a great bull-like guy to it and he'd break every record. . . . You must have some greater thing than yourself to push it."

Landy believed that the track conditions and his running form were enough to give him the edge he needed. Two days before his race, Wes Santee provided some extra incentive by running a 4:01.3, the second-fastest mile in history. He had the pacemaking help of his two teammates, Lloyd Koby and Art Dalzell, through the first three laps. Now another miler had beaten Landy past the longtime mark held by Gundar

Haegg, and the Kansan was likely to better this time in early June once he recovered from a leg muscle strain and faced the tough competition at the Compton Invitational.

When Landy arrived at Turku's stadium on May 31, meet posters tacked to the walls had a banner running across the top that read: "Come and See the World Record Broken." He hoped to live up to the advertising. With ten thousand people in the stands, Landy stepped to the line with three Finns: Denis Johansson, Urho Vaharanta, and Olavi Vuorisalo. Much had changed in the two short years since his last overseas race. Unlike his experience at the Olympics, the spectators knew his name and expected a mile time out of him that none of their countrymen could equal. Landy was as charged and confident as he had ever been. Although he would have preferred to run the mile record in his hometown, doing so in front of Finns, who were the most devoted track fans in the world, was a close second.

Vaharanta bolted from the start into an early lead, but Landy kept close. In the backstretch he overtook the Finn and took charge of the race, finishing the first lap in a blazing fifty-six seconds. His time was read over the public-address system in English, but Landy couldn't make out the words. He thought his first lap was fifty-eight seconds. In the second lap Johansson tried to stay close to Landy, attempting to spark a little competitive struggle to help him. The Australian was maintaining too fast a pace, however. He finished the second lap in fifty-nine seconds, giving him a half-mile time of 1:55. Again Landy thought he was two seconds slower, but so eager was he to be racing that his legs were fooling his head.

By the bell Landy's time was 2:57, a second and a half faster than he had planned to run the first three laps, and he began to pay for his lack of pace judgment. In the backstretch he began losing momentum, and his face contorted into a mask of torture. The effort to continue onward was enormous. The encouragement from the stands glanced off his leaden legs, and for the last one hundred yards he looked altogether finished. Still, when he broke through the tape, the stopwatches registered his best time ever: 4:01.6.

Johansson finished next, ten seconds behind him. Landy was unusually candid about what he thought of the race and his future chances. Yes, he had poorly managed his pace, but he considered himself at a level as good as—and in terms of training probably better than—Bannister or Santee. "I'm not a four-minute miler yet," Landy said after the run, "but I soon will be."

"If you hooked Bannister onto the Twentieth Century Limited [train], he couldn't beat Santee." The young Kansan referred to himself in the third person in his statements to a crowd of reporters before he boarded a plane to Los Angeles for the Compton Invitational. He explained that he had never felt in better shape.

"Why do you think you could defeat the first four-minute miler?"

"Bannister ran his super mile without pressure. . . . I am confident that I can beat any and all comers in a mile footrace."

"Will you set a new record on Saturday?"

"California weather and track conditions are just right for championship running. I intend to run extra fast on the coast."

It was Thursday, June 3, and Santee felt the noose tightening around what remained of his running career. He had graduated, and real life loomed. He needed to report for Marine officer training day in Quantico, Virginia, in ten days. He had only two races left: the Compton Invitational, which Bannister would not make because of his medical board exams, and the open mile at the Southern Pacific AAU meet, where Josey Barthel would challenge him. Santee still desperately wanted to break the four-minute mile, and he also wanted to have the chance to run against the Briton and the Australian, perhaps even at the Empire Games in Vancouver if it could be arranged with the AAU and British Empire officials. Bannister and Landy had been his rivals too long to not have a showdown among them. If Santee did not run a record mile, this was not likely to happen. Easton was engaged in a letter campaign to get the Marines to allow Santee further leave, and if Santee had a sub-four-minute mile to his name, the publicity he would earn for the military by racing against Bannister and Landy might be worth it. With milers Ingvar Ericcson (the Swedish champion) and Russ Bonham (the Whittier College star) slated to challenge him that Saturday, he was hopeful that he might get that chance. It might be his last.

The month of May had been defined by endings. On May 6, of course, his dream of being the first to break the four-minute barrier was finished. He had to suffer endless reports of Bannister's run. It was emblazoned on theater signboards thanks to Fox Movietone News, which had distributed the BBC film footage across the country. At his next meet he set a new collegiate two-mile record and then led his Jay-hawks to their third straight—and his last—Big Seven outdoor track and field championship. Two days before the month's end he represented the University of Kansas in his final race as a student, clocking his best mile time of 4:01.3. Because Easton had made an error on his application for the NCAA championships during Santee's freshman year, the AAU had banned the miler from competing in the NCAA Championships his senior year. No doubt Santee would have won, but his collegiate athletic career had to conclude without that victory.

But none of this would matter to Santee if he managed a record run in Compton. When he arrived in California, Al Franken gave him the star treatment once again. There were numerous television and radio appearances and time spent on the set of a Mitzi Gaynor and Ethel Merman picture. But Santee had a single focus: being the first American to break the mile barrier. It was not quite the first ever, but sadly there was nothing he could do about that now. Although none of his countrymen were as close as he was, an unknown runner could burst on the scene—much as Landy had done almost eighteen months before. Santee would not rest easy until he had run under four minutes himself.

On the afternoon of June 5 he sat in the locker room at Ramsaur Field, ten minutes before his race. He had already done his warm-up jog and sprints, and Easton was taping up his shoes for him, pulling the tape from the outside step, over the spikes, and tight around the instep. This added strength to the arches of Santee's feet.

"How do you feel? Everything okay?" his coach asked. Santee nodded, quiet as ever before a race. Easton patted him on the shoes and said, "Go get 'em."

It was, for California, a cool June afternoon, barely sixty degrees. In the stands, Santee's wife and her parents were watching him through field glasses. They had driven through the night from Kansas to be there. Santee left the locker room and arrived at the starting line just as the race was about to begin. Easton had followed him out to find a place to stand on the back straight.

Track officials, timekeepers, photographers, and television camera-men crowded the infield by the starting line. The timekeepers were reminded to start their watches at the sight of smoke out of the gun, not at the sound of the bang itself, to account for any delay between the shot and its sound reaching them. Everything had to be right for his attempt.

The runners positioned themselves along the line, Santee in the inside lane, his left arm up, his right foot back, facing straight ahead. His former high school rival, Billy Tidwell, who had beaten him in his senior year, was ready to help pace Santee for as long as he could hold, but they certainly had no strict lap schedule planned out as Bannister had done. They shot from the line, Marty Montgomery of the University of Southern California moving into an early lead in the first lap. Montgomery knew he needed to give it everything he had in order to challenge the "Ashland Antelope." Santee stayed back in third position, Bonham just ahead of him. The crowd of eight thousand, at least one in five of whom were waving the Jayhawk symbol, were quiet.

By the end of the first lap Montgomery had run himself out. Tidwell strode past Santee, then Bonham, then Montgomery, taking the lead a few yards into the second lap. Santee continued to hold back, having decided with Easton that he would wait until the second half-mile before he really took off. Still, his first lap was run in 58.1 seconds, pretty quick. As they moved into the back straight, however, his coach yelled out. "It's not fast enough. Not fast enough." Santee heard Easton, but he wanted to ride Tidwell out as long as he possibly could. By the start of the third lap, having run the first half-mile in 1:58.2, Santee knew he would have to take the lead. Tidwell simply couldn't keep the pace fast enough. As Santee made his way into the turn, he was already past his former rival, alone now against the clock. He felt a surge of energy. He was going for the mile record.

The crowd began to chant his name. "Santee! Santee! Santee!" Applause started to mount. Danna and her parents sensed that this could be it.

Santee stormed around the track, pushing himself to clock a good time in the third lap. It had always been his most difficult. At that point Ericsson and Bonham were barely clipping at his heels, and it was unlikely they would challenge him. Coming out of the first turn, Santee heard Easton again, "Faster! Faster!" At the bell Santee was under three minutes by a second. He had managed the third in 60.3 seconds.

"Santee! Santee! Santee!" the crowd called in unison.

One more lap. He just needed to run it in under sixty-one seconds. This was the moment to kick, to put aside the pain and give it everything.

In the back straight Easton shouted: "Go! Go, Wes, go!"

As the miler went into the last turn he was tiring badly. Each stride was harder than the one before. He was pumping his arms higher to keep up his speed. His breathing was heavier in his chest. He could barely hear the crowd now—it felt as if he were running in a tunnel. With only a hundred yards to go, he suddenly felt cold. His hands were clammy, and his shoulders seemed to shake. He sensed himself losing feeling in his arms and legs. Still he drove on, past the 1,500-meter mark at the top of the curve where a timekeeper was stationed. Now he just had the straight, and it would be over.

"Santee! Santee! Santee!" The stands were thundering.

He was long past exhaustion as he neared the tape. His legs continued to drive, almost with their own will. This was everything he had. At the finish he pushed his shoulders forward, and the timekeepers punched their stop buttons. Santee continued down the track as he slowed into a jog. His first thought was, Have I done it?

He turned back to the timekeepers, Easton rushing to his side. "I think we're close," he said. "We're really close."

Finally the crackle of the public-address system quieted down the stands. They were going to announce his time. "Wes Santee has set a new world record in the 1,500 meters with a time of 3:42.8." Easton and his miler shared a look. That was good, but they wanted the mile time.

"Santee! Santee! Santee!" went the crowd again.

Then the stadium went silent as the announcer came back over the speakers. "Now the mile time . . . a new stadium record of four minutes and six-tenths of a second."

It was agonizingly close. Six-tenths of a second close. It was nothing: a flicker of time, an instant faster jump at the start, a slightly favorable breeze, a half-stride, a deeper lean into the tape. It was nothing, but still it was everything.

Santee waved toward Danna, who came hurrying down to the edge of the track. He hugged and kissed her before he had to turn to the bustle of reporters, eager to know what had happened. He had broken the world record for the 1,500 meter, but true greatness had escaped him in the public eye. He was six-tenths of a second shy.

A few days after the race he learned from Easton that the Marines had denied his request for summer leave. He wouldn't have the chance to race Landy and Bannister.

· · ·

On the evening of June 20 John Landy walked around the track at Tur-ku's stadium with Chris Chataway. Twilight was darkening the clear sky, and the air was warm and crisp. The weather promised to be much the same for the mile race the following day. The English runner had flown into the city's small airport earlier in the morning, where Landy and Johansson had greeted him in the simple wooden terminal building.

Only a week before Chataway had won a 1,500-meter race in Amsterdam and afterward sat down with a *News Chronicle* journalist to declare, "I should very much like to race against Landy sometime in the next fortnight. . . . I would not go [to Finland] just as a pacemaker. I would prefer to make a real race of it." After the Iffley Road triumph, Chataway had asked Bannister and Brasher to help pace him in a world-record two-mile attempt. On June 6, in front of forty thousand fans at White City Stadium, Chataway failed in his bid by a mere three-fifths of a second. Both Brasher and Bannister, tired from competing the prior day in mile and half-mile races, respectively, had not been able to assist him as much as they would have liked. After the race Chataway said, "I much prefer racing against men than against the clock. It is much more fun."

Prompted by Denis Johansson, the Turku Athletic Association almost immediately issued Chataway an invitation through the British AAA. Coincidentally, Bannister's world mile record was ratified on the same day. Before Chataway accepted the offer, he made one request: he wanted the 1,500-meter race on June 21 changed to a mile. Everyone agreed. It was obvious to most that Chataway might prove the missing ingredient in Landy's pursuit of a record mile. If Landy managed to beat Bannister's time only weeks later—and without the help of pacing—the achievement at Iffley Road would be diminished in many minds, including Bannister's own. Before Chataway left England, Bannister told his friend, "If you do go, it makes it certain that he will break the four-minute mile." Chataway said there was no such certainty about it. He simply wanted to see how he would fare against the Australian. Although bothered by Chataway's participation in the race, Bannister said nothing else, knowing he had no right to tell another athlete—let alone a friend—when to compete.

In the four races Landy had run since arriving in Scandinavia, he had yet to find what he needed to break a world record, whether the mile or any other distance. In Stockholm a week after his 4:01.6 mile in Turku, Landy ran the same time again, despite having the added support of the presence of his father (who was traveling through Europe with John's uncle and aunt). Perhaps this was the best Landy could do, and Bannister's widely reported prediction that others would soon follow him into sub-four-minute mile territory was simply not true. On the afternoon of June 11, the same day Landy tried and failed to claim a 1,500-meter record in Helsinki, Wes Santee came agonizingly short again, clocking 4:00.7, despite the fact that Olympic gold medalist Josey Barthel was there to challenge him. With his Marine commitment, it looked like the American might not get another shot. Landy didn't have much time left himself to keep cracking his head against his own four-minute barrier. On June 16, although feeling tired from too much racing, Landy managed a 5:12.6 in a 2,000-meter race—eleven seconds faster than his best—but this hardly helped his mile chances.

While walking with Chataway the evening before their race, Landy stopped at the side of the track and looked at the British miler. The Australian knew Chataway had come not in an attempt to pace him, as some in the press had said. Chataway was there to beat him. "I could change into shorts and spikes now," Landy said, "and run a mile in 4:02 with nobody watching and with no competition."

Chataway believed that Landy could do exactly what he said. Unlike himself and Bannister, Landy had trained hard enough to run good times week after week without much strain. This gave him a toughness, physically and mentally, that Chataway felt he simply didn't have. The English runner would have to run the best mile of his life if he was to have any chance at winning, particularly since his fastest mile was 4:07.2.

The next afternoon Landy had a late lunch with Johansson, enjoying a beer with his Finnish host and feeling confident. Before Chataway arrived in Turku, Landy had run three time trials—200 meters in twenty-three seconds, 300 meters in thirty-seven seconds, and 400 meters in forty-nine seconds—showing how sharp his speed was. As he later said, he was "fit as a trout." With the British miler threatening him, Landy believed that in his seven o'clock race he might well make his own bit of history. Johansson agreed, having timed Landy in his trials. The Finn offered to arrange for a pacesetter in the race, but Landy declined. He wanted to do it on his own.

At seven o'clock, forty-six days after Bannister broke through the barrier that had withstood decades of assault, Landy wished his competitors good luck and settled into his lane at the starting line. He wore white shorts and his Geelong Guild singlet with number 2 pinned to his chest. Chataway was number 1 in all white, and Johansson number 3 in all black. Three other milers, including the young Finnish ace Antte Kallio, were lined up alongside them. June 21 was the longest day in the year, and the sun was still bright in the sky. The weather was ideal: seventy degrees and no wind. Eight thousand Finnish fans jammed into the small Turku stadium, anticipating a great race, particularly with this redheaded Chataway fellow who had served as hare for the first four-minute miler. A number of journalists, many of whom had flown in for the event, were also in attendance.

As the gun trailed smoke from its barrel, the six runners bolted from the line. Kallio, who started third from the post, quickly angled his way toward the inside line past Chataway. Moving into the first turn, Landy positioned himself a stride behind Kallio's right shoulder, letting him take the lead. Landy wanted to run as evenly paced as possible, in contrast to his May 31 race. Three-quarters of the way through the first lap, they maintained this position, with Chataway in third place, two strides back, and Johansson in fourth. Landy finished the first lap in 58.5, Kallio ahead by half a second. The Australian was running smoothly, his form ideal—high knee lift, eased shoulders, center of gravity balanced, heel-to-toe roll as his shoes hit the track. He was a very different runner from two years before.

At a lap and a half Landy decided to take the lead. He had waited longer than usual, but Kallio looked to be tiring from such a strong early pace. Nearing the halfway mark, Landy was decidedly in control, with Chataway ten feet behind him. Kallio, Johansson, and the rest of the field were forgotten. It was a two-man race. Chataway thought that if he held close to Landy, he could dash ahead of the Australian in the final straight. At the start of the third lap, the stopwatches registered an average 1:57.9—an ideal pace. Landy thought he had the race in hand. He had been in this position many times, and his competitors always folded by the first turn in the final lap.

The third lap was steady and sure. Landy's rhythm was good, and he continued to run relaxed. The sound of his feet striking the cinder track had the steady beat of a metronome. This was the pause before Landy gathered the focus and determination that he would need to maintain a fast pace through the last lap. The lead did not change, and the two milers further distanced themselves from the field. The crowd was expectant, but with Landy, they had been here before. They knew enough of middle-distance running to understand that the proof was in the final lap.

At the bell the time was impressive—2:56. Landy was surprised to hear Chataway so close behind him at this late stage in the race. He was two strides back—incredible, given the pace. Nobody had ever been able to keep up with him this far. Nonetheless, Landy did not break. Yes, the British runner was good, but he had to fail soon, another hundred yards at most. If Landy broke too fast too soon, he would not have the drive to finish strong. He had seized up around the last turn into the final straight too many times before.

When Landy reached the second-to-last turn, three-quarters of a lap from the finish, the indefatigable Chataway was still on his shoulder. This was it, Landy thought. If he slowed, the British runner would surely pounce. Landy had to go. He got onto his toes and said to himself, NOW! As Landy accelerated away from him, Chataway never had a chance to hold: five yards and then ten separated them in what seemed a blink of the eye. It was incredible to Chataway. Bannister had needed him and Brasher to carry him around the track for over three laps before he made his kick. On the other hand, Landy managed nearly the entire race from the front and still had the reserve to drive toward the finish with such speed. It was an amazing display of self-reliance.

Suddenly the crowd realized what was happening. They began chanting, "Landy! Landy! Landy!"

The Australian had to be tiring, but he maintained his rhythm as he moved into the last turn heading toward the finish line. The stands boomed his name louder and louder. Timekeepers positioned at the 1,500-meter mark looked at their watches after he passed. It was world-record fast—3:41.8. Blistering.

Landy did not hear the crowd or know his time. Having broken away from Chataway, Landy focused solely on fighting the pain and tension to sustain form. Don't fight the stride, he told himself. His legs continued to drive down the track. It was impossible to know if they were slowing. He willed himself faster, though the effect was only to maintain his speed. When he broke through the tape, there was no great leap forward. He looked almost as if he planned to continue down the track.

Turning, he saw Chataway finish almost forty yards behind him. Landy had no idea what he had run. It felt fast, maybe 4:01 or 4:02. The Finnish miler Vuorisalo passed the finish line next, then Johansson.

Kallio came last. The eight thousand spectators waited anxiously for the time. Finally, the announcer came on to the public-address system and spoke a few words in Finnish. Pandemonium erupted throughout the stadium. Landy didn't understand the words but knew he had done something spectacular to evoke this response. Johansson angled toward him as the stands emptied and hundreds of cheering Finns surrounded Landy.

"A new world record," Johansson yelled to him. "3:58!"

Landy was stunned but had only a moment to register that he had beaten Bannister's time by over a second and a half before he was hoisted onto the shoulders of a mass of people. The Finns raised him up and down like a trophy over their heads. Camera flashbulbs exploded ahead of him. He was carried forward, nearly horizontal, arms above his head. He had finally done it.

Eventually the crowd let his feet touch the track again, and Johansson told him he should run the "Lap of Honor." Landy found Chataway, who had run his best time of 4:04.4, and asked him to come along. There was no way he could have done it without him, Landy said.

"No, no. It's your achievement," Chataway said. "It's you they want to see."

Finally Landy threaded his way out of the crowd and began running slowly around the track. Thunderous applause followed him, and the Australian flag was raised over the stadium. After two years of concentrated effort and countless races run well but deemed failures, the mile record was his and by a staggering margin.

16

The possibilities in racing tactics are almost unlimited, as in a game of chess, for every move there is a counter, for every attack there is a defence. . . . The runner's greatest asset, apart from essential fitness of body, is a cool and calculating brain allied to confidence and courage. Above all, he must have a will to win.
—FRANZ STAMPFL
Franz Stampfl on Running (1955)

HALF AN HOUR after Landy crossed the finish line, Bannister answered the door at his Harrow home to field questions from journalists. He was expecting them, having heard on the radio the report of the 3:58 mile.

"Roger, what do you think of Landy's run?" asked one of the journalists crowded at his doorstep, notebook in hand.

"It is a wonderful achievement, and I send Landy my heartiest congratulations," Bannister said. He artfully masked his shock that the Australian had managed to bring down his record by such a decisive degree. He had expected Landy to run under four minutes because of Chataway's presence, but not by two seconds. "Landy had tried so hard, and I am very glad that he has now succeeded. It shows that times can always be broken."

"What next?"

The moment Bannister heard the radio announcement he knew that everything had changed. The race against Landy in the Empire

Games would no longer be just another race. That he had broken the barrier first was almost meaningless now, particularly if the Australian beat him in face-to-face competition.

"I look forward very much to racing against Landy in Vancouver in August," Bannister explained calmly. "But I don't expect that his time will be broken in a race of that kind with twelve men running."

"Will you try to break Landy's record in the near future then?"

He smiled. "I don't know."

When Bannister finally managed to close the door on the reporters, he faced the fact that his greatest race was not six weeks in the past but rather six weeks in the future. Beating 3:58 was, if not completely impossible, the least of his worries. Though he continued to go to the Duke of York's Barracks, he had allowed his training to lose focus; his running, as he described it, was in the "doldrums." Since May 6, he had been pulled in every direction except toward the track.

A few days after his Iffley Road triumph he was shipped off to the United States for what could only be called a victory tour encouraged by the British Foreign Office. Upon landing at New York's Idlewild Airport, he was beset by controversy. The television program *I've Got a Secret* had paid for the trip, and since the show was commercially sponsored—and by none other than a cigarette manufacturer—Bannister risked losing his amateur status if he appeared on it. The appearance had to be canceled, and his expenses repaid. Still, he participated in a number of interviews, reaching a reported total of 75 million people and answering questions such as "Do you think you will be knighted by the queen?" ("Good gracious me!") and "What do you think of American girls?" ("They have a certain uniformity as you see them on the street, but I am sure that individually they are delightful.") Then he stumbled into another mess when the Olympic Committee of Southern California presented him with the "Miracle Mile Trophy," which had been created years before for the first athlete to run the landmark achievement. A firestorm erupted when reporters discovered that the trophy was worth £178—exactly £166 more than an amateur could accept in prizes. Bannister returned to England with a miniature replica valued at £12.

Once back in London he plunged into his medical exams. "You sweated blood over them," a contemporary of his at St. Mary's explained. First was a series of three-hour essay tests in medicine, surgery, obstetrics, pharmacology, and several other fields. Second was the practical exam in which he was presented with a patient and had forty-five minutes to take a history and do a full examination. At the end he had to give a diagnosis and treatment plan. If he missed something serious, he failed. After eight years of preparation, there was a great deal at stake.

His studies left little time for a social life, but during the summer he began to see a young Swedish woman named Moyra Jacobsson, a talented artist with a studio in St. Albans Grove in London. Her father was chief economist for the Bank for International Settlements. She was decidedly underwhelmed by Bannister's achievements on the track. He joked, "I am quite sure she was under the impression that I had run four miles in one minute." No doubt she was intriguing for this reason as well as for her striking looks and wide-ranging interests. The two had a chance to meet only a couple of times that summer, but Bannister wanted to get to know her better once he qualified as a doctor and returned from Vancouver.

When Bannister participated in races, his results were lackluster at best. At the British Games on June 4 at White City Stadium he ran the half-mile and lost to Czechoslovakia's Stanislav Jungwirth. The next day he saw his picture on the front page of newspapers, his jersey spattered with mud while Jungwirth breasted the tape in front of him. "Here's Mud in Your Eye," Bannister joked to himself about what the headline would read, knowing how fickle the press was. Two days later he tried to help Chataway claim the two-mile world record and struggled through the second half of the race, finishing sixth. As Bannister expected, the British press seized on these failures, particularly with Jungwirth, as evidence that Bannister was better against the clock than man to man. It appeared that they were just as good at toppling kings as they were at making them. Some thought Bannister was scared of the infighting and jockeying for position, the type of rough competition that made mile races so appealing to fans. The *Daily Mirror* wrote most pointedly:

There is a world of difference between racing for time and racing to win. The white line and clear course are needed for the one; generalship, ability to change pace, and track tactics for the other. And Bannister is not strong in these latter qualities. For that he can blame his policy of keeping actual racing to a minimum.

If the miler was going to have a chance at the Empire Games and the European Championships, the pundits recommended that he start running in more races to get the feel of competition. Now that Landy had claimed a new world record, a "titanic clash" between the two milers was expected in Vancouver. Bannister had to get cracking. After all, in many circles he was now perceived as the underdog.

Bannister, in typical fashion, ignored the press's advice. Nonetheless, he started preparing in earnest for his showdown with Landy immediately after the news arrived from Turku. He quickly reintensified his training efforts. But more important, he began strategizing about how to run against this miler who had crossed the finish line in 3:58, and moments afterward, according to Chataway, looked like he had simply gone out for a Sunday afternoon jog.

In the evening after Landy ran the fastest race of his life, he retreated uncomfortably from the spotlight. Of the glare of publicity he later said, "It's not really life. You have to see it for what it is. It's not what it's all about." His motivation had always been to excel, but it was not about acclaim or records for their own sake. The attention was simply something to cope with as best as he could. He attended a celebratory party, thrown for him in a house on a lake, but after a few beers he left early, surprising Chataway and Johansson. He knew they didn't understand his lack of elation. His 3:58 mile brought him a strong sense of accomplishment, yet he had run it without much strain, and as he explained, "It was done. Finished. Next thing."

He was the only one to take the record with equanimity. Such was his achievement that Finland's prime minister, Urho Kekkonen, who was a former Olympic high-jumper and friend of Paavo Nurmi, presented Landy with the Kekkonen Cup, an honor never before awarded to anyone other than a Finnish athlete. His friends back home literally cheered into their radios as they listened to the June 21 race. His family was awakened in the middle of the night with the news. The phone in their East Malvern home rang nonstop until the morning, and Landy's mother sent a telegram to her son that read: "Thrilled with superb run [stop] Best news ever [stop] Mother." The Australian papers reveled in their great hero, who predicted, "I can do even better." Landy was noted for his "unquenchable, indomitable spirit," and the observation was made that "perseverance should be his middle name." In the *Melbourne*

Sun, his 3:58 mile was shown in comparison to previous world-record times, the illustration detailing how in a race he would have finished ten yards ahead of Bannister, twenty-five yards ahead of Gundar Haegg, and over sixty-five yards in front of Wooderson and Cunningham. An *Age* editorial remarked that Landy had bolstered national pride and then explained that "sportsmen, as well as statesmen, carry a heavy responsibility for our good name. So long as they are of the Landy type, they will not let us down." Over Melbourne's Town Hall the same Australian Olympic flag that had been flown at Helsinki was raised high once again, this time in honor of John Landy, and Victorian amateur officials suggested naming Olympic Park after the great miler. When reporters tracked down Percy Cerutty, he once again took credit for coaching this national treasure and also explained that "I have always said that Landy could run 3:57. No miler in the world has covered the training miles in twelve months that John has."

The next day Landy escaped the crush of attention thanks to Johansson, who arranged for a trip to Naantali, a small, secluded island outside Turku where the miler could relax and take a hike along the wooded shoreline. Over the next week the story about the upcoming clash with Bannister at the Empire Games gathered momentum in the news. Still, Landy did not want to talk about his running. When Geoff Warren, who had been competing in England and Norway prior to Vancouver, came to visit him in Finland, Landy barely let his friend utter a word about the 3:58 record before shifting the conversation to Warren's recent 5,000-meter race in Oslo. Landy knew about it in detail. "It took a major effort to be able to get him to hear my congratulations," Warren later said.

Despite his reluctance to discuss his running, in the three weeks before his arrival in Vancouver on July 15 Landy himself thought plenty about it. His "next thing," the second of his two ambitions, was winning the mile race in the Empire Games against Bannister. He knew it would be a big deal: the die was cast when he beat Bannister's time. As Landy later described it:

The race had the ingredients for a world title fight. On the one hand, they said you couldn't run four minutes, and there's a guy who does it. Seven weeks later someone betters his time. They're both going to represent their countries. There was no pacing, no artificiality. I was going to try to win from the front. He was going to try to hang on. It was almost an unbelievable set of circumstances.

Running a mile was an art form created from speed and stamina. Illustrating that these two elements could be applied very differently, Bannister and Landy pursued diametrically opposed styles. From what Bannister had read and heard of the Australian—and he tried to learn as much as possible—Landy was a "front-runner," the kind of miler, in track and field parlance, who sets a breakneck pace from the beginning, leaving his foes choking on his dust and unable to catch him in the last lap. Landy relied on his pace judgment and confidence in his superior fitness to crush his opponents. Bannister was a "racer," or "positional runner," who stayed back, letting milers like Landy carry him around the track, making sure to stay close enough—or "in contact"—so that by the bell he could strike with a fast finishing kick. Both styles had advantages and disadvantages, and in the mile all decisions on how fast to set the pace, when to break contact, and when to start one's kick had to be made quickly through a haze of exhaustion. But an athlete could prepare in advance to improve his chances. He simply had to begin the race from the understanding that, much like an artist sketching the lines of a painting, he could not know which colors and shades of color would best play off one another until the first brush strokes were made.

In developing his strategy, Bannister had Chataway, who had not only brought back Landy's times broken down in hundred-meter splits from his races in Finland but knew what it was to compete against him. Prior to this, the most insight that Bannister had into the Australian was from Percy Cerutty's overblown statements that he had read in track and field journals: that in Landy there was a "ruthlessness, lack of feeling for others, and a ferocity and antagonism, albeit mostly vented on himself, that makes it possible on occasions for John to rise to sublime heights of physical endeavor." Chataway had experienced Landy firsthand. He had walked around the track with him the night before his 3:58 mile and seen the Australian after his record run. "It was a solemn moment for him," Chataway would later recall:

All the people gathered around him were not looking at it the same way he was. He was not ebullient or over the moon. It was as if this was an entirely private achievement, something he wanted, worked for, struggled for one hell of a lot of time, and suddenly it had arrived. It was almost like having the world's press descend on your wedding night. This was entirely private to him.

The Australian was driven by a demand to push himself to the limit. He drove fast from the beginning, never looking back. A race was less about what others were doing and more about personal challenge. Part of this had to do with the fact that Landy was never threatened in Australia—and this was thus the only kind of racing he knew—but part of it came from the kind of person he was as well. There was no doubt that in Vancouver he would take the lead and try to run the legs out from under Bannister.

To make sure this was his strategy, Bannister decided to send a message to Landy. The Australian might have been physically tougher, but Bannister had the ability to deliver a withering finish out of sheer will. At the AAA Championships on July 10, a day after he qualified as a doctor, he ran the first three laps of the mile race at a moderate pace, staying back in the pack. One hundred yards after the bell he burst forward into the lead and drove at a flat-out pace to the finish, clocking a last lap at 53.8 seconds for a mile time of 4:07.6. If Landy had questions about Bannister's kick, they were answered now.

In the woods outside Quantico, Virginia, Santee was kneeling in the dirt, fumbling with the straps of his backpack for yet another hourlong hike through the woods in the hot mid-July sun. His M-1 rifle was leaning against a nearby tree.

"Candidate," a voice said sternly above him.

Santee looked up to see J. D. Roberts, the former Oklahoma football star, towering above him and wearing the stripes of a lieutenant. "Yes, sir," Santee said.

"We want you to carry that rifle. It's not to be away from your body. You sleep with it. You take it to the latrine. Do you understand?"

"Yes, sir," he said, throwing his backpack over his shoulder and grabbing his rifle as the others in his platoon began moving away. He followed quickly behind them, his shirt sticking to his chest from a long afternoon of marching. It was his third week of boot camp, but this was his first day of training. While the others in his platoon had already been taught how to fire their rifles and pack their gear in the previous two weeks, Santee had been busy elsewhere.

The past month had been a whirlwind. On June 11 at Memorial Stadium in Los Angeles he had entered into the final lap of his race against Josey Barthel two strides behind. Three minutes flat had elapsed on the clock, and once again he was in perfect position to be the first American to run the magic four-minute mile. Barthel then surged ahead, looking as if he wanted to break away from Santee by the backstretch. Santee knew he needed to maintain an even pace if he was going to run under four minutes, but he couldn't risk Barthel winning the race. Halfway down the back straight, 220 yards from the finish, Santee coiled and sprang past Barthel like "a shot out of a gun." The crowd was mad with excitement as Santee decisively retook the lead. But one hundred yards from the finish, Santee lost speed, albeit only a fraction. His burst to gain the lead had tied up his legs. He broke the tape in 4:00.7 — once again just tenths of a second too slow.

After the race Barthel came up to him. "Why did you go past me? I was setting it up for you." It took Santee a moment to realize what Barthel had just said. He was stunned. The Luxembourg miler had moved past him in the final lap in an effort to pace him to the finish. If Santee had just hung on to him until the last one hundred yards instead of running his legs out on the backstretch, he could have had his record. Afterward Santee had very little to say to reporters. It was devastating for him to come so close for the second time, but he kept that to himself. "I'm leaving my running to the Marines this summer," he told them. "I hope they will let me get away for a few meets but I certainly don't want to be a coddled athlete."

A couple of days later Santee and his wife packed their clothes in Lawrence and said their good-byes. When Santee went to the ROTC center to pick up his orders, a Marine major stopped him at the door. "I know you think you're a big hotshot athlete," he said, "but you're going down there to do your basic training. Got that?" Santee nodded his head, "Yes, sir."

In Quantico, only moments after arriving and in the process of collecting his boots and fatigues, a jeep pulled alongside his platoon and the driver yelled out, "Candidate Santee?"

He stepped forward. "Here, sir."

"Come here."

Santee was carrying his boots and an armful of shirts. "What am I supposed to do with this stuff?"

"Leave it there."

Minutes later Santee stepped into the office of General Clifton Cates, commandant of the Marine Corps School—or "God," as some called the steely-eyed, sixty-one-year-old three-star general who had first distinguished himself at the Battle of Verdun in World War I. "Nice to meet you, Wes," the general said, shaking his hand and then moving back behind his desk. "Good to have you here. We're proud to have you as a Marine. Now next weekend we're having the All Marine Corps track meet at Camp Lejeune in North Carolina. If you represent Quantico, we can win this thing."

"Thank you, sir. But I'm here to do my military training."

"I know, but we have all kinds of Marines coming in for the meet. We can win this thing if you run."

"I need to get my military duty out of the way, sir." Santee looked to his right, where a Marine major was shaking his head up and down, indicating that he should say yes or suffer the consequences. "When I left Kansas, I was told that I couldn't do any running down here. What am I supposed to do?"

"Hey, look," the three-star general said calmly. "If I say it's okay . . . it's okay."

An hour later Santee was in a staff car on his way to North Carolina. He did not even have time to call Danna to tell her that he was leaving. She had to read about it in a newspaper, after which she drove down to join him. At the meet Santee raced in the mile, the half-mile, and the relays. He won them all and earned Quantico a first-place trophy. That night he received a phone call from General Cates. "Fine job. . . . By the way, stay down another week, because we're going to host the All-Services Championships."

While Santee was in North Carolina, news of Landy's 3:58 broke, and the press hounded Santee for a comment. Given how close the Australian had come in the previous month, Santee was not surprised. "People who have concentrated in the manner that Landy and Bannister have may eventually run a mile in 3:55," the cadet said. He resented that he had not been able to do the same. When he was allowed to focus himself in the same way, an opportunity that would have to wait until his three-month Marine training was completed, Santee advised reporters not to exclude him from the list of milers capable of the feat. He already had his plan: in the fall he would do intensive, cross-country training mixed with short sprints on the track; in the winter he would race on the indoor circuit to sharpen his speed; and in the spring of 1955 he would be ready. "I'm going to train as hard as I can and sacrifice everything I have to bring the mile record back to the United States," he promised.

When Santee returned to basic training after leading the Marines to triumph in the All-Services Championship, thoughts of four-minute barriers and mile races were lost to the demands of Quantico. He had to play catch-up learning how to be a soldier, and lieutenants like Roberts offered no special treatment for Santee now that General Cates was finished with him. Although the Kansas miler was in better shape than others in his platoon—he handled the long marches like he was out for a stroll—boot camp had other challenges. Week after week, as Santee was instructed on marksmanship, orienteering, survival skills, and hand-to-hand combat, his name disappeared from track and field headlines and his hopes of a great showdown with Bannister and Landy faded.

After Landy set his mile record in Turku, he began training again in earnest for the Empire Games, slated to start on July 30. Mostly he concentrated on speed work, running repeat 800 meters with two laps of jogging in between. He had been in racing form since December 1953, a long period in which to keep at top pitch without a break, but his relentless training kept him going.

As for his strategy, there was never really any question of how he would run his race. Even when he read of Bannister's July 10 last lap of 53.8, which Landy interpreted automatically as a statement from the British miler that "you have no alternative, mate, you have to lead," he did not think of surprising Bannister by playing a waiting game in Vancouver. Johansson advised Landy not to set the pace from the beginning, as he had in his races in Finland. The Finnish miler told him that unless he was able to establish a huge lead running from the front, Bannister would be able to catch him with his kick. Although Landy threw the letter away, Cerutty had much the same advice, telling him to pace the first lap like it was a warm-up and then run like it was a three-lap race.

Tactically, Landy did not have much experience. He had not lost a mile race in almost two years, and every one of those he had led almost from the start. He liked running his opposition into the ground and thought that as long as he set a fast enough pace, Bannister would not have enough leg in the last lap to deliver his kick. This was what Landy had done with Chataway, who finished forty yards back from him in Turku. Landy had read up on Bannister's times, and though he was fit, Landy was fitter. Tactics were fine and good but critical only if the race was settled by a matter of yards. If Landy had his way, he would be so far in front of Bannister that the British miler would have no room to maneuver. More important, Landy simply didn't want to run a slow, jockeying race. He wanted to control it from the start.

On July 11, in response to Bannister's statement at the British Championships the day before, Landy wanted to send a message of his own. In his last race in Finland before leaving for Vancouver, he produced a witheringly fast 1,000-meter run, only half a second shy of the world record in 2:20.9, despite a strong wind and a short 300-meter track. That was the kind of speed that Bannister would have to contend with in their showdown. As Landy later explained, "I felt that this might confuse the issue as to who was going to take the lead in the Vancouver race. Maybe I was going to run a quite different race [than Bannister expected] and use my speed to win tactically by lurking behind him."

Two weeks before the Empire Games were to start, Santee was with his platoon marching with his rifle in one of Quantico's outlying camps when he was told by his commanding officer that he was wanted at company headquarters. A jeep transported him "Mainside," and he was ushered into the office of public affairs. Santee had no idea what to expect.

Santee saluted the Marine captain in charge of the office and stood at attention in front of his desk. The captain went straight to the point. "There's the Bannister and Landy race in Vancouver on August seventh, and NBC wants you to come to New York and do some commentary on it."

Santee swallowed the news. He had no choice in the matter and said, "Yes, sir." For a competitor like him, who had spent years training to be the best in the world in the mile, this was a cruel request. He did not want to watch these two on a monitor and announce the race. He wanted to run it. But because of his Marine obligations and international racing ban, he had no recourse.

"Do you have a dress uniform?" the officer asked.

"No," Santee said. He had spikes and a singlet, he wanted to say, but this was not what he had been asked. Santee must have wondered whether this meeting might have been about his competing against Bannister and Landy if he had found a way to knock six-tenths of a second from his Compton Invitational mile. He had come so close. His AAU fight, his Marine obligation, and his Jayhawk team commitments had kept him from achieving his own ambitions.

A jeep returned him to his platoon. Crawling quickly through the mud underneath strands of barbed wire was the only racing he would be doing in the upcoming days.

On July 15 Landy flew into Vancouver, circling past the city of skyscrapers and the bay's crystal-blue waters dotted with yachts before the airplane's wheels touched down on the tarmac with a screech. While the plane taxied into the airport, Landy looked out the window to see what some called his "film star" welcome. It was simply a mob. Hundreds of fans, autograph seekers, journalists, and cameramen swarmed around the miler, pushing aside the four other Australian athletes traveling with him. And because Landy was proving an economic boom to the city — ticket sales spiked the day after Landy ran his own sub-four-minute mile and had since sold out — Vancouver's mayor had also come to welcome him. Finally the police stepped into the melee, escorting Landy to a waiting car before he was glad-handed to death. But when the official responsible for transporting him to the Empire Village got the door closed, he discovered that only he and Landy were inside. "Oh," the official said. "Where are the other Australians? Can't forget them."

Once the others were found and herded into the car, a motorcycle police escort led them to the Empire Village, where a press conference was waiting. Everyone wanted to know what Landy thought of his chances in the race now being labeled "the Mile of the Century."

On Friday, July 23, Roger Bannister knocked on the door of Franz Stampfl's apartment on King's Road and was welcomed inside. Coach and athlete sat together on the couch while Stampfl's wife made a pot of tea in the small adjoining kitchen.

The Austrian coach had ignored the hype after Bannister's Iffley Road triumph, preferring to slip away quietly and get back to London to train other athletes. He didn't need to stand around and get his picture taken by Bannister's side, and he made no claims that the four-minute mile had been achieved through strict adherence to his coaching. As Stampfl told Pat the evening of May 6, he would have liked to escape from London for a few days because "the heavens are going to open." The only satisfaction Stampfl got from the publicity was the knowledge that it would encourage more athletes to train with him.

Bannister was leaving for Vancouver the following day. Stampfl could not afford to travel with him, nor did he want to be hassled about his role as Bannister's coach. This was therefore their last chance to speak before the Empire Games. Stampfl was convinced that Bannister could beat the Australian, but the coach had to hope that the confidence the English miler gained from May 6 would hold out for his race against Landy.

Over tea and the rumble of the King's Road traffic outside, the two talked strategy. It was largely a conversation of "what ifs." What if Landy played a waiting game? What if the pace was too strong to maintain contact? What if Bannister broke too early and ran out of steam before the finish? Fundamentally, the focus was on this final question. There was no doubt that Landy would maintain a severe pace through the first three laps, leaving Bannister simply too tired to keep within striking distance. If Bannister started his kick at three hundred yards out, the typical distance at which he made his move (and there would be only the one opportunity for a move), he would find it difficult, if not impossible, to keep driving to the finish at that top pace. His best chance then might be to wait, to make sure he never lost contact, and to let Landy draw him around the track until the final turn going into the homestretch. "That's when the damage must be done," Stampfl told Bannister. "Not before." Coming out of the bend, Bannister should strike, enjoying the brief psychological advantage of passing Landy ("a blow in the stomach," as Stampfl described the effect of being passed) and not giving Landy the chance to make a countermove.

Bannister could have arrived at this strategy on his own, but developing it with Stampfl helped convince him it was possible. His coach assured him that he had the strength and competitive will to "unleash just that extra energy" needed at the end of the race to win — as he had at Iffley Road over two months before. Yes, Landy had run better times with more consistency. Yes, if they had to compete against one another week after week, Landy would probably win more races than he lost. But for this one race, Bannister could summon the mental focus to win.

The effect of his talk with Stampfl was profound, as it had been the morning of May 6. Chris Chataway best explained what these conversations with their coach provided:

> It was a sort of pre-race mental calisthenics. I would say I was tired, and he would explain why he was absolutely convinced that my finishing burst would be strong. In a way, I knew that he didn't know any better than I did whether or not I would win, because it was a total unknown quantity, but just hearing someone say the things — by then I knew what he would say — was useful.

Bannister left Stampfl that afternoon certain that he would win, perhaps by less than a stride — but a stride was all he needed.

17

What happens when a 3:59.4 miler matches strides with a 3:58 miler? It is not an academic question like the time-honored poser: What would happen if Jack Dempsey fought Joe Louis? Bannister and Landy are contemporaries, and no one will have to wait long for an answer.

— *New York Times*, August 1, 1954

IN LONDON Bannister and a large group of British athletes, including Chataway and Brasher, boarded a plane for their flight to Vancouver. Their first stop was supposed to be Montreal, but twelve hours after takeoff, because of a brisk headwind, they had to stop over at Goose Bay in Labrador, an isolated patch of land usually frozen in ice, to refuel. Since the layover was several hours long, Bannister disembarked and began jogging around the fifty-square-yard compound in which they were restricted. Other athletes soon followed him, and as marathoner Jim Peters described the scene, "we paced backwards and forwards like convicts during their daily exercise period." When they eventually landed in Montreal, in the middle of the night, they slept in what amounted to an army barracks whose only luxury was a Coca-Cola machine that took English sixpence coins and gave the change in Canadian money worth more than what they had paid. For amateurs given only a few pounds a day in expense money, this was a windfall.

The following morning they reboarded the plane for the ten-hour journey to Vancouver. The boredom was relieved by a pillow fight in the back of the plane, where Bannister was sitting, and by the sight of the Rocky Mountains, with the pilot pointing out the various peaks of the vast and awe-inspiring mountain range. Bannister had procured a melon and sliced it into pieces for his teammates, some of whom, never having seen the fruit before, refused the delicacy, not daring to upset their carefully calibrated diets.

Finally they landed in Vancouver on July 26. Over one thousand people and a troop of bagpipe players were on the tarmac waiting for their arrival. The athletes filed out of the airplane in strict order, team captain Jim Peters the last to leave. After nearly two days of quiet anticipation, they were thrown into the carnival atmosphere of the Empire Games. As his teammates dispersed into the crowd, the press flocked to the main and only attraction, the newly minted doctor Roger Bannister. His salient comment before jumping into a car was, "I will be out to win, not break records." One particularly observant reporter noted that Bannister was wearing a wristwatch with the twelve letters P-E-N-N-S-Y-L-V-A-N-I-A in place of numerals for the hour markings. He had earned the watch by winning the 1951 Benjamin Franklin Mile, one of his first great victories on the international stage.

After leaving the airport in Vancouver, Bannister and Chataway dropped off their bags at the University of British Columbia campus, the site of the Empire Village, and headed off to take a swim at the pool built for the Empire Games. As they walked past the training track, on their way to the pool, Bannister spotted Landy on the track.

The two had not met since the Helsinki games in 1952, yet for nearly two years they had followed each other's every move. It was inevitable that they would speak before their race, and Bannister wanted to get it out of the way. He was not known for befriending his rivals. Landy must have been aware of this, since it was his own countryman Don Macmillan who had told Bannister years before, "Roger, you only become really friendly with your opponents after you've beaten them!"

Bannister and Chataway walked down to the track. Landy was running sprints on the grass, barefoot and wearing only a pair of white shorts. He saw them and came across the field. He was darkly tanned and as fit as any miler Bannister had ever seen.

"Hello, John," Bannister said, feeling awkward.

"Roger," Landy said. He shook his hand vigorously and hardly seemed fazed.

Fortunately for Bannister, Chataway was there to ease the tension. He greeted the Australian as an old friend.

"Seen the track at the new Empire Stadium?" Bannister inquired.

"Yes," Landy said. "It looks a bit clayey. If the weather gets hot, it'll get very hard."

The three spoke of the weather (sunny and smashing, they said) and the arrival of Landy's father to see the race (wonderful, they agreed), but nothing was said of their upcoming race. They were two prize-fighters talking about everything except what mattered most.

"Are you going to have a run tonight?" Landy asked.

"No, we're off for a swim," Bannister said plainly. And after a few more pleasantries, Bannister and Chataway walked off and Landy continued with his training run. It was the most they would say to one another until after their race two weeks later. Before they had gone their separate ways, however, a pair of *Vancouver Sun* photographers slipped over to catch the two in a picture that was splashed across newspapers the following day under headlines such as "Mile Stars in Guarded Meeting." The great showdown had begun.

On October 30, 1891, five years before the revival of the ancient Olympic Games, the Reverend J. Astley Cooper proposed in the *Times* a "Pan-Britannic Festival" of sport that would bring together all the countries of the British Empire. There were many who thought that Britain owed her greatness on the world stage to the ideals her people learned in amateur athletics. The concept took some time to gather momentum, but eventually, in honor of King George V's coronation two decades later, an awkwardly titled "Festival of Empire" was held that featured, among other exhibitions, an inter-Empire sports competition between Great Britain, Australia, South Africa, and Canada. It was not until 1930, however, that the first true Empire Games were held, in Hamilton, Canada. Teams from seven countries, all English-speaking and united under the Union Jack flag, competed in track and field, swimming, boxing, wrestling, rowing, and lawn bowls. Only male athletes were allowed to compete, and the mile race was won by England's R. H. Thomas in 4:14. Much had changed in the twenty-four years since: now women competed alongside men; twenty-four countries were represented instead of the original four; athletes arrived by airplane instead of ship; competitions were followed throughout the world by radio and television as well as newsprint; electronic devices decided sprint finishes instead of the naked eye; and the two men competing in the mile event had already broken the four-minute mile.

The Vancouver games opened on July 30 to a parade of athletes, the hoisting of flags, the release of pigeons, and the firing of guns. The focus of attention was a far cry from Cooper's original vision of unifying Empire countries under the shared principle of sport. The only thing people wanted to read, see, and hear about was the meeting of the two sub-four-minute milers. Henry Luce, the famed publisher who founded *Time, Fortune,* and *Life,* had sent his best writer and photographer to Vancouver to cover the race for the inaugural issue of his magazine *Sports Illustrated.* Luce had arranged for a plane to be waiting on standby at the airport on the day of the mile final to fly the color pictures of the finish to the magazine's printers. To televise the event across the United States and Canada, NBC took the extreme measure of building a number of permanent radio relay towers between Vancouver and Seattle because the Canadian Broadcasting Company, whose first television station had been launched only two years before, had yet to build a coast-to-coast relay. From Seattle, the images would then be transmitted by relay to Portland, Salt Lake City, Denver, Omaha, Chicago, Buffalo, and finally New York. Meanwhile, 560 radio stations in the United States and hundreds of others around the world had cleared time slots on their schedules for the event's broadcast.

For the estimated 100 million people expected to tune in to the "Dream Race" on Saturday, August 7, the rest of the games were window-dressing. And John Landy and Roger Bannister knew it. Literally hundreds of journalists and radio men from over twenty countries were assigned to follow their every move, whether it was on the track, around the city of Vancouver, or in the Empire Village. Their faces were plastered on posters and newspapers everywhere they went. The media frenzy they had attracted in their respective home countries prior to this event was child's play in comparison.

In the two weeks before August 7 the two milers handled the attention as differently as they planned on running their races. In the morning Landy walked to the training tracks, signing autographs and speaking to the press along the way—more out of an obligation to his fans than a desire for the spotlight. In front of over five hundred people who had assembled at the track solely to watch him train, he knocked off a series of quarter- and half-miles at a pace that drew the crowd's applause. As race day approached his sessions drew more and more people. Though at one point he had to enlist several of his Australian team-mates to encircle him on the way to the track—so as not to be stampeded—he continued to train in the open. Reports of his sessions reached Bannister, and they were intimidating. After a half-mile trial in 1:58, an athlete who saw Landy's run commented to the press, "He was as fresh as when he started. He certainly is a machine." Each session won headlines such as "Landy Claps on the Pace" and "Landy: Speeds Up Training." And when he killed a three-quarter-mile trial in 2:59.4, reporters speculated that the Australian planned on running faster than the 4:02 mile he previously predicted would win the race against Bannister.

"Where's Roger the Dodger?" Posed by an admittedly biased Steve Hayward from the *Melbourne Herald*, the question was on everyone's mind. So seldom was he seen around Vancouver that autograph seekers rated one of his signatures to be worth four of Landy's. Bannister was indeed training, albeit in secret. Instead of visiting the public track at the University of British Columbia, he conducted his sessions with Chataway on a pine tree–lined golf course late in the afternoons. Though he ran the risk of being hit by stray golf balls, the course was not besieged by reporters. He ran his time trials on a cinder track ten miles outside of the village in Balaclava Park, earning him headlines like "Bannister Stays Out of Sight." On July 31 Norris McWhirter, on location in Vancouver for the *Star*, wrote that Bannister, Chataway, and Brasher "slid out of the camp with collars turned up and in dark glasses" to train. Bannister's absence led Landy to approach McWhirter to ask, "What is Roger up to? He never comes here." If Bannister had Landy guessing, all the better. One time the press mistook a British sprinter for Bannister on the Empire Village training track and were amazed at the swiftness of his 220-yard sprints, which they promptly reported the next day. Perhaps Landy saw this article; Bannister certainly hoped he had. He knew that Landy could run repeat quarter-miles with better speed, shorter intervals, and more ease than he could. Still, the Englishman believed he probably held the tactical advantage.

On Thursday, August 5, the day of the mile's qualifying heats, the anticipation over "the Mile of the Century" was beginning to reach an even higher level. The debates, whether over meals in the Empire Village dining hall or on the newspaper editorial pages, gathered momentum. Would Bannister's stinging finish win out over Landy's astounding stamina, or would it be the other way round? Odds were posted, giving stamina a three-to-one advantage over a fast kick. On this fifth day of seven in the competition, athlete after athlete was breaking records in other events, with England leading overall in point totals. Still, very little warranted mention apart from the mile race. The qualifying heats, normally a routine event, packed the newly built stadium and prompted columns of newspaper print.

Bannister was set against Australia's Geoff Warren and Don Macmillan, England's David Law and John Disley, Canada's Richard Ferguson, and New Zealand's Murray Halberg, whom many considered the dark horse in the upcoming showdown. It was debatable, between track aficionados, whether Bannister or Landy had the easier heat, but Geoff Warren planned to exhaust his countryman's rival more than he would have liked. Hoping Bannister would take the bait, Warren took off strong from the start and ran a 2:00.4 first half. But the English miler wasn't biting and let Warren tire himself out by the third lap. Bannister ran an even race throughout and finished third in what McWhirter called a "nonchalant" 4:08.4. Halberg was first, Ferguson was second, and Law, in fourth, was the final qualifier.

Landy faced England's Chris Brasher and Ian Boyd, Canada's William Parnell, the defending champion, Northern Ireland's Victor Milligan, and New Zealand's William Baillie. This heat was slower than the previous one, with Baillie commanding the lead for most of the race; he finished first in 4:11.4 with Milligan, Landy, and Boyd crossing only inches behind him two-tenths of a second later. Brasher finished last, and since the Empire Games did not include the steeplechase, his competitions were over.

Reporters tried to pry from Landy and Bannister what the heats meant for the forthcoming race, but neither was talking. "Crack Milers Take It Easy" was the next day's headline in the *Daily Mail*, which admitted at the end of the article that "as a guide to what is likely to happen on Saturday, the heats were completely useless." Newspapers sold off the racks regardless.

As if the atmosphere was not charged enough, reports spread through the village that some television executives had hatched a plot to have Wes Santee run the mile race against Bannister and Landy by satellite, in Quantico, Virginia. The scheme involved starting Santee at the exact time the gun went off in Vancouver, and by virtue of a split-screen device, thirty million American viewers could watch to see if their star miler would finish first. The fact that Santee would be in New

York broadcasting the race for NBC seemed neither to quiet the rumor nor halt the preparation of official protests.

No doubt the Reverend Cooper would have blushed had he witnessed the media circus and spectacle undermining his noble concept of the Empire Games, but his principle held strong for the two milers set to face one another forty-eight hours later. As amateurs, they wanted only to represent their countries as best they could and to prove they were the best. There was no other reward.

Behind a bedroom door in the Empire Village, one whose number had been switched by teammate Geoff Warren to throw off the press, Landy was restless. It was three o'clock Friday morning, the day before the mile final. Like the athletes' quarters in Helsinki, the room was sparsely furnished, but Landy had only one roommate this time, high-jumper John Vernon. Vernon was sleeping easily in the next bed. Landy decided to take a walk outside to get some fresh air and stretch his legs. It was the only time of the day when he could be alone; besides, he was unable to sleep.

Because of the heightened press attention in the past week, Landy had not been able to relax and enjoy Vancouver with the same freedom he had on first arriving. His every appearance was chronicled the next day in the newspapers. Meanwhile, his teammates were out touring the city and seeing movies. Knowing he was restricted, one of his teammates usually stayed behind to keep him company, though they suspected he was perfectly capable of entertaining himself by reading. One afternoon a couple of Vancouver girls with a car asked Geoff Warren if he and some of his friends wanted to see the sights. Warren finally convinced Landy to join the group, and they piled into a car, but it became clear very quickly that the car was too small for all of them. The girls said they could get a bigger car, and they drove to one of their houses. When the young men were asked inside, the father seemed to recognize Landy—exactly the kind of situation he had wanted to avoid. Warren and several of the other athletes started talking about their particular events, but the father was interested in Landy. "What about you?" he asked. One of the Australians, marathoner Bryce Mackay, answered for him. "He's a boxer. Johnny the Kid." The father looked Landy over suspiciously. "A boxer?" Landy evaded the question, but Mackay piped up again. "Oh, John's a fine boxer." The father then replied, "Let's see some boxing then." Landy did not want to be discovered, so he started shadow-boxing. The father gave him a look that said, "I think you're John Landy," but they then made their escape. Except to train or see athletic events at the stadium, Landy did not venture out much again.

For all his patience with the hoopla surrounding him in these Empire Games, Landy wanted nothing more than to be left alone to concentrate on his contest with Bannister. His friendliness at the track masked what was going on inside, where he was gathering the determination he needed to win the race. He was "an iron fist in a velvet glove," explained Warren. Or as Landy described himself, "I'm vicious underneath." To him running was more than just a sport. In the past few years it had become an obsession. As he later said:

> In any running event, you are absolutely alone. Nobody can help you. But short races are run without thought. In very long races you must go a great distance simply to be present in the laps that really count. But almost every part of the mile is important—you can never let down, never stop thinking, and you can be beaten at almost any point. I suppose you could say it is like life. I had wanted to master it.

Since he had arrived in Vancouver, advice about how he should run the race had come from every direction. His roommate Vernon and Don Macmillan, two friends and athletes he respected greatly, had tried to shake him from his decision to run from the front. If he played a waiting game, they said, he would have a better shot at winning.

"Roger's going to sit you . . . and then jump you," Macmillan had said, having competed against Bannister more than any other Australian. "That's all he'll do. He'll sit, sit, sit. John, you'll be a sitting duck."

Landy had appreciated the advice, but his answer was clear and shut down further conversation: "I'll run it my way."

Nonetheless, as he stepped off the veranda outside his room in the middle of the night, he was still nervous about the race he planned to run. He knew front-running was psychologically more exhausting. As the hunted, he would have to worry about whether he was setting a fast enough pace and would only be able to guess at how the others were running. On the other hand, the hunter, Bannister, could hold back and decide when and how fast to make his strike. Until then, his only responsibility would be to stay close enough.

While jogging barefoot on the grass, trying to relax from the weight of these thoughts, Landy suddenly felt a sharp stab of pain in his left foot. He lifted it up to see a gash on his instep; on the grass was a broken photographer's flashbulb. As he stumbled back toward his room, blood gushed from his foot. Finally, he rested on his bed, a trail of red on the floor. His foot was sliced open, two inches long. The light woke up Vernon, who propped himself up in bed.

"I've cut my foot. It's pretty bad." Landy grimaced.

Vernon was as calm as possible, knowing what this could mean. "We'll sort something out."

"We can't tell anybody," Landy said. Above everything, he did not want to have to give an excuse for Saturday's race if it failed to go as planned. Whether he would be able to run in it at all seemed secondary at that moment.

They bandaged the cut as best they could and tried unsuccessfully to get to sleep. A few hours later, as the other athletes began stirring and passing through the corridor, Don Macmillan came into the room. Blood was smeared on the bedding and floor.

"What the hell is this?" Macmillan asked.

"Nothing, nothing," they both said.

"Oh, nothing?" Macmillan was obviously unconvinced.

"He cut his foot," Vernon said. "He stepped on a flashbulb."

Finally the three decided that the cut had to be looked at by a doctor, but again Landy was insistent that it needed to be kept secret. Macmillan and Vernon left the room and found a mounted policeman, who arranged for a car to pull up next to a side door so they could avoid the press, who were camped outside. They drove to the University of British Columbia health center. A doctor was called and sworn to secrecy before he treated the cut. He wanted to stitch the diagonal gash, which ran from the instep of Landy's foot to his heel, and told the miler he could not run. But Landy was convinced that the cut would not affect his running given its location. Finally the doctor agreed to tape the gash instead, and Landy returned quickly to the Empire Village. For the rest of the day Landy remained in his room. When several teammates inquired as to why he didn't visit the track, Vernon said that he was resting.

In the afternoon Andy O'Brien, a reporter commentating for the National Canadian Film Board, came to interview Landy. He found a Canadian Mountie posted outside the door, who told him Landy was sleeping and not to be bothered. O'Brien backed down, but then returned an hour later to hear the miler's voice behind the door. He insisted on speaking to Landy, since the miler had already agreed to the interview. Finally he forced his way into the room to find Landy. The miler stepped away from his bed and left a smear of blood on the floor.

"I know you will think this is awful," Landy said. "But I cannot do what I promised." There was no way he could do an interview.

O'Brien saw the blood.

"I will tell you why—only on your promise not to tell a soul. Right?"

O'Brien nodded.

Landy told him what had happened and then said, "I am determined to run. I cannot let down my team and the fans now."

The reporter promised not to publish the news and then left. Landy wanted no alibis. Since the cut was on the underside of his instep rather than the pad of his foot, he believed it would not make a difference in his stride. At dinner that night he neglected to tell even his father, who had flown to Vancouver to support his son. His father made it a practice of not interfering with his son's running endeavors, a fact that John appreciated. He was simply glad to have his father there. In any event, John planned on beating Bannister, gash or not. That the accident failed to rattle his determination and confidence showed just how much iron was inside that velvet glove.

Late in the afternoon on August 6, Wes Santee and his wife drove through the Holland Tunnel and surfaced in Manhattan. This was Danna's first trip to New York City, and heading uptown, they marveled together at the Chrysler and Empire State skyscrapers and the bustling sidewalks where the sun seemed to never shine. They got turned around a few times trying to find their hotel—to Santee, negotiating his way through traffic seemed more difficult than herding a hundred cattle through a gate—but he eventually maneuvered onto Park Avenue and stopped in front of the Waldorf Astoria. NBC had arranged a room for them at the luxury hotel, which at fifty dollars a night was an extravagance they never could have afforded on their own.

This was the first opportunity they had had since Santee entered boot camp to spend much time together alone. But it was impossible to escape the feeling that they never should have been there in the first place. Santee wanted to be in Vancouver, preparing for the race of a lifetime. In his mind, as well as with Easton back in Kansas, he had played out how he would have run against Bannister and Landy. He felt certain that he was good enough to beat them both, and more than anything in the world he wanted the chance. Instead, he was in New York City, and although comforted by Danna, who was as surprised and disappointed as he was that it had come to this, the next day he had to face sitting in a studio to narrate a race that should have been his to win.

The two had a quiet dinner at their hotel and then went to bed early. They did not even have the chance to go sightseeing or listen to the Cuban band playing in the Waldorf's Starlight Room or take in the new motion picture *On the Waterfront* at a nearby theater. An NBC car was expected early in the morning to bring them to the studio.

The night before the race Bannister was struggling against a chest cold that he had recently caught. He was producing sputum and worried that the cold would affect his running. During his qualifying heat he had been afraid of being overcome by a fit of coughing but managed to run his mile without much strain: a hopeful sign, but by no means convincing. In his race against Landy he would have to work his lungs much more severely. Even if his cold took just 1 percent off the oxygen exchange, there were consequences. For the past few days he had entertained many such scenarios.

Except for participating in the mile heats, his time in Vancouver had been little more than a painful waiting game, particularly after he stopped training the previous Sunday. For the busy medical student who had little—if any—free time back in London, this gave his mind unusual leisure. As much as possible he tried not to occupy it with thoughts of his upcoming race. Instead, he toured the city and surrounding countryside in an Austin car loaned to him (and several other British athletes) by a Canadian publisher; he swam at the Empire Village pool; he read; he went to dinner with Chris Chataway and his girlfriend, a television producer; he attended parties thrown by local residents; and he used his free stadium pass to watch some of the other events. He avoided the press as much as possible.

On August 3 he went to see Chataway compete in the three mile. Since their arrival on July 26, they had taken several long walks together to discuss the tactics of their respective races. One afternoon after a session of repeat quarter-miles in sixty seconds, they ran a trial that they hoped would serve them both in their finals. The plan was for Bannister to run 220 yards in approximately half a minute, upon which Chataway would stride past him as fast as possible, at the moment in his race when he hoped to seize the lead. After following Chataway around the final turn, Bannister would then sprint past him at the top of the home-stretch, the place where he hoped to take over Landy. The trial went exactly as planned, and they ran the last 220 yards in twenty-five seconds. In his three-mile final Chataway benefited from this trial: he took over the lead in his race a half-lap from the finish and broke through the tape first, exacting revenge on Freddie Green, who had literally inched him out in a shocking upset at the AAA Championships in July. "The great Mr. Second"—as the *Evening Standard* once labeled him for his help in Bannister's and Landy's four-mile attempts—had finally triumphed. Just as Chataway's 5,000-meter Olympic defeat had boded ill for Bannister in Helsinki, he saw Chataway's victory in Vancouver as an "encouraging omen."

But even with all these diversions and promising signs, Bannister still had too much time on his hands. Much of it was spent in the room he shared with Chataway, especially in the last twenty-four hours before the race. Chataway was used to his friend's nervousness before a big race and suspected that his cold was at least in part psychosomatic. He had suffered a similar one before May 6. As much as Chataway drank, smoked, and tried to lighten the mood with jokes about how Bannister couldn't possibly be worried about being beaten by anyone other than a good Englishman, he knew his friend was revving himself up for his race and there was nothing to be said that would make much of a difference now. As he described Bannister to a reporter before his clash with Landy:

> Roger hates the idea of having to beat Landy—of having thousands of people expecting him to do it. But he'll do it. Nobody gets in such an emotional pitch before a race as he does. Roger may tell you he has slept before a race, but he hasn't. When he goes out to run, he looks like a man going to the electric chair. There are times the night before a race when he actually makes involuntary sounds, like a man being tortured. But Roger is a hard man to comfort—if you try, he'll give you a look that goes right through you.

With each hour, whether taking a walk, pacing his room, or lying in bed, Bannister became more and more fired up to win. He was the underdog in this race, but that was fine with him. In Helsinki he had been favored to win, and that had done nothing to improve his chances. His focus was intense. He ran the race over in his head, convincing himself each time that when his muscles told him to stop in the last lap, he would refuse to listen. Everything else in his life diminished and faded away. He later admitted that it was an "abnormal state of attention." But for this brief moment in time his race against Landy at 2:30 P.M. the following day was the most important thing in the world—and would continue to be until one of them broke through the finishing tape first.

18

Now bid me run, and I will strive with things impossible.

—SHAKESPEARE, *Julius Caesar*

T
HE SUN ROSE over the snow-capped mountains surrounding
Vancouver. The waters of Burrard Inlet lightened, and a few
early-to-rise sailors pointed their boats out toward the deeper
bay. Morning strollers walked along the beaches, and the towering
Lion's Gate suspension bridge began to see the first cars in what would
be a tough day for traffic. The flags of twenty-four competing nations
from throughout the British Empire lined the streets leading to the stadium. A horseshoe-shaped wonder of steel and concrete, the stadium
had been built, along with a bicycle velodrome and a swimming center,
especially for the 1954 Empire Games. Inside the stadium the groundsmen raked the broad jump pit and took special care rolling the six-lane
clay track. The athletes for the final day of events would soon arrive to
test their spikes on it. With the forecasts predicting an afternoon of
sunshine and warm temperatures, the track promised to be the perfect
setting for the heralded mile race.

On newsstands from Vancouver to New York and from London to
Melbourne, the race was headlined on front pages and dominated sport
sections. "Landy, Bannister in Epic Clash at Games Today," read the
Sun-Herald in Australia. "Mile of the Century at Vancouver Today,"
bannered the *Daily Telegraph* in England. "Landy, Bannister Primed for
'Miracle Mile,'" proclaimed the *New York Herald Tribune*. Hyperbole

was at a premium. One newspaper predicted that the "whole athletic world will be tuned to Vancouver with eyes, ears and heart." Another expanded this audience and labeled that day's mile "the race the whole world is waiting for." Landy and Bannister were profiled and compared on every score—their birth dates, heights, weights, and fastest half-mile, mile, and two-mile times. Images of the two running were placed next to each other. Final quotes from the two were published. Landy said, "I have reached my peak." "We may get down to four minutes," Bannister offered. And last-minute predictions were made: Australian papers tipped Landy to win; British papers gave Bannister the advantage, while the American press took the middle road, simply saying that this race was the "supreme test" between the two milers.

When Landy awakened early that morning after a surprisingly restful night's sleep, his roommate Vernon, who felt nervous for his friend, asked, "How does your foot feel?" Landy replied, "Fine," but said little else. But the dressings were soaked with blood. The cut had continued to bleed through the night, and Landy knew that he needed to get it looked at again. Though his race against Bannister was only a few hours away, he returned to the university hospital. Somehow he managed to elude reporters. The same doctor from the night before told him he needed stitches, race or no race. Landy abdicated. After stitching his foot, the doctor insisted that the miler couldn't run in his condition, but the miler was determined. He was running. The doctor dressed and padded his foot, and Landy returned to have lunch with a few of his Australian teammates. Despite his foot's tenderness, he did not let it affect his gait.

When he arrived at the stadium, the stands were quickly filling to their capacity of thirty-five thousand. In the locker room nobody said anything to Landy about his cut foot, proof that the reporter O'Brien had kept his word. Twenty minutes before the race was to start Landy put on his spikes, carefully slipping on his left shoe so as not to disturb the dressings. His only choice was to believe that the cut would not bother him. If the cut had been an inch over on his heel or on the ball of his foot, he could never have raced. Before he went out onto the field to warm up, the doctor who had stitched his foot approached him, offering to give Landy a local anesthetic for the pain. Landy said he could manage without it.

All roads had led to this moment: training at Portsea with Cerutty, the lessons of Zatopek, his surprise 4:02.1 at Olympic Park, the months and months of uninterrupted training, his failure to bring his time down further in Australia, and then his triumph in Turku. But here finally was the race that mattered most. Aside from the pressure of leading from the front with Bannister and the six other runners poised behind him, just waiting to pounce, he had to deal with the hope of his teammates and millions of Australians that he would bring victory to what had otherwise been an unsuccessful Empire Games for his country. He also had to contend with the fact that every stride, move, and countermove would be watched, broadcasted, reviewed, and dissected by millions. It was difficult to handle. As the race approached, however, he concentrated solely on his game plan. He would run a moderately quick first half, followed by a very fast third lap in which he believed he could break Bannister. It wasn't a complicated strategy, but he felt that it was the only one that would work. There would be nobody more fit than him on the track, and he was tremendously motivated to win.

Before leaving for the stadium, Bannister carefully packed the same track shoes he had worn at Iffley Road on May 6. He decided to take the team bus so as not to risk an accident if he drove himself. His mind was too preoccupied. Surrounded by his teammates on the bus, he watched the crowds of people descending on the stadium, knowing they had all come to see him and Landy race. In the locker room, with its cement-gray walls and wooden benches, he looked pasty and white; his cold was less severe than the night before, but still tight in his chest. As a *Vancouver Sun* journalist later reported, other athletes in the locker room were not much better off:

> One was inconspicuously chewing his fingernails; another held his head upon his knees, as if praying to someone above for strength for the coming race; yet another was sitting stonily on a bench in a far corner, taking in everything without a reply to anything; another was unconsciously turning from side to side; another just sat still, throwing examining glances around the room; and finally, one sat alone on a bench with a nervous smile affixed upon his face.

Bannister felt the same tension. The past few hours had been almost unbearable for him. As he had eaten a light breakfast and taken a short walk in the Empire Village earlier, he felt as if his whole future, as he later described it, was "hanging on a knife edge." He didn't want to endure the agony of willing his body beyond its breaking point. He feared coming under the glare of so many people again and knew that as he stepped up to the starting line he would feel weak and almost unable to stand. It was intolerable, and yet there he was, a warm-up away from race time.

Bannister had never expected to be running competitively at this point in his life. If he had won in Helsinki two years before, he would have been happy to hang up his spikes and dedicate himself fully to medicine. But the sting from his devastating loss at the Olympics had driven him to continue running and to seek the four-minute mile as evidence that his approach to sport still had merit. When he ran his 3:59.4, he thought that this would have been triumph enough, but Landy did him one better at Turku, and without pacing. No, this race today was the climax. He had to win it. Failure would confirm the critics who called him supercilious for following his own methods and not theirs. Failure would taint his May 6 race and validate the claim that a British newspaper had printed that same morning, telling him that he had "never won a really important race when the others weren't in there to help you." He had to get in there today, spikes flying and elbows pushing, and beat Landy and the rest of the field in a race in which anything could happen. The pressures were much the same as they had been in Helsinki—expectant British public, big crowd, critics waiting to pounce—but Bannister was not the same man anymore. He had a mentor in Stampfl, training partners in Chataway and Brasher, and a more complete understanding of how important it was to have faith in himself. The question remained, however: how good was Landy? And could Landy change gears at the race's end to fight off Bannister's kick?

As the starter called the milers out to the track, Bannister remembered that he also had six other runners to deal with, each with his own plan to win. Unless Landy played a waiting game, he would not have to vie for position in the pack, but Bannister would. If he was blocked off by one or two of them, it would ruin his chances. English runners David Law and Ian Boyd, both Oxonians, had best mile times of 4:08 and were not likely to prove too much of a challenge. Irishman Victor Milligan, his country's team captain and mile champion, and Canadian Richard Ferguson, a strong runner whose best distance was two miles, had no allegiance to either Bannister or Landy and would be fighting for their own space in the field. The ones Bannister had to watch most carefully were New Zealanders William Baillie and Murray Halberg. Halberg, twenty years old and winner of the Benjamin Franklin Mile in Philadelphia, had already clocked a 4:04.4 mile. Rumor had it that the

Kiwis might set an early pace for Landy; regardless of that, Halberg was likely to be a risk throughout the race.

Five minutes before the race the concrete stands encircling three sides of the track were packed to capacity. A helicopter chartered by *Life* magazine and the *Vancouver Sun* loomed at a distance, the sound of its spinning blades reverberating around the bowl-shaped stadium besieged by hundreds of parked cars and the continuing advance of trams dropping off more and more spectators outside its walls. From the helicopter's aerie perch, the crowds looked like a calm sea of white shirts and hats. Up close, however, particularly at the entrances, it was chaos: scalpers were selling tickets for a hundred dollars; fire wardens tried to impose order on the lines still gathered at the gates; and schoolboys scaled the four ticket booths to secure a view of the race.

Everyone's eyes were glued to the milers as they jogged around the track and began taking off their sweats. The other finals held that day, including the field events and the 440-yard race, might as well have taken place on the sidelines. The mile race was all-consuming. The Duke of Edinburgh, who had seen Bannister race in London and Landy in Australia, arrived to watch the final, with a twenty-one-gun salute announcing his presence. He was seated in the decorated royal box, having already inspected the Seafourth Highland Regiment in their crimson jackets, kilts, and high feathered caps while bagpipes played behind him on the infield.

Under the steel roof at one end of the stadium Norris McWhirter was ready with his stopwatch to help call the race for BBC Radio with journalist Rex Alston, who, McWhirter knew, had very little understanding of the intricacies of the race despite being a former Cambridge runner. McWhirter would not have made it to the stadium in time had he not been staying at the Duke of Edinburgh's hotel. With his brother Ross and a few others crammed into an Austin 7, they pulled away from the hotel at the same time as the duke's limousine and proceeded to follow in the wake of his police escort, cutting through the snarl of traffic descending on the stadium. In the radio commentary box next to Norris, his brother was preparing to help call the race for the Australian Broadcast Network. Adjacent to him was Chris Chataway, lured there by a Canadian broadcaster. Everyone was waiting for the race to begin.

It was late evening in England, and Bannister's parents, recently returned from a fortnight in Cambridge, were listening to the race on the radio at their Harrow home. Their daughter Joyce, who had sent her brother a "good luck" telegram the day before, was in her Bristol home, tuned to the same station. Stampfl sat still at the kitchen table in his King's Road apartment, the radio on. His wife, Pat, was fidgeting, as nervous as he was, just showing it differently. Despite receiving several postcards about Landy's extraordinary fitness from athletes he had coached who were in Vancouver, Stampfl remained convinced that Bannister could win, but the waiting was torture. At St. Mary's hospital the night shift was also tuned in to the BBC to listen to the race. To many, Bannister exemplified the best of what it was to be an Englishman: he was well rounded, masterfully disciplined, an explorer of new territory, and brave enough, as he said himself, to run "into extinction."

It was Sunday morning in Australia when the race was scheduled to begin. The Landy family, apart from John's father, who was with him in Vancouver, had congregated at their East Malvern house to listen to the radio broadcast. Landy's mother had decided not to send John a telegram wishing him luck, thinking it might be just more pressure for him to handle.

Percy Cerutty was in his Domain Road house off the Botanical Gardens, eager to hear whether Landy would follow the instructions he had sent about how to run the race. So far Landy had not responded to his letters, despite the news in the Melbourne press that his former miler was running the Vancouver race according to Cerutty's "Secret Plans." Those athletes who were close to Landy but not in attendance at the Empire Games, including Les Perry and Robbie Morgan-Morris, were also sitting anxiously in anticipation of the broadcast. The whole country was anchored in the moment as well. "Australia considered Landy unbeatable," sportswriter Adrian McGregor later commented. "He was all we mythologized about ourselves. Gallant, modest, idealistic, but beneath it all a champion equipped with [a] destructive will."

At dinnertime in New York, Wes Santee was staring at the camera in front of him at the RCA Exhibition Center. Instead of a singlet and spikes, he was dressed in a tan Marine uniform and dress shoes. Half the age of the four other men at the table with him—Asa Bushnell and Kenneth Wilson, secretary and president, respectively, of the U.S. Olympic Committee; Jesse Abramson, the *New York Herald Tribune*'s lead sports columnist; and Ben Grauer, NBC's talking head—Santee twisted uncomfortably in his seat. He felt as if he were getting ready for the race himself. He watched it unfold in his head. Danna was off the set and in the shadows, but he was at least comforted to have her there.

"Any word yet from Edinburgh?" Grauer asked into the phone, obviously having trouble coordinating the transmission delay. "I mean Vancouver."

Santee knew that the race was about to begin and, as with the 1,500-meter Olympic trials in Los Angeles two years before, he was on the sidelines. The American miler knew how it would be run. Bannister had the faster kick, and Landy could set a brutal pace. If Bannister failed to hang on to the Australian by the end of the third lap, he was finished. But as Santee waited for the transmission from Empire Stadium to appear on the monitor to his side, the race he imagined on the darkened screen included him toeing the line. Landy went out first, Santee right behind him, and Bannister in third, ten yards back. Santee stayed in the middle, all the way through three and a half laps. The pace was fast, but he had the conditioning to hold. With a half-lap to go, Santee struck, a Mal Whitfield technique. Landy and Bannister expected him to make his move coming out of the last curve, not going into it. By the time they realized what he had done, Santee was past the two milers in a flash; they never had a chance. With sixty yards to home, Bannister delivered his kick, but he was too late. Santee had already started on his. It was Santee through the tape first, then Bannister or Landy—it didn't matter who came in second.

This was the race as it should have happened, but Santee felt he had been robbed of the chance. The closest he could get to a battle against Bannister and Landy was via radio signal from Vancouver, through Seattle, and into New York. He knew that when the screen finally flickered in the exhibition hall, showing the runners in Vancouver pacing in front of the starting line, the race would already have started in real time.

In Empire Stadium, two minutes before 2:30 P.M., the scheduled start of the mile event, the sun cleared from behind a bank of clouds and the stands and track were enveloped in light. It was seventy-two degrees, with mild humidity. The faintest of breezes stirred the air in the stadium. Officials in green coats cleared the track as Bannister and several others peeled off their sweatsuits on the infield. Bannister wanted to stay as warm as possible until he had to stand, exposed, at the starting line. Landy was the first one ready, walking back and forth on the track, head down, rubbing his deeply tanned arms. His light jog during warm-up proved to him that his foot would be okay, and this improved his confidence. Before the start, he returned to the infield and shook hands with Bannister, who was perspiring and appeared deathly pale as he kicked off his sweatpants. Landy stepped back onto the track, focusing on the effort ahead. He walked away from the others, for a moment on his own. He knew he needed to run so fast that nobody "was going to be left standing."

Bannister was one of the last runners on the track. He checked the bottoms of his track shoes, making sure that no cinders had clumped to his spikes while warming up. It was almost time. Tense and anxious to start, he seemed unaware that anyone else was in the stadium. He told himself that if Landy went off fast in a fifty-six-second first lap and then ran the next lap in sixty seconds, he was unlikely to have the stamina to finish the next two laps in sixty seconds each. He would have to slow some, coming back to Bannister. As long as Bannister ran evenly, he would conserve energy and be able to win.

The eight runners settled in their lanes five yards behind the start. At last the two great sub-four-minute milers were facing off against one another. In the inside position, Landy wore green shorts and a white singlet. Halberg was in all black next to him. Ferguson, from Canada, was in the third lane, Milligan in fourth. Bannister had the fifth lane, wearing all white with the rose of England on his breast. His countrymen Boyd and Law were in the two lanes outside of him, and Baillie of New Zealand was in the outside lane. The spectators made a steady rumble of noise, punctuated by shouts like "Go Landy!" and "Come on, Bannister!" but most cheered for Ferguson, the host country favorite. Cameramen on elevated platforms in the infield directed their lenses at the starting line, ready to broadcast this battle to millions from coast to coast. Hundreds of journalists waited with open notepads to record their impressions for the following day's papers. The team of timekeepers readied their new $8,000 Omega watches, which had been checked, double-checked, and verified for accuracy.

Next to McWhirter in the radio commentary box, Rex Alston spoke into the microphone, his clear, sharp voice reaching across oceans. "There is a tremendous feeling of excitement and tension here on this beautiful summer's day, [with a] bit of a breeze."

Down on the infield, the starter shouted over the crowd: "To your marks!"

The eight runners moved forward to the line. Bannister ran his fingers through his hair and glanced toward Landy. They settled at the line. Landy shot his own look toward Bannister and then crouched down, facing straight ahead, preparing to be the hunted. The surge of adrenaline made any pain in his foot insignificant. Bannister positioned himself at a slight angle toward Landy. He was standing nearly erect. Nothing else in the world mattered but what he had to do in the next four minutes. It had all come down to this.

A track official raised his arms over his head, signaling for the crowd to quiet down. A hush fell over the stadium.

"Set!" The starter yelled. He raised his pistol up to the sky with his right arm.

Bannister took a deep breath, bending slightly forward. His long thin legs looked frail. Landy deepened his crouch, ready to burst ahead. The world waited for the bark of the gun. Its sound echoed around the stadium as the milers swept forward, a wave of flying arms and legs all breaking toward the inside lane. Gun smoke and a cloud of clay dust trailed in their wake. As they went into the first turn the burly New Zealander Baillie angled into the lead, his taller, more fair-haired countryman Halberg behind him. Landy was third, Law was fourth, and Bannister clawed for room in fifth. The field remained tight as they moved around the turn, strides lengthening and shortening while they fought for position. Law cut in between Landy and Halberg to move into third. As Law surged toward the back straight he stutter-stepped, and his right shoe went flying off his foot, landing in the third lane. He kept running and moved into first down the back straight. Positioned at the outside edge of the pole lane, Bannister remained a few yards behind Landy, expecting him to take the lead soon.

As they approached the 220-yard mark at the end of the back straight Landy was ready to move ahead of Baillie and Law. He looked like a man impatiently waiting to get through a narrow doorway with two people blocking his way. The pace wasn't fast enough. At the mark Don Macmillan, who had previously arranged with Landy to call out his split times, yelled out "28.9!" and "Three yards behind!" Hearing his time and Bannister's position, Landy increased his tempo, realizing that he had to take the lead now and set the pace. From the inside edge of the second lane he shifted past the two milers as if they were standing still.

The crowds bordering the track gasped as the Australian made his move. High in the stadium, Rex Alston spoke quickly into his microphone as the race unfolded. "Landy has decided that he must crack on the pace and has taken over the lead with 150 yards to go to the end of the first lap. Landy in his green shorts for Australia . . . slim, sallow, curly dark hair . . . and he is setting out a very fast pace."

Landy was clearly into his rhythm, his arms and legs moving smoothly as he distanced himself from the field into the home straight of the first lap. Halberg was second, Baillie third, and Bannister fourth. Law, having lost his shoe, slowed almost to a stop. Bannister didn't want to be trapped behind Baillie or Halberg when they made the first turn of the second lap, so he moved ahead, increasing his speed almost imperceptibly as he passed the two. Landy finished the first lap in 58.2 with Bannister five yards and six-tenths of a second behind him. The other runners, including Halberg in third and Ferguson in fourth, looked incapable of keeping the pace that Landy continued to set. The race between the two sub-four-minute milers had finally been joined in earnest, and the crowd cheered.

In New York Santee watched the race unfold on the monitor. He pictured himself on the track equidistant between Landy and Bannister. He would let Landy continue to set the pace, but make sure not to let the Australian get too far ahead. Bannister would continue to trail at Santee's heels, waiting for the last lap to make his move. Santee would be there to block him out and surge ahead to victory. The four men at the table with him in the studio could see in his eyes that he wanted very much to be someplace else.

In the second lap Landy turned on the heat, his cut foot forgotten. For the first quarter he had held back, conserving his strength. But now he meant to stretch his lead yard by yard until he broke Bannister. As he rounded out of the turn the gap lengthened. He didn't want to see Bannister's shadow or hear his breath for the rest of the race. If Bannister was near him in the last lap, Landy knew he would have trouble holding off the English miler's kick.

At the 660-yard mark the Australian, striding purposefully and smoothly, was eight yards ahead of Bannister. In the turn Landy picked up even more speed, increasing his lead to ten yards. It was a huge distance between the two milers. Bannister knew Landy was going too fast for him. A few more yards, and Bannister would lose contact. Psychologically it would be the end of his race. As it was, with this gap between them, Bannister suffered the absence of someone to pull him around the track. In a sense he was running as much on his own as the Australian was. He couldn't panic, though. If he got up on his toes to catch

Landy too soon, it would be suicide. Bannister had to believe he could still win.

"Landy comes down the straight for half-distance," Alston told his BBC listeners, his voice edged with anxiety. "Bannister with his prancing, high-stepping stride, ten yards behind, ready, poised." McWhirter, who was very worried about the distance separating his friend from Landy, showed his stopwatch to Alston as the Australian crossed the starting line for the second time. "Here goes Landy now has passed half-distance, Bannister second, Ferguson third, Halberg fourth, Milligan fifth, Baillie sixth, Boyd seventh, and Law has dropped out and limping. Landy is doing what I think a lot of people thought he would do. . . . At-half distance, 1:58.2. Bannister has done 1:59.4."

In the nearby box Chataway was enraptured by the showdown. He knew these two milers better than anybody and chattered anxiously into the microphone. "Dangerous gap there between Landy and Bannister. Landy is looking stronger and Roger has got to close that gap, and soon, if he's going to be there at the finish, with his no doubt superior finishing burst."

Santee was barely able to keep his legs still. Landy was fifteen yards ahead, a distance that the Kansas miler never would have let his competition get. At this point in the race he would have been three or four yards back at the most. And given the pace, Santee knew he would have had enough in reserve to kick past in the final lap. Bannister would still have some fire left too. He had yet to challenge, but unless he moved up, and did so quickly, he was out of the race.

Tens of millions around the world had stopped what they were doing to listen to the race or to watch it on their televisions. In homes and bars conversations paused, children hushed, and bridge games were delayed, pool cues abandoned, forks put down, and drinks left untouched. The collective silence was profound. Those rooting for Landy hoped that he could keep to his fast pace. Those behind Bannister prayed he could bridge the gap.

The crowd in Empire Stadium began to cheer wildly. Both milers were under two minutes for the first half-mile. Landy heard his time called. At this pace he expected to cross the three-quarter-mile mark in 2:58. He had not seen or heard from Bannister but still needed to keep the pressure intense. This was the critical lap for Landy. He ran hard yet kept his stride economical and relaxed. From the stands he looked inexhaustible.

Two more minutes of struggle, Bannister told himself going into the third lap, then it would be over. It would be all over. He was running to his schedule but was far back, and his rival was amazingly maintaining his pace. Bannister felt his confidence weaken. What if Landy never slowed and came back to him? What if Landy was capable of a 3:56 or better? At this point fifteen yards separated them; he needed to be at Landy's shoulder by the last lap, or it was over. Unless Bannister adjusted his speed, unless he relinquished the pace he had planned to run for the one being forced on him by Landy, he would lose. Into the turn Bannister increased the tempo of his circular stride, but in such small measures that from the stands it was nearly impossible to notice he had accelerated. He was like a ball gathering momentum down a hill. First he took one yard from Landy, then two, then three, closing the gap gradually so as not to exert too much energy. His legs ached from the effort, but by the back straight he was only five yards back.

As they sped into the turn Bannister felt himself connected again to Landy. He watched the Australian's stride, almost mesmerized by the steady, rhythmic strike of Landy's spikes on the cinder track. In his mind, Bannister had drawn a "cord" around Landy, and as they moved around the turn he pulled himself closer and closer.

"Here they come into the straight," Alston said enthusiastically. "Bannister is striding up to Landy . . . he's running absolutely beautifully, a much bigger stride. Fifty yards to go to the bell, and Bannister is at Landy's elbow. . . . Now what's going to happen?"

At the bell Landy clocked 2:58.4, and Bannister was only three-tenths of a second behind him. Ferguson was twenty yards back in third place, followed closely by the rest of the field, but everyone's attention was on the two leaders. Photographers lined the infield snapping shots. Newsreel cameras whirred, and tens of thousands of spectators jumped up and down, many shouting until their throats went hoarse. The race was everything they had expected, and more. At this pace the two milers might break four minutes too.

Santee was witnessing a race playing out exactly as he had suspected it would. He desperately wanted to be there to take advantage of the strategy he had devised for this final lap. He could almost see himself in the monitor, running just a half-lane wide of Landy so as not to step on his heels. If Bannister wanted to pass Santee, the English miler would have to step out into the second lane, and this would force him to run

just enough extra distance to prove fatal. If Santee had been there—
and this was what was so hard to bear—he knew he would have been
in exactly the right position to make his break in the final curve. His
kick was as good as Bannister's, or better, and Landy would have been
too tired from playing the rabbit to counter. By the start of the fourth
lap Santee knew that victory would have been his to grasp.

Landy turned into the first bend, shooting a glance over his shoulder. He saw Bannister's shadow and heard his breathing. His hunter
had pulled close, too close. This was the race now. Bannister was not yet
run off his feet. Landy had to hope that his rival had become exhausted
from drawing himself back in contention. It was time to go. Landy
fought gallantly to drive down the track at a greater pace than before.
This was his move. Now was the moment to crack Bannister. Out of the
turn into the back straight, Landy pulled away again from Bannister—
one yard, two, three. Landy's shadow lengthened in front of him into
the next lane. He could not see Bannister's. As Landy approached the
final 220-yard mark the noise from the crowd drowned out Macmillan's call. But he could see his Australian teammates gesturing wildly, as
if to say, "Keep it going, you've got him." Bannister should have made
his move by now. When is it? Landy thought, looking back yet again.
When is the kick going to come? Perhaps he had finally stolen Bannister's kick. Landy began to lose momentum, knowing he had given everything, but hoping it was enough.

"Landy has got a lead of three yards," Alston said, gripping his microphone. "Two hundred twenty yards to go—I don't think Bannister
will be able to catch him. Landy is running beautifully."

Bannister dashed into the final turn, shocked that Landy was still
driving so hard. This man was a machine. Because Bannister had abandoned his even pace in the third lap, he was more tired at this point
than he had expected to be. They had run so fast, for so long. Bannister
had to win, though. He had too much to prove to himself and to others.
His finishing kick had to be there in the end. It had not been in Helsinki. Every hour of training, every race, every sacrifice, every bit of his
love for running, had come down to this final moment, this final half-
lap around the track. When they came out of this bend into the final
straight, he had to be close enough to strike. Once again he drew a bead
on Landy's back. His legs had to be deadening, Bannister told himself.
Stride by stride, Bannister closed the gap between them. If Landy had

only known how much he had exhausted his competitor, he might have found the strength to go faster, but he didn't know. The front-runner never did.

As they neared the home straight, Bannister marshaled his remaining kick. This was his final chance. This was the point in the race he and Stampfl had decided Landy would never anticipate, this was the strike he had practiced with Chataway. Bannister needed to win. He *had* to win. The Australian could run as an expression of the best that was within him, but Bannister ran to be better than anyone else. This was the moment to reveal that he was. Ninety yards from the tape, Bannister swung his arms high and lengthened his stride. He urged his tired muscles into action. The effort took every shred of will and heart he had left. When he passed Landy, he wanted to do so fast.

Coming out of the bend, Landy thought he had finally shaken Bannister. He could no longer see Bannister's shadow. Good thing, since Landy knew he had no more strength in his legs. He looked over his left shoulder to make sure he had succeeded.

Exactly at that moment Bannister hurled himself around Landy on the right in two long strides, seeing the Australian glance the other way and knowing that the hesitation would cost him, if only the smallest fraction of a second. At seventy yards to the tape, Bannister seized the lead. It was exhilaration. It was triumph. Although excruciatingly painful to keep his speed, this was the moment he loved most in running, the moment when his spirit fused with the physical act of running. The roar of the crowd pushed him onward. Everything was a blur but the finish line. He sped down the track, momentum carrying him now. Landy tried to kick again down the homestretch but knew that his legs were finished.

"Bannister has passed Landy," Alston shouted excitedly, losing any sense of unbiased composure. "He comes into the straight. It's going to be Bannister's race. Landy is flagging. Here comes Bannister, striding absolutely magnificently. He's got a lead of two yards, three yards, four yards, about fifteen yards to go, and Bannister. . . ."

The English miler sprinted to the finish, his long stride unfailing. With a last drive off his right foot, he leapt forward, head back in sheer exultation. He broke through the tape, victory his at last.

"He's done it! He's done it!" Chataway exclaimed into the microphone, tens of thousands of Canadian listeners sharing in his excitement.

A stride and a half past the tape, Bannister was in a state of collapse. The will that had held his legs up was now spent. Landy finished second, five yards behind. His shoulders slackened, and he closed his eyes briefly, as if he wanted to be anywhere at that moment but there. He slowed and walked forward as the English team manager, Leslie Truelove, kept Bannister, whose face was deathly pale, from falling. The track was swallowed up with officials and athletes. Ferguson came in third, Milligan fourth, Boyd fifth, Halberg sixth, and Baillie seventh, but they were forgotten. In the stands guards kept a feverish crowd from rushing the track.

Landy tried to step clear of the melee, but too many people surrounded him. He had run his hardest, done everything he could, yet Bannister never broke. "Hard luck, John. . . . Great run, though, great effort." He gave his well-wishers a smile, but there was little anyone could say to quell his disappointment.

Bannister drew in several deep breaths, still held up by his team manager. People surrounded him, congratulating him, patting his back, shaking his hand. When his legs finally regained some strength, there was only one person he wanted to see. He stood upright, loosened himself from Truelove, and jogged forward, filled with the glory of his triumph. Weaving through the mass of bodies, he found Landy between two policemen and threw his arms around him.

"You were colossal, Roger." Landy smiled.

"I knew that if I did beat you, it would take everything I had," Bannister said, keeping his left arm around the Australian, knowing the anguish he must have been feeling.

Photographers herded around them to get a shot of the two together. Fans were pushing and pulling to get at them. Bannister leaned backward to draw more breath. He nearly collapsed again, and Landy, looking absent of strain, held him strong.

In the infield, away from the pandemonium, the four timekeepers who had clicked their stopwatches when Bannister broke through the tape and the three who clocked Landy settled on the official time. The three timekeepers stationed at the 1,500-meter mark had already agreed that Landy, who had led the race 120 yards from the finish, was only one-tenth of a second shy of his world record of 3:41.9 set in Turku. The official times for the top three finishers, Landy, Bannister, and Ferguson, were decided and given to the announcer to read over the public-address system. Over the loudspeaker the announcer declared what most in the stadium already knew unofficially. Nonetheless, a quiet descended throughout the stands. "Winner of event six, the mile, Roger Bannister, in a time of 3:58.8. . . . Second place, John Landy, in a time of 3:59.6. . . . Third place . . ."

Cheers and applause boomed through the stadium as Bannister and Landy jogged around the track, waving at the stands. In the race of the century, in the contest between the first two milers ever to break four minutes, both runners had once again crossed the threshold. It was perfection in sport.

In New York Wes Santee was alight with excitement as he spoke into the camera. "It was a magnificent race, and I think the better man won. . . . Those two boys just threw everything into it, and the result was this greatest of mile races ever run. Bannister was magnificent, but so was Landy." As the other panelists commented on the race, Santee looked off wistfully. The two milers had run tremendously, and he would call them later to say so, but Santee still believed that had he been in the thick of the battle he would have breasted the tape first. Sitting there in the studio, he was worn out, as if he had actually run in the race himself. As he later explained, "I was more exhausted because I hadn't been there."

In Melbourne Landy's family was deflated by the outcome. Reporters were keen for their comments, but they held off for the moment. Les Perry, agonized by his friend's defeat, called the Landy house to say how sorry he was that John had lost. He found that Landy's mother was philosophical, not full of lament. They were proud of John, with or without a victory. Cerutty, who usually used these big occasions to pontificate on his insights into Landy, was absent of comment. Robbie Morgan-Morris, who idolized Landy and was given the miler's singlet after his December 1952 run, best described what millions in his country felt that morning after hearing the news: "When Landy lost in Vancouver, the whole of Australia cried."

In London newspaper editors were already preparing the next day's headlines. Franz Stampfl, who had known Bannister would win from the moment Landy proved unable to shake him loose on the last turn, was quietly satisfied. For Stampfl the race was a triumph of the individual will, and he was simply glad to have helped in the effort. When he went to bed that night, still unable after all those years to sleep under sheets because of his memories of confinement, he himself was testament to this triumph, though he never would have admitted it.

In Vancouver, ten minutes after the race had finished and the crowd was starting to calm itself after the bedlam, Bannister donned his track suit with "England" stitched across its front and moved to the winner's stand. A green-capped official had placed the results of the mile race on the results board, including their times, below the oversized portrait of a saluting Queen Elizabeth. Bannister stepped up onto the top position, Landy to his right, Ferguson to his left. Bannister looked out across the stadium, overwhelmed by the sight of it all. It was his finest moment. He had beaten the best of competitors in John Landy. He had brought glory to his country. He had captured victory in a race greater than any numerical barrier. Roger Bannister had run the perfect mile.

EPILOGUE

And thick and fast they came at last
And more and more and more

— LEWIS CARROLL,
Alice's Adventures in Wonderland

TWENTY MINUTES AFTER Bannister crossed the finish line ahead of Landy in one of the most triumphant moments in sport, tragedy struck. Thirty-five-year-old English team captain Jim Peters ran into the stadium for the last few hundred yards of the marathon. The favorite to win, he was more than a mile in front of his nearest competitor, and the crowd rose to its feet to cheer him around the track. But something was wrong with Peters. He looked uncertain on his feet and almost blissfully unaware of where he was. The crowd hushed.

Peters took a few steps forward, weaving from side to side like a drunk, and then collapsed. He rolled to his side, his white singlet stained by the track's clay dust, and pushed himself to his feet. His arms were listless, his legs akimbo, and his face blanched. He struggled forward another few yards and then he stopped. Wavering, he took one more beleaguered step and then fell. He sat on the track, looking toward the sky before once again finding his way to his feet. His legs then buckled again and he dropped back down. Everyone in the stadium watched in horror, suddenly aware of the scorching sun and thick air and seeing the effect of those conditions on a runner gallantly trying to finish his race. As Peters attempted to stand yet again, people buried their heads into each other's shoulders; they covered their faces with their hats and wept; they begged for him to stop or for someone to help him. Please help him.

Bannister and Landy stood next to each other on the infield. For two runners who time and time again had pushed themselves to the extreme, they understood why Peters drove himself onward. At this level of competition an athlete had to ignore the body's call to stop. After years of punishing training, it was instinct.

For almost fifteen minutes Peters stumbled, staggered, and at times crawled forward, making his way 150 yards around the track before dropping for the twelfth time. This looked to be the end, but then he pushed himself back to his feet, zigzagging another twenty yards forward to where he thought the finish line was. Just as Peters was about to collapse again, the British trainer gathered him in his arms. The finish line was still two hundred yards away, and the British team manager, Leslie Truelove, had seen enough.

A stretcher was called, and Peters was carried into the dressing room, barely conscious. "Did I win?" were his first words to the nurse before the ambulance arrived. To the thousands in the stadium waiting to hear of his condition, Peters was a painful reminder of how far these athletes were willing to go to capture victory. Rarely in the history of sport had tragedy and triumph been juxtaposed in such a short space of time.

The next day newspaper front pages chronicled the extraordinary climax of the Empire Games, some carrying side-by-side columns: "Triumph!" and "Disaster!" Mostly, though, editors led with the dramatic mile race. "The Mile of the Century—And Bannister Wins for England!" headlined the *News of the World*. "Bannister Wins Greatest Mile Race of All" bannered the usually understated *Times*. "Bannister Outruns Landy" detailed the *New York Times* on the front page above the fold—quite a placement considering there was no American in the race. The *Chicago Tribune* and *New York Herald Tribune* gave similar prominence to the story. "The Great Finish! One of Us Had to Crack: John" read the *Melbourne Argus*. "Bannister's Triumph in Empire Mile" led the *Sydney Morning Herald*, but not without a sub-banner that said, "Bannister Collapses!" Of the many stories from the day, one evoked the mile race's importance best. British marathoner Stanley Cox, delirious from the heat, ran headlong into a telephone pole in the twenty-third mile of his race. When he finally came to, he wanted to know one thing: "Did Bannister make it?" After hearing that he had, Cox said, "God bless him," and then lay back down.

After the closing ceremonies in Vancouver, Roger Bannister did not return immediately to London with the rest of the team but instead did what any good doctor would have done: he stayed on to help tend to Jim Peters, who had been hospitalized for severe heat stroke and dehydration, which precipitated the end of his running career. Bannister flew back with Peters in case there were any complications during the marathoner's journey. Peters and Bannister were scheduled to fly into London Airport a week later, where a press contingent was waiting. A thick fog caused their plane to be diverted, and they landed in Kent in almost complete anonymity. One of the world's most famous athletes, back from claiming glory for his country, had to wait for over an hour to clear customs. Later, when Bannister arrived in Harrow by car, he was able to enjoy a small celebration with his friends and family. The next day he ran alone around the Harrow cricket field, pleased to be home and away from the crush of media attention.

Two weeks after returning from Vancouver, Bannister traveled to Berne, Switzerland, for the European Championships. The 1,500-meter final was almost a replay of the race he had lost two years before in Helsinki. As Bannister later said, the race promised "a crowded field, lots of barging, twelve runners, all Europeans, and the best in the world. . . . It was an act of completion that I felt I needed." From the gun, Bannister ran a tactical race, staying back in sixth position through the first 400-meter lap and allowing Czechoslovakia's Stanislav Jungwirth, West Germany's Werner Lueg, and Denmark's Gunnar Nielsen to carry the lead. By the end of 800 meters Bannister had moved into second place behind Jungwirth, with Nielsen in third place. At 1,200 meters they held the same positions, but the Czech was flagging. The Dane appeared to be the lone runner who could challenge Bannister. Into the back straight, with only two hundred meters left to go, Bannister unleashed his kick—nearly in the same place he had hoped to burst ahead in Helsinki. This time his kick did not falter, and he pulled quickly away from Jungwirth and Nielsen. The Dane tried to recover some of the gap, but Bannister was unfailing. He drove to the finish, long stride after long stride, and won easily. Nielsen, who claimed the silver medal, told reporters after the race that he was giving up middle-distance running to take up lawn tennis. Such was the devastating nature of Bannister's finishing kick. But Nielsen would soon have no reason to fear the great English miler, because after the final Bannister announced that he had run his last race. He was retiring from athletics to devote himself to medicine.

In the span of 112 days Bannister had broken the mile barrier, graduated from St. Mary's, passed his medical board exams, courted his future wife Moyra, beaten John Landy in the "Mile of the Century," claimed the 1,500-meter European crown, and won his future residency as a doctor. In a word, he had done it all.

At the Savoy Hotel on the last day of 1954, he was honored with the "Sportsman of the Year" award by Lord Brabazon, who in his magisterial voice summarized what the whole of Britain now felt for Bannister: "I'd like to say, Bannister, we have taken you to our hearts. . . . In your bearing, in your approach to sport, in your modesty, you are an example to the world of our ideal sportsman. . . . It is given to very few people to do something in this world which will be forever remembered. That is what you have done."

John Landy later succinctly characterized his loss at Vancouver: "It was the race I had to win, but I didn't." Directly after the race he was the consummate gentleman, praising Bannister for a terrific run and telling the press that the better man had won. A day later he told the press that he had accepted a teaching job at Geelong Grammar School and that his future as a miler was "hazy." But this announcement was drowned out by the report that his foot had been cut prior to the race and that he had said nothing about it. Andy O'Brien, the sportswriter who had promised to keep Landy's cut foot a secret, broke his word and told what he knew on a nationwide Canadian broadcast. At first Landy tried to discount the story. A *Melbourne Herald* correspondent approached him in the Empire Village and asked, "Did you stand on a flashbulb on Thursday?"

"How do I know if I stepped on a flashbulb? All I'm saying is that I went to the mile start 100 percent fit." Landy moved away, favoring his right leg over his left.

"Are you sure that limp isn't due to a cut?" The correspondent stopped him.

"If I can run a 3:59.6 with a limp," Landy said, "I've got possibilities as a runner."

The story was too big to hide, however. Journalists tracked down the doctor who had tended to Landy. They confronted the Australian team manager to see what he had known (nothing). Finally Landy admitted the truth but remained adamant that it had made no difference in the race. None. His story would never change, and the fact was that he *did* run a sub-four-minute mile in the final.

When Landy returned to Australia, he discovered that his zeal for racing was gone. He had no intention to run unless it was at the best of his ability. "Everybody beat me when I got home," he said.

A schoolboy beat me in a quarter-mile. I could see no reason for going on. Running is not a big sport in Australia, and I had run against the best in the world on the best tracks in the world. At home I faced the prospect of running badly on mediocre tracks against mediocre competition in little meets attended by three people. It was too much. Running is not a life; I had to quit sometime. I decided that the time had come to scrub it.

The headmaster at Geelong Grammar, Dr. J. R. Darling, provided Landy with a retreat. He had started a branch of the school in Timbertop, a secluded enclave in the Victorian Alps, where each student was required to live for a year. Darling needed a biology teacher, and Landy accepted the post. The first seven months were a dark period for the miler, one often spent hiking alone through the woods. He was away from family and friends and found himself constantly reliving that moment when Bannister passed him. Gradually, though, the desire to race took hold of him again, and he began training. In sand shoes, Landy ran along meandering trails and up and down hills, with no destination or end point in mind. He abandoned his schedules and for the first time in a long while enjoyed running again.

On January 4, 1956, Landy returned to Olympic Park for his first race since his defeat by Bannister. Melbourne newspapers had a heyday, announcing, "Landy to Run Next Week," in a tall linotype. Landy ran in the half-mile against the world-record holder in the distance, Len Spurrier. Landy lost by only inches. At month's end in the Victorian Championships, he blistered the Olympic Park track, doing what he had never been able to do before in Australia: run under four minutes. He clocked a 3:58.6, the second-fastest mile in history, second only to his own world record, set in Turku, which had yet to be improved. The next day he won the 880-yard title in his fastest time in the distance,

1:50.4, showing newfound speed and besting a sixteen-year-old Australian record. A few weeks later he beat his own record in the three-mile event by eleven seconds. Melbourne's favorite son was back, better than before, and with the 1956 Olympics set to be held in the city, a 1,500-meter Olympic gold was likely to be theirs.

At the Australian Championships in early March Landy was slated to go for a new mile record. A new crop of milers, including Robbie Morgan-Morris, Ron Clarke, and Merv Lincoln—all of whom had been inspired by his efforts in the four-minute mile pursuit—were set against him. Over twenty thousand people showed up at Olympic Park. By the end of the second lap Morgan-Morris was in the lead, having run 2:02, with Clarke in second place and Landy in third. The race looked to be unremarkable.

Into the second turn of the third lap, however, with the entire field muscling for position to go into the bell lap, Clarke unexpectedly tumbled to the track. Landy was right behind him and tried to jump clear of him. The rest of the field shot ahead. Instead of continuing, Landy stopped and turned back to see if Clarke was all right. Although Landy had spiked Clarke's arm with his shoe, the nineteen-year-old miler got back to his feet, said he was okay, and then rushed past Landy to rejoin the race. At this point Landy had lost roughly seven seconds and was forty yards back from Lincoln, now in first position. Nonetheless, Landy chased after the leaders. He sprinted the remainder of the third lap to get within striking distance. Into the turn he was only fifteen yards back, having already passed Clarke. By the back straight he had come within five yards, and around the last turn he burst past Lincoln and sprinted to the finish to win the race by twelve yards in 4:04.2.

The renowned sports journalist Harry Gordon wrote an open letter to Landy in the *Melbourne Sun*, summarizing what many felt after seeing the race:

> Dear John,
>   The fellows in the Press box don't have many heroes. Often they help to make them—but usually they know too much about them to believe in them. Up in the Press seats they don't usually clap. . . . Mostly, they've mastered the art of observing without becoming excited. On Saturday at 4:35 P.M., though, they forgot the rules. They had a hero—every one of them. And you were it. In the record books, [today's race] will look a very ordinary run for these

days. But, for my money, the fantastic gesture and the valiant recovery make it overshadow your magnificent miles in Turku and Vancouver. It was your greatest triumph.

A couple of months later Landy flew to California to help promote the Melbourne Olympics. He ran back-to-back sub-four-minute miles, became a hero to American track and field fans, and boosted ticket sales for the 1956 Olympics. But the trip, which Landy took more out of obligation than desire, cost him dearly. At a time when he should have been resting, he had flown halfway around the world, done countless interviews, and run on the hard California tracks, which aggravated the tendonitis he had developed. At the 1,500-meter Olympic final he placed a disappointing third. Ron Delany, whom Landy had crushed in one of his races in California, won the gold. As with Vancouver, Landy never uttered a word of complaint about his misfortune. After the Olympics he ran a couple of more races, but then retired in February 1957 at the age of twenty-six.

Wes Santee never broke the four-minute mile, nor did he participate in the 1956 Olympics, both ambitions that he had set out to achieve when he finished Marine boot camp at summer's end in 1954.

In November 1954 track and field expert Cordner Nelson predicted that "1955 should be a great season for the ex-Kansan. He will not have to run two to four races every weekend. Instead he'll concentrate on the mile, and if he doesn't break 3:58, I'll be disappointed." The Marines supported Santee in his efforts, permitting him a schedule that allowed him to enter competitions. After all, his running brought them good press. He trained as religiously as ever, and though Danna was expecting their first child, his focus remained sharp. During the winter season he set a new world indoor record with a 4:03.8 mile. At his first outdoor meet at the Texas Relays, he shaved one-tenth of a second off his best mile time with a 4:00.5. A sub-four-minute mile looked guaranteed, and Bill Easton, who continued to coach Santee, said after the race, "If you got this close the first time you tried outdoors this season, you can't miss. It will come." Unfortunately, this was the fastest he would ever run the mile.

On June 1 a *San Francisco Chronicle* article reported that in a series of West Coast meets in 1955 — including the West Coast Relays (May 14), the Coliseum Relays (May 20), and the California Relays (May 21)

—Santee had received $3,000 in expense money. AAU rules allowed athletes only $15 per day. The *Chronicle* article neglected to mention that Santee had recently turned down an invitation to run in a meet sponsored by the newspaper in which the miler was offered much more than his AAU limit in expenses. Santee refused because he had a previous speaking engagement at a Catholic high school in Redding, Pennsylvania. Whether or not the *Chronicle* article was hypocrisy or vendetta, Santee was in trouble. Dan Ferris and the AAU demanded an immediate investigation. The Missouri Valley AAU, which had jurisdiction over the matter, looked into the allegations and determined that Santee had taken at least $1,200 in expenses. They permanently suspended him as an amateur athlete.

Santee appealed; since he was in Quantico, Easton went in his stead to argue the case. His coach did not dispute that Santee had accepted the money, but he pointed out that the meet promoters, most of whom were AAU officials, had freely offered it to him. Years later Santee explained it this way: "It was as if I handed my grandson a candy bar, he ate it, and then I slapped him for eating it." Easton asked the simple question: if it was illegal, why were these officials giving him the excess expense money in the first place? The obvious answer to the question was that amateur officials wanted Santee at their meets to sell tickets. However, no such explanation was forthcoming. Instead, the Missouri Valley AAU simply annulled Santee's suspension by a twenty-one-to-seven vote. Perhaps they were unwilling to expose the underbelly of what sports historian Joseph Turrini referred to as their "underground-labor-relations system in track." Santee considered the matter resolved and turned his attention to the 1956 Olympics. But Dan Ferris and the AAU were not finished. The miler and those rallying around his cause, including Frank Carlson, an influential U.S. senator, were threatening the AAU's control of amateur athletics. This was intolerable. In December 1955 Ferris reopened the case, even after the time allotted by AAU procedures to pursue the investigation further had passed. Santee continued to race, but his focus was distracted by the legal wrangling.

Early in 1956 Ferris privately asked Santee to quit amateur athletics before things got even uglier, but he refused. In fact, Santee, aided by Charles Grimes, a bulldog former New York City district attorney who had taken the case pro bono, warned Ferris that he would sue the AAU for an illegal investigation. This did not help. On February 19, 1956, the AAU banned Santee from amateur athletics. Ferris told reporters that the young Kansan would "never run in another track meet in which the AAU [was] involved." Only after Grimes complained to the press did the AAU turn over the evidence to support its secret investigation. It claimed that in 1955 Santee took $2,355 more in expenses than allowed. He was also punished for using a "booking agent" in California, namely Al Franken. Franken denied the accusation and later said that the idea of Santee requiring "a booking agent was like Muhammad Ali in his heyday needing someone to speak for him." None of the AAU officials who had given Santee the expense money received more than a slap on the hand.

Santee continued to fight. On March 1, 1956, he received a temporary injunction on his ban from the New York State Supreme Court. More and more people came to Santee's defense, including Glenn Cunningham and several other prominent athletes who knew well the hypocrisy and unchecked power of the AAU. The wife of Jim Thorpe, who was the most famous American athlete to be banned by the amateur officials, asked that every American "protect this man from the bloodsucking octopus of the AAU." A survey conducted in California found that only one person among the 4,639 polled thought that the AAU was in the right on this matter. When Santee competed at events, the stadium cheered his name and booed the AAU. Unfortunately for Santee, however, this matter was about power, not popularity.

The AAU immediately went to court to have the injunction lifted. Meet directors and athletes feared that if they invited Santee or ran against him, they risked punishment. In March 1956 Santee went out to his lawyer's house on Long Island. The athlete wanted to testify. Grimes asked him what he planned to testify to and Santee said, "That all of us got more money than the rule book allowed." Grimes, taking on the role of the AAU lawyer, asked, "How do you know?"

Santee told Grimes that he had seen many athletes take money from the AAU over the years, some of whom were to be on the 1956 Olympic team. And then he suddenly understood Grimes's question. If Santee were to testify, he would have to name names, something he refused to do. In court the next day Santee did not testify in his own defense. The AAU lawyer excoriated him in his summation, saying, "He can run a mile, but he cannot walk twenty feet to the witness stand in his own defense. He makes a confession by not calling a single witness in his own behalf." The judge lifted the injunction, and Santee was again banned from amateur athletics, this time for life.

Enraged at the injustice of the AAU's action, he telephoned Easton. "What do we do now, coach?"

Easton knew the fight was over. His tone was resigned. "I don't know what to do, Wes. There's nothing you can do."

Though Santee was the best middle-distance runner in America, he was not going to the Olympics. As for his four-minute dreams, even though Al Franken tried to get him together with Roger Bannister and John Landy in a professional race, the idea never got off the ground. Santee had been tangled up in the middle of a sporting world in transition, where amateur officials were fast losing control to the rising tide of professionalism. Santee was its victim.

On May 28, 1955, Dr. Roger Bannister, now retired from athletics, went to White City Stadium to support Chris Chataway in the British Games mile race. Chataway's fiercest competitors were his countryman Brian Hewson and Hungary's Laszlo Tabori. At the three-quarter-mile mark Hewson held the lead in a time of 3:02. In the back straight Chataway and Hewson were neck and neck, with Tabori in third. Then the Hungarian began to kick; the two British milers answered with their own increase in pace. With sixty yards to the tape, the three were within inches of each other. They fought to the finish, Tabori stretching out a lead of four yards by the tape to win. Chataway and Hewson crossed the line in the same time. All three ran under four minutes, and Bannister, having lost his world mile record to Landy almost a year before, now found that he no longer laid claim to the fastest mile in Britain.

"Après moi, le déluge," Bannister said in the days after he made history at the Iffley Road track in Oxford, referring to the famous statement by Madame de Pompadour, intimate of Louis XV. With the barrier of the four-minute mile removed, the flood began. First Landy, then Tabori, Chataway, and Hewson. Was Bannister's prediction accurate because he had removed the psychological obstacle that the four-minute mile might not be impossible? Or had the barrier's fall simply been a matter of progress—of runners training better and more frequently? The answer probably falls somewhere in between, but there is no doubt that the four-minute mile turned out to be little more than a stepping-stone taken by the fastest milers of today, fifty years after Bannister's feat, on their way to greatness.

Progress on the world mile record has been steady since 1954. Landy held his record for two days shy of four years when Derek Ibbotson from Yorkshire ran 3:57.2 in London, fulfilling a promise he had made to his wife on the birth of their first daughter a month before. On August 6, 1958, Herb Elliott from Australia, the much-heralded new prodigy of Percy Cerutty, obliterated Ibbotson's time by nearly three seconds with a 3:54.5 mile in Dublin. Of his astounding run Elliott later remarked, "It was just another time, another progression." Naturally enough, that was not how Ibbotson felt. Elliott had been staying with him before he left to go to Dublin. When the Australian returned to gather his things, he found them on the doorstep. "What's my case doing out here?" Elliott asked. Ibbotson said, "If you think you're staying here after taking my record you can piss off." In 1962 New Zealander Peter Snell, whose workout schedule included twenty-two-mile Sunday runs in the mountains around Auckland, lowered Elliott's time by one-tenth of a second. And in 1964 he lowered his own record by three-tenths of a second to 3:54.1. He was bested by half a second a few months later by Frenchman Michel Jazy (3:53.6), who then lost his crown in 1966 to Jim Ryun (3:51.3), a Kansas native and the first American to hold the record since Norman Taber in 1915. Ryun was also the first high school student to run the mile in under four minutes. His coach, Bob Timmons, had inspired him by telling him stories of *Roger Bannister.*

It took eight more years before Ryun's time was bested by Tanzania's Filbert Bayi, who held the record for four short months until New Zealand's John Walker ran 3:49.4 on August 12, 1975. Then the great rivalry between the United Kingdom's Sebastian Coe and Steve Ovett saw the record pass back and forth between the two over the course of twenty-five months. Their battles recalled the days of Haegg and Andersson. Coe ended with the best time of 3:47.33 in August 1981 (records now being parsed to the hundredth of a second). His countryman Steve Cram followed him with a 3:46.31 mile in 1985; Algeria's Noureddine Morceli ran 3:44.39 in 1993; and then Morocco's Hicham El Guerrouj delivered a 3:43.13 mile in Rome on July 7, 1999. If Bannister had been in the same race, he would have finished almost a quarter of a lap behind. When El Guerrouj seized the world mile record, almost one thousand individuals had run under four minutes.

So much for a barrier.

This progress begs the question: how fast can the mile be run? If it can be run in less than four minutes, can it be run in less than three and a half? The prognosticators of the past — those who wagered bottles of champagne with Joseph Binks that the four-minute mile was a fantastical dream, those like Brutus Hamilton who banked their reputations on a "perfect record" that stopped at 4:01.6—have all been proven wrong. As for how far off the mark they were, one has to excuse them for not foreseeing synthetic tracks, high-tech shoe design, two-a-day workouts, engineered diets, high-altitude training, and a field of milers selected from countries far and wide, the very best of whom find a prosperous career and not a little fame in running. This is to say nothing of those who will dare push the body's limits through performance-enhancing drugs, hormone replacement, and—don't be surprised—genetic modification. The only sure bet as to how fast the mile will be run is to acknowledge the wisdom of the old cliché: "Records are made to be broken." The longer a record stands, the surer one can be that some ambitious young kid will put it in his or her sights.

But the methods and reasons for pursuing ever-faster miles have changed in the past half-century. If one is to become an elite athlete today, there is little room for anything else. The best train four or five hours a day, and their lives completely revolve around running. When some discover that their times fail to improve no matter what kind or amount of training they undergo, they turn to drugs that not only threaten their expulsion from competition if they are caught but also have dangerous side effects.

Of course, the rewards for being a top-flight runner seem to mitigate the sacrifices involved in becoming one. Allan Webb, the first American to break Jim Ryun's high school mile record, dropped out of the University of Michigan after his freshman year to earn six figures a year in sponsorship deals. El Guerrouj socks away more than a million dollars a year in appearance fees, sponsorships, and prize money. Beyond a desire to be the best, today's runners have many such commercial reasons to claim the fastest mile in the world. But the steady encroachment of commerce into modern athletics over the years has taken some of the romance out of the mile record. There was more honor in pursuing it for no other reward than knowing one had pushed through the boundary of what was possible.

No matter how far the record falls, people will look back to the breaking of the four-minute barrier and the showdown between Landy and Bannister in Vancouver as two defining moments in the history of the mile—and of sport as well. On May 6, 1954, Roger Bannister, an amateur who trained little more than an hour a day and for whom running was nothing more than a passionate hobby, achieved greatness on a cinder track he had helped to build, in front of a small crowd, a handful of journalists, and a lone camera crew that had to be persuaded to attend. Only three months later, in a modern concrete and steel stadium, Landy and Bannister battled each other in a heavily promoted race covered by an army of journalists and camera teams and broadcast to millions of homes worldwide, with their fiercest rival as a commentator. The "Mile of the Century" had all the hallmarks of a professional sporting event except that not one of its competitors earned a penny in the process. If the first race sounded the death knell of amateurism, the second race struck one of the first notes of sport's future.

Fifty years later Wes Santee, John Landy, and Roger Bannister live only a short distance from where each ran his first fast miles. Walking around the tracks at the University of Kansas, Olympic Park, and Iffley Road, they must hear the echoes of the past: the pop of the starter's pistol, the rhythmic strike of steel spikes into cinder, the crescendo of the crowd's cheer, the crackle of the public-address system as everyone hushes for the mile time, wondering whether today would be *the* day.

Our sporting heroes often strike us as ageless. We remember them in their prime, their faces unblemished, their bodies still taut with power. If a measure of a person is how he lives his whole life and not simply his youth, then these three men deserve our regard for what they did after their pursuit of the four-minute mile as well. Wes Santee had a long and distinguished career serving as a Marine reservist while running his own insurance business. He remains a champion of the University of Kansas and continues to support youth programs in sport. After his teaching stint at Geelong Grammar, John Landy joined the chemical company ICI as a rural scientist and was head of its rural research and development division by the time he retired. He served on the Melbourne Olympic Committee, chaired a task force to promote Australian athletics, led the Australian Sports Drug Agency, and also wrote a couple of books on natural history. In 2000 he was appointed governor of Victoria. Once retired from athletics, Roger Bannister dedicated himself to medicine, becoming a noted neurologist. He sidelined as an official on Britain's Sports Council, where he led two major campaigns: first, building recreational centers throughout the country; and second, discouraging athletes from taking performance-enhancing drugs through random testing. In 1975 he was knighted for his efforts in medicine and sport. Bannister also wrote one of the most evocative books on running and was the master of Pembroke College at Oxford University.

Bannister, Landy, and Santee look back at their competitive running days with a blend of pride and "oh not that old story again." Santee remains stung by his fight with the AAU. Landy is wistful for what might have been in Vancouver. Bannister still exudes the determination and aggression that gave power to his finishing kick. Dramatic as their efforts were to many millions of people, the three speak pointedly about what sport gave to them, regardless of four-minute barriers and miracle miles.

Landy says, "Running gave me discipline and self-expression. . . . It has all the disappointments, frustrations, lack of success and unexpected success, which all reproduce themselves in the bigger play of life. It teaches you the ability to present under pressure. It teaches you the importance of being enthusiastic, dedicated, focused. All of these are trite statements, but if you actually have to go through these things as a young man, it's very, very important."

Santee would agree. "Hard work pays off," he says. "You have to be just as disciplined to run a business as you do to train for an athletic event. You have to eat right, still have to get up early and work more than others. Great athletes usually spend extra time in the weight room, shoot extra baskets, run extra sprints, whatever. And that whole thing translates into larger life. . . . When I'm going to give a speech, like to young Marines, I will plan my whole day around that so I am mentally and physically alert. You can't separate these when you're performing, same as if I was running an event. I still eat my tea, toast, and honey."

And as Bannister came to understand, "sport is about not being wrapped up in cotton wool. Sport is about adapting to the unexpected and being able to modify plans at the last minute. Sport, like all life, is about taking your chances."

AUTHOR'S NOTE

WHEN AN AUTHOR sets out to investigate a legend—and there are few stories as legendary in sport as the pursuit of the four-minute mile—it is initially difficult to see the heroes around whom events unfold as true flesh-and-blood individuals. Myth tends to wrap its arms around fact, and memory finds a comfortable groove and stays the course. What makes these individuals so interesting—their doubts, vulnerabilities, and failures—is often airbrushed out and their victories characterized as faits accomplis. But true heroes are never as unalloyed as they first appear (thank goodness). We should admire them all the more for this fact.

Getting past the panegyrics that populate this history has been the real pleasure behind my research. No doubt there have been some very fine articles written about this story, but only by interviewing the principals—Roger Bannister, John Landy, and Wes Santee—and their close friends at the time does one do justice to its depth. Their generosity in this regard has been without measure. These interviews, coupled with contemporaneous newspaper and magazine articles and memoir accounts by several individuals involved in these events, serve as the basis of *The Perfect Mile*. With this material, the story almost wrote itself.

I have included a collective reference for those interested in knowing the source behind particular conversations and scenes. No dialogue in this book was manufactured. All dialogue is directly quoted from either a secondary resource or an interview. That said, a half-century has passed since this story occurred. On some occasions dialogue was represented as the best recollection of what was probably said. Furthermore, memory has its faults, and in those situations where interview subjects contradicted one another, I almost always went with what the principal recollected. In those instances when contemporaneous sources (mainly newspaper articles) did not correspond with memory, I primarily went with the former, particularly when there were several sources indicating the same facts. Having inhabited this world of paper and interview tapes for the past eighteen months, I feel I have been a fairly accurate judge of the events as they happened. I hope that I have served the history of these heroes well.

ACKNOWLEDGMENTS

When beginning *The Perfect Mile*, I was inspired by the words of Alan Hoby, who in 1954 documented the role of a good sportswriter:

> It is not simply to write a technical treatise in which the performer is dissected like some laboratory specimen. . . . It is much more. It is heat and fire, drama and high excitement. It is victory and disaster. It is perspiration and the pungent whiff of liniment. It is the roar of the crowd. . . . Above all, it is recapturing for the reader the supreme effort of the [athlete]—the very heartbeats of the particular triumph or tragedy the reporter is striving to word-paint.

Re-creating the events of a story that occurred fifty years ago in this manner is no small feat, and any success I have had is thanks to the patience and forthrightness of Roger Bannister, John Landy, and Wes Santee. They each sat through several interview sessions, responded to scores of questions, and then entertained follow-up phone calls and correspondence providing further detail. I never could have written this book without them, and they have my heartfelt appreciation and respect.

In my travels to visit each of the principals I also connected with their friends, running mates, and acquaintances from the time, many of whom invited me into their homes and discussed days past. Thank you to Chris Chataway, Norris McWhirter, Nicolas Stacey, Ronald Williams, John Disley, Peter Hildreth, Terry O'Connor, and Pat Stampfl for regaling me with stories of Roger Bannister. Thank you to Len McRae, Geoff Warren, Trevor Robbins, John Vernon, Don Macmillan, Les Perry, Julius Patching, Ron Clarke, Robbie Morgan-Morris, Merv Lincoln, Kev Dynan, and Murray Halberg for sharing their recollections of John

Landy. And thank you to Tom Rupp, Dick Wilson, Al Frame, Lloyd Koby, Bob Timmons, Bill Mayer, Don Humphreys, and Herbie Semper for their many helpful insights and anecdotes about Wes Santee.

I would still be researching if it were not for sportswriter Dave Kuehls, who signed on at this book's inception to help me through each stage in the process. He tracked down interview subjects, guided me through the world of track and field, offered suggestions on each draft, and was truly my right-hand man from start to finish. Thanks to Liz O'Donnell, doyenne of the written word, who was my first reader and made critical edits in each chapter. I also want to acknowledge Todd Keithley, Bruce McKenna, and Joe Veltre for their early reads as well. And I would be remiss in not mentioning my friend Jim Catlin, who got me out of Dodge and housed me in his too-swank Milan flat for a month while I began this book.

Throughout I have been enthusiastically guided by my literary agent, Scott Waxman. He has a great eye and, most important, is a good man to have in your corner. Thanks also to Judi Heiblum, Justin Manasek, Joel Gotler, Danny Baror, and Susan Mindell.

I have had the pleasure of working with two fine publishers on this book, Houghton Mifflin in the United States and HarperCollins in the United Kingdom. At Houghton Mifflin I first want to thank my editor Susan Canavan. She possesses a terrific sense of narrative flow, wields a mean line-edit pencil, and has been a great champion of this book from the beginning. Thank you also to her assistant Sarah Gabert, as well as to Gary Gentel, Bridget Marmion, Lori Glazer, Carla Gray, and Megan Wilson. Drinks are on me when I come to Boston. At HarperCollins UK, I owe a great deal of gratitude to Michael Doggart, publishing director of CollinsWillow. He fired my imagination as to what this book could be and has been a great support throughout. Thank you also to Tarda Davison-Aitkens and the rest of the team in London.

This book is dedicated to Diane and her unyielding faith in what is possible.

NOTES

Prologue

page
ix *"How did he know"*: Roger Bannister, personal interview.
    "seemed so perfectly round": "The Milers," *Sports Illustrated*, June 27, 1994.
x   *Running the mile was an art form*: "Four-Minute Men," *Sports Illustrated*, August 16, 1994.
    "He just flat believed": Wes Santee, personal interview.
    "I'd rather lose a 3:58": Arthur Daley, "Listening to John Landy," *New York Times*, May 22, 1956.
    Running revealed to him: John Landy, personal interview.
    They spent a large part: "The Milers," *Sports Illustrated*, June 27, 1994.
xi *If they weren't training*: Chris Chataway, personal interview.
xii *"tapestry of alternating triumph and tragedy"*: Norris McWhirter, National Centre for Athletics Literature interview, University of Birmingham [n.d.].

Chapter 1

3   *"Bannister had terrific grace"*: Terry O'Connor, personal interview.
    Some said he could: Peter Hildreth, personal interview.
4   *Bannister loved that moment*: Roger Bannister, *The Four Minute Mile* (Globe Pequot Press, 1955), p. 59.
    He held his thumb: Norris McWhirter, personal interview.
    They were three years older: ibid.
    There lies the body: Norris McWhirter, "The Man Who Made History," *World Sport*, June 1954.
5   *"At least, Norris, you"*: Chris Chataway, personal interview.
    But he knew one way to make sure: Dr. Ronald Williams, personal interview.
    When the twenty-three-year-old Bannister: Arthur Daley, "Listening to a 4-Minute Mile," *New York Times*, May 14, 1954.
6   *"Roger . . . they put in a semifinal"*: Dr. Ronald Williams, personal interview.
    He was to be the hero: Terry O'Connor, personal interview.
    "It is gone": quoted in John Montgomery, *The Fifties* (George Allen and Unwin, 1965), pp. 46–47.

7   *"we still bathed":* quoted in Juliet Gardiner, *From Bomb to the Beatles* (Collins and Brown, 1999), p. 30.

It was so cold: Alfred Havighurst, *Twentieth-Century Britain* (Harper & Row, 1966), p. 399.

"the largest, saddest and dirtiest": quoted in ibid., p. 35.

8   *"just like Britain":* ibid., p. 52.

Crowds wearing black armbands: Harry Hopkins, *The New Look: A Social History of the Forties and Fifties in Britain* (Secker and Warburg, 1963), pp. 283–84.

"England has owed": J.E.C. Weldon, headmaster of Harrow, 1881–95, quoted in Richard Holt, *Sport and the British: A Modern History* (Oxford University Press, 1990), p. 205.

Yet even in sport: ibid., pp. 105–6.

"United, Euphoric": Peter Lewis, *The Fifties* (Heinemann, 1978), p. 15.

After that the country: Hopkins, *New Look*, pp. 283–84.

For a country that considered: Holt, *Sport and the British*, pp. 276–77.

He didn't come: Roger Bannister, American Academy of Achievement interview, October 27, 2000.

9   *All Roger knew:* Bannister, *Four Minute Mile*, p. 46.

Only later in life: Radio 4, "A Conversation Piece with Sue McGregor," May 17, 1990.

"I was startled and frightened": Bannister, *Four Minute Mile*, pp. 11–12.

When he was ten: Roger Bannister, American Academy of Achievement interview, October 27, 2000.

As an awkward, serious-minded twelve-year-old: Bannister, *Four Minute Mile*, pp. 32–35.

The next day Bannister eyed the favorite: ibid., p. 34.

10   *"You'll be dead before":* ibid., p. 38.

His new school: ibid., pp. 38–44.

Bannister intended to study: George Smith, *All Out for the Mile* (Forbes Robertson, 1955), pp. 144–45.

"If there was a moment": BBC, "Suspense: The Four-Minute Mile," July 18, 1954.

11   *"Stop bouncing":* Bannister, *Four Minute Mile*, pp. 50–51.

"over-stride in a series": ibid., p. 51.

The cruel winter: Smith, *All Out for the Mile*, pp. 144–45; Bannister, *Four Minute Mile*, pp. 56–61.

"You mean the Jack Lovelock": Bannister, *Four Minute Mile*, p. 60.

Six weeks later, on June 5, 1947: ibid., pp. 64–78.

12   *He had taken a coach:* Roger Bannister, American Academy of Achievement interview, October 27, 2000.

Bannister had spent the two previous years: Bannister, *Four Minute Mile*, pp. 88–118.

13   *First he flew to New Zealand:* ibid., pp. 124–29.

"No manager, no trainer": ibid., p. 136.

In front of forty thousand: "British Miler Beats Wilt; Gehrmann 3D," *Chicago Sunday Tribune*, April 29, 1951.

"worthy successor to Jack Lovelock": "Franklin Mile to Bannister," *New York Herald Tribune*, April 29, 1951.

"He's young, strong": "Bannister Hailed for Mile Triumph," *New York Times*, April 30, 1951.

"Anyone who beats him": Joe Binks, "Bannister's Race My Oslo Memory," *News of the World,* June 24, 1951.

14   *"Go Back to Your Own Distance, Roger"*: Doug Wilson, "Bannister Can Still Learn Much," *News of the World,* August 12, 1951.

    To escape the attention: Bannister, *Four Minute Mile,* pp. 149–50.

    Throughout the winter: ibid., pp. 153–59.

    "space-eating stride": "Bannister's Half-Mile in 1 Min 53 Sec," *Daily Mail,* May 29, 1954.

15   *"more sensitive, often more"*: L. A. Montague, "Why R. G. Bannister's Training Methods Are Right," *Manchester Guardian,* June 9, 1952.

    "Don't Worry About Bannister's Defeat": James Stagg, *Daily Mirror,* July 7, 1952.

    "No alibis": Norris McWhirter, "Bannister Will Have No Alibis," *Star,* May 3, 1952.

    "Victory at Helsinki": Bannister, *Four Minute Mile,* p. 159.

    A part of him suspected: ibid., pp. 159–60.

    "We will not let Britain down": "British Athletic Team Reach Helsinki," *Daily Telegraph,* July 16, 1952.

    His friend Chris Chataway: "Goggles for Chataway," *Star,* July 16, 1952.

    "I could hardly believe": Bannister, *Four Minute Mile,* p. 162.

Chapter 2

17   *In the narrow concrete tunnel:* Wes Santee, personal interview.

18   *"Boy, this building"*: ibid.

19   *His countrymen had cleared:* Red Smith, "Red Smith in Helsinki," *New York Herald Tribune,* July 19, 1952; Graem Sims, *Why Die? The Extraordinary Life of Percy Cerutty* (Lothian Books, 2003), pp. 113–14.

    Peerless Paavo: Jesse Abramson, "Nurmi," in *The Realm of Sport,* ed. Herbert Warren Wind (Simon & Schuster, 1966), pp. 629–33.

20   *From a distance: Manchester Guardian,* July 21, 1952.

    If his father: Wes Santee, personal interview. Many of the details of Santee's early life were checked against newspaper and magazine articles written about him in the early 1950s.

21   *"I just don't like to fiddle around"*: Bob Hurt, "Sure I'll Run the Four-Minute Mile," *Saturday Evening Post,* September 26, 1953.

25   *Santee did not bring his arms:* Wes Santee, personal interview; Bill Easton, "Santee's Stride" [n.d.], Archives of William Easton, University of Kansas.

    Led by Santee, the freshman: "KU Freshman Track Team Rated," *Daily Kansan,* February 1951.

    While some athletes were hesitant: Wes Santee, personal interview.

    "I want to make the Olympic team": Jerry Renner, "Wes Santee, KU Track Star," *Daily Kansan,* October 2, 1951.

26   *"Look what it says"*: Profile of Wes Santee [n.d.], Archives of William Easton, University of Kansas.

    "He's wilting in the sun": Wes Santee, personal interview.

    "Santee's not human": Bob Hurt, "Writers Name Santee as Drake Relays Star," *Daily Capital,* April 28, 1952.

    "Santee stuck out above": ibid.

    "Santee is the greatest": ibid.

27 *"win as he pleases":* U.S. Olympic Team meet schedule, Archives of William Easton, University of Kansas.

"*Wes, I'm sorry":* Wes Santee, personal interview.

Only the previous week: Dwain Esper, "Four Records Fall in AAU Championships," *Track and Field News,* July 1952.

The coach had the stocky build: James Gunn, "Second Isn't Good Enough: A Day in the Life of Bill Easton," *University of Kansas Alumni Magazine,* May 1959.

28 *The three weeks between the trial:* Wes Santee, personal interview.

He ran in an exhibition: Stan Hamilton, "Wes Santee" [n.d.], article in Santee's scrapbook.

Chapter 3

29 *All was quiet:* Norman Banks, *The World in My Diary: From Melbourne to Helsinki for the Olympic Games* (William Heinemann, 1953), pp. 54–55.

At fifty-seven: Harry Gordon, *Young Men in a Hurry: The Story of Australia's Fastest Decade* (Landsdowne, 1961), p. 18.

30 *Prancing around Motspur Park:* Graem Sims, *Why Die? The Extraordinary Life of Percy Cerutty* (Lothian Books, 2003), p. 118.

"So you're Bannister": ibid., p. 118.

"Others can run faster": ibid., p. 117.

On arriving in Helsinki: ibid., p. 117.

Earlier that evening: J. H. Galli, "Man of the Miracle Mile," *Sport,* August 1954.

31 *In London he had placed:* William T. J. Uren, *Australian Olympic Team at Helsinki 1952* (Australian Olympic Committee, 1952), pp. 58–59.

"paralyzing burst": Ron Carter, "Sprint Star Breaks Own in Final," *Melbourne Argus,* June 23, 1952.

"had not seen a runner": Bruce Welch, "Woman Athletes Star in Belfast," *Melbourne Age,* June 27, 1952.

He had even set: "Record 2-Mile by John Landy," *Melbourne Herald,* July 1, 1952.

"runners were oddities": Trevor Robbins, personal interview.

32 *The country had a long track and field tradition:* Geoff Warren, personal interview.

"Olympic Park [was] a depressing shambles": Joseph Galli, "Landy's Mile," *Amateur Athlete,* January 1953, pp. 17–18.

It has been noted that for every thirty words: Wray Vamplew and Brian Stoddart, *Sport in Australia* (Cambridge University Press, 1994), p. 11.

In the early 1950s: "Australians 'Most Avid Sports Fans,'" *Sydney Morning Herald,* July 23, 1953.

Total attendance in the minor rounds: Vamplew and Stoddart, *Sport in Australia,* pp. 11–13.

33 *"world champion":* "Fastest Man in the World," *Sun-Herald,* June 27, 1954.

Landy enjoyed a comfortable childhood: John Landy, personal interview; Les Perry, personal interview.

Young John Landy: John Landy, personal interview.

"prefects whack[ed] the boys": Paul O'Neil, "Duel of the Four-Minute Men," *Sports Illustrated,* August 1954.

John was part of a group: John Landy, personal interview.

In his final year: Joseph Galli, "Victorian John Landy May Soon Become Our Greatest Middle-Distance Runner," *Sports Novels,* April 1952.

34 *When he enrolled:* ibid.

The club captain: John Landy, personal interview.

"You're not fit": Len McRae, personal interview.

The two went over: Sims, *Why Die?* pp. 100–101; Percy Cerutty, *Sport Is My Life* (Stanley Paul, 1966), pp. 34–35.

35 *The first was Les Perry:* Sims, *Why Die?* pp. 80–86.

A year later: Les Perry, personal interview.

When Macmillan: Sims, *Why Die?* pp. 86–93; Don Macmillan, personal interview.

36 *"What did you say your name was?":* Sims, *Why Die?* pp. 100–101; Cerutty, *Sport Is My Life,* pp. 34–35; Joseph Galli, "Landy Will Set More Records, Says Coach," *Amateur Athlete,* August 1954; John Landy, personal interview. This scene, including the dialogue, is drawn from a combination of these sources.

When Landy left, Cerutty: Galli, "Landy Will Set More Records."

It took three weeks: Robert Solomon, *Great Australian Athletes: Selected Olympians 1928–1956* (R. J. Solomon, 2000), p. 163. Solomon has done an extensive study of John Landy's times in this book.

On May 22, 1951: John Landy, personal interview.

Landy had natural coordination: Galli, "Man of the Miracle Mile."

37 *Almost from the day:* Keith Dunstan, *Ratbags* (Sun Books, 1979), pp. 148–50; Sims, *Why Die?* pp. 7–33; Graeme Kelly, *Mr. Controversial: The Story of Percy Wells Cerutty* (Stanley Paul, 1964), pp. 35–67.

"I can't heal you": Sims, *Why Die?* p. 35.

He restricted his diet: ibid., pp. 34–56; Alan Trengrove, *The Golden Mile: The Herb Elliott Story* (Cassell, 1961), pp. 34–37.

38 *"I've come down to have a run":* Sims, *Why Die?* p. 49.

The road hadn't been easy: Trengrove, *Golden Mile,* p. 38.

"Thrust against pain": ibid.

The gate to the property: Trevor Robbins, personal interview; Sims, *Why Die?* pp. 105–10.

His parents were circumspect: John Landy, personal interview.

He had brought a sleeping bag: Trevor Robbins, personal interview; Sims, *Why Die?* pp. 105–10.

39 *"primitive man":* John Vernon, personal interview.

"Move your bloody arms": Sims, *Why Die?* p. 229.

40 *"Realization that":* Dunstan, *Ratbags,* p. 148.

"There. Did the cat": Trevor Robbins, personal interview.

41 *The first night Landy:* ibid.

"It's pretty tough out here": Don Macmillan, personal interview.

"He undervalues himself": Sims, *Why Die?* pp. 103–4.

"It is bad luck": "Cheers Were Mile[d]," *Melbourne Argus,* January 14, 1952.

42 *If Landy and a few others:* Julius Patching, telephone interview.

John heard the news: John Landy, personal interview.

"I don't know just what": Galli, "Victorian John Landy."

And he was very sensitive: Les Perry, personal interview.

Chapter 4

43   *The rain of the opening ceremonies:* The *Official Report of the Organizing Committee for the Games of the XV Olympiad, Helsinki 1952* (Werner Soderstrom Osakeyhtio, 1952), p. 247.

Santee awakened in his room: Wes Santee, personal interview.

44   *It was quite certain:* Jesse Abramson, "U.S. Athletes Are Favorites in Ten Events," *New York Herald Tribune,* July 6, 1952.

Late that afternoon: "U.S. Olympic Track Squad in Helsinki," *Topeka Capital,* July 10, 1952.

On the first day: Lainson Wood, "Zatopek Storms Home in Olympic 10,000 Metres," *Daily Telegraph,* July 21, 1952.

45   *"mobilized to win":* "Muscles Pop Through Iron Curtain," *Life,* July 28, 1952.

No effort was spared: Alan Hoby, *One Crowded Hour* (Museum Press, 1954), p. 41.

46   *When he saw Fred Wilt:* Wes Santee, personal interview.

47   *Sitting in the stands:* John Landy, personal interview.

48   *He was in the fourth:* "Track and Field Prospects: New World's Record Probable in Great 1,500 Meters," *Manchester Guardian,* July 16, 1952.

"there's nothing graceful": Jim Denison, ed., *Bannister and Beyond: The Mystique of the Four-Minute Mile* (Breakaway Books, 2003), p. 24.

He had failed to qualify: Robert Solomon, *Great Australian Athletes: Selected Olympians 1928–1956* (R. J. Solomon, 2000), p. 167.

When the gun went off: ibid., pp. 25–35; Cordner Nelson, "Profiles of Champions —Emil Zatopek," *Track and Field,* December 1953; Raymond Krise and Bill Squires, *Fast Tracks: The History of Distance Running* (Stephen Greene Press, 1982), pp. 119–20; Lainson Wood, "Chataway Cracks Within Sight of the Tape," *Daily Telegraph,* July 25, 1952.

"apoplectic fit": Hoby, *One Crowded Hour,* p. 25.

50   *Landy himself was impressed:* John Landy, personal interview.

"mad scramble": ibid.; "Hot Field," *Melbourne Herald,* July 25, 1952.

"No man or woman": "Olympic Athletes Criticised: Not Fit Enough," *Melbourne Age,* March 14, 1954.

51   *When Perry first arrived:* Graem Sims, *Why Die? The Extraordinary Life of Percy Cerutty* (Lothian Books, 2003), pp. 123–25; Les Perry, personal interview.

After his 1,500-meter loss: Geoff Warren, personal interview.

"Piped Piper of Hamelin": John Landy, personal interview.

"When I was in the 1950 European Championships": Les Perry, personal interview.

"I shall learn to have a better style": Frantisek Kozik, *Zatopek: The Marathon Victor* (Artia, 1954), p. 93.

52   *Roger Bannister was too exhausted:* Roger Bannister, *The Four Minute Mile* (Globe Pequot Press, 1955), pp. 168–80; Chris Chataway, personal interview; Nicholas Stacey, personal interview; Roger Bannister, personal interview.

"While he goes for a twenty-mile training run": Bannister, *Four Minute Mile,* p. 171.

53   *"Bannister had watched":* ibid., p. 172.

"eat a pair of spiked shoes": Nicholas Stacey, telephone interview.

"Don't Worry, We Are Still in the Fight": Daily Mirror, July 22, 1952.

"rarely bothered about picking": ibid.

But his legs hurt: Bannister, *Four Minute Mile*, pp. 168–80.

54 *"Good luck, Don"*: Don Macmillan, personal interview.

When the Duke of Edinburgh arrived: A. J. Liebling, "Letter from the Olympics," *The New Yorker*, August 9, 1952.

"There was a peculiar loneliness": Christopher Brasher, *Sportsmen of Our Time* (Victor Gollancz, 1962), p. 20.

Chris Chataway was also in the stands: Chris Chataway, personal interview.

Though tense and sapped: Roger Bannister, personal interview.

After Finnish middle-distance runner: Liebling, "Letter from the Olympics."

Suddenly they were off: Roger Bannister, personal interview; Bannister, *Four Minute Mile*, pp. 175–80; Chris Chataway, personal interview; R. L. Quercetani, "1,500 Meters," *Track and Field* August 1952; Brasher, *Sportsmen of Our Time*, pp. 20–21; Liebling, "Letter from the Olympics"; Douglas Wilson, "Bannister's Gallant Failure," *News of the World*, July 27, 1952; "Bannister Fourth in 1,500 Metres," *Times*, July 28, 1952.

55 *"He is not running"*: "Commentary by Harold Abrahams — 1,500 meters," 1952 Helsinki Olympic Games, BBC Sound Archives, July 1952.

56 *"A disaster is something"*: Brasher, *Sportsmen of Our Time*, p. 21.

Chapter 5

57 *"every morning in Africa"*: Bernd Heinrich, *Racing the Antelope: What Animals Can Teach Us About Running and Life* (Cliff Street Books, 2001), p. 9.

"symbolized laying claim": Edward Sears, *Running Through the Ages* (McFarland & Co., 2001), p. 14.

58 *Other early societies*: John Marshall Carter and Arnd Kruger, eds., *Ritual and Record: Sports Records and Quantification in Premodern Societies* (Greenwood Press, 1990); Allen Guttmann, *From Ritual to Record: The Nature of Modern Sports* (Columbia University Press, 1978). These are two illuminating books about early sporting traditions and how they were recorded and quantified.

A Greek citizen named Coroebus: John Kieran, "Olympic Games," in *The Realm of Sport*, ed. Herbert Warren Wind (Simon & Schuster, 1966), pp. 625–29.

Sporting ability was integral: John Blundell, *The Muscles and Their Story from the Earliest Times* (Chapman and Hall, 1864), p. xvii.

The Romans favored: ibid., p. 24.

mille passus: George Gretton, *Out in Front* (Pelham Books, 1968), pp. 83–84.

59 *By the nineteenth century*: Sears, *Running Through the Ages*, pp. 50–56.

Running a mile in less than five minutes: ibid., pp. 80–111.

For most of the nineteenth century: ibid., pp. 113–19.

60 *It was impossible to know*: ibid., pp. 110–213; George Smith, *All Out for the Mile* (Forbes Robertson, 1955), pp. 37–87. The history of the progress of the four-minute mile and the quotes in this short section are taken from these two sources. Smith's book is the best history of the mile and of the runners who achieved predominance that I found in my research. It contains rare interviews and profiles that have never been reproduced elsewhere. *Running Through the Ages* by Sears proved indispensable in my research on the history of running and contains innumerable anecdotes of great fun to anyone interested in running.

62   "the other side": Jim Denison, ed., *Bannister and Beyond: The Mystique of the Four-Minute Mile* (Breakaway Books, 2003), p. 11.

    Over the course of three and a half years: Roger Bannister, personal interview. The chart is from Smith, *All Out for the Mile*, p. 86.

63   *can the mile be run:* Lawrence J. Baack, ed., *The Worlds of Brutus Hamilton* (Tafnews, 1975), pp. 64–67.

    "When we stop this nonsense": Colonel Strode Jackson, *Collier's*, 1944.

    "The Poles had been reached": Frank Deford, "Pioneer Miler Roger Bannister and Everest Conqueror Edmund Hillary," *Sports Illustrated*, January 3, 2000; Denison, *Bannister and Beyond*, p. 13.

    Less than forty-eight hours: Bill Brown, "British Empire Versus U.S.A.," *Athletic Review*, September 1952.

    The stadium had staged: Norris McWhirter, personal interview.

    The stadium was now used: Terry O'Connor, personal interview.

64   *"every time we had stepped":* Wes Santee, personal interview.

65   *"I couldn't understand how":* Don Humphreys, personal interview.

    "Wesley Santee has recently": Wes Santee's scrapbook.

    Only days after: Bob Hurt, "Sure I'll Run the Four-Minute Mile," *Saturday Evening Post*, September 26, 1953.

    John Landy had a different announcement: John Landy, personal interview.

66   *For his stride:* Graem Sims, *Why Die? The Extraordinary Life of Percy Cerutty* (Lothian Books, 2003), pp. 136–44; John Landy, personal interview.

    On the flight back: John Landy, personal interview; Len McRae, personal interview.

    "He thoroughly deserved his success": "Travelling Too Much," *Melbourne Argus*, August 10, 1952.

67   *Save for a horse:* A. W. Ledbrooke, *Great Moments in Sport* (Phoenix House, 1956), pp. 39–43.

    "Hang out the crepe": Cecil Bear, "Bravo Helsinki!" *World Sports*, September 1952.

    "Britain was failing to win": Hyton Cleaver, *Before I Forget* (Robert Hale, 1961), p. 176.

    "Roger Bannister could have won": "Give Them Some REAL Competition," *Daily Mirror*, August 9, 1952.

    Not only did Bannister: Christopher Brasher, *Sportsmen of Our Time* (Victor Gollancz, 1962), p. 16.

68   *"greater degree of self-determination":* ibid., p. 21.

Chapter 6

71   *In Melbourne's Central Park:* John Landy, personal interview; Steve Hayward, "Mile Star Shows Technique," *Melbourne Herald* [n.d.], from Len McRae's scrapbook; Paul O'Neil, "A Man Conquers Himself."

72   *Cerutty had promoted:* Steve Hayward, "Run Like a Rooster, Says the White Sage," *Melbourne Herald* [n.d.], from Len McRae's scrapbook.

    "They don't run on their toes": *Sporting Globe*, November 19, 1952.

73   *"The mind is always selling":* John Landy, personal interview.

    "It's like a car starting": ibid.

    On a typical night: Fred Wilt, ed., *How They Train* (Tafnews, 1973), pp. 102–3;

John Landy, personal interview; Ron Clarke, ed., *Athletics: The Australian Way* (Lansdowne, 1976), pp. 53–57.

On a typical day: John Landy, personal interview.

74   *In this schedule:* "Fastest Man in the World," *Sun-Herald*, June 27, 1954.

"The harder, the better": "Landy Runs 4:02.1," *Track and Field News*, December 1952.

"I just go out there": "Runners Are Getting Nearer the Four-Minute Mile," *Sydney Morning Herald*, February 10, 1954.

"There is no gray": O'Neil, "A Man Conquers Himself."

Landy's resolve: Adrian McGregor, "The Greatest Mile of the Century," *National Times*, August 18, 1979, p. 14.

How fast is this bloke: Robbie Morgan-Morris, personal interview.

75   *"This is terrific sort of training":* Les Perry, personal interview.

"I'm taking no more advice": Harry Gordon, *Young Men in a Hurry: The Story of Australia's Fastest Decade* (Lansdowne, 1961), p. 104.

In the history of athletic training: Wilt, *How They Train*, pp. 9–10; Edward Sears, *Running Through the Ages* (McFarland & Co., 2001), pp. 32–33; John Blundell, *The Muscles and Their Story from the Earliest Times* (Chapman and Hall, 1864), pp. 196–97.

The ancient Romans had their own ideas: Walter Thom, *Pedestrianism: An Account* (Aberdeen and Frost, 1813), pp. 221–27.

76   *By the seventeenth century:* Sears, *Running Through the Ages*, p. 47.

Training techniques looked like: ibid., pp. 62–65; Thom, *Pedestrianism*, pp. 228–31.

"Not all training is good": Adolphe Abrahams, *The Human Machine* (Pelican, 1956), p. 104.

Some physicians thought: Tim Noakes, *The Lore of Running: Discover the Science and Spirit of Running* (Leisure Press, 1991), p. 670.

77   *"First, I figured out":* ibid., p. 115.

"Monday a mile with a fairly good": John Graham, *Practical Track and Field Athletics* (Fox, Duffield and Co., 1904), p. 41.

The trials and the errors: Noakes, *Lore of Running*, pp. 135–65.

78   *"it's not unusual":* ibid., p. 449.

79   *"Two- and three-mile events":* Ken Moses, "Landy Wins Easily," *Melbourne Argus*, November 17, 1952.

Three days later he entered: Steve Hayward, "Run for Record Praised," *Melbourne Herald*, November 19, 1952.

On December 12: John Landy, personal interview; Les Perry, personal interview; Sears, *Running Through the Ages*, p. 142.

80   *John Landy put in his half-day:* John Landy, personal interview.

81   *Olympic Park was the center:* Trevor Robbins, *Running into History: A Centenary Profile of the Malvern Harriers Athletic Club* (Malvern Harriers, 1996), pp. 169–71.

By two o'clock Landy: John Landy, personal interview; Les Perry, personal interview.

"I think they called": John Landy, personal interview.

"Nobody will cross over": Robbie Morgan-Morris, personal interview.

Each club team stood: Trevor Robbins, personal interview.

82   *"Then I went":* John Landy, personal interview.

83 *"You ran 4:03"*: ibid.

"Most of the credit must go": Ken Moses, "Landy Chasing Records," *Melbourne Argus*, December 15, 1952.

While Landy explained: Les Perry, personal interview; Graem Sims, *Why Die? The Extraordinary Life of Percy Cerutty* (Lothian Books, 2003), p. 143.

84 *"Here's a bloke who's come home"*: ibid.

When he went home: John Landy, personal interview.

Chapter 7

85 *On December 14, 1952*: Norris McWhirter, personal interview. Roger Bannister, personal interview.

86 *Bannister was stunned*: Roger Bannister, *The Four Minute Mile* (Globe Pequot Press, 1955), p. 184.

"Never in the history": Arthur Daley, "With a Grain of Salt," *New York Times*, December 24, 1952.

"No hope of catching him": "Wells on the Track," *Melbourne Age*, January 5, 1953.

"Ever since Irving and Mallory": *Athletics World*, December 1952.

87 *"no good being second to run"*: Norris McWhirter, personal interview.

In the middle of interviews: Dr. Ronald Williams, personal interview.

88 *When Bannister arrived*: Roger Bannister, personal interview; Dr. Ronald Williams, personal interview; Anthony Carthew, "The Man Who Broke the Four-Minute Mile," *New York Times*, April 19, 1964.

"unfinished business": Roger Bannister, personal interview.

"To say, however": Bannister, *Four Minute Mile*, p. 188.

89 *The darkness was not*: Roger Bannister, personal interview.

Since mid-December: Roger Bannister, personal interview.

Oxford sprinter Bevil Rudd: Chris Chataway, personal interview.

90 *Does it work?*: Roger Bannister, personal interview.

"art of taking more out": ibid.

Arterial pCO_2, blood lactate: R. G. Bannister, Dr. Cunningham, and Dr. Douglas, "The Carbon Dioxide Stimulus to Breathing in Severe Exercise," *Journal of Physiology*, 1954; R. G. Bannister and Dr. Cunningham, "The Effects on the Respiration and Performance During Exercise of Adding Oxygen to the Inspired Air," *Journal of Physiology*, 1954.

91 *"The efficient integration of the human body"*: Roger Bannister, personal interview.

"Do you think you could": Norris McWhirter, personal interview.

92 *"black waves of nausea"*: G. F. D. Pearson, ed., *Athletics* (Nelson, 1963), p. 28.

At six minutes: ibid.; Bannister, Cunningham, and Douglas, "The Carbon Dioxide Stimulus to Breathing in Severe Exercise"; Bannister and Cunningham, "The Effects on the Respiration and Performance During Exercise of Adding Oxygen to the Inspired Air"; Roger Bannister, personal interview.

Afterward, in the laboratory: Bannister, *Four Minute Mile*, p. 120.

93 *Based on body types*: Roger Bannister, personal interview; "Science Predicts Athletic Prowess," *New York Times*, August 16, 1951.

Bannister had long since: Roger Bannister, "How to Run the Mile," *World Sports*, December 1954; A. V. Hill, "Where Is the Limit?" *World Sports*, August 1952.

94 *In 1953 Bannister had*: Carthew, "The Man Who Broke the 4-Minute Mile."

Many decades would pass: James Fixx, *The Complete Book of Running* (Random House, 1997); Charles Houston, *Going Higher: The Story of Man and Altitude* (Little, Brown, 1987); Fred Wilt, ed., *How They Train* (Tafnews, 1973); Tim Noakes, *The Lore of Running: Discover the Science and Spirit of Running* (Leisure Press, 1991). These four books provide a comprehensive and in-depth investigation of the fascinating science behind running, chemical reactions and all.

"Psychologically the rest of life": Norris McWhirter, personal interview.

95   *"his eyes firmly fixed":* "Round and About," *Athletic Review,* January 1953.

Chapter 8

96   *While the Third Infantry:* Dick Wilson, personal interview; Wes Santee, personal interview.

97   *"Coach, let's drop out":* Wes Santee, personal interview.

98   *"Hi ya, ya bum":* Bob Asbille, "Prayed All Year We'd Get Revenge," *Des Moines Tribune,* April 25, 1953.

    At the Texas Relays: Ed Fite, "Kansas Runners Dominate Relays," United Press, March 28, 1953.

    "It was a season-launching": "Santee Finds Short Race Is His Forte," *New York Herald Tribune,* March 29, 1953.

    "The guy has a lot": Bill Moore, "Track Experts See Him as the Fastest Mile Runner," *Kansas City Star,* April 5, 1954.

99   *His statement shocked them:* Wes Santee, personal interview; Dick Wilson, personal interview; Tom Rupp, personal interview; Bob Timmons, personal interview.

    "When Easton told you": Dick Wilson, personal interview.

    He gave written instructions: Bill Easton, "Letter to Athletes Prior to Texas Relays," April 2, 1955, Archives of William Easton, University of Kansas.

    "You are college men": Bill Easton, "Letter to Athletes Prior to Oklahoma A&M Trip," October 19, 1951, Archives of William Easton, University of Kansas.

100   *"Go get him to run":* Wes Santee, personal interview.

    "We need to talk.": ibid.

102   *"You're not running the way":* Dick Wilson, personal interview.

    "We're gonna have some fun": Tom Rupp, personal interview.

103   *They had met the year:* Wes Santee, personal interview.

    Easton frowned on his athletes: Wes Santee, personal interview; Dick Wilson, personal interview; Tom Rupp, personal interview.

104   *"so that you will be ready":* Bill Easton, "Letter to Athletes—Merry Christmas," December 13, 1952, Archives of William Easton, University of Kansas.

    "1-man record demolisher": "Santee and Mates Take on Missouri," *University Daily Kansan,* February 19, 1953.

    "Mincing Menace of Mount Oread": "All Eyes on KU Ace" [n.d.], Dick Wilson's scrapbook.

    "Knowing how determined he can be": statement by William Easton [n.d.], Wes Santee's scrapbook.

    "We can take him": Bill Mayer, "Colorful Santee Whips Frat Team," *Lawrence Journal-World,* December 15, 1952.

105   *"For world-wide interest":* Gerald Holland, "The Golden Age Is Now," *Sports Illustrated,* August 16, 1954.

The exuberance in American sport: Karal Ann Marling, *As Seen on TV: The Visual Culture of Everyday Life in the 1950s* (Harvard University Press, 1994).

106 *Children flocked to baseball diamonds:* Holland, "The Golden Age Is Now."

107 *"I don't know when":* Bob Hurt, "Sure I'll Run the Four-Minute Mile," *Saturday Evening Post,* September 26, 1953.

As an amateur college athlete: Wes Santee, personal interview.

"I didn't think you acted": ibid.

Chapter 9

110 *"Will man ever run":* Max Crittenden, "A Four-Minute Mile," *Melbourne Argus,* January 6, 1953.

By April 1953: John Landy, personal interview.

111 *"There are more important":* ibid.

"but having his morning shower": Robert Solomon, *Great Australian Athletes: Selected Olympians 1928–1956* (R. J. Solomon, 2), p. 170.

"I say, John": Graem Sims, *Why Die? The Extraordinary Life of Percy Cerutty* (Lothian Books, 2003), p. 103.

112 *Some joked that:* Len McRae, personal interview.

"Maybe too much salt": Arthur Daley, "Too Much Salt," *New York Times,* December 29, 1952.

A relaxed mental outlook: Frank Tierney, "Landy Will Need Help in Pacing," *Sydney Morning Herald,* January 18, 1953.

"If he feels hungry": Steve Hayward, "Butterflies for Speed," *Sydney Morning Herald,* January 22, 1953.

113 *"I'll do my best":* Ben Kerville, "Landy Lost No Prestige in Missing His Record," *Perth Daily News,* January 28, 1953.

Blunders by officials: John Landy, personal interview; Ken Moses, "Blunder Upsets Landy," *Melbourne Argus,* February 18, 1953.

At another mile race: Globe, January 28, 1953.

114 *By the conclusion:* Solomon, *Great Australian Athletes,* p. 171.

"About this four minute mile business": "John Has Had It," *Melbourne Argus,* February 23, 1953.

"It was just a clinker": Norris McWhirter, personal interview.

Bannister raised the money: Roger Bannister, personal interview; Norris McWhirter, personal interview; Roger Bannister, *The Four-Minute Mile* (Globe Pequot Press, 1955), pp. 49, 73.

115 *Early in the nineteenth century:* George Gretton, *Out in Front* (Pelham Books, 1968), pp. 27–51.

"traced back to the Renaissance": Randy Roberts and James Olson, *Winning Is the Only Thing: Sports in America Since 1945* (Johns Hopkins University Press, 1998), p. 3.

"wherever he goes": Gretton, *Out in Front,* p. 35.

116 *"We have not journeyed":* Frank Deford, "Pioneer Mile Roger Bannister and Everest Conqueror Edmund Hillary," *Sports Illustrated,* January 3, 2 .

The annual AAA: John Disley, personal interview.

Those in the know: Chris Chataway, personal interview; Bannister, *Four Minute Mile,* pp. 192–93.

"Chataway Should Avenge": Harold Palmer, "Chataway Should Avenge Mile Defeat by Bannister," *Evening Standard*, April 30, 1953.

Chataway was better suited: Chris Chataway, personal interview; Bannister, *Four Minute Mile*, pp. 192–93.

117 *In the two months*: ibid.

After an Easter break: Bannister, *Four Minute Mile*, pp. 190–91.

"most intensive start": "Big Start to the Athletic Season," *Daily Telegraph*, May 1, 1953.

Bannister took his usual: Roger Bannister, personal interview.

"to release every ounce": ibid.

118 *"Only the silky-striding Bannister"*: Norris McWhirter, "Bannister Runs 4:03.6 for AAA," *Athletics Weekly*, June 1953.

"a hard-working medical student": E. W. Stanton, "Do Players Give Enough Thought to the Game?" *Daily Telegraph*, May 4, 1953.

"poised high up on the frozen": Bill Clark, "High Endeavour," *Athletic Review*, June 1953.

119 *"the four-minute mile was not"*: Bannister, *Four Minute Mile*, p. 193.

"I think Santee will someday": Bill Mayer, "Sport Talk," *Lawrence Journal-World*, June 1 and June 5, 1953; Wes Santee, personal interview.

120 *Its leader was Avery Brundage*: Roberts and Olson, *Winning Is the Only Thing*, pp. 9–11.

"troop of trained seals": ibid., p. 11.

121 *Any decisions made by the AAU*: Wes Santee, personal interview.

"Transatlantic Oceanic Hitchhikers": ibid. This statement was ascribed to Phog Allen, the coach of the University of Kansas basketball team. In addition, I heard the term from Bob Timmons, the coach who succeeded Bill Easton as the Jayhawk track coach.

"I caught my quarters right": Norris Anderson, "Santee Sets National Mark in Mile," May 24, 1953, Wes Santee's scrapbook; "Santee Sets Mile Mark as Kansas Wins Title," *New York Herald Tribune*, May 24, 1953.

"I hope he read": Bill Mayer, "Sport Talk," *Lawrence Journal-World*, June 1, 1953.

122 *"That's okay by us"*: Bill Mayer, "Sport Talk," *Lawrence Journal-World*, June 2, 1953.

At the Kansas City airport: Wes Santee, personal interview.

123 *"the greatest ever to run"*: Al Franken, "Compton's Meet — Best Yet!" in *Compton Invitational Program — June 1953*, Wes Santee's scrapbook.

While Santee prepared for the race: Wes Santee, personal interview.

124 *In the third lap Johansson sped quickly past*: "Oh, That Compton Meet," *Track and Field News*, June 1953; "Fastest American Mile," *Time*, June 15, 1953.

125 *"You guys are crazy"*: Wes Santee, personal interview.

"I didn't think it": *Track and Field News*, June 1953.

"We're getting closer": "Santee Runs Mile in 4:02.4," *New York Herald Tribune*, June 7, 1953.

"He taught me not": Maxwell Stiles, "Denis Praises Santee," *Los Angeles Mirror*, June 6, 1953.

126 *"This was the ultimate"*: Bob Hurt, "Santee Cracks Record," *Daily Capital*, June 6, 1953; "Santee Admits Getting Closer to Four-Minute Mile," *Wichita Eagle*, June 6, 1953.

Chapter 10

127 *In the small community:* Les Perry, personal interview; Geoff Warren, personal interview.

128 *The closest Landy came:* Geoff Warren, personal interview.
"It won't be any good": Joseph Galli, "John Landy Goes into Training," *Track and Field News,* March 1953.
The details of his program: John Landy, personal interview; Fred Wilt, ed., *How They Train* (Tafnews, 1973), pp. 102–3. Wilt's book documents Landy's training sessions from August 1952 up through his race in Turku, Finland, in June 1954.
He spent so much time: Harry Gordon, *Young Men in a Hurry: The Story of Australia's Fastest Decade* (Lansdowne, 1961), p. 110.

129 *"over the ground":* Percy Cerutty, "3:53 Mile Is Possible," *Track and Field News,* May 1953.
He knew that come his first race: "Runners Are Getting Nearer the Four-Minute Mile," *Sydney Morning Herald,* February 10, 1954; John Landy, personal interview.
Although his studies: John Landy, personal interview.
He would have preferred: Don Macmillan, personal interview.
"Roger, here. Roger Bannister": Don Macmillan, personal interview.

130 *"I think you can":* "His Faith in Santee," Associated Press, June 24, 1953, Wes Santee's scrapbook.

131 *"It's becoming quite a tyranny":* "They All Plan My 4-Min. Mile — Except Me," *Evening Standard,* May 15, 1953.
On May 23 at White City Stadium: George Smith, *All Out for the Mile* (Forbes Robertson, 1955), p. 104.
"We know the race might": Roger Bannister, personal interview.
"Santee's going to do": ibid.

132 *"It was the manner of this triumph":* Richard Holt, *Sport and the British: A Modern History* (Oxford University Press, 1990), pp. 279–80.
"The British are the best": Kenneth and Valerie McLeish, *Long to Reign over Us: Memories of Coronation Day and of Life in the 1950s* (Bloomsbury, 1992), p. 103.
By the morning of June 27: Smith, *All Out for the Mile,* pp. 105–6; Norris McWhirter, "The Story of Bannister's 4:02," *Athletics World,* July 1953; Don Macmillan, personal interview; Bert Johnson, "Bannister Strikes Again," *Athletic Review,* July 1953. Immense attention was paid to this race, but these four reports are the most authoritative.

133 *"Hope for the best":* Don Macmillan, personal interview.
"an amputee getting used": Norris McWhirter, "The Story of Bannister's 4:02," *Athletics World,* July 1953.
"Wide open, Don": ibid.
"climb the ladder": Don Macmillan, personal interview.

134 *"Only five yards outside":* Bert Johnson, "Bannister Strikes Again," *Athletic Review,* July 1953.
"Maybe I could run a Four-Minute Mile": Jesse Abramson, "Views of Sport," *New York Herald Tribune,* July 1, 1953.
"The world obviously would": ibid.

136 *"It was work":* Wes Santee, personal interview.
A few days before: Lloyd Koby of the Amateur Athletic Union, letter to Bill Eas-

ton, February 4, 1954, Archives of William Easton, University of Kansas.
"You're a damn liar": Wes Santee, personal interview.

137 *"I've run seven races—one every other day":* "Pirie Beats Santee in 4:06.8," *New York Herald Tribune,* August 9, 1953.

Chapter 11

138 *Wearing jackets and ties:* Norris McWhirter, personal interview.

139 *But by September 1953:* Roger Bannister, *The Four Minute Mile* (Globe Pequot Press, 1955), pp. 203–4; Christopher Brasher, "Christopher Brasher Recalls the Day," *Observer,* May 5, 1974.
"has been compelled": "Bannister's Record," *Manchester Guardian,* July 13, 1953.
In hindsight, he knew: BBC, "Suspense: Four-Minute Mile," BBC Sound Archives, July 18, 1954.
Many considered him: Roger Bannister, personal interview.

140 *Bannister appreciated:* "Pirie Beats Santee in 4:06.8," *New York Herald Tribune,* August 9, 1953.
"Pirie is the most extraordinary runner": Joseph Binks, "His Mile Victory over America's Best," *News of the World,* August 9, 1953.
Born in British Guinea: H. A. Meyer, ed., *Modern Athletics by the Achilles Club* (Oxford University Press, 1958), p. 99.
"Enthusiasm was the feature": Chris Chataway, personal interview.
"He was a thrusting sort": Peter Hildreth, personal interview.

141 *Furthermore, he never:* Norris McWhirter, personal interview.
"For me and many others": Norris McWhirter, "This Man Chataway," *World Sports,* August 1955.
"a man of spirit": ibid.
"He invested with magic": Chris Chataway, personal interview.
"Come and join us": BBC, "Franz Stampfl," BBC Sound Archives, British Library, 1994.
or "rubber," as they were called: Norris McWhirter, personal interview.
"It is absolutely necessary": BBC, "The Loneliest Place in the World," BBC Sound Archives, January 1964.

142 *In October, after a day:* Roger Bannister, American Academy of Achievement interview, October 27, 2 .
The training ground was just: Chris Chataway, personal interview; Peter Hildreth, personal interview; Norris McWhirter, personal interview; Terry O'Connor, personal interview.
Born in Vienna, Austria: Pat Stampfl, personal interview; Benzion Patkin, *The Dunera Internees* (Cassell, 1979); Merv Lincoln, personal interview; Peter and Leni Gillman, *Collar the Lot! How Britain Interned and Expelled Its Wartime Refugees* (Quartet Books, 1980); "The Dunera Internees," *Melbourne Age,* September 8, 1979.

143 *"It was not just a job for me":* Patkin, *Dunera Internees,* p. 78.
"the ability to make a man": David Walsh, "The Miracle Mile," *Sunday Times,* January 17, 1999.
Stampfl was unlike anyone: Roger Bannister, personal interview.

144 *"You have to train harder":* Pat Stampfl, personal interview.
In his opinion: BBC, "Franz Stampfl," BBC Sound Archives, British Library, 1994.

"Who do you think you are": John Landy, personal interview.

"While you were at the pictures": Harry Hopman, "Landy Training for Summer," *Melbourne Herald,* April 22, 1953.

From July 21 to September 30: Fred Wilt, ed., *How They Train* (Tafnews, 1973), pp. 102–3.

145 *Throughout this training:* Graem Sims, *Why Die? The Extraordinary Life of Percy Cerutty* (Lothian Books, 2003), pp. 146–47; Harry Gordon, *Young Men in a Hurry: The Story of Australia's Fastest Decade* (Lansdowne, 1961), p. 20.

"Landy Back for Big Mile Series": Steve Hayward, "Landy Back for Big Mile Series," *Melbourne Herald,* November 20, 1953; Bruce Welch, "Crack Miler Resumes," *Melbourne Age,* November 21, 1953. Although Landy ran in a race at his former school, Geelong Grammar, on October 17, this was not part of his competitive interclub athletic season.

"The only thing of which": Jack Dunn, "'Best Ever' Mile Display," *Melbourne Argus,* November 23, 1953.

"Gee, is that true?": Ken Moses, "Helms Award Goes to John Landy," *Melbourne Argus,* December 1, 1953.

146 *"top condition"*: Joseph Galli, "Joe Galli Reports," *Track and Field News,* September 1953.

The immense pressure: John Landy, personal interview; Jack Dunn, "Timing Error Hampers Landy in Record Mile Try," *Melbourne Sun,* December 7, 1953.

From the start, Landy raced: "John Landy Runs 4:02 Mile," *Melbourne Age,* December 14, 1953; Jack Dunn, "Landy Could Be Greatest Ever," *Melbourne Sun,* December 14, 1953; "Landy Plans Short Ease Up," *Melbourne Argus,* December 14, 1954.

147 *The wind ruined:* Jim Denison, ed., *Bannister and Beyond: The Mystique of the Four-Minute Mile* (Breakaway Books, 2003), p. 27.

"No one outside": "Landy: Only 2 More Tries": *Melbourne Herald,* December 14, 1954.

No doubt some of this statement: John Landy, personal interview.

The next day Landy: John Landy, personal interview; Geoff Warren, personal interview; Trevor Robbins, personal interview.

148 *Amazingly to Perry:* Les Perry, personal interview.

"equal pleasure as": John Landy, personal interview.

A blanket of snow: Wes Santee, personal interview; Dick Wilson, personal interview.

149 *"Man, look at this"*: Wes Santee, personal interview.

"The process of running": Jack Clowser, "Record Planned for Wes," *Track and Field News,* January 1954.

"This was chicken feed": Wes Santee, personal interview.

Instead of slowly jogging: Bill Easton, "Workout Sheets—December 19–31, 1953," Archives of William Easton, University of Kansas.

150 *"My break between quarters"*: Wes Santee, personal interview.

"This keeps you going": ibid.

"Wes Santee . . . John Landy . . .": "Santee Spurs Rising Furor over Four-Minute Mile," Associated Press, January 7, 1954.

"The Girl That Finally Caught Wes": "Wes Santee Sets One-Mile Record," *The Letter from Home,* November 1953.

She had traveled down: Wes Santee, personal interview.

First, the AAU had ruled: Bob Busby, "Rule Out Santee," *Kansas City Times,* January 9, 1954.

151   *"Something is hanging over":* "Santee, Whitfield Shunned by Sullivan Award Group," *Evening Eagle,* December 14, 1953.

"I'd like to run for about": Bob Hurt, "Sure I'll Run the Four-Minute Mile," *Saturday Evening Post,* September 26, 1953.

"I hope we've set it up": Wes Santee, personal interview.

152   *"I'm really sorry":* ibid.

Santee's outdoor season didn't begin: "May Ban Whitfield, Santee," *Mirror,* December 15, 1953.

Chapter 12

154   *"Why would you train":* Len McRae, personal interview.

The night before: Steve Hayward, "Landy Will Run Hungry," *Melbourne Herald,* January 21, 1954.

"I'm not a bit worried": "Man of Moment Has No Worries," *Melbourne Age,* January 21, 1954,.

"most retiring world-class performer": Hayward, "Landy Will Run Hungry."

Landy arrived at: John Landy, personal interview; Len McRae, personal interview; Les Perry, personal interview; Peter Banfield, "Landy Goes 'Over,'" *Melbourne Argus,* January 22, 1954.

155   *When Landy took to the track:* John Landy, personal interview.

156   *Nobody could keep up:* Robbie Morgan-Morris, personal interview.

He had a good sense: John Landy, personal interview.

"master power switch": Trevor Robbins, personal interview.

157   *When he returned:* John Landy, personal interview; Len McRae, personal interview.

The next day his run: Jack Dunn, "Applause Cost Landy Mile Record," *Melbourne Sun,* January 22, 1954; "14,500 See Landy Just Miss 4 Min," *Melbourne Age,* January 22, 1954; Peter Banfield, "Magnificent Failure," *Melbourne Argus,* January 22, 1954; Steve Hayward, "No Let-up in Plans," *Melbourne Herald,* January 22, 1954; Joseph Galli, "Landy Below 4:03 Again," *Track and Field News,* January 1954.

"Landy is magnificent": Steve Hayward, "He May Go to Europe," *Melbourne Herald,* January 22, 1954.

So they sent letters to Lloyd Olds: Bill Easton, letter to Lloyd Olds, February 10, 1954, Archives of William Easton, University of Kansas; Wes Santee, letter to Lloyd Olds, February 10, 1954, Archives of William Easton, University of Kansas.

158   *A week later Hurt wrote:* Wes Santee, personal interview.

"The restriction is nothing": Bill Mayer, "Sport Talk," *Lawrence Journal World,* February 24, 1954.

Soon after, Santee: "Who Needs Foreign Stars," *Los Angeles Times,* March 22, 1954.

"For me to drive myself": Wes Santee, personal interview.

After hanging his half-length white coat: Roger Bannister, personal interview.

159   *Stampfl ran them through:* ibid.; Franz Stampfl, *Franz Stampfl on Running: Sprint, Middle Distance, and Distance Events* (Macmillan, 1955), pp. 110–11.

On occasion, he even: Brian Lenton, ed., "Interview with Roger Bannister," in *Through the Tape* (self-published, 1983).

"Do it again!": John Disley, personal interview; G.F.D. Pearson, ed., *Athletics* (Nelson, 1963), p. 28.

"the focus of the week": Roger Bannister, personal interview.

The Austrian coach: Pat Stampfl, personal interview.

From the start, he knew: George Smith, *All Out for the Mile* (Forbes Robertson, 1955), p. 112; BBC, "Franz Stampfl," BBC Sound Archives, British Library, 1994.

"They've got to love it": Pat Stampfl, personal interview.

160 *Stampfl had seen Bannister:* Bud Greenspan, "Bannister's Run Was for All-Time," *Montreal Gazette,* May 8, 1994.

"Training is principally": Stampfl, p. 37.

161 *"The great hurdle was":* Greenspan, "Bannister's Run Was for All-Time"; BBC, "Franz Stampfl," BBC Sound Archives, British Library, 1994.

Stampfl invested: BBC, "Franz Stampfl," BBC Sound Archives, British Library, 1994.

In a very real sense: ibid.

After their sessions: Chris Chataway, personal interview.

Week after week they nervously waited: Roger Bannister, *The Four Minute Mile* (Globe Pequot Press, 1955), pp. 201–2.

The McWhirter twins continued: Norris McWhirter, personal interview.

162 *"greatest double in American track history":* Jack Clowser, "Santee's Relay Efforts," *Track and Field News,* February 1954.

"an almost uninsurable risk": "Prospects for A.D. 1954," *Athletics World,* February 1954.

"obituary notices": "Santee Blazes to 4:02.2," *Athletics World,* January 1954.

"I don't know how": Sir Edmund Hillary, *View from the Summit* (Pocket Books, 1999), p. 26.

Most weekend mornings: Betty Lou Watson, "The Fleet and Fair," *University of Kansas Yearbook,* April 1954.

163 *Three months to the day:* "Pro Bowl Won by East Stars," *University Daily Kansan,* January 18, 1954.

At the first outdoor meet: George Breazeale, "4-Minute (Maybe) Miler Strictly Team Man Here" [n.d.], Wes Santee's scrapbook.

"Some night Santee's going": Edgar Hayes, "Sees 4-Minute Mile Nearing for Santee" [n.d.], Wes Santee's scrapbook.

164 *By two o'clock on Saturday:* Watson, "The Fleet and Fair"; "Track, Exposition, Parade Included in Relays Weekend," *University Daily Kansan,* April 19, 1954.

"Let's try to break it": Wes Santee, personal interview.

165 *Fifteen minutes before race time:* ibid.; Bill Mayer, personal interview. There are conflicting reports as to the weather that day. The news reports make no mention of the rain but do say that there were strong gusts of wind and that the track needed to be rolled several times before the Cunningham Mile began. Santee and Mayer both said it rained before the meet.

Jogging off to the side: Wes Santee, personal interview.

166 *Opposing him in the race:* "Santee Enters Cunningham Mile for First Time," *University Daily Kansan,* April 13, 1954.

He just needed to stick: Wes Santee, personal interview.

"I just can't talk": Lulu Mae Coe, "Santee's Bride Finds Track Tour Exciting Honeymoon" [n.d.], Wes Santee's scrapbook.

Right before the gun: Wes Santee, personal interview.

167 After seeing the time: "Next Best Mile," Kansas City Star, April 18, 1954; "Santee Decided Too Late for Mark," Kansas City Star, April 18, 1954; Dana Leibengood, "Santee Sets Record in Cunningham Mile," University Daily Kansan, April 19, 1954; "Santee 4:03.1," Associated Press, April 17, 1954; "Drake Relays Next Target," New York Herald Tribune, April 18, 1954.

168 "Wes Santee isn't going": Skipper Patrick, "Wedded Wes Santee," Kansas City Star, April 19, 1954.

Chapter 13

169 By mid-April 1954: Roger Bannister, The Four Minute Mile (Globe Pequot Press, 1955), pp. 204–5.
Bannister had always been: Norman Harris, The Legend of Lovelock (Nicholas Kaye, 1964), p. 138.

170 "It is a belief": Franz Stampfl, Franz Stampfl on Running: Sprint, Middle Distance, and Distance Events (Macmillan, 1955), p. 40.
In his view: ibid., pp. 37–40.
Stampfl advised the three: Roger Bannister, personal interview; Chris Chataway, personal interview; Christopher Brasher, "Christopher Brasher Recalls the Day," Observer, May 5, 1974.
Several times before, Bannister had: Bannister: Four Minute Mile, pp. 113–18.

171 At dawn on Saturday morning: Bannister, Four Minute Mile, pp. 204–5.
They got into the adventure: ibid.; Brasher, "Christopher Brasher Recalls the Day"; Christopher Brasher, "Forty Years Ago We Ran into History," Sunday Times, May 1, 1994.
After three more days' rest: Ross McWhirter, "The Long Climb," Athletics World, May 1954.

172 "You, Chris"—he looked: Christopher Brasher, Sportsmen of Our Time (Victor Gollancz, 1962), p. 11. The exact date of this meeting between the four remains uncertain, but in several sources it was noted to have occurred in April. For continuity's sake, I have placed it after the achievement of the 10 x 440 intervals under sixty seconds, when it can be assumed that they were discussing exactly how to run the May 6 race.
In his own mind: Frank Bath, "The Loneliest Place in the World—Speaking with Christopher Brasher," BBC Sound Archives, January 1964.
On the tarmac of an airport: "Landy Off with Big Smile," Melbourne Sun, April 29, 1954; Bruce Welch, "John Landy at Peak in June," Melbourne Age, April 29, 1954; Peter Banfield, "Quest for the Magic Mile," Melbourne Argus, August 28, 1954; John Landy, personal interview.

173 His times since: "U.S. Writer Says Landy Best," Melbourne Argus, April 24, 1954.
On February 11: "Duke's Dash to See Landy Win Mile Title," Sydney Morning Herald, February 12, 1954.
Two weeks later he ran: Peter Banfield, "Landy Romps Home in 4:02.6," Melbourne Argus, February 24, 1954.
And just the previous week: "Great Run by Landy at Bendigo," Melbourne Age, April 20, 1954; John Landy, personal interview.

174 "I had an obligation to perform": Darren Alexander, "An Examination of the Victorian Newspapers' Portrayal of John Landy's Attempts at the Four-Minute Mile Between 1952 and 1954," La Trobe University, 1991.

Whenever he had failed to break: ibid. Darren Alexander's essay is a very thorough record of the media attention paid to John Landy and worthwhile for those interested in knowing more about how the press spiraled out of control.

"Do the winds blow differently": "Critics Storm at Landy 'Alibis,'" *Sun Herald,* February 14, 1954.

"A great runner, the young Australian": Graeme Kelly, *Mr. Controversial: The Story of Percy Wells Cerutty* (Stanley Paul, 1964), pp. 65–66.

But more than anything: Banfield, "Quest for the Magic Mile."

He hoped that Johansson: John Landy, personal interview.

175 *"in one slimly built":* Banfield, "Quest for the Magic Mile."

In the 4 x 1 mile relay: "Santee Does 1:49.8 as Kansas Again Beats U.S. Mark," *Des Moines Register,* April 24, 1954.

"Under our system": "Easton-Santee TV Blackout, Curfew Trouble Cleared Up" [n.d.], Wes Santee's scrapbook.

176 *His Ashland hometown fans:* Bill Murdock, "Wes Santee at Home," Wes Santee's scrapbook.

He had to tune up: Bannister, *Four Minute Mile,* pp. 205–7.

177 *"There was no longer any":* ibid., p. 206.

Every muscle and fiber: ibid., pp. 205–7; Norris McWhirter and Ross McWhirter, "Bannister Does It — 3:59.4," *Athletics World,* May 1954.

After watching the trial: Doug Wilson, "Stand by for a Fast Mile," *News of the World,* May 2, 1954.

"The world's one-mile record": George Smith, *All Out for the Mile* (Forbes Robertson, 1955), p. 114.

Bannister would probably have discounted: Bannister, *Four Minute Mile,* pp. 205–7; McWhirter and McWhirter, "Bannister Does It — 3:59.4"; Norris McWhirter, *Ross: The Story of a Shared Life* (Churchill Press, 1976), p. 129.

178 *"It is not the doing":* McWhirter and McWhirter, "Bannister Does It — 3:59.4."

On April 30 Bannister: Bannister, *Four Minute Mile,* p. 207; Christopher Brasher, *Sportsmen of Our Time* (Victor Gollancz, 1962), p. 12.

As for Brasher and Chataway: Christopher Brasher, "Christopher Brasher Recalls the Day," *Observer,* May 5, 1974.

179 *"You can do it":* Chris Chataway, personal interview.

The evening before the Oxford meet: Pat Stampfl, personal interview.

To this end: Norris McWhirter, "Aim May Be Four Min Mile," *Star,* May 5, 1954.

Yet when he called Peter Dimmock: Norris McWhirter, personal interview; Norris McWhirter, National Centre for Athletics Literature interview, University of Birmingham [n.d.].

Chapter 14

181 *"You don't really think":* Roger Bannister, *The Four Minute Mile* (Globe Pequot Press, 1955), p. 207.

182 *"They should be light":* Raymond Krise and Bill Squires, *Fast Tracks: The History of Distance Running* (Stephen Greene Press, 1982), p. 128.

The resulting pair: Larry Montague, "Preparing for a World's Record," *Manchester Guardian,* May 15, 1954.

Once finished with his spikes: Bannister, *Four Minute Mile,* p. 208.

Bannister wasn't alone: Pat Stampfl, personal interview.

183 *He explained to Stampfl:* Bannister, *Four Minute Mile*, pp. 208–11.
"With the proper motivation": ibid., pp. 209–10; Roger Bannister, personal interview; Radio 4, "A Conversation Piece with Sue McGregor," May 17, 1990; David Walsh, "The Miracle Mile," *Sunday Times*, January 17, 1999. There are a number of versions of what exactly was said at this fateful meeting between Bannister and Stampfl. I have endeavored to convey the words, thoughts, and meanings as best as possible.

184 *When they finally arrived:* Bannister, *Four Minute Mile*, pp. 210–11; Roger Bannister, personal interview; "Star Man's Diary," *Star*, May 7, 1954.
"The day could be a lot worse": Bannister, *Four Minute Mile*, p. 211.
"The wind's hopeless": ibid.

185 *So forty-five minutes before:* Ross and Norris McWhirter, "The Four-Minute Mile Story," *Athletics World*, May 1954; Christopher Brasher, *Sportsmen of Our Time* (Victor Gollancz, 1962), pp. 13–14; Alan Hoby, *One Crowded Hour* (Museum Press, 1954), p. 125.
The crowd of 1,200: E. D. Lacy, "The Four-Minute Mile," *Athletic Review*, June 1954.
In the center infield: Paul Fox, "Sport: Bannister Build-up Begins," *Daily Telegraph*, April 18, 1994.
Norris McWhirter, who had arranged: Norris McWhirter, personal interview.
"By the way, I may": "The World's Most Popular Athlete," *Daily Mirror*, May 8, 1954.

186 *The moment had arrived:* Bannister, *Four Minute Mile*, pp. 212–15; McWhirter, "The Four-Minute Mile Story"; Brasher, *Sportsmen of Our Time*, pp. 11–16; Hoby, *One Crowded Hour*, pp. 122–41; Christopher Brasher, "Christopher Brasher Recalls the Day," *Observer*, May 5, 1974; Smith, *All Out for the Mile*, pp. 112–21; "His Day of Days," *Track and Field News*, May 1954; Syd Cox, "Last-Minute Decision Led to Bannister's Success," *Oxford Mail*, May 7, 1954; Norris McWhirter, *Ross: The Story of a Shared Life* (Churchill Press, 1976), pp. 130–35; Bud Greenspan, "Bannister's Run Was for All-Time," *Montreal Gazette*, May 8, 1994; Terry O'Connor, personal interview; Roger Bannister, personal interview; Norris McWhirter, personal interview.

191 *"Well, we did it":* Terry O'Connor, personal interview.
It was a humid afternoon: Bill Mayer, personal interview.
Santee was finishing: Wes Santee, personal interview.
"I am not exceptionally disappointed": "Santee Hails Great Run," *Kansas City Star*, May 7, 1954.
"Why were you beaten": This exact quote for the question was not detailed in the news reports on Santee's response. No doubt the thrust of the question was the same, though the syntax may have been different.
"Having to compete for": "Santee Lauds Bannister's Performance," *University Daily Kansan*, May 7, 1954.

192 *"We tried":* Wes Santee, personal interview.
At a restaurant in Turku: John Landy, personal interview.
"It's great, great, great": McWhirter, "The Four-Minute Mile Story"; Smith, *All Out for the Mile*, p. 117.
The next day Landy: "World Record Schedule," *Track and Field*, January 1958.
If Bannister had: Jim Denison, ed., *Bannister and Beyond: The Mystique of the Four-Minute Mile* (Breakaway Books, 2003), p. 27.

Chapter 15

197   *As evening fell on May 7:* Roger Bannister, personal interview; Karl Baedeker, *London and Its Environs: A Handbook for Travelers* (Baedeker, 1951), p. 301.

      "No words could be invented": Roger Bannister, *The Four Minute Mile* (Globe Pequot Press, 1955), pp. 215–16.

      That evening on Sportsview: Peter Dimmock, "Four-Minute Mile," BBC *Sportsview,* May 6, 1954.

198   *"adroit modesty":* Norris McWhirter, personal interview.

      "a tall fair girl": "At Last — The 4-Minute Mile," *Daily Express,* May 7, 1954.

      "I can't believe I did it": Norris McWhirter, personal interview.

      "You gentleman are no": Christopher Brasher, "Forty Years Ago We Ran into History," *Sunday Times,* May 1, 1994.

199   *"I've got two better boys":* "Bannister and His Pacemakers Go Dancing Until Dawn," *Evening Standard,* May 7, 1954.

      "The Empire is saved": Red Smith, "Empire Reborn," *International Herald Tribune,* May 8, 1954.

      National hero or not: "Star Man's Diary," *Star,* May 7, 1954; Christopher Chataway, "Chris Brasher — Eulogy," provided by Dr. Ronald Williams.

      In the afternoon: Bannister, *Four Minute Mile,* p. 216; Radio 4, "A Conversation Piece with Sue McGregor," May 17, 1990.

      With London unfolded: Roger Bannister, personal interview.

200   *"Now life in earnest":* ibid.; Chris Chataway, personal interview.

      "We honestly believed": Patrick Collins, "Chris Brasher — 1928–2003," *Marathon News,* April 2003.

      "Heard a rumour": John Landy, letter to Len McRae, May 10, 1954.

201   *Turku was a quiet old city:* Sylvie Nickels, Hillar Kallas, and Philippa Friedman, eds., *Finland: An Introduction* (George Allen & Unwin, 1973), pp. 137–38; *Jussi Kiisseli* (Tampereen Uusi Kirjapaino, 1952), pp. 105–9.

      When Landy arrived: John Landy, letter to Len McRae, May 10, 1954; John Landy, personal interview.

      He was so impressed: MMBW officer's journal, July 1955.

      In the three weeks leading: "World Record Schedule," *Track and Field,* January 1958.

      "Running is not only": "Pride Not Enough," *Sydney Morning Herald,* February 11, 1954.

      Two days before: Bill Mayer, "Sport Talk," *Lawrence Journal-World,* May 31, 1954.

202   *Vaharanta bolted from the start:* Australian Associated Press, "Landy 2.2s Behind Bannister," *Melbourne Herald,* June 1, 1954.

203   *"I'm not a four-minute miler":* "I'll Soon Be a 4-Minute Miler," Australian Associated Press, June 1, 1954.

      "If you hooked Bannister": Skipper Patrick, "Scorned by Santee," Associated Press, June 4, 1954.

      It was Thursday: Bill Mayer, "Final Big Fling by Santee," *Lawrence Journal-World,* May 31, 1954. "Noose tightening" is a close reference to Mayer, who wrote in this article, "The noose is drawing tight on Santee's freedom on the cinders."

      Santee still desperately wanted: Wes Santee, personal interview.

      Easton was engaged: ibid.

204   *"How do you feel?":* Wes Santee, personal interview.

Santee left the locker room: ibid.; "Wes Clips Record for 1,500 Meters," *New York Times,* June 5, 1954; "Santee Runs 4:00.6 Mile," *Chicago Tribune,* June 5, 1954; "Wes Vows to Break 4:00," *Lawrence Daily Journal-World,* June 10, 1954; "Wes Sets 1,500 Meter Mark," *Lawrence Daily Journal-World,* June 5, 1954; "Wind Stops Wes," *Kansas City Star,* June 5, 1954; Ernie Klann, "Valley Sports Corral," *Citizen-News,* June 8, 1954. The account here of this race is drawn from a collection of these sources. Quotes of conversation are directly from my interview with Wes Santee.

207   *"I should very much":* George Smith, *All Out for the Mile* (Forbes Robertson, 1955), pp. 124–25.

"I much prefer": Harold Palmer, "Chataway Beat British Two Miles Record," *Evening Standard,* June 7, 1954.

It was obvious to most: Bannister, *Four Minute Mile,* pp. 223–24.

"If you do go": Roger Bannister, personal interview.

In the four races Landy: Robert Solomon, *Great Australian Athletes: Selected Olympians 1928–1956* (R. J. Solomon, 2), pp. 179–81.

The Australian knew Chataway: John Landy, personal interview.

208   *"I could change into shorts":* BBC, "Suspense: Four-Minute Mile," BBC Sound Archives, July 18, 1954.

"fit as a trout": Adrian McGregor, "The Greatest Mile of the Century," *National Times,* August 18, 1979, p. 14.

The Finn offered: ibid.

At seven o'clock: Chris Chataway, personal interview; John Landy, personal interview; R. L. Quercetani, "Landy's Turn—3:58," *Track and Field News,* July 1954; "Butterfly Chaser Runs a Record Mile," *Life,* July 1954; Smith, *All Out for the Mile,* pp. 126–33; "3:58—and I Can Do Better," *Melbourne Herald,* June 22, 1954; "Landy: My Future Is in the Air," *Melbourne Herald,* June 25, 1954.

211   *"3:58":* In fact, Landy's time was 3:57.9, but fifths, not tenths, of seconds were accepted in official times, so his time was rounded up to 3:58.

"No, no. It's your achievement": Chris Chataway, personal interview.

Chapter 16

212   *Half an hour after:* Roger Bannister, *The Four Minute Mile* (Globe Pequot Press, 1956), p. 224.

"Roger, what do you think": "Now a 3:58 Mile," *Daily Mirror,* June 22, 1954; "He Sets World Record for 1,500 Meters, Too," *Daily Mail,* June 22, 1954.

The moment Bannister heard: Bannister, *Four Minute Mile,* pp. 224–25.

213   *"Do you think you will":* "Bannister Flies Home Triumphant," *Daily Mail,* May 15, 1954.

Then he stumbled into another: "Bannister Clears Trophy Obstacle," *New York Times,* May 14, 1954.

"You sweated blood over them": Dr. Ronald Williams, personal interview.

First was a series: Roger Bannister, personal interview.

214   *His studies left little time:* Anthony Carthew, "The Man Who Broke the 4-Minute Mile," *New York Times,* April 19, 1964; Norris McWhirter, personal interview.

"I am quite sure": Carthew, "The Man Who Broke the 4-Minute Mile."

When Bannister participated: Bannister, *Four Minute Mile,* pp. 222–23.

"Here's Mud in Your Eye": Roger Bannister, personal interview.

Two days later he tried: Bannister, *Four Minute Mile*, pp. 222–23.

"There is a world of difference": Geoffrey Simpson, "Do More Racing, Bannister," *Daily Mail*, June 7, 1954.

215   *"It's not really life":* John Landy, personal interview.

"It was done": ibid.

"I can do even better": "3:58 — and I Can Do Better," *Melbourne Herald*, June 22, 1954.

"indomitable spirit": H. J. Oaten, "Landy Heads Great Mile Trio," *Melbourne Herald*, June 23, 1954.

216   *"sportsmen, as well as":* "Landy's Achievement Builds National Pride," *Melbourne Age*, June 23, 1954.

"I have always said": "Coach Always Confident," *Sydney Morning Herald*, June 23, 1954; "Coach Lauded," *Melbourne Age*, June 23, 1954.

The next day Landy: "Landy Rests on Isolated Island," *Sydney Morning Herald*, June 24, 1954.

"It took a major effort": Geoff Warren, personal interview.

"The race had the ingredients": John Landy, personal interview.

217   *Running a mile was an art form:* Franz Stampfl, *Franz Stampfl on Running: Sprint, Middle Distance, and Distance Events* (Macmillan, 1955), pp. 28–32.

In developing his strategy: John Landy, personal interview.

"ruthlessness, lack of feeling": Bannister, *Four Minute Mile*, p. 201.

"It was a solemn moment": Chris Chataway, personal interview.

218   *To make sure this was his strategy:* Bannister, *Four Minute Mile*, p. 227.

In the woods outside: Wes Santee, personal interview.

219   *On June 11 at Memorial Stadium:* "Wes Shy by .7," *Kansas City Times*, June 12, 1954.

"Why did you go past me?": Wes Santee, personal interview.

I'm leaving my running": Charles Stevenson, "Santee Pacer Is Slow," *Kansas City Star*, June 12, 1954.

220   *"People who have concentrated":* "Bannister Congratulates Landy, Looks Forward to Racing Him," *New York Times*, June 22, 1954.

221   *"I'm going to train":* "Hard Work Basic Ingredient in Santee Bid at Mile Mark," *Lawrence Daily Journal-World*, July 27, 1954.

After Landy set his mile record: "World Record Schedule," *Track and Field News*, January 1958.

"you have no alternative, mate": John Landy, personal interview.

Johansson advised Landy: Percy Cerutty, *Sport Is My Life* (Stanley Paul, 1966), pp. 40–41.

222   *He liked running his opposition:* John Landy, personal interview.

Tactics were fine and good: Ron Clarke and Norman Harris, *The Lonely Breed* (Pelham Books, 1967), pp. 118–23.

On July 11, in response: John Landy, personal interview.

"I felt that this might confuse": ibid.

"There's the Bannister and Landy": Wes Santee, personal interview.

223   *On July 15:* "Police Rescue Landy from Welcoming Mob," *Sydney Morning Herald*, July 16, 1954.

On Friday, July 23: Bannister, *Four Minute Mile*, pp. 226–30; Pat Stampfl, personal interview.

224   *Bannister was leaving:* Pat Stampfl, personal interview.

"what ifs": ibid.

There was no doubt that Landy: Stampfl, *Franz Stampfl on Running,* pp. 104–5.

"That's when the damage": Adrian McGregor, "The Greatest Mile of the Century," *National Times,* August 18, 1979, p. 14.

"a blow in the stomach": Raymond Krise and Bill Squires, *Fast Tracks: The History of Distance Running* (Stephen Greene Press, 1982), p. 131.

His coach assured him: Bannister, *Four Minute Mile,* pp. 227–28.

225   *"It was a sort of pre-race":* Chris Chataway, personal interview.

Bannister left Stampfl: Bannister, *Four Minute Mile,* p. 228.

Chapter 17

226   *In London:* Jim Peters, *In the Long Run* (Cassell & Co., 1955), pp. 182–88.

227   *"I will be out to win":* "Rivals Happy to See Each Other," *Melbourne Age,* July 27, 1954.

One particularly observant: "Bannister, Man with a 10-Second Secret," *Melbourne Herald,* August 1954.

"Roger, you only become": Bannister, *The Four Minute Mile* (Globe Pequot Press, 1956), p. 127.

"Hello, John": "Rivals Happy to See Each Other," *Melbourne Age,* June 26, 1954; "Mile Stars in Guarded Meeting," *Melbourne Herald,* June 27, 1954; Dick Beddoes, "Mile Aces Avoid Talk of Records," *Vancouver Sun,* June 26, 1954.

228   *On October 30, 1891:* "Australia at the British Empire and Commonwealth Games, Vancouver, Canada 1954," *British Empire Games Official Program,* July 30, 1954; John Blanch and Paul Jenes, *Australia's Complete History at the Commonwealth Games* (John Blanch Publishing, 1982).

229   *Henry Luce, the famed publisher:* Norris McWhirter, personal interview.

To televise the event: "TV Mile Thriller Seen by 40, , ," *New York Times,* August 8, 1954.

For the estimated: Arthur Daley, "Dream Race," *New York Times,* August 1, 1954.

In the morning: "Crowd Sees Landy Train," *Sydney Morning Herald,* July 19, 1954.

As race day approached: Geoff Warren, personal interview.

230   *Reports of his sessions:* Bannister, *Four Minute Mile,* p. 232.

"He was as fresh": "Landy: Speeds Up Training," *Sydney Morning Herald,* June 27, 1954.

And when he killed: "Fast Trial by Landy Revives Speculation," *Sydney Morning Herald,* July 28, 1954.

"Where's Roger the Dodger?": "Roger the Dodger Has Not Been Loafing," *Melbourne Herald,* July 30, 1954.

"What is Roger up to?": Norris McWhirter, "Landy Is Kept Guessing by Bannister," *Star,* July 31, 1954.

One time the press: Bannister, *Four Minute Mile,* pp. 232–33.

231   *Bannister was set against:* "Bannister and Landy Are All Set," *Star,* August 6, 1954.

"as a guide to what": "Crack Milers Take It Easy," *Daily Mail,* August 6, 1954.

As if the atmosphere: "Star Man's Diary," *Star,* July 31, 1954.

232   *Behind a bedroom door:* John Landy, personal interview; Geoff Warren, personal interview; John Vernon, personal interview.

Because of the heightened: Geoff Warren, personal interview.

233   *"an iron fist in":* Geoff Warren, personal interview.

"I'm vicious underneath": Paul O'Neil, "A Man Conquers Himself," *Sports Illustrated*, May 31, 1956.

"In any running event": ibid.

"Roger's going to sit you": Don Macmillan, personal interview.

He knew front-running: O'Neil, "A Man Conquers Himself."

235   *"I know you will think"*: "Landy Had Foot Stitched Before Final of Mile Race," *Melbourne Age*, August 11, 1954.

The reporter promised: John Landy, personal interview; John Vernon, personal interview; Don Macmillan, personal interview; John Fitzgerald, "Landy's Cuts Treated at University Centre," *Melbourne Sun*, August 11, 1954; "Landy Did Not Tell His Father," *Melbourne Sun*, August 12, 1954; "Landy Kept Secret from Father," *Melbourne Age*, August 12, 1954. The exact sequence of events related to Landy's cut foot is not entirely clear. Sources contradict one another, as do interviewees. I have represented the events as accurately as possible.

Late in the afternoon on August 6: Wes Santee, personal interview.

236   *The night before*: Roger Bannister, personal interview.

Except for participating: ibid.; Chris Chataway, personal interview.

One afternoon after a session: Bannister, *Four Minute Mile*, p. 234.

237   *In his three-mile final*: "English Track Triumph," *Daily Mail*, August 4, 1954.

"The great Mr. Second": George Smith, *All Out for the Mile: A History of the Mile Race* (Forbes Robertson, 1955), p. 130.

"encouraging omen": Bannister, *Four Minute Mile*, p. 235.

Chataway was used to: Chris Chataway, personal interview.

As much as Chataway drank: Chris Chataway, personal interview; Roger Bannister, personal interview; Bannister, *Four Minute Mile*, pp. 236–37.

"Roger hates the idea": "Four-Minute Men," *Sports Illustrated*, August 16, 1994. In an interview Chris Chataway said that he was probably the one who made this statement, though it was possible, given distant memory, that it was Chris Brasher instead.

238   *"abnormal state of attention"*: Roger Bannister, personal interview.

Chapter 18

240   *"whole athletic world will"*: "Landy, Bannister Primed for 'Miracle Mile' Today," *New York Herald Tribune*, August 7, 1954.

"I have reached my peak": Judy Joy Davies, "Mile of the Century," *Melbourne Argus*, August 6, 1954.

"We may get down to": "Landy Tipped to Take in 3:57," *Sydney Morning Herald*, August 7, 1954.

"How does your foot feel?": John Vernon, personal interview.

the dressings were soaked: "Doctor Tells of Injury," *Melbourne Age*, August 12, 1954.

Twenty minutes before: John Landy, personal interview.

Before he went out: Adrian McGregor, "The Greatest Mile of the Century," *National Times*, August 18, 1979, p. 18.

241   *He would run a moderately quick*: "John Landy: The First Australian to Run the 4-Minute Mile," National Sport Information Centre, Canberra, Australia.

Before leaving for the stadium: Murray Halberg, personal interview; Roger Bannister, personal interview.

"One was inconspicuously chewing": Skip Rusk, "Long Wait Tests Nerves," *Vancouver Sun,* August 7, 1954.

"hanging on a knife edge": Roger Bannister, personal interview.

242   *Failure would confirm:* Peter Wilson, "The Night Before the Mile," *Daily Mirror,* August 7, 1954.

He had a mentor in Stampfl: "The Meaning of the Four-Minute Mile," transcript of panel discussion at Grinnell College, April 5, 1984, p. 20.

As the starter called: Roger Bannister, *The Four Minute Mile* (Globe Pequot Press, 1955), p. 237; "Bannister and His Rivals," *Daily Mail,* August 7, 1954.

243   *Five minutes before:* "In Their Thousands They Came to Cheer the Miracle Mile," *Vancouver Sun,* August 7, 1954.

He was seated in the decorated royal box: "Bannister Beats Landy in 3:58.8 Mile," *New York Herald Tribune,* August 8, 1954.

Under the steel roof: Norris McWhirter, personal interview; Norris McWhirter, *Ross: The Story of a Shared Life* (Churchill Press, 1976), p. 136.

In the radio commentary box: Chris Chataway, personal interview; Norris McWhirter, personal interview.

It was late evening: "Lightning Round the Teapot," *Star,* August 7, 1954.

244   *Stampfl sat still:* Pat Stampfl, personal interview.

To many, Bannister: McGregor, "Greatest Mile of the Century," p. 13.

It was Sunday morning: "It's Suspense . . . and Hope for John's Mother," *Vancouver Sun,* August 7, 1954.

"Australia considered Landy": McGregor, "Greatest Mile of the Century," p. 13.

245   *Santee knew that the race:* Wes Santee, personal interview.

The closest he could get: "TV Mile Thriller Seen by 40, , ," *New York Times,* August 8, 1954.

In Empire Stadium, two minutes: "Vancouver Race" (video), National Sport Information Centre, August 7, 1954; George Smith, *All Out for the Mile* (Forbes Robertson, 1955), pp. 136–39.

246   *"was going to be left standing":* McGregor, "Greatest Mile of the Century," p. 13.

Bannister was one of the last runners: "Vancouver Race" (video), National Sport Information Centre, August 7, 1954; Smith, *All Out for the Mile,* pp. 136–39.

"There is a tremendous feeling": Rex Alston, "British Empire Games—One Mile Race," BBC Video Archives, August 7, 1954.

247   *Bannister took a deep breath:* ibid.; "Four-Minute Men," *Sports Illustrated,* August 16, 1994; Norris McWhirter, "Bannister Slammed in the Clutch," *Athletics Weekly,* August 1954; Erwin Swangard, "Miracle Mile Thrills World," *Vancouver World,* August 9, 1954; Bert Nelson, "Miracle Mile to Bannister," *Track and Field News,* August 1954; Smith, *All Out for the Mile,* pp. 136–39; Bannister, *Four Minute Mile,* pp. 236–40; NSIC, "Vancouver Race"; Ron Clarke and Norman Harris, *The Lonely Breed* (Pelham Books, 1967), pp. 118–23; McGregor, "Greatest Mile of the Century," pp. 13–18; John Landy, personal interview; Roger Bannister, personal interview; Chris Chataway, personal interview. These were the primary sources for this description of the "Mile of the Century" race. I've indicated sources for direct quotes and important specific descriptions as well. In

addition, I've used as a model the race sequence described in Norman Harris, *The Legend of Lovelock* (Nicholas Kaye, 1964), pp. 168–74.

"*28.9!*": Don Macmillan, personal interview.

248 *A few more yards:* Bannister, *Four Minute Mile*, pp. 238–39.

249 "*Dangerous gap there*": Chris Chataway, personal interview.

Tens of millions around: A. W. Ledbrooke, *Great Moments in Sport* (Phoenix House, 1956), p. 57.

250 *Two more minutes of struggle:* Bannister, *Four Minute Mile*, pp. 239–40.

251 "*Keep it going*": Clarke and Harris, *The Lonely Breed*, p. 122.

When is it?: "Landy to Make Attempt on 2 Miles Record," *Sydney Morning Herald*, August 9, 1954.

252 "*He's done it!*": Chris Chataway, personal interview.

253 "*Hard luck, John. . . .*": Clarke and Harris, *The Lonely Breed*, p. 123; Roger Bannister, personal interview.

"*You were colossal*": "Roger, You're Colossal," *Melbourne Argus*, August 9, 1954.

In the infield: "24 Watches Time Mile of Century," *New York Times*, August 9, 1954.

254 "*It was a magnificent race*": "Santee Says Thrilling," *Daily Mail*, August 9, 1954.

"*I was more exhausted*": Wes Santee, personal interview.

"*When Landy lost*": Robbie Morgan-Morris, personal interview.

For Stampfl the race: Pat Stampfl, personal interview.

Epilogue

256 *Twenty minutes after Bannister:* Jim Peters, *In the Long Run* (Cassell & Co., 1955), pp. 195–207; Peter Wilson, "Peters Cries in Delirium," *Daily Mirror*, August 9, 1954; "Bannister Wins Greatest Mile of All," *Times*, August 9, 1954.

258 "*Did Bannister make it?*": "Vain Agony of Peters," *Manchester Guardian*, August 9, 1954.

"*a crowded field*": Roger Bannister, personal interview.

From the gun: Norris McWhirter, *Athletics World*, August 1954.

259 *In the span of 112 days:* ibid.

"*I'd like to say, Bannister*": Lord Brabazon, "Sportsman of the Year Presentation," BBC News Archives, December 31, 1954.

"*It was the race*": John Landy, personal interview.

Directly after the race: Steve Hayward, "Landy to Join Geelong GS," *Melbourne Herald*, August 9, 1954.

"*Did you stand on*": John Fitzgerald, "Landy Runs with Foot Badly Cut," *Melbourne Herald*, August 9, 1954.

260 "*Everybody beat me*": Paul O'Neil, "A Man Conquers Himself," *Sports Illustrated*, May 31, 1956.

The headmaster at Geelong: ibid.

On January 4, 1956: Robert Solomon, *Great Australian Athletes: Selected Olympians 1928–1956* (R. J. Solomon, 2), pp. 194–215.

261 "*The fellows in the Press box*": Harry Gordon, "Landy Runs Back," *Melbourne Sun*, March 11, 1954.

262 *A couple of months later:* Solomon, *Great Australian Athletes*, pp. 194–215.

"*1955 should be a great*": Cordner Nelson, "Track Talk," *Track and Field*, November 1954.

"If you got this close": Joseph Turrini, "Wes Santee—The Four-Minute Mile, and the Amateur Athletic Union of the United States," *Sport History Review,* 1999, pp. 66–67. A very informative overview of Santee's fight with the AAU.

On June 1 a San Francisco Chronicle article: Turrini, "Wes Santee," p. 67; Wes Santee, personal interview.

263   *"It was as if I handed":* Wes Santee, personal interview.

"underground-labor-relations system": Turrini, "Wes Santee," p. 68.

264   *"a booking agent was like":* ibid., pp. 71–72.

"protect this man": ibid., p. 73.

A survey conducted in California: ibid.

"That all of us got more money": Wes Santee, personal interview.

265   *On May 28, 1955:* George Smith, *All Out for the Mile* (Forbes Robertson, 1955), pp. 144–45.

266   *"It was just another time":* Jim Denison, ed., *Bannister and Beyond: The Mystique of the Four-Minute Mile* (Breakaway Books, 2003), p. 63.

"What's my case doing": ibid., p. 37.

In 1962 New Zealander: ibid.

When El Guerrouj seized: James Dunaway, "Running a Four Minute Mile Is No Longer Mythical," *New York Times,* May 4, 2003.

269   *"Running gave me discipline":* John Landy, personal interview.

"Hard work pays off": Wes Santee, personal interview.

"sport is about not": Christopher Brasher, "Christopher Brasher Recalls the Day," *Observer,* May 5, 1974.

INDEX